www.brookscole.com

www.brookscole.com is the World Wide Web site for Brooks/Cole and is your direct source to dozens of online resources.

At *www.brookscole.com* you can find out about supplements, demonstration software, and student resources. You can also send email to many of our authors and preview new publications and exciting new technologies.

www.brookscole.com
Changing the way the world learns®

Learning C++
A Hands-On Approach

Third Edition

Eric Nagler

University of California, Santa Cruz
and
Lawrence Technological University

Australia • Canada • Mexico • Singapore • Spain • United Kingdom • United States

THOMSON

BROOKS/COLE

Publisher: *Bill Stenquist*
Acquisitions Editor: *Kallie Swanson*
Editorial Assistants: *Carla Vera and Aarti Jayaraman*
Technology Project Manager: *Burke Taft*
Executive Marketing Manager: *Tom Ziolkowski*
Marketing Communications: *Margaret Parks*
Editorial Production Project Manager: *Kelsey McGee*
Print / Media Buyer: *Jessica Reed*

Permissions Editor: *Sue Ewing*
Production Service: *Matrix Productions*
Copy Editor: *Sally M. Scott*
Cover Designer: *Denise Davidson*
Cover Image: *Image State*
Cover Printing: *Phoenix Color Corp.*
Printing and Binding: *Maple-Vail Manufacturing Group*
Compositor: *G&S Typesetters, Inc.*

United States of America
1 2 3 4 5 6 7 06 05 04 03 02

For more information about our products, contact us at:
Thomson Learning Academic Resource Center
1-800-423-0563
For permission to use material from this text, contact us by:
Phone: 1-800-730-2214
Fax: 1-800-730-2215
Web: http://www.thomsonrights.com

Library of Congress Control Number: 2002114117

ISBN 0-534-38966-X

Brooks / Cole — Thomson Learning
511 Forest Lodge Road
Pacific Grove, CA 93950
USA

Asia
Thomson Learning
5 Shenton Way #01-01
UIC Building
Singapore 068808

Australia
Nelson Thomson Learning
102 Dodds Street
South Melbourne, Victoria 3205
Australia

Canada
Nelson Thomson Learning
1120 Birchmount Road
Toronto, Ontario M1K 5G4
Canada

Europe / Middle East / Africa
Thomson Learning
High Holborn House
50/51 Bedford Row
London WC1R 4LR
United Kingdom

Latin America
Thomson Learning
Seneca, 53
Colonia Polanco
11560 Mexico D.F.
Mexico

Spain
Paraninfo Thomson Learning
Calle / Magallanes, 25
28015 Madrid, Spain

To those the author loves

Contents

Transitioning from C to C++ 1

4   Reference Variables   49

5   Dynamic Memory Allocation   60

6   Introduction to Classes   72

7   Constructors and Destructors   113

8   More Class Features   163

9 Exception Handling   211

10   Function Overloading   245

11   Inheritance   287

12   Templates   335

13 Runtime Type Information   399

14   Iostream Output   410

15   Iostream Input   435

16   Manipulators   452

17   File Input/Output   462

The **string** Class and the Standard Template Library   481

++

Preface

A Bit of History

Welcome to the third edition of *Learning C++: A Hands-On Approach*. I hope that using this book will greatly enhance your ability to learn the C++ language, and at the same time provide a convenient reference document for many years to come.

This book was first published in June 1993 and completely revised in 1996 for the second edition. I am very pleased that many colleges and universities have adopted it as the textbook for their C++ courses. It's been 7 years since the second edition, and many changes have been made to the C++ language since 1996 (including standardization in 1998), so you easily can see that this latest edition of the book is long overdue.

For a long time, people referred to the language definition as the "C++ Draft Standard," but now it's simply the "C++ Standard." The technical document that describes the language in excruciating detail is "ISO/IEC 14882 Programming Languages–C++." You may purchase a copy directly from the American National Standards Institute (ANSI): **http://webstore.ansi.org/ansidocstore**.

If you need assistance directly from ANSI, you may call 212/642-4900 or e-mail them at **storemanager@ansi.org**.

What's Inside

This hands-on introduction to C++ programming uses a learn-by-example method. Its more than 400 examples are short and easily understood and the book serves as your classroom notes, tutorial, and reference. *Learning C++* employs a careful and steady progression of skills and concepts, going beyond the level of detail of most C++ books. It can be used either independently or in the classroom, in which case it serves as your notes as well as a textbook and reference guide.

Because I believe in the KISS ("Keep It Simple, Students") approach to learning, I provide many examples of relatively short and easy-to-comprehend C++ code. I support each idea or point that I make by a code snippet or a complete coding example. When the code constitutes a compilable and executable program, the output is shown at the end. At the end of each important topic, I include a brief summary that highlights the essential point.

If you're sitting in a classroom with the book in front of you, you should have to take very few notes, although a highlighter might prove useful. I am most comfortable with this approach when I teach C++, and over the past 13 years I've taught it more times than I can remember. In effect, it's a matter of following the notes and examples (i.e., the book itself) and discerning the major points. After the class session, you can review the examples and read the text with more care and detail. Some instructors prefer that students get more actively involved by taking lots of notes and copying as much code as possible. I find that this introduces errors and is a great distraction from the points that I am trying to make. That is, it's very difficult for you to pay attention to my words and to me when you have your head buried in a notebook as you busily copy everything I say. To liven things up and retain your attention, I always use my laptop in the classroom to compile and run the programs in the book, and even to dream up new code that everyone can help write and debug.

Prerequisites

This book assumes that you have a working knowledge of the C language. That is, you must already be familiar with the concepts of the C language keywords, primitive types, structures, pointers, dereferencing, arrays, calling functions, operators, and so forth. Other good C++ books review these concepts first, before delving into the semantics of C++ itself, but this book does not. Instead, it picks up where C leaves off. If you need a good book that covers the C language, rest assured that many are available. It's merely a matter of finding one that appeals to you. Nevertheless, in covering the various topics in C++, it's impossible to get away from the C language, so you'll receive a nice review anyway, especially in Chapter 1.

Coding Style

I am fully aware that if you put five programmers in a room and ask about coding style, you would get at least nine different opinions. Nevertheless, I use this style in this book:

1. All opening and closing braces are vertically aligned, with all of the contained code indented. I have always found this style easy to read and debug, especially when tons of error messages are emitted because of a missing or extraneous brace. The only exception is when a function body or class definition (e.g., a constructor), is empty, in which case, I might write { } on one line. In addition, I might use only one line of code to spell out a simple enumeration (e.g., **enum color { red, white, blue };**).

2. At the end of a **for** loop, the counting variable is incremented or decremented *prefix* style. While most C and C++ books use *postfix*, the results will be no different using prefix, and it's a good habit to get into in preparation for user-defined types, in which the prefix usage is much more efficient. How many times have you seen code that tries to increment a counter through a pointer like this: ***ptr++**? Of course this statement will not yield the desired result because parentheses surrounding ***ptr** are mandatory to get the job done: **(*ptr)++**. Without the parentheses, you would be dereferencing **ptr** and then adding 1 to **ptr**, not to the object to which **ptr** is pointing. Using prefix notation, however, you would get the correct result with or without the parentheses, that is, both **++*ptr** and **++(*ptr)** work.

3. Classes have been modularized within a given example so that there is a clear separation between the class's header file and its definition file. Thus, the code can easily be broken apart and copied into separate files within some IDE, for example, Borland or Microsoft. To perform a flat file compilation (with the header file embedded within the definition file as a single translation unit), certain **#include** statements, such as those that include the class's header file, must be removed or commented out.

4. In a declaration statement involving a reference or pointer, the **&** or ***** token is associated with the name being declared (the declarator), *not* the type (the declaration specifier). For example: **T *ptr**, *not* **T* ptr** and *not* **T * ptr**. Besides, two pointers of type **T** need to be declared as **T *ptr1, *ptr2**, which conforms to my declaration of a single pointer. The same rule holds for declaring functions. For example, here are two functions, both of which return a pointer to a **T**:

   T *func1(), *func2();

5. In any statement with the keyword **const** in the declaration specifier or as part of the return type, **const** is always written last. For example, **char const *ptr**, not **const char *ptr** and, **int const size = 10**, not **const int size = 10**. The compiler, of course, doesn't care one way or another because such modifiers as part of the declaration specifier may appear in any order. It certainly reads better right to left, that is, "**ptr** is a pointer that points to a **const**(ant) **char**(acter)" and "size is a **const**(ant) **int**."

6. In naming classes and variables, I consistently tried to follow the Java convention: (a) starting class names with a capital letter, (b) starting variable and function names with a lowercase letter, and (c) capitalizing all subsequent words in multi-word names.

Compliance with the C++ Standard

The code in this book has been tested primarily with the Comeau 4.2.45.2c compiler in strict mode, as well as Borland CBuilder 6 (compiler version 5.6). The Comeau compiler is virtually 100% ANSI C++ Standard compliant, and I have yet to find a bug in it. (See **www.comeaucomputing.com** for more details if you're interested in this compiler. I highly recommend it.) If you compile the code in this book with another compiler (e.g., Microsoft Visual C++ 6.0 or .NET, or GNU C++), and get a compiler or linker error or a different run-time result, please do not hesitate to contact me if the reason is not clear. In this regard, be aware that some C++ compilers, erroneously, do not place their C language header files in the standard (std) namespace (see Chapter 2 for more details). Thus, to write code that will work for these compilers and still be compliant with the C++ Standard (which dictates that all C language header files exist in the std namespace), you should write code similar to the following example that retrieves the length of a string:

```
#include <cstring>
#include <cstddef>
#ifndef MY_COMPILER // Whatever macro is valid for your compiler
   using std::strlen;
   using std::size_t;
   // Other using declarations as needed
#endif

void func(char const *str)
{
   size_t length = strlen(str);
}
```

If you are using a compiler other than your own (in which case the C language header files are indeed in the **std** namespace), then the two using declarations will bring the names **strlen** and **size_t** into the global scope, and the code in **func**() will compile just fine. If you're using your own compiler (in which case the C language header files are still in the global namespace), then the two using declarations will be bypassed, and once again the code in **func**() will compile successfully.

I do not point out deficiencies in various compilers, although I know they exist. This is because (a) I do not know if or when the deficiencies might be fixed and (b) legal liability might be involved if I were to say that something does not work and it does. I do say something like "your compiler may not yet support this feature."

Acknowledgments

Although this book is an expansion and enhancement of the second edition, I still needed a lot of help from other people to bring it to fruition. First, I would like to thank

Gerald Cahill of Antelope Valley College, Barbara Goldner of North Seattle Community College, Robert Koss of Object Mentor, Mansur Samadzadeh of Oklahoma State University, and Simon Walker of Northern Alberta Institute of Technology, who took the time and effort to review the preliminary copy and give me their feedback on what needed improvement. In particular, I want to acknowledge the other contributions of Bob Koss, who used his expert knowledge of object-oriented analysis and design to help me with the chapter on inheritance and with class design in general. My friend and C++ guru, Jim Fischer, used his expertise to delve into the darker corners of the language and correct a lot of my small errors, especially in I/O. As a result, the technical accuracy of the book improved immensely, and I slept a lot better. Finally, for many years I have been directing questions to Ed James-Beckham at Borland International, who has patiently answered all of them.

As mentioned earlier, I used the Comeau C++ compiler as my primary testing tool, especially for the code in the chapter on templates. Whenever I had a question, I knew that I could always ask Greg Comeau about it, and I would get an answer, usually within a few hours. Indeed, this happened many times. His quick assistance was invaluable in helping me write the template chapter, easily the longest and most difficult one in the book.

A project of this magnitude is impossible without a good publisher, and I am fortunate to have one of the best. First and foremost, my editor, Kallie Swanson, has been working with me for well over a year on this edition. I have also been aided by other people at Thomson/Brooks Cole: Valerie Boyajian, Aarti Jayaraman, Kelsey McGee, Bill Stenquist, Burke Taft and Carla Vera. Furthermore, Merrill Peterson of Matrix Productions guided me through the processes of copyedit and of proofing the final pages.

Finally, teaching is not a one-way street. Although most of the knowledge in this course goes from me to students, a lot of it comes back to me in the form of questions and comments that never occurred to me. I incorporate these remarks into the next edition so that it becomes even better. I thank all of you who have bought and used either the first or the second edition of the book and have given me feedback on what you think.

How to Contact Me

Please do not hesitate to contact me with any questions that you might have. You can reach me easily via e-mail at *epn@eric-nagler.com*. You may visit my website at *www.eric-nagler.com* for an errata list (let's hope there aren't too many!) and other news about the book and me. Brooks/Cole supports a Web site for this book at www/brookscole.com and you may reach my editor, Kallie Swanson, at Brooks/Cole. Good luck!

Eric Nagler

About the Author

Eric Nagler earned his B.A. in mathematics from the University of Michigan and immediately joined the federal government as a computer programmer and systems analyst. He has worked in data processing ever since. He moved to California in 1972, began to teach computer languages at a local community college in 1980, and taught his first C++ course in 1990. Eric taught C, C++, and Java for the University of California, Santa Cruz Extension and at numerous companies in the San Francisco Bay area and throughout the United States. He has spoken on technical issues at C++ conferences. He joined the staff of Lawrence Technological University and ITT Technical Institute in Michigan in 2002.

1

Transitioning from C to C++

Introduction

Bjarne Stroustrup of AT&T Bell Laboratories invented the C++ language as an extension and enhancement of the C language in 1979; it has now evolved into a unique language. It supports several styles of programming, including the following:

▲ *C-style,* which supports C's flexibility and efficiency with enhanced type checking;

▲ *Data abstraction,* which allows you to create user-defined types for whatever kind of problem needs to be solved;

▲ *Object-oriented programming,* which involves class hierarchies and runtime polymorphism;

▲ *Generic programming,* which entails using parameterization of functions and classes.

After many years of struggle and debate, the C++ Standards Committee approved the language definition in November 1997. It was voted into existence by the participating members in July 1998 (officially called ISO/IEC 14882 Programming Languages— C++) and published in September 1998. Does this mean that C++ is what it is, and always will be? Well, no. As you read this, work is proceeding on eliminating ambiguities in the standard and on enhancing the standard library. This version of the language is called C++0X. Stay tuned for more details.

 The C++ standard was approved in 1998, even though work is continuing on the language and the libraries.

1

C versus C++

For the sake of backward compatibility, you can usually take your existing C programs and compile them successfully using a C++ compiler. I say "usually" because, strictly speaking, C++ is not a "superset" of C but rather an extension and enhancement, and there are some subtle differences that you must know. This chapter will cover those differences. In addition, C++ adds some useful miscellaneous features to C, which are also covered in this chapter. This is sometimes called "using C++ as a better C." Let's get started.

SUMMARY   C++ is an extension and enhancement of the C language, not a "superset."

How Does the Compiler Recognize a C++ Program?

Because many C++ compilers can compile a program written in either C or C++ , they must have a way to determine the type of code they are processing. Typically, in a Windows/DOS environment, the file name extension **.cpp** is associated with files that contain C++ source code. If you pass your C++ compiler the name of a file that ends with **.cpp**, therefore, the compiler assumes you want to do a C++ compilation. In addition, it's fairly standard in a Unix environment to use **.cc** or **.C** as the file name extension of a C++ source file. Otherwise, unless the extension is something recognizable, such as **.lib**, **.obj**, **.asm**, **.def**, and so forth, any other extension implies that a C compilation will be done. In a Unix environment, the type of compilation might depend on the particular command you enter and is case sensitive. If your first C++ program produces, say, several dozen error messages, you'll know where to look first!

SUMMARY   Be aware of how your compiler tells the preprocessor to process either a C or a C++ program.

How Does the Preprocessor Know the Environment?

The preprocessor (which honors those statements beginning with a # symbol) occasionally needs to ask the question, "Am I running in a C or C++ environment?" For example, if you're running in a C language environment, and try to **#include** a C++ header file, you had better believe that something bad is going to happen. The preprocessor answers this question by looking at the macro _ _**cplusplus** (note the *two* leading underscores). A C++ compiler automatically defines the _ _**cplusplus** macro to the value **199711L** when compiling a C++ translation unit. This macro is not defined for non-C++ translation units. (The term *translation unit* typically means a C++ source file.)

This macro will always be true whenever you are compiling a C++ program. If you are compiling a C program using a C++ compiler, it will be false.

 The macro _ _**cplusplus** tells the preprocessor what environment it's running in.

A New Style of Commenting

C++ defines a new style of commenting that consists of two forward slashes (//). Whenever the compiler encounters this token, it will ignore everything that follows it to the end of the current line. The comment does not extend across more than one line, like a C-style comment. Of course, C-style comments continue to be valid for purposes of backward compatibility.

By the way, some C++ purists insist that it's bad style, if not downright ugly, to write a C++ program and include C-style comments. I do not share that opinion, and in fact I will be using C-style comments in this book where they are appropriate. For example:

```
void someFunction(/* Function arguments go here */);
```

Just be careful that you don't try to nest C-style comments, as follows:

```
void someFunction()
{
  /* Temporarily ignore the following loop:
  int total = 0;
  for(int i = 1; i <= 10; ++i)     /* Sum the digits 1
                                       through 10 */
    total += i;
  */
}
```

It should be obvious that the first comment is terminated by the */ of the second comment, so when the compiler finds the final */ it will get very confused and vent its frustration on you.

 In addition to the C-style comment, you can use a C++ comment, which is a double forward slash (//).

Never Assume! (The Implicit Use of Type int)

Ever since its creation, C++ has honored the C tradition of assuming type **int** in situations where an explicit type would normally be written but in fact is absent.

This style of coding has been deemed invalid, however. Therefore, you should always explicitly specify type **int** where appropriate. The quintessential example is the declaration of the **main()** function, which you often see as one of the following two lines:

```
main(void)      // or...
main(int argc, char *argv[])
```

The correct declarations in C++ are the following:

```
int main(void) // or...
int main()      // same meaning as above, or...
int main(int argc, char *argv[])   // or...
int main(int argc, char **argv)    // same meaning as above
```

And please note that the following code,

```
void main()
```

is invalid because a return type of **void** is invalid. Be sure that **main()** is correctly declared to return type **int**.

 The term "invalid" in C++ can be a bit misleading. Sometime it means "deprecated" (deemed obsolete, so stay away), and sometimes it means "won't compile." Where applicable, I will try to be clear on its exact meaning.

 If you want to use type **int**, be sure to write it explicitly. Never assume that a missing type is type **int**.

The Default Return Value from **main()**

Normally when a function promises to return a value of a particular type, you must, in fact, return such a value lest you incur the wrath of the compiler (unless, of course, you decide to call **exit()**, throw an exception, or take some other drastic measure of escape). The one exception to this rule is the function **main()**. Even though it promises to return an **int** (per the previous section), you can omit a **return** statement, in which case the compiler will generate a return value of 0 as the last statement. Because not all compilers support this feature, you will never go wrong by having **main()** explicitly return a 0 (assuming, of course, that you want to indicate a status of success).

 In **main()**, even if you return nothing, a return of 0 will be generated by the compiler.

The Difference between a Declaration and a Definition

A *declaration* in C announces to the compiler that a particular object is to be deemed valid but its definition lies elsewhere. For example, the following lines all constitute declarations:

```
extern int x;
void someFunction();
struct ADT;
```

A *definition,* on the other hand, inherently consists of a declaration as well as additional code that (usually) reserves memory. Although the compiler only wants declarations in order to be kept happy, the linker needs definitions. (An exception to this rule is when you want to create an instance of a structure or class; then, the compiler must have already seen the structure or class's *definition.*) The previously cited declarations can be turned into definitions by writing the following:

```
int x = /* Some optional value */;
void someFunction()
{
    // Code here
}
struct ADT
{
    // Code here
};
```

 A *declaration* keeps the compiler happy, whereas a *definition* is needed by the linker.

Formal Argument Names in Function Declarations

As in C, formal argument names in function declarations are always optional. The compiler doesn't care one way or the other. But if you feel they improve the documentation of the declaration, then by all means provide some names.

```
double power(double, double);       // Same as...
double power(double base, double exponent);
```

SUMMARY▶ In both C and C++, formal argument names in function declarations are always optional.

Formal Argument Names in Function Definitions

It's a different story when it comes to writing function definitions, however. In this case, the C language demands that you provide formal argument names. Otherwise, how else could you refer to a parameter? C++ eliminates this requirement because often there is simply no need to ever refer to the argument itself (e.g., due to the concept known as *function overloading,* which will be discussed extensively in Chapter 10).

```c
void someFunction(int, double)// Invalid in C, valid in C++
{
    // Function body
}
```

 Formal argument names in C++ function definitions are optional.

All Functions Must Be Declared before Being Called

Be aware that in C++ *all* functions *must* be declared before you are entitled to call them. If you fail to do so, the compiler will complain long and loudly. And don't forget that in C any primitive type can always be implicitly converted to any other primitive type (excluding pointers). Of course, the compiler might emit a warning message if significance will be lost during the conversion, but it's *never* going to give you a fatal error. For example:

```c
void someFunction(int);

int main()
{
    someFunction(39);          // OK
    someFunction('A');         // OK
    someFunction(53.73);       // OK, but may emit a warning
}
```

 All functions *must* be declared before being called.

The Meaning of Empty Parentheses

In C++, the following two function declarations are identical insofar as the compiler is concerned:

```c
void someFunction(void);
void someFunction();
```

Certainly **void** in C means "no arguments can be passed in," and so do empty parentheses in C++. (In C, empty parentheses mean "I'll take anything you want to give me.") Therefore, there's no need to write **void** if the function does not expect to receive any arguments. After all, you want the world to think that you're a C++ programmer, not a C programmer, right?

SUMMARY   Empty parentheses in a C++ formal argument list are the same as **void**.

Default Function Arguments

In C, there is no such concept as a "default function argument." In effect, all arguments are mandatory. That is, if you declare a function to receive four arguments, then the user is obligated to call it with exactly four arguments. End of story.

In C++, however, an argument can be specified as being a *default*. This means that the user has the option to either (1) accept the default value already provided, or (2) override the default with a different value.

A default argument is declared by writing an equal sign and a default value following the type in any function declaration. For example:

```
void someFunction1(int = 0);
void someFunction2(double pi = 3.1416);   // 'pi' is optional
```

When a function declaration contains both mandatory and default arguments, the mandatory arguments must come *first,* and the default arguments must come *last.* For example:

```
void someFunction1(char, int = 0);                    // OK
void someFunction2(float f, double pi = 3.1416);      // OK
void someFunction3(char eol = '\n', char *buffer);    // Error
```

When the time comes for you to override any default arguments, you must do so strictly from left to right, with no jumping or skipping:

```
void someFunction(int x = 0, double pi = 3.1416);
// ...
someFunction();              // OK; take both defaults
someFunction(1);             // OK; override the int only
someFunction(2, 3.14159);    // OK; override both defaults
```

Note that in the second call with one argument, it is impossible to accept the first default and override the second. Instead, the only choice is to override the first default value.

CAUTION   Ensure that all default values appear in the function *declaration* so that these values are made available to the compiler. Never write default values in function definitions because such definitions could eventually be compiled into object format and thus are unavailable to serve as declarations.

Default function arguments always appear in a function declaration after the mandatory arguments and are specified by writing an equal sign followed by the default value. They are overridden strictly from left to right.

The Difference between Initialization and Assignment (and Why It's Important)

Before proceeding any further, it is critical that you understand the difference between the processes of (1) declaration and initialization and (2) assignment. Knowing this difference has important ramifications in C++, and you will pay a handsome price in terms of time and space if you don't know which is which. This guideline is applicable even in C because, when initializing a variable, try to define and give the variable its initial value in just one operation instead of defining it with no initial value and then assigning to it later.

Let's look at this in more detail. First, *declaration and initialization* constitute the process in which an object is declared (i.e., provides a valid name to the compiler) and then is given some initial value. It is essentially a one-step process. For example, in the following code the variable **data** is declared and initialized with the value 1:

```
int data = 1;
```

On the other hand, *assignment* is the process in which an existing object is overwritten with the contents of some other object. Nothing is being created. For example, in the following code **data** is being assigned the value 2, which replaces the previous value of 1:

```
data = 2;
```

Despite the fact that an equal sign appears in both statements, the compiler can easily differentiate one from the other by asking if the statement begins with a declaration specifier, that is, a type (excluding modifiers such as **static** and **const**). If the answer is yes, then it's a declaration (possibly followed by initialization); if no, it's an assignment. The first example,

```
int data = 1;
```

begins with the type **int**, so it's an initialization statement. The second,

```
data = 2;
```

does not begin with a type, so it's an assignment statement. Why is this distinction important? Because when user-defined types are involved, different functions will be called when performing these processes, and issues of efficiency will come into play. Trust me on this—it's important. Therefore, what you need to remember is to Prefer (declaration and)

Initialization To Assignment whenever possible. This rule, which I'm going to call the PITA rule, is very important.

 Know the difference between a declaration and an assignment statement. When possible, always prefer (declaration and) initialization to assignment (the PITA rule).

Where to Place Your Variable Declarations

In C, whenever you write a block of code, the variables must be declared at the beginning, before any executable statements. If you want to create a new variable, you must start a new block (scope) by typing an open brace. For example, the following function will not compile in C because the variable **data** appears after the **puts**() statement:

```
#include <stdio.h>

void getData(void)
{
   puts("Enter a value: ");
   int data;    // Error in C, OK in C++
   scanf("%d", &data);
}
```

In C++, however, this code is perfectly valid. There is no restriction that variables must be declared at the start of a scope. This is a wonderful feature because it allows you to defer declaring (and possibly initializing) a variable until you're ready to use it. Do you take out and "declare" your credit card to the waiter in a restaurant as soon as you sit down? Or do you wait until you're ready to pay the bill? I assume it's the latter, which is the way you should be programming. But going beyond that nicety, it's actually a C++ requirement that you be able to do this because of the necessity to declare *and* initialize user-defined types in one line of code, as opposed to declaring them at the beginning of a scope and then assigning to them later on. (Remember the PITA rule?)

 In C++, variables can be declared anywhere within a block of code, not just at the beginning (as in C).

Variable Declarations inside a **for** Loop

Within a **for** loop, it is now possible to declare and initialize the counting variable as the first step (instead of simply assigning into a previously declared variable). Why was this made possible in C++? The PITA rule! In other words, instead of declaring the counting variable in one place (outside the loop) and then assigning into it (inside the loop), you can combine these two operations. For example:

```
// C style 'for' loop
int const dimension = 5;
int total = 0;
// 'i' is declared outside the loop
int i;
for(i = 0; i < dimension; ++i)
  total += i;
```

```
// C++ style 'for' loop
int const dimension = 5;
int total = 0;
// 'i' is declared within the loop itself
for(int i = 0; i < dimension; ++i)
  total += i;
```

It's important to point out that, when the counting variable is declared within the loop itself, the scope of the variable is restricted to the loop. That is, the following code is perfectly valid even though the counting variable **i** is used in both loops:

```
int const dimension = 5;
int total = 0;
for(int i = 0; i < dimension; ++i)
  total += i;
for(int i = 0; i < dimension; ++i)
  total -= i;
```

CAUTION In the early days of C++, the counting variable remained in scope after the **for** loop ended. If your compiler has not been upgraded, either use a different counting variable when writing a new loop, or apply the following macro as a temporary solution:

```
#define for if(false) { } else for
```

 In a **for** loop, the counting variable can be declared within the loop itself, and it goes out of scope when the loop ends.

The Tag Name Becomes the Type Name

In C, suppose you have a structure definition called **Person**, and later you wish to create an instance of this definition called **student**. You could write something like this:

```
struct Person
{
  char name[100];
```

```
    int age;
};
struct Person student;
```

The job would then be done. However, you can shorten this process by using a **typedef** so that the type name becomes **Person** instead of **struct Person**:

```
typedef struct
{
   char name[100];
   int age;
} Person;
Person student;
```

Fortunately, in C++ the need to **typedef** a structure is no longer necessary because the tag name of a structure automatically becomes the type name as soon as it's encountered by the compiler. In other words, in C++ you can simply write the following:

```
struct Person
{
   char name[100];
   int age;
};
Person student;
```

You have thereby obviated the need for a **typedef**. This feature also applies to the keywords **enum**, **union**, and **class**.

 In C ++, the tag name of a **struct**, **enum**, **union**, or **class** automatically becomes the type name.

How Enumerated Types in C++ Differ from C

In C, you can initialize or assign or increment an enumerated value with any type whatsoever, and the compiler will not complain:

```
enum color { red, white, blue };
void someFunction(enum color c)
{
   c = 9;              // OK in C, error in C++
   c = 'A';            // OK in C, error in C++
   c = 54.631;         // OK in C, error in C++
   ++c;                // OK in C, error in C++
}
```

In C++, however, these assignments are deemed invalid because they make no sense. What is the color 9, or the color A, or the color 54.631, or the color that is one more than blue? Therefore, the compiler will now produce either a warning or a fatal error. For purposes of backward compatibility, however, in order to make the code compile, you're going to need a cast:

```
enum color { red, white, blue };
void someFunction(color c)
{
  c = (color)9;
  c = (color)'A';
  c = (color)54.631;
  c = (color)(c + 1);
}
```

By the way, did you notice the use of **color** instead of **enum color** in the formal argument?

Of course, going in the opposite direction, from the enumeration into some other integral type, is considered to be a promotion, and it is always valid:

```
enum color {red, white, blue};
void someFunction(color c)
{
    int someColor = c; // Always valid
}
```

CAUTION   How an enumerated type is represented internally is strictly compiler dependent. All that is guaranteed is that it's some kind of integral type. There is no way to determine if its size is the same as a **short**, **int**, **long**, and so on.

SUMMARY   Enumerated types are more strongly typed in C++ than in C.

Initialization of Global Variables

In C, global variables might be initialized only to constant values, that is, values whose addresses are known at compilation time. In C++, however, they might be initialized to the value of an expression, provided that the expression can be computed:

```
/* At the global scope... */
int a = 1;                     // legal in both C and C++
int b = a;                     // legal only in C++
int c = puts("Ready to start"); // legal only in C++
```

CAUTION   This feature is mandatory in C++ because, when a user-defined instance is declared at the global scope, a function will be called to perform initialization.

Nevertheless, you should avoid using global objects whenever possible. Even though the language supports them, globals can couple otherwise nondependent functions. If one function uses a global in a way that another function isn't expecting, an error is introduced—one that is hard to track down. This becomes more and more likely as the size of the code base grows, and name collisions will increase. The problem with the global space is that there is only one of them. Finally, link time can become significant as more functions depend on the global space.

In C++, global variables can be initialized with expressions and function calls, not just constants.

Array Initialization

In C, the values of all of the initializers in an array declaration must be known to the compiler. For example, a list of constants works just fine. An array of pointers-to-characters is also a good example because the compiler knows the address of each string as it is stored in global memory, not on the stack or in dynamic memory. Therefore, the following line of code compiles correctly in both C and C++:

```
char const *array[] = { "C++", "is", "great" };
```

On the other hand, if the initializing values are on the stack or in dynamic memory, C cannot initialize the array. For example, the following function does not compile in C because the variables **a** and **b** reside on the stack, and their values are *not* known at compilation time.

```
void someFunction(void)
{
    int a = 1, b = 2;
    int someArray[] = { a, b };        // Error in C, OK in C++
}
```

As you might expect, C++ has no trouble whatsoever compiling this function. That is, the initializers no longer need to be known at compilation time. This feature will prove to be useful later on when an array of pointers to user-defined objects needs to be initialized with the addresses of objects on the free store.

Unlike C, the values of array initializers in C++ do not need to be known at compilation time.

Incidentally, C++ now supports empty braces as a way to initialize an array to all zeroes (as opposed to your having to write at least one explicit 0 between the braces):

```
int array[10] = { }; // OK; all zeroes in the array
```

Empty braces can be used to initialize an array to all zeroes.

The Boolean Type **bool**

First the bad news: the C language never explicitly incorporated a Boolean type and corresponding values to represent *false* and *true*. Sure, every primitive type (including pointers) could be implicitly converted to a Boolean type (with all bits off meaning false, and anything else meaning true), but that was about the extent of it.

Now the good news: C++ has remedied the situation by introducing the type **bool** and the associated literals **false** and **true**. Any primitive type (including pointers) is freely convertible to type **bool**, and vice versa. For display purposes, **false** appears as a 0, and **true** appears as a 1:

```
void someFunction()
{
  bool b = false;
  b = true;
  b = 0;        // b is now false
  b = 5;        // b is now true. A display of b produces a 1
}
```

If you're still in the habit of writing **int** when the type should be **bool**, you should break that habit now. For example, to find out if **x** is greater than **y**, you should write the following:

```
bool isGreater(int x, int y)      // Return type bool, not int
{
  return x > y;      // Relational operators yield type bool
}
```

And while we're on the subject, please do not write the preceding function as follows:

```
bool isGreater(int x, int y)
{
  return x > y ? true : false;    // Too verbose!
}
```

or, even worse than that:

```
bool isGreater(int x, int y)
{
  if(x > y)            // Way too verbose!
    return true;
  else
    return false;
}
```

Unless you get paid by the word, clean, concise code is a joy to behold. Don't get carried away with your keyboarding skills.

Get into the habit of using type **bool** and its corresponding values **true** and **false** where appropriate.

void * Pointers

The **void** * pointer is unique in the sense that it can point to any object. That is:

```
int x = 0;
void *ptrVoid = &x;          // Point to an int *
double y = 56.34;
ptrVoid = &y;                // Now point to a double *
```

In C, the opposite is also true; a **void** * pointer can be assigned to any other kind of pointer, as in the following:

```
void *ptrVoid;
int *ptrInt = ptrVoid;            // Store void * into int *
double *ptrDouble = ptrVoid;      // Store void * into double *
```

However, in C++ this code will not compile for the simple reason that it's not a safe thing to do. For example, consider the following:

```
char const *ptrChar = "C++";
void const *ptrVoid = ptrChar;            // OK
double const *ptrDouble = ptrVoid;        // Error in C++
```

If the last line were to compile (as it would in C), you would be in the unenviable position of having a pointer-to-**double** pointing to an array of characters. When you decide to increment this pointer by one, where are you in the array? Beats me. Of course, if you're determined to do it, a cast will force the compiler to accept your decision.

In C++, implicit conversions from type **void** * are no longer allowed.

Use 0, Not the Macro NULL

C++ guarantees that a constant expression that evaluates to 0 will be converted to a pointer type whenever a pointer is expected. In C++, therefore, there is really no problem using 0, whereas in C you would use the macro **NULL.** The standard C++ library defines a macro named **NULL** (see the header file **cstddef**), but in general try to stay away from the preprocessor when you can.

Use 0 instead of the macro **NULL.**

The Keyword **const**

The keyword **const** is a C++ creation that was later adopted by ANSIC. As you know, it is a modifier that deems an object to be constant, that is, an object whose value can never be modified. Stated differently, you can never assign into a constant object.

Incidentally, as noted in the Preface, my preference is to write this keyword *last* in a declaration specifier, for several reasons. For one thing, it makes more grammatical sense when reading the declaration specifier of a line of code from right to left. For example:

```
int const data = 0;
```

Here, **data** is the declarator (the object being declared) and **int const** is the declaration specifier. Thus, the line would be read as "**data** is a **const**(ant) **int**(eger)."

 The keyword **const** deems an object to be constant.

All Constants Must Be Initialized

This should be obvious. If you fail to initialize a constant at its point of declaration, how would you or could you ever assign a value to it later? Besides, doesn't this conform to the PITA rule anyway?

```
int const x;          // Error
int const y = 1;      // OK
```

 All constants must be initialized in order to conform to the PITA rule.

What It Means to Pass Arguments to a Function by **const**-Value

When you **const**-qualify arguments that are passed by value to a function, you are effectively not buying yourself much of anything. A copy is made of the object being passed in, and **const**-qualifying the argument simply means that the function cannot modify the argument itself. It has nothing whatsoever to do with the original object. To the caller of the function, it makes no difference whatsoever that you've decided to add **const** to the argument. As a matter of fact, in a function declaration the following two lines are identical:

```
void someFunction(int);
void someFunction(int const);        // Harmless redeclaration
```

The second declaration causes no harm. Unless you've got a good reason for doing so, therefore, don't bother **const**-qualifying your arguments.

CAUTION This type of **const**-qualifying the argument is called a "top-level" **const**-qualifier because the word **const** pertains to the formal argument itself. When pointers are discussed in the section "How **const** Affects Pointers," you will see how **const** can pertain to the caller's object as well.

 const-qualifying arguments to a function that are passed in by value doesn't do you much good.

What It Means to Return Arguments from a Function by **const**-Value

It's pretty much the same story when it comes to *returning* a **const**-qualified object from a function by value. That is, it doesn't do you much good. In other words, the following two declarations are effectively the same:

```
int someFunction();
int const someFunction();
```

Whatever value comes out is considered nonmodifiable, whether it's **const**-qualified or not.

Later you will see that, when returning a *user-defined* type by value from a function, it makes a difference if you **const**-qualify it or not.

 const-qualifying the return type of a function that returns an object by value doesn't do you much good.

How **const** Affects Pointers

When dealing with pointers, the situation becomes a little more confusing because now two objects are involved: the pointer itself and the object to which the pointer points.

First, to make constant the one or more characters being pointed at, write the word **const** to the left of the asterisk. Reading from right to left, you would say, "**ptr** is a (modifiable) pointer, and it points to one or more **const**(ant) characters," as in the following:

```
void someFunction(char const *ptr)
{
    *ptr = 'A'; // Error
    ptr = 0;    // OK
}
// ...
char const *ptr = "C++";
someFunction(ptr);
```

This situation is quite common because it's how a pointer is used to *support constant objects*. This particular topic is very important because, if you don't adhere to it, you will be writing a lot of erroneous code. (Using the keyword **const** correctly is also sometimes called writing "**const**-correct" code.) For example, what if you neglected to write the word **const**, and instead wrote the following?

```
void someFunction(char *ptr)        // No support of const objects
{
   // ...
}
// ...
char const *ptr = "C++";
someFunction(ptr);    // Compiler error
```

The body of the function is irrelevant because the call itself will not compile. Why? Because you're asking the compiler to perform an implicit conversion from type **char const *** into type **char ***, and there is no such conversion. (If there were, the function would be able to change the content of the string itself. Not good.) That's why it's necessary to write the word **const** when declaring the function's formal argument.

In addition, you could use the keyword **const** twice to make the pointer itself constant and to support a constant character string. Simply write **const** again to the right of the asterisk. Now "**ptr** is **const**(ant), it's a pointer, and it points to one or more **const**(ant) **char**acters":

```
void someFunction(char const *const ptr)
{
   *ptr = 'A'; // Error
   ptr = 0;    // Error
}
// ...
char const *ptr = "C++";
someFunction(ptr);
```

SUMMARY ▶ Where you write the word **const** in a pointer declaration affects what is deemed constant.

How an Array of Characters in C++ Differs from C

In the C language, you can create an array of characters and point to it with a statement similar to the following:

```
char *ptr = "C++";
```

You can then proceed to make changes to the array of characters by writing the following:

```
*ptr = 'D';
```

However, the C++ Standards Committee decided that, by default, any string literal in C++ should automatically be deemed *constant*. Therefore, its type is no longer **char**[]

("array of characters"), but rather **char const**[] ("array of constant characters"). Because using an array (such as "**C++**") in this example generates a pointer to the first element, you're first implicitly converting from **char const**[] to **char const** *, and then asking the compiler to perform another implicit conversion from **char const** * on the right to **char** * on the left (the type of **ptr**). Of course, the compiler will not do this (i.e., it will not ignore the **const** qualifier).

Consequently, the declaration for **ptr** above is correctly written as:

```
char const *ptr = "C++";
```

Now the characters surely are protected from modification. Of course, if you're determined to (eventually) modify one or more characters in the string literal, you can always cast away the **const** part of the pointer:

```
char const *ptr = "C++";
((char *)ptr)[0] = 'D';      // or...
*(char *)ptr = 'D';
```

However, a professional C++ programmer would write this as follows, using a new-style casting operator:

```
char const *ptr = "C++";
const_cast<char *>(ptr)[0] = 'D'; // or...
*const_cast<char *>(ptr) = 'D';
```

We'll cover the new casting operators of C++ later, in the section "New Styles of Casting."

 Your compiler might not even emit a warning message if you fail to **const**-qualify your **char**[] declarations.

 An array of characters in C++ is automatically deemed to consist of *constant* characters.

How to Support an Array of Type char const *

If you have an array consisting of a number of elements, each of which is type **char const** *, then, when the array is converted to a pointer pointing to the first element, the correct way to ensure that everything remains constant is to store the pointer into type **char const ***const** * ("pointer to constant pointer to constant characters"). Therefore, the characters themselves *and* the pointers that point to the characters are made constant:

```
void func(char const *const *ptr)
{
   *ptr = 0;             // Error
   **ptr = 'a';          // Error
}
```

```
int main()
{
    char const *languages[] = { "C", "C++", "Java" };
    func(languages);
}
```

 Declare a function to receive type **char const *const *** to support an array consisting of type **char const ***.

The Difference in How C and C++ Handle **const**

The primary difference between how C and C++ handle constants is that the fundamental (built-in) type constant values in C++ are kept in a separate compiler-only table and substituted into the code as literal constants, similar to how **#define** works. If you were to take the address of a constant object in C++ and store this address into a pointer variable, then storage for the constant itself must be reserved. On the other hand, in C the value of a **const** is *not* determined until execution time.

One good use of the way C++ handles **const** is in specifying the dimension of some array that will exist on the stack or in the global space. Of course, in C this would cause a compilation error because, as was just stated, the variable does not get its value until execution time:

```
int const dimension = 5;
double array[dimension];    // Error in C, OK in C++
for(int i = 0; i < dimension; ++i)
    // Do something with the array
```

 In C++ the value of a **const** might be known at compilation time.

Use **const** instead of **#define**

"So what's wrong with a **#define**?", you ask. For one thing, it involves the use of the preprocessor. The problem is that the preprocessor doesn't understand language or scoping rules whereas the compiler does. Thus, the compiler is a better choice for defining constants in C++. Here is an example that illustrates what can go wrong when using the preprocessor:

```
#define dimension 5
void firstFunction()
{
    double array[dimension]; // Fine
}

void secondFunction()
```

```
{
   int dimension = 10;        // Oops...
}
```

Of course, this will not compile because, after the textual substitution in the second function, you would be left with the following:

```
void secondFunction()
{
   int 5 = 10;                // Oops...
}
```

This is syntactical nonsense. The use of a constant in the first function, however, provides scope and thus avoids the problem:

```
void firstFunction()
{
   int const dimension = 5;
   double array[dimension];  // Fine
}

void secondFunction()
{
   int const dimension = 10; // Fine; no conflict
}
```

 Prefer the use of **const** to **#define** when defining constants.

Linkage of const Variables

By default, **const** values in C at the global scope have external linkage. This means that the linker sees them and can use them in a file that has an **extern** declaration. In C++, however, the default is internal:

```
// At the global scope...

int const x = 0;            // External in C, internal in C++
extern int const y = 0;     // External in both C and C++
static int const z = 0;     // Internal in both C and C++
```

The implication in C++ is that, if several different compilation modules each include a header file that has a constant defined at the global scope and all such constants have the same name, the linker will *not* produce a duplicate definition error message because it knows nothing about these constants.

 Global constants in C and C++ have different default linkages.

New Styles of Casting

Bjarne Stroustrup, the creator of C++, has called the C style of casting a "sledgehammer," and he's right. This is because it can be unclear to someone reading your code why you are performing a cast. For example:

```
void someFunction(void const *v)
{
    int *ptr = (int *)v;
}
```

Is it obvious that two conversions are taking place on the casting line? We are converting from a **void** * type to an **int** * type, and at the same time we are removing the "**const**-ness" of the object being pointed at.

This confusion has been solved by the new style of casting that C++ provides. Stroustrup maintains that the goal of the new casts is to minimize and localize unsafe and error-prone programming practices.

 Prepare to get into the habit of using new styles of casting.

The Difference between a Cast and a Conversion

First, let's make sure that you've got the terminology correct and that you understand the difference between a *cast* and a *conversion*. A conversion occurs when the compiler changes the type of an object. This can involve changing the bits that represent the object (e.g., the conversion from a **double** to an **int**), or it can mean simply reinterpreting the same bits (as in a conversion from an **int** to an **unsigned**), or the conversion from an **enum** to an **int**. The compiler is allowed to do some conversions whenever they are needed. These are called *implicit conversions,* such as converting the **double** to an **int**.

On the other hand, the compiler is allowed to do other conversions only when you give it "permission." These are known as *explicit conversions,* such as, converting from a **void** * to a **char** *, or converting a pointer-to-a-constant-object to a pointer-to-a-non-constant-object. You give the compiler "permission" to do an explicit conversion by using a cast.

 Know the difference between a conversion and a cast.

The Generic Format of a Cast

The generic format for the new style of casting is always the following:

```
typeOfCast<newType>(valueToBeCast)
```

where the **typeOfCast** is one of the following C++ keywords (and a new operator):

- ▲ **static_cast**
- ▲ **reinterpret_cast**
- ▲ **const_cast**
- ▲ **dynamic_cast**

Note the angle brackets surrounding the **newType** and the mandatory parentheses around the **valueToBeCast**. One thing is for sure: that's a cast!

A brief description of the first three casts follows. The fourth cast, **dynamic_cast**, is used to navigate safely down a class hierarchy and will not be discussed until Chapter 13.

static_cast

The **static_cast** keyword is used to perform a conversion that requests an "equivalent" value in a different representation. For example, you would use a **static_cast** to find the "equivalent" type **int** value of a **double** value. Any implicit type conversion that the compiler would normally do can be written using a **static_cast**. Note that using a **static_cast** eliminates any warning message that the compiler might emit, such as when significance would be lost:

```
double const value = 74.39;
int x = value; // OK; may produce a warning message
int y = static_cast<int>(value);   // Never produces a warning
                                   // message
```

Now suppose that you're doing integral arithmetic with type **int**. If you fear the possibility of overflow, it is incumbent upon you to use greater precision, such as arithmetic involving a **long** value. Thus, to ensure that **long** arithmetic is being used, you can cast one of your values to type **long** using a **static_cast**:

```
long someFunction(int x, int y)
{
   return static_cast<long>(x) + y;
}
```

If you're doing a division using integral types, and you want a fractional quotient, then one of the operands must be converted into a floating-point type using a **static_cast**:

```
double someFunction(int x, int y)
{
   return static_cast<double>(x) / y;
}
```

Although a **static_cast** can be used where an implicit type conversion would normally suffice, it must be used when the opposite direction is traversed, even if a cast is required to make the conversion. A perfect example occurs when using enumerated types:

```
enum color {red, white, blue};
void someFunction(color c)
{
    int x = c;                       // Promotion
    int y = static_cast<int>(c);     // Cast optional
    c = static_cast<color>(9);       // Cast required
    c = static_cast<color>('A');     // Cast required
    c = static_cast<color>(54.631);  // Cast required
    c = static_cast<color>(c + 1);   // Cast required
}
```

Another good example would be the conversion to and from a **void *** or **void const *** type:

```
char const *ptrChar = "Some string";
// Cast optional
void const *ptrVoid = static_cast<void const *>(ptrChar);
// Cast required
double const *ptrDouble = static_cast<double *>(ptrVoid);
```

A **static_cast** is used to request an equivalent value in a different type. It is a "safe" cast.

reinterpret_cast

The **reinterpret_cast** keyword is used to cast a value so that the bits, while not changing, take on a totally different meaning. Without a cast, this conversion is always a compiler error because, in essence, it is an unsafe cast. For example, the conversion of an **int *** to a **char *** requires a **reinterpret_cast**.

```
char const *ptrChar = "C++";
int const *ptrInt = ptrChar;       // Error
int const *ptrInt = reinterpret_cast<int const *>(ptrChar);   // OK
```

For all practical purposes, you will almost never have occasion to perform a **reinterpret_cast** (although one is used in Chapter 17).

A **reinterpret_cast** doesn't change the bits but instead gives them a totally different meaning. It is an "unsafe" cast.

const_cast

The **const_cast** keyword is how C++ explicitly casts away the **const**-ness or **volatile**-ness of an object. It can also be used to add **const**-ness or **volatile**-ness to an object, even though a cast is not required to do so.

```
int x = 0;
int *ptr1 = &x;
// Cast optional
int const *ptr2 = const_cast<int const *>(ptr1);
// Cast mandatory
ptr1 = const_cast<int *>(ptr2);
```

SUMMARY The **const_cast** adds or takes away the **const**-ness of an object.

You Can't Go Wrong

The beauty of the new-style casts is that the compiler will not let you use the wrong one in any particular situation:

```
// static_cast needed
double const value = 74.39;
// Errors
int y = reinterpret_cast<int>(value);
int y = const_cast<int>(value);

// reinterpret_cast needed
char const *ptrChar = "C++";
// Errors
int const *ptrInt = static_cast<int const *>(ptrChar);
int const *ptrInt = const_cast<int const *>(ptrChar);

// const_cast needed
int x = 0;
int *ptr1 = &x;
// Errors
int const *ptr2 = static_cast<int const *>(ptr1);
int const *ptr2 = reinterpret_cast<int const *>(ptr1);
```

SUMMARY The compiler ensures that you always use the proper cast.

CAUTION Even with these new-style casts, casting is still frowned upon. C++ is a type-safe language; when you cast, you are circumventing the type system. Sometimes casting has to be done, but always ask yourself why you are doing it and if it is really needed.

C and C++ Keywords

The following list contains all 74 keywords used in C and C++. Those in bold-face type are specific to C++:

and	**and_eq**	asm	auto
bitand	**bitor**	**bool**	break
case	**catch**	char	**class**
compl	const	**const_cast**	continue
default	**delete**	do	double
dynamic_cast	else	enum	**explicit**
export	extern	**false**	float
for	**friend**	goto	if
inline	int	long	**mutable**
namespace	**new**	**not**	**not_eq**
operator	**or**	**or_eq**	**private**
protected	**public**	register	**reinterpret_cast**
return	short	signed	sizeof
static	**static_cast**	struct	switch
template	**this**	**throw**	**true**
try	typedef	**typeid**	**typename**
union	unsigned	**using**	**virtual**
void	volatile	**wchar_t**	while
xor	**xor_eq**		

2

Namespaces

Introduction

Your C++ code typically consists of a collection of definition (or implementation) files, which contain any number of **#include** statements to bring in the requisite header files. Each header file includes preprocessor guards in the following form:

```
// File header.h

#ifndef HEADER_H
#define HEADER_H
/* All code in the header file */
#endif
```

In this code, the macro **HEADER_H** uniquely identifies this header file among all other header files in the current translation unit. When the header file is first included into the translation unit, the preprocessor has not yet **#define**'d a macro named **HEADER_H**. Consequently, the first time the preprocessor encounters the **#ifndef HEADER_H** directive (i.e., "if the preprocessor has not yet defined a macro named **HEADER_H** ..."), the directive evaluates to true. As a consequence of the **#ifndef** directive's true outcome, the preprocessor now begins processing the lines of code that lie between the **#ifndef HEADER_H** directive and its matching **#endif**. Therefore, the next line of code seen by the preprocessor is the **#define HEADER_H** directive, which defines a macro named **HEADER_H** within the current translation unit. Now note the following: If for some reason this header file is again **#include**'d into the current translation unit, the preprocessor directive **#ifndef HEADER_H** evaluates to false this time, because a macro named **HEADER_H** is currently defined in this translation unit. As a consequence of the **#ifndef** directive's false outcome, the preprocessor now bypasses all of the code that lies between the **#ifndef HEADER_H** directive and its matching **#endif**. Preprocessing then continues with the line of code that follows the **#include** directive that once again included this header file into the current translation unit.

The Problem

Now let's look at a troubling example:

```
// File header1.h

#ifndef HEADER1_H
#define HEADER1_H

int const x = 1;
void someFunction();
// ...

#endif

// File header2.h

#ifndef HEADER2_H
#define HEADER2_H

int const x = 2;
int someFunction();
// ...

#endif

// File main.cpp

#include "header1.h"
#include "header2.h"

int main()
{
    // ...
}
```

Because both header files happen to contain a constant with the same name, the compiler will object and yield a multiple declaration error. In addition, **someFunction()**

cannot be redeclared with only a variation in the return type. Oops. You've got a big problem on your hands.

The good news, however, is that namespaces provide a solution to this dilemma. A *namespace* is a C++ mechanism that is designed to partition the global space into individually named spaces. Each space then defines its own unique scope. This avoids naming conflicts that can arise from the vast number of declarations that typically reside in the global space, such as class names, function declarations, and so forth.

 Namespaces provide a solution to the problem of duplicate names in the global space.

How to Create a Namespace

A namespace is created by writing the C++ keyword **namespace** followed by some name of your choosing, followed by a pair of braces that define the scope of the namespace itself:

```
namespace A
{
    // Stuff in the namespace
}
```

A single namespace can be split among many different header files. In point of fact, this is exactly how the namespace called **std** (meaning "standard" and discussed in Chapter 3) is defined.

 Use the keyword **namespace** and a pair of braces to define a namespace scope. More than one namespace with the same name are merged into just one namespace.

The Scope Resolution Operator

C++ introduces a new operator called the *scope resolution operator*. This operator consists of two colons (::) written together as a single token. As with other operators such as plus (+), minus (−), asterisk (*), and ampersand (&), the scope resolution operator exists in two forms: unary and binary.

▲ In its *unary* form, the operand is written on the right-hand side; it instructs the compiler to look for the name in the global scope.

▲ In its *binary* form, the first operand on the left-hand side represents a scope (such as a namespace or a structure), and the second operand on the right-hand side represents a member in that scope, which could be yet another namespace (e.g., a nested namespace, a nested structure, etc.). It's quite possible to "chain" uses of the scope resolution operator together in order to access a particular member within a given namespace.

The scope resolution operator is a C++ operator that exists in both unary and binary forms.

How to Access Members of a Namespace

You can access members of a namespace in any of three different ways.

Accessing Namespace Members Directly

In the first method, simply use the binary scope resolution operator with the namespace name on the left and a specific member name on the right.

In the following example, notice how the variable **x** needs to be scoped to tell the compiler which namespace is to be accessed. If no scoping is provided, the compiler first looks to the local scope, then to the global scope; failing to find an **x** declared in either scope, it produces a fatal error. It's the same story for the structure **ADT**.

```
namespace A
{
   int x = 1;
   struct ADT
   {
     enum color { red, white, blue };
   };
}

namespace B
{
   int x = 2;
   struct ADT
   {
     enum color { green, yellow };
   };
}

void someFunction()
{
   int y = x;                           // Error
   int a = A::x;                        // OK
   int b = B::x;                        // OK
   ADT::color c1 = ADT::white;          // Error
```

```
    A::ADT::color c1 = A::ADT::red;        // OK
    B::ADT::color c2 = B::ADT::yellow;     // OK
}
```

CAUTION The ISO/IEC/ANSI C++ standard and other C++ texts use the term "fully qualified name" instead of "accessing members directly."

SUMMARY Use the scope resolution operator to directly access members within a namespace.

Using Declarations—Another Way to Access Namespace Members

The second way to access namespace members involves a *using declaration*. This entails writing the keyword **using** followed by a particular scoped member name, as in the following:

```
namespace A
{
   int x = 1;
   void f(int);
   void f(double);
   struct ADT
   {
      enum color { red, white, blue };
   };
}

namespace B
{
   int x = 2;
}

void someFunction()
{
   using A::x;            // A::x is brought into scope
   int a = x;             // OK; no need to qualify x
   using B::x;            // Compiler error; two x's in scope
   int x;                 // Compiler error; two x's in scope
   void f(char);          // Declare another f()
   f(1);                  // OK; call f(char)
   using A::f;            // Bring all A::f()'s into scope
   f('A');                // OK; call f(char)
   f(1);                  // OK; call f(int)
   f(645.7);              // OK; call f(double)
```

```
   using A::ADT;                 // A::ADT is brought into scope
   ADT::color c = ADT::red;  // OK
}
```

A using declaration injects a name into that particular scope so that this name can then be used without any qualification. If a function name is declared, then all functions having that name are brought into scope. Any attempt to create another object with that same name produces a compiler error.

A using declaration obeys normal scoping rules so that if it goes out of scope, its effect goes away:

```
namespace A
{
   int x = 1;
}

namespace B
{
   int y = 1;
}

using B::y; // Bring B::y into global scope

void someFunction1()
{
   using A::x;         // Bring A::x into function scope
   x = 5;              // OK; A::x = 5 (local using declaration)
   y = 5;              // OK; B::y = 5 (global using declaration)
}

void someFunction2()
{
   x = 2;         // Compiler error; no x in scope
   y = 2;         // OK; using declaration is still in effect
}
```

 A *using declaration* names a particular namespace member and implicitly declares it in the current scope.

Using Directives—Another Way to Access Namespace Members

The third way to access namespace members involves a *using directive*. This entails writing the two keywords **using namespace** followed by a namespace name, as in the following:

```
namespace A
{
   int x = 1;
```

```
    struct ADT
    {
      enum color { red, white, blue };
    };
}

void someFunction()
{
  using namespace A;
  x = 0;                 // OK; use A::x
  int x = 1;             // OK; declare a local x
  x = 0;                 // OK; use local x
  A::x = 0;              // OK; use A::x
  ::x = 0;               // Error; no x at the global scope
  ADT::color aColor = ADT::white;  // OK
  aColor = ADT::red; // OK
}

void anotherFunction()
{
  int b = x;   // Error; no x is in scope
}
```

The effect is to make all members of that namespace available without qualification at the point where the using directive occurs. As with a using declaration, a using directive obeys scoping rules. Unlike a using declaration, however, a function can still declare names identical to those made available by a using directive.

SUMMARY ▶ A *using directive* makes all names in a namespace available without qualification.

Be Careful to Avoid Ambiguous Situations

A member with the same name as one that exists in a namespace might reside at the global scope, but a using directive now creates an ambiguous situation. Therefore, explicit scoping must be used:

```
int x; // At the global space

namespace A
{
  int x = 1;
}

void someFunction()
```

```
{
   using namespace A;
   x = 0;        // Error; x is ambiguous
   A::x = 0;     // OK; use A::x
   ::x = 0;      // OK; use global x
}
```

 A using directive can easily lead to ambiguous situations.

Unnamed Namespaces

A namespace might be unnamed. The effect is to make its member names available without qualification:

```
namespace      // No name here
{
   int x = 1;
}

void someFunction()
{
   int a = x;   // OK
}
```

Of course, two such unnamed namespaces containing the same name is ambiguous:

```
namespace
{
   int x = 1;
}

namespace
{
   int x = 2;            // Error
}
```

So why bother with unnamed namespaces? Because an unnamed namespace can be used to replace the (now deprecated) definition of a static (linkage) data member at the global scope. That is, instead of writing the following:

```
static int x = 1;    // Visible only in this translation unit
```

```
void someFunction()
{
    int a = x;    // OK
}
```

you should instead write this:

```
namespace
{
    int x = 1;    // Visible only in this translation unit
}

void someFunction()
{
    int a = x;    // OK
}
```

The linker, of course, knows nothing about the member **x**, and that's just what you want to happen.

 An unnamed namespace allows unrestricted usage of its members and provides internal linkage for them.

Namespace Aliases

If a namespace name is too cumbersome to use, you always have the option to create an alias for that name. Just write the keyword **namespace**, the alias name, an equals sign, and the name to be aliased:

```
namespace AmericanTelephoneAndTelegraph
{
    int x = 0;
}

void someFunction()
{
    namespace ATT = AmericanTelephoneAndTelegraph;
    using ATT::x;
    x = 1;
}
```

 A namespace alias can be used to create a shorter name for a namespace.

The Koenig Lookup Rule

The Koenig lookup rule (named after Andrew Koenig, one of the pioneers of the C++ language) states that if a member of a namespace is used in an expression, then that namespace is automatically included in the lookup for any function calls using that particular member. For example:

```
namespace NS
{
   struct X { };
   void someFunction(X const *);
}

int main()
{
   NS::X x;
   someFunction(&x);
}
```

Because the call to **someFunction**() uses the member **x**, which is an instance of struct **X** in the namespace **NS**, then the search for the declaration for **someFunction**() will automatically include the namespace **NS**. I'll mention this rule again when it comes up in Chapter 3.

SUMMARY The Koenig lookup rule allows function declarations to be looked up automatically in a namespace.

EXERCISE 2.1

Given the following namespace definition,

```
namespace NS
{
  int greater(int first, int second)
  {
     return (first > second) ? first : second;
  }
}
```

first employ *explicit scoping*, then a *using declaration*, and finally a *using definition* to make the following **main**() function compile successfully:

```
int main()
{
  int answer = greater(3, 5);
}
```

3

Input/Output Basics

Introduction

I hate to be the bearer of bad news, but it's time to say good-bye to your old friends **scanf()**, **printf()**, **gets()**, **puts()**, and the rest of the **stdio** functions. In this chapter you will learn how to use the basic capabilities of a new input/output library called **iostream**. This library will serve you quite well once you start dealing with user-defined objects. And besides, you don't really like **scanf()** and **printf()** that much, do you?

 stdio functions are being replaced with a better way to do input/output.

Why Switch to Something New?

Perhaps you are wondering the justification for abandoning the **stdio** library and switching to something new. Several good reasons exist for doing so.

For example, although **scanf()**, **printf()**, and the rest of the functions in the **stdio** library can handle fundamental types just fine, they cannot be modified to accommodate user-defined types. The member functions in **iostream** are extensible, however, so that the input or output of an instance of some class can be written exactly the same way as that for a fundamental type. The implementation of this feature will be shown in Chapter 10.

In addition, the functions **scanf()** and **printf()** are prone to error (in case you hadn't noticed), as shown in the following:

```
long data;
scanf("%d", data);    // Two errors
printf("You entered %d", data);    // Error
```

With **scanf()**, you have to remember to write an ampersand in front of a variable name (except in the case of an array). With **printf()**, you have to remember that if you're printing an **int**, the conversion specification must be "**%d**"; if you're printing a **long**, then it must be "**%ld**". For floating-point types, both a **float** and a **double** are displayed with "**%f**", whereas a **long double** is displayed with "**%Lf**". When using **scanf()**, however, a **float** is described with "**%f**" and a **double** with "**lf**". Got all that? If you make a mistake, then you may get incorrect input or output. Fortunately, this problem goes away when you use **iostream** functions because the argument type itself determines how it is to be displayed. For example,

```
long data;
cin >> data;
cout << "You entered " << data;
```

translates the previous erroneous example into valid C++ code and gives you a quick preview of what lies ahead.

 There are many reasons to replace **stdio** functions.

Header File-Naming Conventions

Before proceeding with input/output, it's important that you understand how the library header files are named in C++. First, all header files that once had the suffix **.h** no longer have this suffix. Second, C language header file names have been modified so that they begin with the letter **c**. Thus, **stdio.h** now is called **cstdio**, **string.h** now is called **cstring**, and so on. Don't forget to use angle brackets (<>) when including library header files, and use double quotes ("") when including user-defined header files.

 Adhere to the new header file-naming conventions.

The **iostream** Header File

The first step in using **iostream** functions is to include the header file called **iostream** (and, as just noted, there is no **.h** extension):

```
#include <iostream>
```

You *must* include this header to use the facilities of the **iostream** library because it allows you to perform the most fundamental input and output operations. The header contains the definitions for several classes, and it provides you with a *public interface* to the functions of the classes. If all this object-oriented terminology sounds a bit confusing, don't worry about it now. It will all become much clearer in Chapter 6.

 Include the header file **iostream** to do the fundamental input/output operations.

The **cout** Object

Your terminal screen is just an object, and in object-oriented programming work is done by sending messages to objects. With **iostream** functions, the screen (or wherever the standard output has been routed) has been "attached" to an object called **cout** (meaning "console **out**put"). This object has been instantiated (created) from a class whose name is **ostream**.

Here's where it gets interesting. Virtually all C and C++ library functions, classes, and objects (including **cout**) exist in a namespace called **std**. (This is why it was important to discuss namespaces in Chapter 2.) Therefore, within the header file **iostream**, you will find code similar to the following:

```
// File iostream

namespace std
{
   extern ostream cout;      // Declare the terminal screen
   // etc.
}
```

This statement *declares* (rather than defines) the object **cout** to be of type **ostream**, and it makes its name available to anyone who includes the header file. (The object **cout** itself is actually *defined* in a definition file that has already been compiled into object format.) Why can't the **cout** object be defined (instead of declared) in the header file? Because then it would be violating the *one definition rule* (also known as the "ODR"). This rule states that the linker must encounter no more than one definition for any given object or function. If a header file were to contain definitions, and more than one translation unit included this header, then, when the object code for all of the translation units went into the linker, so would all of these duplicate definitions. Therefore, you must *never* place any definitions into header files (with the exception of structure and class definitions, which are okay because they do not reserve any space and are not something to be "resolved" by the linker).

CAUTION The **std** namespace also contains declarations for the error-logging instances **cerr** and **clog**, which by default will direct their output to the terminal screen. In addition, three other instances called **wcout**, **werr**, and **wlog** are used to accommodate wide character output of type **wchar_t**. A discussion of wide character output (as well as input) is not included in this book.

 The instance **cout** typically represents the terminal output device and lives in a namespace called **std**.

The Insertion Operator

In object-oriented programming, you send messages to objects to get the work done, and the most fundamental message you can send to the **cout** object is *insert*. It is written using an overloaded bitwise left-shift operator (<<). This is the *insertion operator*. (Operator function overloading is discussed in much more detail in Chapter 10.) Following this operator, you write the data (variable name or constant) that you wish to be displayed on your screen. This data can be any type that was handled previously by the **stdio** function **printf**(). For example:

```
cout << "C++";
```

 The insertion operator is used to send data to the **cout** device, meaning that this data will be displayed on the device.

Explicitly Qualifying the **cout** Object

The following code shows one way in which you could display the value of two variables of type **int**. The compiler is smart enough to know that the left-shift operator in this context means to "insert" the **int**s into the **cout** object and not somehow bitwise left-shift the **int**. Of course, if you really do want to perform a bitwise left-shift operation, you must use parentheses, as shown in the second line. Note also how the **cout** object needs to be explicitly qualified with its namespace in order to be accessed:

```
#include <iostream>

int main()
{
  std::cout << 4 << 2 << '\n';
  std::cout << (4 << 2) << '\n';
}

/* Output:

42
16

*/
```

Note that more than one insertion operator can be used in a single output statement. This means you don't have to write more than one **cout** statement to display one line of output. Because the insertion operator really generates a function call, and the **cout** object always appears to the left of the insertion operator, it should be apparent that the function returns the **cout** object itself. How this is accomplished will be explained in Chapter 8.

Explicitly qualifying the **cout** object with its namespace name **std**, and then using the insertion operator, is one way to perform output.

Accessing the **cout** Object with a Using Declaration

Here is the previous example again with a *using declaration*, which was discussed in Chapter 2. Because this using declaration appears in the global space, it will remain in scope so that the unqualified name **cout** could be used in other functions that might appear:

```
#include <iostream>
using std::cout;

int main()
{
   cout << 4 << 2 << '\n';
   cout << (4 << 2) << '\n';
}

/* Output:

42
16

*/
```

Do you remember the Koenig lookup rule from the previous chapter? Even though the insertion operator exists in the namespace **std**, its name does not need to be scoped to, or declared in, the namespace because the use of the **cout** object automatically tells the compiler to look in **std** for a prototype of the insertion operator.

A using declaration can be used to bring the **cout** object into the current scope.

Accessing the **cout** Object with a Using Directive

Finally, a *using directive* can be used to achieve the same result:

```
#include <iostream>
using namespace std;
```

```
int main()
{
   cout << 4 << 2 << '\n';
   cout << (4 << 2) << '\n';
}

/* Output:

42
16

*/
```

A using directive for the namespace **std** can be used to make the **cout** object available without qualification.

EXERCISE 3.1

Write a C++ program that displays your name and age on the terminal screen. Try experimenting with explicit scoping, then a using declaration, and finally a using directive.

A Suggestion for Proper Usage of the std Namespace

Given the three ways in which members of a namespace can be accessed, which one should you use? There are differing opinions on this subject among various C++ gurus, but this book will employ the following strategies:

1. Because a using directive is essentially the opposite of encapsulating members within a namespace scope, it defeats the purpose of a namespace and opens the door for conflicts at the global scope. Therefore, a using directive will never be used.

2. In all header files, only explicit qualification of namespace members will be used. The reason is that, because a typical implementation (.**cpp**) file might include a lot of header files, using declarations at the global scope can lead to possible conflicts. For example, two different namespaces might contain members with the same name, and you need both. Two using declarations would not work. Besides, header files typically do not contain a lot of code (perhaps with the exception of class templates using the inclusion model) and don't reference the **std** namespace very often, so explicitly qualifying all usages from the **std** namespace is not really a burden. Even if a particular type is used frequently (e.g., **std::ostream &**), a **typedef** can simplify the code.

3. In all definition files, using declarations will be used at the global scope unless there is so little code that explicit qualification would not be a burden. However, because

a definition file can very well contain a lot of references to members in the **std** namespace (e.g., **cout**, **cin**, **ostream**, **endl**, etc.), it might be too cumbersome to explicitly qualify all such usages. Thus, conflicts are still possible. If this should ever occur, however, the compiler will, of course, produce a duplicate declaration error at the point of the conflict, and explicit qualification can be used on one or both of the conflicting member names.

 For this book, in a header file all members from a namespace are explicitly scoped. In a definition file, the namespace members are explicitly scoped or brought into scope with using declarations.

Be Aware of Operator Precedence

When an operator such as bitwise left-shift is overloaded (as it is inside the class **std::ostream**), several syntax rules must be followed. One of them states that operator precedence cannot be changed. (Other rules state that the operator's associativity and "narity" cannot be changed either. That is, bitwise left-shift will always be left-to-right associative and will always be binary.) Therefore, when an output statement contains operators that are *lower* in precedence than left-shift, they must be enclosed in parentheses to avoid ambiguity at best and a compiler error at worst. If an operator (such as +) is *higher* in precedence than left-shift, parentheses are optional:

```
#include <iostream>

int main()
{
   bool b = true;
   std::cout << (b ? "true" : "false") << '\n';  // Parentheses
                                                  // mandatory
   int x = 1, y = 2;
   std::cout << x + y << '\n';      // Parentheses optional
}

/* Output:

true
3

*/
```

 Be aware of the operators that are lower in precedence than bitwise left-shift; parentheses will be required.

Formatting the Output

The formatting of the output to make it look presentable will be discussed in great detail in Chapter 14. For now, however, it's enough to use **iostream** functions in their simplest form.

 See Chapter 14 for details on how to format the output.

The cin Object

In a very similar manner to that of **cout**, your computer's keyboard has been "attached" to an object called **cin** (meaning "console **in**put"), which also lives in the namespace **std**. The **cin** object is an instance of the class **istream**. Thus:

```
// File iostream

namespace std
{
    extern istream cin;        // Declare the keyboard object
    // etc.
}
```

Sending messages to the **cin** object thus achieves the goal of getting terminal operator input.

 The instance **cin** in the namespace **std** typically represents the keyboard, and it is used to get terminal operator input.

The Extraction Operator

The most fundamental message you can send to the **cin** object is *extract,* and it is written using an overloaded bitwise right-shift operator (>>). Following this operator, you write the name of the variable into which the data from the keyboard is to be stored. Interestingly, you must *not* write an ampersand in front of the variable, as you would do for **scanf()**. Here's a quick example:

```
int data;
cin >> data;
```

The type of this data can be any type that is handled by **scanf()**. As with the insertion operator, extraction messages can be chained together using the same or different types of data because the output of the call to extract is the **cin** object itself.

For example, the following is how you could enter and display the value of some variable. As with the **cout** object, chaining calls to the extraction operator can be done because each call returns the **cin** object itself:

```
#include <iostream>
using std::cout;
using std::cin;

int main()
{
    cout << "Enter an integer and a double: ";
    int i;
    double d;
    cin >> i >> d;
    cout << "You entered " << i << " and " << d << '\n';
}

/* Sample output:

Enter an integer and a double: 45 975.406
You entered 45 and 975.406

*/
```

CAUTION   By default, the extraction operator ignores leading whitespace characters (blank, tab, new line, etc.) and separates one input value from another by the occurrence of (1) at least one whitespace character, or (2) a character that cannot be part of the variable being formed. For example, reading 123ABC as a number will stop when the character "A" is seen, and the characters "ABC" will remain in the input system stream. Your program will not resume execution until all program variables have received values and the <ENTER> key has been pressed.

SUMMARY   The extraction operator is an overloaded bitwise right-shift operator. Sending the extract message to the **cin** object gets keyboard input.

EXERCISE 3.2

Write a program that reads your name and age from the keyboard and then displays them on the terminal screen.

Checking for End-of-File

The termination of input data is usually denoted when an end-of-file character is encountered. In DOS and Windows environments, this is done by pressing <CTRL>-Z on the keyboard. In Unix environments and on Macintosh computers, it's done by pressing <CTRL>-D.

CAUTION Because of a bug in some compilers, you might need to enter <CTRL>-Z twice in order for it to take effect.

The class **std::istream** contains a function called **eof()** (inherited from the class **ios_base**) that returns the **bool** value **true** if end-of-file was entered, and **false** if not. If end-of-file is found, then the content of the variable into which you are reading is not modified.

Recall from the C language that the dot operator is used to fetch individual members from a structure object. (If you have a pointer to a structure, then you can use the arrow operator.) In a similar fashion, the dot operator is used to call a function inside a class (because the function has been logically encapsulated inside the class, just like the data members).

While we won't be too concerned about checking the validity of the input data, note that the following statement,

```
if(cin >> someValue)
```

will return the **bool** value **true** if good numeric data was entered. Otherwise, it will return **false**.

Thus, if you wish to set up a loop to enter some data, and iterate until the operator enters end-of-file, you should use a **do/while** loop that is something like this:

```
#include <iostream>

using std::cout;
using std::cin;
using std::cerr;

int main()
{
  do
  {
    cout << "Enter an integer: ";
    int someValue;
    if(cin >> someValue)
       cout << "You entered " << someValue << '\n';
  }
  while(!cin.eof());
  cout << "\nEnd-of-file";
}

/* Sample output:

Enter an integer: 123
```

```
You entered 123
Next integer: ^Z
End-of-file

*/
```

CAUTION In Chapter 15, when error checking is expanded, this will be enhanced to accommodate all possible invalid conditions and to avoid the endless loop that results from entering invalid (nonnumeric) data.

CAUTION Some Windows operating systems do not allow any output to occur to the terminal screen once end-of-file has been encountered using **std::cin** unless and until a new-line character (**\n**) is subsequently output. This character does *not* cause a carriage return/line feed to occur, but it does allow any following characters to be displayed properly.

SUMMARY The encapsulated function **eof()** is used to see if an input device has reached end-of-file.

EXERCISE 3.3

Modify Exercise 3.2 so that your name and age are entered from the keyboard continually until end-of-file is entered. Be sure to use function chaining in your code.

EXERCISE 3.4

Modify Exercise 3.3 so that your code is broken into three functions: **main()**, **readData()**, and **displayData()**. The **main()** function and two declarations are as follows:

```
bool readData(char name[], int *ptrAge);
void display(char name[], int age);
int main()
{
  int const length = 256;
  char name[length];
  int age;
  while(readData(name, &age))
    displayData(name, age);
}
```

EXERCISE 3.5

Write a C++ program that computes and prints the first 20 Fibonacci numbers. A Fibonacci number is a number that is computed by adding the two previous numbers in the sequence.

Prompt the terminal operator for the starting two numbers (typically 0 and 1), so that the first few numbers should be 1, 2, 3, 5, 8, 13, 21, 34, 55, and so on. (Use type **long int**.) Then display the newly computed number and its predecessor, and display the ratio of this new number divided by the predecessor. You should observe the convergence to the Golden Mean (also known as the Golden Ratio) of 1.61803.

Be sure to test with different starting numbers. When end-of-file is entered, terminate the program.

4

Reference Variables

Introduction

A reference variable (or, simply, a reference) in C++ is something that C does not have, and it fills a big void left by the C language. What a reference variable does is allow you to create *aliases* to variables and objects, thereby simplifying your coding job, while providing a more intuitive interface for the users of your functions and classes. In this sense, it is like a constant pointer to another variable that is automatically "dereferenced" by the compiler when you use it. Reference variables are used so frequently and are so important that they deserve to be discussed in their own chapter.

SUMMARY A reference variable creates an *alias* to variables and objects.

What's the Problem?

Consider the case in which you need to write a function whose job is to add 1 to some variable in the calling routine. First, let's try to pass this variable (called **someVariable**) into the function *by value:*

```
#include <iostream>

void addOne(int arg)
{
   ++arg;
}
```

```
int main()
{
   int someVariable = 0;
   addOne(someVariable);
   std::cout << someVariable << '\n';
}


/* Output:


0


*/
```

Clearly this does not work because passing by value means that a *copy* of the variable gets made and that is what gets modified in the function, not **someVariable**.

Next, let's do this by passing the address of **someVariable**:

```
#include <iostream>

void addOne(int *arg)
{
   ++(*arg);
}

int main()
{
   int someVariable = 0;
   addOne(&someVariable);
   std::cout << someVariable << '\n';
}

/* Output:


1


*/
```

Much better. Now the correct answer is produced. However, C++ provides a cleaner way to write this code:

```
#include <iostream>

void addOne(int &arg)
{
   ++arg;
}
```

```cpp
int main()
{
    int someVariable = 0;
    addOne(someVariable);
    std::cout << someVariable << '\n';
}


/* Output:

1

*/
```

Note the use of the ampersand (&) as part of the declaration of **arg** in the function, and the elimination of all asterisks in the function. This is your first taste of a reference variable in C++. Although you could argue (and be correct) that a reference variable is not strictly required here to get the right answer, you will soon see many examples in which references must be used. I hope it's obvious that there's not much point in creating a reference to a variable in the same scope as the variable itself. Its main use, as shown in the previous example, is to pass an alias of a variable into some other scope.

 Reference variables make your coding life much simpler.

How to Create a Reference Variable

The creation of a reference variable in C++ is nothing more than the creation of an *alias*. This is done by writing an ampersand after some type, similar to writing an asterisk after a type to declare a pointer. For example:

```cpp
int data = 6;
int &refData = data;
```

Here is a picture of how a reference works. The use of the reference always automatically takes you to the "real" object to which the reference acts as an alias.

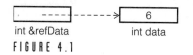

int &refData   int data

FIGURE 4.1

 Just as an asterisk creates a pointer, writing an ampersand as part of the declarator after the type creates a reference.

All References *Must* be Initialized

Because a reference, or alias, by definition must refer (or bind) to some "real" object, the C++ compiler insists that your reference variable *always* be initialized at the same time that it's created (from Chapter 1, the PITA rule again!). If you fail to do this, you will get a compilation error;

```
int &ref;              // Compiler error; no initialization here
```

Of course, the solution is to initialize (bind) the variable to some variable of the same type:

```
int someVariable = 1;
int &ref = someVariable;    // OK now
```

Because **ref** is simply an alias for **someVariable**, whenever **ref** is used in your code **someVariable** is really the object being accessed. If you understand that statement, then you have an excellent grasp of what references are all about.

Note also that once a reference variable is declared and initialized, it can never refer (alias) any other variable as long as it (the reference) remains in scope. Also, if a reference is used as a formal argument in a function declaration, the initialization issue takes care of itself because the reference will be initialized (and perhaps alias different objects) each time the function is called. (Remember that when the function terminates, the reference, being on the stack, will automatically go out of scope.)

SUMMARY All references *must* be initialized when they are created, and they must refer to some "real" variable or object.

What's the Point of All This Work?

Creating a reference in the same scope as the object to which it refers really doesn't give you very much. After all, what's the point of accessing an object through an alias if you can access the object directly? Where references really shine, however, is when they're used as formal arguments in a function; they then allow you to gain access to the calling parameters (which exist in a difference scope) without the messiness of a C language pointer declaration and dereference.

Let's look again at the program shown in the beginning of this chapter. The function **addOne**() does just that—it adds 1 to the object to which its formal argument refers:

```
#include <iostream>

void addOne(int &arg)
{
    ++arg;
}
```

```
int main()
{
  int someVariable = 0;
  addOne(someVariable);
  std::cout << someVariable << '\n';
}

/* Output:

1

*/
```

SUMMARY ➤ References are useful when passing an argument into a function, and the function needs to modify the argument.

const-Qualifying a Reference

There is certainly nothing wrong with adding a **const** qualifier to a reference variable, and indeed it is sometimes mandatory that you do so. In this case, it means that insofar as the reference is concerned, it can support constant (and temporary) calling arguments; the object to which the reference refers is deemed constant. This is not to say the object really is constant, just that it's constant in the eyes of the reference. For example:

```
#include <iostream>

void display(int const &ref)
{
  // The object to which 'ref' refers is constant here
  std::cout << ref << '\n';
}

int main()
{
  int someVariable = 1;
  display(someVariable);                      // Not constant
  int const anotherVariable = 2;
  display(anotherVariable);                   // const-qualified
  display(2);                                 // Constant
  display(1 + 2);                             // Temporary
  display(static_cast<int>(3.14159));         // Temporary
}
```

```
/* Output:

1
2
3
4

*/
```

Is the **const** qualifier for **ref** really necessary here? Yes, it is, because the caller of the function always has the option to provide an object that is (1) **const**-qualified, (2) constant, or (3) temporary, and the function being called *must* support such objects.

In the previous example, if the function were to be declared as,

```
void display(int &ref)
```

then the last four calls would have generated errors because the compiler will not bind a non-**const** qualified reference to a **const**-qualified object, a literal constant, or a temporary object.

 Be sure to **const**-qualify a reference when you need to support constant and temporary objects.

When Not to Use a Reference

Admittedly, using a reference can be a bit of overkill. After all, if you have no intention of modifying the object, then you still have the option to pass it into the function *by value,* thereby causing the compiler to make a copy and preventing the function from reaching out and modifying the actual argument itself, as in the following:

```
#include <iostream>

void display(int copyOfSomeVariable)
{
    std::cout << copyOfSomeVariable << '\n';
}

int main()
{
    int someVariable = 1;
    display(someVariable);
    display(2);
}
```

```
/* Output:

1
2

*/
```

 When user-defined types are introduced in Chapter 6, you will see how the guidelines for passing objects of these types will change slightly because of the overhead involved.

 Prefer pass-by-value semantics when a primitive type is deemed "read-only" by the function being called.

There Is No "Constant Reference"

By the way, note that there is no such concept as a "constant reference" because, unlike a pointer, writing the keyword **const** after the ampersand and before the variable name is a syntax error. The actual object being aliased can still be modified and the name itself is already "constant" in the sense that you cannot bind the variable to anything else. See the following:

```
int someVariable = 0;
int &const ref = someVariable;      // Illegal code
```

 Do not attempt to **const**-qualify the reference name itself.

Making a Reference to a Pointer

Making a reference to something other than a simple primitive type works the same way—just add an ampersand immediately in front of the reference name, ensuring that it appears as the last token. For example, the following program uses a function to "initialize" a pointer. Without the use of a reference variable, you would be forced to declare a pointer-to-pointer and to use a dereferencing operator to get the job done. Do you really want to do that, or does using a reference make your job simpler?

```
#include <iostream>

void initialize(char const **ptrPtr)
{
   *ptrPtr = "C-style pointer-to-pointer ";
}
```

```
void initialize(char const *&refPtr)
{
  refPtr = "C++ reference-to-pointer";
}

int main()
{
  char const *ptr;
  initialize(&ptr);          // C style pointer-to-pointer
  std::cout << ptr << '\n';

  initialize(ptr);           // C++ reference-to-pointer
  std::cout << ptr << '\n';
}

/* Output:

C style pointer-to-pointer
C++ reference-to-pointer

*/
```

Even if the reference-to-pointer syntax appears to be a bit messy, don't forget that a **typedef** usually bails you out of such messiness:

```
#include <iostream>

typedef char const *PTR_CHAR;
void initialize(PTR_CHAR &refPtr)
{
  refPtr = "C++ reference-to-pointer";
}

int main()
{
  PTR_CHAR ptr;
  initialize(ptr);
  std::cout << ptr << '\n';
}

/* Output:

C++ reference-to-pointer

*/
```

You can easily refer to a pointer variable as well as to the simple primitive types.

Making a Reference to an Array

Although it's not something you're probably anxious to do, you can bind a reference to an array using the following syntax:

```
int const dimension = 5;
double array1[dimension] = { 0.0 };
double (&refArray1)[dimension] = array1;
// ...
double const array2[dimension] = { 0.0 };
double const (&refArray2)[dimension] = array2;
```

 You can create a reference to an array.

Returning a Reference from a Function

A function can also return a variable by reference, with or without the **const** qualifier. Without the use of a **const** qualifier, the function then returns a modifiable *lvalue* and thus can be modified.

CAUTION In C++, any named region of storage is called an *lvalue*. Unlike in C, this storage can be either modifiable or nonmodifiable. An unnamed region of storage, such as a temporary object created on the stack, is called an *rvalue;* if it's a primitive type, it can never be modified. If it's a user-defined type, however, then it can be modified and thus is called a *modifiable rvalue.*

The following program uses the function **addOne()** to add 1 to the variable **someVariable**, and then 1 is added to the output of **addOne()** itself in **main()** by the increment operator. Because **addOne()** returns **ref** by reference (thereby creating a modifiable lvalue), the net result is that **someVariable** gets incremented twice:

```
#include <iostream>

int &addOne(int &ref)
{
   return ++ref;
}
```

```
int main()
{
  int someVariable = 0;
  std::cout << ++addOne(someVariable) << '\n';
}

/* Output:

2

*/
```

Of course, if the function **addOne()** had returned **ref** by value or by reference-to-**const**,

```
int addOne(int &ref)         // Return by value
int const &addOne(int &ref) // Return by reference-to-const
```

instead of by reference (to non-**const**), a compilation error would have resulted because the increment operator in **main()** is no longer being applied to a modifiable lvalue.

CAUTION   Make sure that when you return from a function by reference, you are not referring to something that will go out of scope, such as a local automatic variable.

SUMMARY   You can return a reference from a function.

EXERCISE 4.1

Write two functions called **swapByPointer()** and **swapByReference()** that use pointers and references, respectively, to swap the contents of two integer variables in the calling routine. Use the following **main()** to test:

```
#include <iostream>

int main()
{
 int first = -5, second = 4;
 swapByPointer(&first, &second);
 std::cout << "First = " << first << " Second = "
          << second << '\n';
 swapByReference(first, second);
 std::cout << "First = " << first << " Second = "
          << second << '\n';
```

```
}
```

EXERCISE 4.2

Given the **main**() function,

```
#include <iostream>
#include <cstddef>

int main()
{
  int const array[] = { 5, -6, 21, 15, -8 };
  std::size_t const dimension = sizeof(array) / sizeof(*array);
  int min, max;
  find(array, dimension, min, max);
  std::cout << "min = " << min << '\n';
  std::cout << "max = " << max << '\n';
}
```

Write a prototype and define the function **find**() that finds the minimum and maximum values in the array and stores the answers in the **min** and **max** variables. Be sure to use reference variables only where appropriate.

5

Dynamic Memory Allocation

Introduction

C++ has introduced a new technique for allocating and releasing dynamic memory. As you will soon see, the way of handling this task in the C language via the functions **malloc()** and **free()** must now be abandoned. You are about to enter the world of user-defined types, and **malloc()** and **free()** will not be able to handle the tasks that need to be done.

 The C language functions **malloc()** and **free()** will no longer be used.

How to Allocate Dynamic Memory for a Single Object

Dynamic memory is typically needed when the amount of space for your data cannot be determined at compilation time. For example, if you were creating a linked list data structure containing nodes, you don't know the number of nodes at compilation time; each node would therefore have to be dynamically allocated (as opposed to residing on the stack or in the global space).

Somewhat like the **malloc()** function in C, the C++ keyword **new** is used to allocate contiguous, unnamed dynamic memory at execution time. In its simplest form, the keyword **new** is followed by whatever type of data (primitive or user-defined) you want to allocate. This is called a *new expression* and is a unary operator. It secretly generates a function call to the function **operator new()**; what you get back from this function is a pointer to the object that was allocated. The important fact to remember is that the allocation of an object of type **T** always generates a pointer-to-**T**, regardless of the type of **T**. This is illustrated in Figure 5.1.

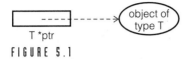

T *ptr

FIGURE 5.1

The following shows an example:

```
int *ptrInt = new int;              // One int
double *ptrDouble = new double;     // One double
float **ptrPtrFloat = new float *; // One pointer-to-float
```

 The term *heap space* refers to that part of dynamic memory reserved by calls to **malloc()**, **calloc()**, and **realloc()**. This is a separate region of memory from the *free store*, which is that part of dynamic memory reserved by using the keyword **new**.

Unlike **malloc()**, you no longer need to use the **sizeof** keyword to specify the exact number of bytes needed. Instead, you merely specify a particular type. The fact that different types occupy different amounts of storage is handled automatically by the compiler.

CAUTION C++ does not provide functions analogous to the C language functions **calloc()** and **realloc()**. Therefore, should you want to emulate these functions, you will have to write your own versions.

CAUTION If the call to **new** cannot find the requested amount of free space, an exception will be thrown. This topic is covered in Chapter 9.

SUMMARY Write the C++ keyword **new** followed by a type to allocate a single object of that type on the free store. You will get back a pointer to the allocated instance.

How to Initialize a Primitive Type

Recall from Chapter 1 how important it is, in C++, to be able to *initialize* your objects as opposed to first creating them and then assigning to them later (the PITA rule). Happily, you have the option to initialize whenever single objects are allocated from the free store. You do this by following the specified type with the initial value enclosed within parentheses. For example:

```
int *ptrInt = new int(123);
double *ptrDouble = new double(3.1416);
```

```
float *ptrFloat = new float(47.054F);
float **ptrPtrFloat = new float *(ptrFloat);
```

 To adhere to the PITA rule, follow the type name with a value between parentheses. The free store will then be initialized with this value.

The Meaning of Empty Parentheses

You can write empty parentheses after the type in a **new** expression, but note the difference between the following two lines:

```
int *ptrInt1 = new int;     // Value is unknown
int *ptrInt2 = new int();   // Value is zero
```

In the first case, an **int** is created on the free store, and its value is unknown. In the second case, however, the value will be initialized to whatever value an **int** at the global space would have. And since all global fundamental types have their initial values set to zero by default, a zero is placed in that location on the free store. This works the same way for all the primitive types. A **bool** type with empty parentheses will default to the value **false**, which implicitly converts to zero.

 The use of empty parentheses after the type causes the space to be initialized with that type's default value.

How to Release the Free Space for a Single Object

As someone once observed (and subsequently wrote a best-selling book), if you open it, you close it; if you borrow it, you return it; if you . . . well, you get the idea. And when it comes to the free space, the rule is also quite simple: If you allocate it, you release it. Of course, this is no great revelation, but sometimes we get sloppy in our code and just "let the operating system" clean up after us. In this case, it's just not a good idea to let other folks do your work for you.

The way to release your free space is to write the keyword **delete** followed by the address of the space that was returned when you called **new**, as in the following:

```
int *ptrInt = new int(123);
// ...
delete ptrInt; // OK; releases the free space
```

Note that the content of the pointer itself will not be changed. And it should be obvious that you are not allowed to release free space that you never owned or that you no longer own.

Use the C++ keyword **delete** to release the space that was allocated by **new**.

Deleting a Zero-Based Pointer

There is something else you should know about **delete**. When the pointer itself contains 0, a **delete** issued against this pointer, although doing no useful work, is a guaranteed safe operation:

```
int *ptrInt = 0;
// ...
delete ptrInt; // OK; does no harm
```

This is an important feature, as you will soon see. Incidentally, some programmers like to zero out their pointers after releasing the free store in case they accidentally attempt to release the (presumed) space a second time. If this happens, no harm will be done (although they might want to do some serious debugging of their code!).

Deleting a zero-based pointer is always a safe operation.

How to Allocate Free Space for an Array of Objects

Perhaps your program needs to allocate not just one object but rather an array of objects of some type. To get memory for an array of some fundamental type, write the keyword **new**, the type name, and the number of array elements enclosed within square brackets (not parentheses!). This number can be either a constant or some expression whose value is determined at execution time (but see the restrictions associated with multi-dimensional arrays, given later in this chapter). What you will get back is a pointer to the first element of the array. This is shown in the following figure:

```
┌──────────┐         ┌────────┬────────┐       ┌────────┐
│   ----   ├┄┄┄┄┄┄┄┄►│ Elem. 0│ Elem. 1│  ...  │ Elem. n│
└──────────┘         └────────┴────────┘       └────────┘
   T *ptr                  Array of 'n' T objects
```
FIGURE 5.2

For example:

```
// Array of 5 ints
int *ptrInt = new int[5];
// Array of 6 doubles
int dimension = 6;
double *ptrDouble = new double[dimension];
```

If the value of the expression between the square brackets is zero, an array with no elements is allocated, and the pointer returned by the new expression is non-zero and distinct from the pointer to any other object. If the value is determined to be invalid at execution time, then the results are unpredictable.

 Use square brackets with a dimension to allocate an array of objects on the free store. You get back a pointer to the first element.

No Initialization of an Array Is Possible

Yes, you read that right. Despite the fact that you've been hit over the head with the importance of initializing objects in C++ (the PITA rule), there is no syntax in the language to allow true initialization of the individual elements of an array on the free store. Therefore, for all primitive types the value of each element will be unknown, and the best you can do is to assign into each element after the array has been created, as in the following:

```
int const dimension = 5;
// Allocate space for 5 ints, all uninitialized
int *ptrInt = new int[dimension];
// Provide some meaningful values
for(int i = 0; i < dimension; ++i)
   ptrInt[i] = i;
```

 An array of user-defined types on the free store can indeed be initialized, but only in a limited fashion. This will be explained in Chapter 7.

 An array of primitive types on the free store cannot be initialized.

How to Release the Free Store for an Array of Objects

The syntax to release an array of objects on the free store is similar to that of a single object, but with one important addition: You *must* write empty square brackets immediately after the keyword **delete**. Thus, for some generic type **T**,

```
T *ptrT = new T[ /* some dimension */ ];
// ...
delete [] ptrT;      // Note square brackets
```

The brackets are required to tell the compiler to expect an array of objects. This has important ramifications when you need to delete an array of user-defined objects (discussed in Chapter 7).

As with a single object, issuing a **delete** against a pointer that contains zero is a guaranteed safe operation:

```
T *ptr = 0;
// ...
delete [] ptr; // OK
```

When deleting an array of objects, be sure to write empty square brackets.

Keep Things in Balance

In summary, the primary rules involving **new** and **delete** are quite simple: (1) Balance every **new** with a **delete**. (2) If you did not use brackets in the **new** statement (meaning that you allocated a single object), do not use brackets when writing **delete**. (3) If you did use brackets in the **new** statement (meaning that you allocated an array of objects), you must use brackets when writing **delete**.

 Be sure to use the correct form of **delete** whenever you use **new**.

How to Use **new** and **delete** to Store Strings on the Free Store

Now let's put it all together. In the following program example, the user is asked to enter string data from the keyboard. The input is captured into a buffer area of some fixed length, after which it is copied onto the free store. Note that exactly the right amount of free store is allocated to store each string. Using an array of pointers keeps track of the individual strings; this array is stored on the free store and dynamically grows as each new string is entered. After all strings have been entered, they are printed and their space released via **delete**. This is illustrated in Figure 5.3.

The key data element is **ptrString**, which is a pointer-to-pointer that allows the array of pointers — needed to keep track of the strings—to grow dynamically on the free store. Note the use of the reference type in the function **getStrings()** to avoid a triple (!)

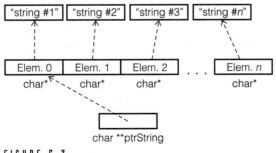

FIGURE 5.3

dereferencing situation. To avoid having to write asterisks all over the place, **typedefs** are used:

```cpp
#include <iostream>
#include <cstring>
using std::cout;
using std::cin;

typedef char *ptrChar;
typedef ptrChar *ptrPtrChar;

void getStrings(ptrPtrChar &refPtrString,
                unsigned &refNumberOfStrings);
void displayStrings(ptrPtrChar ptrString,
                    unsigned numberOfStrings);
void releaseStrings(ptrPtrChar ptrString,
                    unsigned numberOfStrings);

int main()
{
  ptrPtrChar ptrString = 0;
  unsigned numberOfStrings = 0;
  getStrings(ptrString, numberOfStrings);
  displayStrings(ptrString, numberOfStrings);
  releaseStrings(ptrString, numberOfStrings);
}

void getStrings(ptrPtrChar &refPtrString,
                unsigned &refNumberOfStrings)
{
  cout << "Enter your string: ";
  unsigned const bufferSize = 256;
  char buffer[bufferSize];
  while(!(cin >> buffer).eof())
  {
    ptrChar newString = new char[std::strlen(buffer) + 1];
    std::strcpy(newString, buffer);
    ptrPtrChar array = new ptrChar[refNumberOfStrings + 1];
    for(unsigned i = 0; i < refNumberOfStrings; ++i)
      array[i] = refPtrString[i];
    array[refNumberOfStrings++] = newString;
    delete [] refPtrString;
    refPtrString = array;
    cout << "Next string: ";
  }
```

```
      cout << "\n\n";
}

void displayStrings(ptrPtrChar ptrString,
                    unsigned numberOfStrings)
{
   if(numberOfStrings == 0)
     cout << "Nothing to display\n";
   else
   {
     cout << "The strings:\n";
     char const quote = '\"';
     for(unsigned i = 0; i < numberOfStrings; ++i)
       cout << quote << ptrString[i] << quote << '\n';
   }
}

void releaseStrings(ptrPtrChar ptrString,
                    unsigned numberOfStrings)
{
   for(unsigned i = 0; i < numberOfStrings; ++i)
     delete [] ptrString[i];
   delete [] ptrString;
}
```

How to Allocate and Delete Multidimensional Arrays

Instead of allocating space for a one-dimensional array, you can allocate space for an array of any dimension. For example, to allocate space for a two-dimensional 3×5 array of **doubles,** you would write:

```
int rows = 3;
int const cols = 5;
double (*ptr)[cols] = new double[rows] [cols];
// ...
delete [] ptr;
```

A picture of this array is shown in Figure 5.4.

   This example requires a little explanation. First, the elements of a two-dimensional array are simply a collection of one-dimensional arrays (the rows). Consequently, the parentheses surrounding ***ptr** are mandatory in order to create just one pointer that points to the first one-dimensional array, which is five **doubles** long (the number of

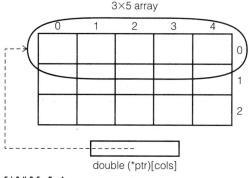

3×5 array

double (*ptr)[cols]

FIGURE 5.4

columns). In other words, this array consists of 3 elements, not 15, and **ptr** points to the first element, which is a one-dimensional array. To prove this, if you were to add 1 to the content of **ptr**, its address would increase by 40 bytes (5 * **sizeof double**, assuming a **double** comprises 8 bytes). This represents the start of the second one-dimensional array (row 1, column 0), not the second **double** (row 0, column 1).

Second, when allocating an array from the free store using **new**, *all* dimensions must be known by the compiler *except* the first, and they must be positive. That's why **rows** could be determined at execution time (perhaps by operator input), but **cols** must be constant so that the compiler knows its value. This means that, for a two-dimensional array, you cannot write a program that prompts the operator for the number of rows and columns and that then proceeds to allocate this array on the free store using **new**. The best you can do is to prompt only for the number of rows.

When it is time to delete the array, note that the format of the **delete** statement is the same as that of a one-dimensional array. In other words, the number of columns does not need to be specified.

By the way, if the declaration of the pointer to the two-dimensional array shown here seems a bit confusing, it's a simple matter to use a **typedef** instead so that **ONE_DIM** represents the type "one-dimensional array of **doubles**." Therefore, **ptr** is now just a pointer to a one-dimensional array of the new type, but in reality you're still creating a two-dimensional array:

```
int rows = 3;
int const cols = 5;
typedef double ONE_DIM[cols];
ONE_DIM *ptr = new ONE_DIM[rows];
// ...
delete [] ptr;
```

SUMMARY When creating a two-dimensional array on the free store, the number of columns must be known at compilation time. Use a **typedef** to simplify the syntax.

Name That Space!

No, it's not the latest TV quiz show. When you allocate an object in the free store by using **new**, you get back a pointer to that object; you then dereference that pointer in order to gain access to the object. But it's possible to refer to an object on the free store without using the dereferencing operator. To do this, dereference the address returned by **new** and create an alias to it. Then simply use the alias to refer to the object. Because **delete** requires the address of the allocated free store space, note carefully the use of the address-of operator (&):

```
double &refFreeStore = *new double(3.1416);
refFreeStore = 3.14159;      // Change the content
// ...
delete &refFreeStore;        // Release the space
```

SUMMARY You can refer to an object on the free store by creating an alias to it.

Do You Understand?

To find out if you have a good grasp of references, make sure you understand the output of the following two programs. In the first example, the reference **refFreeStore** creates an alias to the object (i.e., the storage region) that the program allocates from the free store:

```
#include <iostream>

int main()
{
  int *ptrFreeStore = new int(1);
  int &refFreeStore = *ptrFreeStore;
  std::cout << refFreeStore << '\n';
  ptrFreeStore = new int(2);
  std::cout << refFreeStore << '\n';
  delete &refFreeStore;
  delete ptrFreeStore;
}

/* Output:

1
1

*/
```

In the second example, the reference **refPtrFreeStore** creates an alias to the pointer to the free store:

```
#include <iostream>

int main()
{
    int *ptrFreeStore = new int(1);
    int *&refPtrFreeStore = ptrFreeStore;
    std::cout << *refPtrFreeStore << '\n';
    delete refPtrFreeStore;
    ptrFreeStore = new int(2);
    std::cout << *refPtrFreeStore << '\n';
    delete refPtrFreeStore;
}

/* Output:

1
2

*/
```

EXERCISE 5.1

Write a program that interactively asks the terminal operator to enter an **int** value. Then allocate an array of **double**s on the free store with this dimension. Fill the array with **double** values that are entered interactively. When this has been done, iterate across the array and display all of the values. Then display the highest and lowest values, the total of the values, and the average of the values. Don't forget to release the free store before you exit the program.

EXERCISE 5.2

Modify Exercise 5.1 so that, instead of being fixed length, the array of **double**s on the free store grows dynamically as each new value is entered.

EXERCISE 5.3

Given the following **main()** function that emulates the creation of a two-dimensional array on the free store dimensioned **rows** by **cols**,

```
int main()
{
    int **ptr;
```

```
int rows, cols;
while(!allocate(ptr, rows, cols))
{
    fill(ptr, rows, cols);
    display(ptr, rows, cols);
    release(ptr, rows);
}
}
```

write the function (1) **allocate**() that first allows the user to specify values for the **rows** and **cols** arguments, and then allocates an array of pointers, each of which points to an array of **int**s (the function returns **false** if end-of-file is entered); (2) **fill**() that fills the array elements with the product of the row and column numbers; (3) **display**() that displays all elements of the array; and (4) **release**() that releases all of the allocated space on the free store.

6

Introduction to Classes

Introduction

Now that you have completed Chapters 1 through 5, you are ready for the "main event"—classes. Without a doubt, the ability to create a class in C++ is the most important enhancement that was made to the C language. As a matter of fact, C++ was originally called "C with classes." Classes are needed to support object-oriented programming because they enable the programmer to create a *user-defined* type that can be used almost like the built-in (primitive) type variables. In the realm of top-down procedural design, the focus is on the function. In the realm of data structures, the focus is on the data. But in the realm of object-oriented programming, the focus is on the class and how it can be used to model everyday objects.

SUMMARY ▶ Classes in C++ are used to model everyday objects.

Thinking about Structures in C

Let's start by thinking about several structure objects in C that are designed to abstract a circle using a point and a radius:

```
typedef struct
{
    int x, y;
} Point;
```

```
typedef struct
{
  Point center;
  int radius;
} Circle;
```

Here, we are first creating a **Point** type (for the x,y coordinates), and then creating a **Circle** type that contains members of type **Point** for the center point and type **int** for the radius.

You can now create objects of the **Circle** type and use C style initialization to provide some meaningful values:

```
int main(void)
{
  Circle circleInstance = { 50, 60, 10 };
  // Do something with circleInstance
}
```

In this case, 50 and 60 become the **x** and **y** coordinates, respectively, and 10 becomes the radius.

SUMMARY ▶ A structure object can be used to hold data to abstract a circle.

Global Functions to the Rescue

In order to perform operations on the object **circleInstance**, you need global functions that have knowledge of the object, which is usually passed to the functions by address. This is certainly preferable to passing the object by value, which could incur a lot of overhead. And if you need to make changes to the object, you have to pass its address anyway. But as with any pointer, to support constant **Circle** objects and to prevent the function from making changes, you must add a **const** qualifier.

For example, the following are several global functions to perform manipulations on a **Circle** object:

```
void storeRadius(Circle *ptrCircle, int newRadius)
{
  if(newRadius > 0)
    ptrCircle->radius = newRadius;
}

int getRadius(Circle const *ptrCircle)
{
  return ptrCircle->radius;
}
```

```
double getArea(Circle const *ptrCircle)
{
    double const pi = 3.1416;
    return pi * ptrCircle->radius * ptrCircle->radius;
}
```

SUMMARY ▶ Global functions are used to manipulate structure objects.

The Problem with C

Note the loose connection between the global functions and the **Circle** object itself. That is, **circleInstance** lives within the scope of **main**(), which means that the object somehow has to be "passed" to the functions in order to get any work done. In addition, there is nothing to prevent a new function from modifying the **Circle** object in some disastrous way, such as storing a negative radius, as shown in the following:

```
void disaster(Circle *ptrCircle)
{
    ptrCircle->radius = -5;    // Bad news
}
```

And things just keep getting worse. Suppose that you change your mind and decide that it would be better to represent the **Circle** object using polar coordinates (a radius and an angle) rather than Cartesian coordinates. Or perhaps you want to change the name of the radius variable to, say, **circleRadius**. Now all the functions in a big project that have abstracted a **Circle** using Cartesian coordinates, or that have hard-coded the name of the radius, will have to be painstakingly modified.

In addition, it should be obvious that the **Circle** object is completely passive in nature; it has no life of its own and is essentially "brain-dead." Thus, any action that needs to be done involving the **Circle** object ("move," "get area," "draw," "report your coordinates," etc.) cannot be performed because there is nothing inherent within the **Circle** structure to perform these actions. That's why you need to write global functions. A program written in C, therefore, consists of a series of global functions, designed in some top-down fashion, that pass fundamental data and structure objects back and forth in order to get the problem solved. This is also known as *top-down procedural programming*.

The implication is that modeling a **Circle** object with a structure in C is not a good idea because typically objects are not dependent on outside "forces" to make them "do something," and they should not have to be tossed around like ping-pong balls. Instead, objects should contain within themselves the wherewithal to perform the necessary actions to accomplish some goal or task.

SUMMARY ▶ Top-down structured code is not a good model to use for structure objects because the data is not protected in any way and any changes could have a major impact on users.

A First Look at Encapsulation

There is a big difference between C and C++ in how a structure object is handled; specifically, in C++ the object can contain functions as well as data elements. Thus, by calling functions contained within the object, the object will respond in some predetermined way. Combining member data and the functions that operate upon this data into one composite type is called *data encapsulation*. That is, the data and functions that manage and manipulate the data are encapsulated (packaged together) in one nice, neat bundle called a C++ structure. As a result, an object no longer needs to be dependent on any "outside" (global) functions to alter its state or behavior because these functions are already part of the object itself. In other words, using object-oriented terminology, the object can receive messages (function calls) and act on these messages via its function bodies. The structure object can also send messages to other structure objects.

The bringing together of data and functions into a single structure scope is called *encapsulation.*

The Revised **Circle** Abstraction

The following is what the **Circle** structure shown earlier looks like after the global functions have all been encapsulated with the data members **center** and **radius**:

```
struct Point
{
   int x, y;
};

struct Circle
{
   Point center;
   int radius;

   void storeRadius(int newRadius)
   {
     if(newRadius > 0)
        radius = newRadius;
   }

   int getRadius() const          // Note the word 'const'
   {
     return radius;
   }
```

```
    double getArea() const    // Note the word 'const'
    {
       double const pi = 3.1416;
       return pi * radius * radius;
    }
};
```

There are a couple of important items here:

▲ The encapsulated functions no longer need to take an explicit pointer-to-a-**Circle** object in their formal argument lists because they are in "direct communication" with the data that comprises the abstraction of the **Circle** object itself. (In reality, the functions take a hidden pointer. Chapter 8 discusses this subject in more detail.) That is, when the member function **getRadius()** refers to the **radius** variable, the compiler resolves it by referring to the **radius** variable that exists within the structure.

▲ Recall from Chapter 1 that a **typedef** is no longer needed because both **Point** and **Circle** are inherently valid type names.

 The functions have unrestricted access to the data through an automatically generated hidden pointer to the structure object.

You Must Support Constant Objects

Look again carefully at the previous program example. The keyword **const** has been written as part of the signature lines of the functions **getRadius()** and **getArea()**. This is how member functions of a structure or class in C++ *support constant objects*. Let's explore this topic further. Member functions can be categorized into two types: those that can legally modify the object for which they are called (mutator functions), and those that cannot (constant functions). The constant functions are used to support the constant objects of a structure or class. Think about it: Does it make sense to send a *mutator* message to a *constant* object? Of course not. So that leaves only the *constant* messages that can be sent to a *constant* object. And constant messages are implemented by constant functions, which are designated as such by writing the keyword **const** after the closing parenthesis. You must be absolutely clear that usage of **const** in this context has nothing whatsoever to do with **const**-qualifying the return type of the function, should you ever want to do that.

However, can a constant message be sent to a mutable object? Yes, that's perfectly normal. Just remember that, for the duration of the member function, the object is deemed to be constant and cannot be modified. So, you ask, what happens if a constant function does indeed attempt to modify part of the object for which it is called? The answer is simple—the compiler will emit a nasty error message.

This particular topic—that of supporting constant (and temporary) objects — is so important that we will be visiting it many times throughout this book. I'm going to call it the SCO (Support Constant Objects) rule.

Your member functions must support constant (and temporary) objects of the structure or class of which they are members.

A Structure versus a Class

Perhaps you are justifiably confused about the terms *structure* and *class,* which I have been tossing around quite liberally. Just be aware that in C++ a structure is identical to a class, with two small exceptions in the area of accessibility. The first of these two exceptions will be discussed later in this chapter under the heading "Access Specifiers." We won't mention the second exception until Chapter 11, during the discussion on inheritance. Consequently, the primary change from C to C++ lies in the enhancements that were made to what a structure can contain and what it can do. In other words, a structure in C++ is a far cry from a structure in C. From now on, I will be talking about classes, unless I specifically want to differentiate them from structures.

 In C++, a structure can do anything a class can do, and vice versa. There are only two minor differences in the area of accessibility.

The Purpose of a Class

The concept of a class allows you to define a new type of data according to the needs of the problem to be solved, and to define operators to act upon this type. This is also called *abstract data typing,* or ADT. For example, a string literal in C is not one of the predefined types. Instead, it is made up of various characters followed by the null terminating character (\0). It logically follows that the operators =, +, −, and so forth have absolutely no meaning with regard to string handling, which is why, for example, you need a function such as **strcpy()** in order to copy one string into another, as opposed to using the more intuitive = operator.

With C++, however, it's now possible to define a new type (which is really a class) called **String** (or whatever name you want to give it) that contains the data and requisite operators (member functions) to accomplish the normal tasks associated with string handling. Therefore, the user of the class no longer needs to be concerned with the intricacies of the **cstring** library functions; instead, the user merely has to manipulate **String** objects just like objects of the fundamental types using a much better interface. We will be doing exactly this in Chapter 10.

Many reasons exist for using classes in your C++ programs. For example, they encapsulate design decisions that might involve machine dependencies, such as how a floating-point number is represented internally. In addition, classes represent well-known data structures or algorithms that are of general use when writing programs, such as complex numbers and dates. They also allow the user to write in a more convenient notation by using infix rather than functional notation to imply concepts such as addition, assignment, and so on. Finally, classes have the ability to provide automatic construction and destruction of their variables (discussed in Chapter 7).

 Classes provide a much friendlier interface to the users, and they hide the underlying messiness that these users would normally have to face.

The Components of a Class

You've already seen how a class can encapsulate both data and member functions. Nevertheless, there are two types of data, nonstatic (also known as *instance variables*) and static (also known as *class variables*). Similarly, there are both nonstatic member functions and static member functions. For now, we will concentrate on only the nonstatic data and functions; the static data and functions will be discussed in Chapter 8. Of course, a class can also contain things other than data and functions, such as **typedefs**, enumerations, and even other classes.

 A class can contain both nonstatic and static data and member functions.

How to Write a Class Definition

Because a class is structure, and vice versa, it should come as no surprise that a class definition is written much like the way in which you write a structure definition. For example, a simplified view of some class called **Circle** might appear as the following:

```
class Circle
{
    // All data and member functions inside the Circle
};
```

As you can see, the only difference is that the keyword **class** replaces the keyword **struct**. Also, the structure tag is now called the *class name*.

CAUTION   It is a common mistake to forget to write the semi-colon after the closing brace of a class or structure definition. If the compilation of your definition file produces a lot of errors that make no sense to you, be sure to examine all user-defined header files for correct syntax.

Note that this class definition (like a structure definition) reserves no memory and is usually located at global or namespace scope so that all functions within a program can have access to it. Also, as with a structure definition, it is not possible to initialize the data members at the point of declaration, for the simple reason that no memory exists that can store the value of a hypothetical initialization statement. This means, for example, that you cannot write the following:

```
class Circle
{
  int radius = 10;                  // Error
  Point center = { 50, 60 };        // Error
};
```

CAUTION Exactly how data members of a class are initialized (remember the PITA rule?) will be shown in Chapter 7, which deals with constructors and destructors.

SUMMARY Writing a class definition is virtually identical to writing a structure definition. Use the keyword **class** instead of the keyword **struct**.

Class Declaration versus Class Definition

By the way, note that the creation of a class, from the keyword **class** to the closing brace and semi-colon, is called a *definition*; a class *declaration*, however, involves writing only the keyword **class**, followed by the name, and then a semicolon. This is different from C, in which the term "definition" usually means that space has been allocated.

For example, this is how you would first declare and then define a **Circle**:

```
class Circle;           // A class declaration

class Circle            // A class definition
{
  // All members of the class
};
```

CAUTION Technically, the class declaration shown here is called a *forward declaration*. Furthermore, when a C++ program defines a class, it also "declares the class's existence" to the C++ compiler. Consequently, many C++ books use the term "class declaration" when referring to what this book calls a "class definition," so be careful and make sure you understand the difference in terms.

SUMMARY Know the difference in syntax between a class declaration and a class definition.

When to Use a Class Declaration

When do you need a class declaration? A (forward) declaration of a class name would suffice when, for example, a pointer or reference to that class name is used as a data member. In this case, the only thing the compiler needs to know is that the type name is indeed valid. Nothing else about the class is required.

For example, the definition of a linked list class called **List** contains pointers to the head and tail of objects of the class **Node**. Simply declaring (not defining) the **Node** class is sufficient in the following case:

```
class Node;  // Declaration of the Node class
class List
{
  Node *head, *tail; // Declaration works here
  // ...
};
```

In addition, if a class member function receives a pointer or reference to some class type, then once again only a (forward) declaration of the class is needed. For example, the function **setTail**() receives a pointer to a **Node**:

```
class Node;    // Declaration of the Node class
class List
{
  Node *head, *tail;
  void setTail(Node *newTail)     // Declaration works here
  {
    tail = newTail;
  }
  // ...
};
```

 Use a class declaration when only a pointer or reference to that class is needed.

When to Use a Class Definition

So when is a class *definition* needed? First, when a class contains an instance of some other class, the definition of the class needs to be seen by the compiler. Otherwise, you will get a compilation error. This is because the compiler needs to know the cumulative size of any class it compiles, and therefore it needs to know the size of (recall the keyword **sizeof**) the individual instance variables. If the definition of a contained instance has not yet been encountered, it is impossible for the compiler to perform the computation shown here:

```
class Node;    // Declaration of the Node class
class List
{
  Node dummyNode;    // Error; size unknown
  // ...
};
```

Instead, the correct code is:

```
#include "node.h"    // Include the class definition
class List
{
  Node dummyNode;    // OK now
  // ...
};
```

Another time when a class definition is needed is when a member function or data member in a class needs to be accessed; the compiler needs to see the class's definition. For example, if the **List** class includes a member function to display the head **Node** object, then the compiler needs to know that a member function called **displayNode()** does indeed exist within the **Node** class:

```
class Node; // Forward declaration of the Node class
class List
{
  Node *head, *tail;       // OK
  void someFunction()
  {
    head->displayNode();   // Error; class Node is undefined
  }
  // ...
};
```

Such information comes only with the inclusion of a class definition:

```
// File node.h

#ifndef NODE_H
#define NODE_H

class Node
{
  void displayNode()
  {
    // ...
  }
};

#endif

// File list.h

#ifndef LIST_H
#define LIST_H
```

```
#include "node.h"          // Include the class definition

class List
{
  Node *head, *tail;
  void displayHeadNode()
  {
    head->displayNode();   // OK; member function is known
  }
};

#endif
```

The general rule in C++ is that you should only *declare* a class if that's good enough to get the program compiled. Including a class's complete *definition* makes compiles take longer, which can be significant in large projects.

  Include a class's definition when another class contains an instance of this class or when it needs to call a member function of this class.

What about the Input/Output Classes?

The same principle about declaring and defining classes holds true when talking about the input/output (I/O) classes. Up to now, you've been including the header file **iostream** whenever you needed to perform any kind of input or output operation, but you should not be doing this if all you really need is a declaration of an I/O class. In this case, you should include the header file **iosfwd**. This file contains declarations for all of the I/O classes and is much more efficient than including **iostream**. Do *not* attempt to forward-declare the I/O classes yourself. Of course, when it comes time to start invoking I/O functions, you must, of course, include **iostream**.

For example, a header file might contain declarations for functions that operate upon input and output stream objects. In this case, only **iosfwd** is needed. The corresponding definition file includes **iostream**:

```
// File format.h
#include <iosfwd>

std::istream &formatInput(std::istream &);
std::ostream &formatOutput(std::ostream &);

// File format.cpp
#include <iostream>

std::istream &formatInput(std::istream &stream)
```

```
{
   // Format the stream device by sending messages to it
   return stream;
}

std::ostream &formatOutput(std::ostream &stream);
{
   // Format the stream device by sending messages to it
   return stream;
}
```

SUMMARY Do not include **iostream** if including **iosfwd** will suffice.

Principle of Data Hiding

One of the key elements of the C++ language is the *principle of data hiding*. To understand the need for this principle, let's go back to the **Circle** class example and do the following:

```
struct Circle
{
   int radius;
   Point center;

   void storeRadius(int newRadius)
   {
      if(newRadius > 0)
         radius = newRadius;
   }
};

int main()
{
   Circle circleInstance = { 50, 60, 10 };
   circleInstance.radius = -5;
}
```

The user of the class has circumvented the **storeRadius()** member function and has attacked the **radius** data member directly by storing −5 into it. The compiler happily accepts this code, but it should be obvious that the integrity of **circleInstance** has just been destroyed. What is a circle with a negative radius? As a matter of fact, something as innocuous as this,

```
int main()
{
    Circle circleInstance = { 50, 60, 10 };
    circleInstance.radius = 5;
}
```

is still a very dangerous act to allow. After all, even though the new radius is now a positive 5, perhaps the designer of the **Circle** class has deemed that the only valid radii are between 1 and 4. Fortunately, data hiding in C++ solves this problem quite nicely.

Data hiding means that the data members of a class are *inaccessible* to those functions that are not part of the class itself. (That's why the term *data hiding* is a misnomer. The data members are not "hidden" at all, simply inaccessible.) Data hiding is advantageous because, once a class has been written, debugged, and placed into a library, there is no danger of a nonmember function's accessing the data and perhaps modifying the state of the class object in some unexpected or erroneous way. Put another way, the class object is guaranteed to be correctly manipulated by the member functions of its own class. For example, if a class member function is designed to display the object in a certain way, this behavior will always work properly and the user has no need to write some global function to accomplish this task. If the user of the class accidentally or intentionally tries to violate the principle of data hiding by directly addressing a class member, the compiler will emit an error message.

For example, the following code shows how the **main()** function is attempting to violate data hiding by directly accessing the "private" **radius** member of the **Circle** class:

```
class Circle
{
    // ...
      private:
    int radius;
    Point center;
};

int main()
{
    Circle circleInstance;
    circleInstance.radius = 5;        // Compiler error
}
```

Of course, all of this wonderful theory assumes that all the member functions of a class do their jobs properly and without error. For example, it assumes that, indeed, a member function within the class is designed to change the radius. But it is then incumbent upon this member function to perform a validity check on the input argument (the new radius) to ensure that it is valid.

The principle of data hiding implies the following: The internal representation of a class instance is none of the user's concern. For example, how a floating-point number is represented internally does not really matter to you, does it? All you want is the ability to manipulate floating-point numbers in some fashion and get the correct result. If the internal representation is subsequently changed, your code should not be affected. Going back to the **Circle** class again, if you were allowed to manipulate the data members directly, and if the names of these members changed or took on a completely different meaning, then of course your code would be broken.

SUMMARY ▶ The principle of data hiding ensures that users of your class are not able to manipulate the data members directly.

Working through the Public Interface

You might very well be asking yourself, "If I, as the user of a class, cannot access the data members of that class, then how do I make changes to any object or instance of that class?" The answer is that you will always access the public member functions (the public interface) of that class in order to accomplish your task. These member functions will, in turn, access the data members for you to get the work done.

In top-down structured design, you learned that a function should do one thing and one thing only. This property is called *high cohesion* and is considered to be a good thing. In object-oriented design, functions become members of a class, but the rules of good function design are still valid. A member function should do just one thing, the whole thing, and nothing but the thing. Often, when writing a public member function, you might notice that it is doing more than one thing. You will produce much more maintainable software if you refactor the function to call other "helper" functions instead of doing it all in one big function. These helper functions are an implementation detail and should not be visible to the clients of your class. Hence, you should make them private.

SUMMARY ▶ To gain access to the data of a class, the clients must work through the public interface. Also, ensure that a class does just one thing.

Access Specifiers

The principle of data hiding is very nice except for one problem: It means nothing to the compiler. In other words, you are responsible for telling the compiler explicitly which class members obey the principle of data hiding and which do not. This is done using access specifiers within the class definition, each of which is a keyword in C++ :

▲ *private*

▲ *public*

▲ *protected*

To write an access specifier within the class definition, use the appropriate keyword, followed by a colon, before the class members to which the specifier applies. Because this specifier is very important to both you and someone reading your class, it should either be indented, outdented, or just plain "dented" so that it stands out clearly. For example:

```
class Circle
{
    public:
  // Code
    protected:
  // More code
    private:
  // More code
};

// Or...

class Circle
{
public:
  // Code
protected:
  // More code
private:
  // More code
};
```

Use the keywords **private**, **public**, and **protected** to designate the access privileges of your class members.

private Keyword

The first access specifier is called **private**. This is the *default specifier* for a class, which means that all members written first are automatically **private** and you don't have to say anything one way or the other. The rule with **private** class members is that they can be accessed only by the member functions of that class. Consequently, you use the **private** keyword to enforce the principle of data hiding.

CAUTION In Chapter 8, you will see how a friend function is also able to access the private members of a class.

Unless you have an excellent reason for not doing so, all data members of your class should be **private**. Some member functions can be **private** if you do not want them to be accessible to nonmember functions.

Also note that a member function can access the **private** members of some other instance of the *same class*. This other instance would probably be passed into the member function as an explicit formal argument. For example, in the following class, the function **makeCopy()** has access to the private data member **radius** first as part of the object to which the **makeCopy()** message is being sent, and second as part of the object **arg** that is being passed in:

```
class Circle
{
  int radius;
  void makeCopy(Circle const &arg)
  {
    radius = arg.radius;
  }
  // ...
};
```

SUMMARY The **private** keyword is used to enforce the principle of data hiding; it allows only the member functions of a class to have access to them.

public Keyword

The second access specifier is called **public**. This is the *default specifier* for a structure so that a C program that uses structures can be compiled under C++ and still grant unrestricted access to the user.

The rule with public class members is simple: They can be accessed by any function in your program. This is the means by which you communicate with an object—by sending messages to the public member functions of that object. Such member functions are called the class's *public interface*. For example, in the following class, the function **storeRadius()** serves as the public interface for any nonmember function that wishes to change the radius value:

```
class Circle
{
  int radius; // private member (by default)
    public:
  void storeRadius(int newRadius)
  {
    // Validity check newRadius
```

```
        radius = newRadius;
    }
    // ...
};
```

 The **public** keyword allows unrestricted access to the members that follow; it provides the public interface to the users of a class.

protected Keyword

The third access specifier, **protected**, grants access to the class's own member functions and to the member functions of some new class that is derived from this class. This specifier will be discussed in more detail in Chapter 11, so you don't have to worry about it now.

 The keyword **protected** pertains to member functions of a derived class and will be discussed in Chapter 11.

CAUTION   A class can repeat an access specifier any number of times, but this is not a good idea. Also, the access specifiers can occur in any order.

Choose Your Coding Style

To summarize what has just been said, consider the following four ways in which to define the class/structure **Circle** so that all access privileges are identical to all of the **private** and **public** members:

```
// Style #1
class Circle
{
  // All private members
    public:
  // All public members
};

// Style #2
class Circle
{
    public:
  // All public members
    private:
  // All private members
};
```

```
// Style #3
struct Circle
{
    private:
  // All private members
    public:
  // All public members
};

// Style #4
struct Circle
{
  // All public members
    private:
  // All private members
};
```

So what's your pleasure? Should you spend the rest of your (C++) life writing structures or classes? By unwritten convention, most people in the C++ community write classes, not structures. After all, this is C++, not C, that we're dealing with here, right? At the same time, no one will arrest you if you write a structure using C++, and this will be done occasionally throughout this book, particularly when all of the members are public.

The other consideration to bear in mind is whether the **public** or **private** parts of a class should be listed first. Once again, most of the C++ community prefers to write the **public** part first on the theory that this is what the user of the class is most interested in, so why not have it first? As a matter of fact, it's quite common to have the members of your class listed in order of decreasing accessibility. You can then only hope that when users come to the **private** part, they will avoid looking any farther and totally ignore your class abstraction, but there is nothing stopping them from doing so.

SUMMARY ▶ Prefer classes to structures, and list class members in order of decreasing accessibility.

Modularity and Implementation Hiding

Until now, all member functions have been encapsulated in classes in their entirety. That is, the complete definitions were simply lifted from the global space and dropped into their classes. However, this usually makes for a poor class design. To *modularize* a class definition means to split it apart into a header file and definition file; the header file contains only the member function *declarations*, and the definition file contains the member function *definitions*.

This concept is really no different from what happens in the C language with a library function. In this case, the function is first coded and then compiled into object format and placed into a system library. Eventually the linker will find it to resolve any calls to this function. All that is needed for someone to use this function is its declaration, which can always be found in the appropriate system header file. The function has therefore been modularized into a declaration and definition. The advantage of this should be obvious: Would it make sense to include the source code for a library function, such as **printf**(), for every program that needed it? Of course not, which is why the same principle will now be applied to class member functions.

Good object-oriented design makes a big deal out of separating interface from implementation. That is, you want to make a clear distinction between what an object does (its interface) from how it does it (its implementation). The first technique for achieving this is to keep the interface of the class definition in the header file and the implementation of the member functions in a separate file.

SUMMARY ➤ Member functions of a class should be modularized so that the user knows about only the function declarations, not the definitions.

How to Do Modularization

Now let's get back to classes in C++. You first create a header file that contains the class definition, and inside this definition you provide only the declarations of the class member functions. By convention such a file has an extension of **.h**, but it could be something else. Let's do this now for the **Circle** class, focusing only on the member functions to manipulate the **radius** data member. Don't forget to place preprocessor guards around your class definition to prevent its inclusion more than once in a single definition file (which would cause a compilation error):

```
// File point.h

#ifndef POINT_H
#define POINT_H

class Point
{
   int x, y;
};

#endif

// File circle.h

#ifndef CIRCLE_H
#define CIRCLE_H

#include "point.h"
```

```
class Circle
{
    public:
  void storeRadius(int newRadius);        // Declaration
  int getRadius() const;                  // Declaration
    private:
  Point center;
  int radius;
};
```

```
#endif
```

Next, you create another file, called a definition (or implementation) file, that contains the actual member function definitions. This file typically has an extension of **.cpp**, but sometimes the extension is system dependent. In this file you must include the class's header file that you just created:

```
// File circle.cpp

#include "circle.h"

void storeRadius(int newRadius)    // Oops, a global function!
{
  if(newRadius > 0)
    radius = newRadius;
}

int getRadius() const        // Oops, a global function!
{
  return radius;
}
```

As you can see, the two functions (by default) are *global* in scope, thereby having nothing whatsoever to do with the function declarations inside the **Circle** class. Consequently, the compiler is unable to resolve the references to the **radius** data member.

The problem now is to *associate* these function definitions with the class declarations. Do you remember the binary scope resolution operator (::) from Chapter 2? There it was used to scope members from a namespace—that is, to uniquely identify a member of a particular namespace. Now it will be used to scope members from a class. Simply write the class name, the scoping operator (::), and the name of the member function:

```
// File circle.cpp

#include "circle.h"

void Circle::storeRadius(int newRadius)  // Correct
```

```
{
  if(newRadius > 0)
    radius = newRadius;
}

int Circle::getRadius() const              // Correct
{
  return radius;
}
```

This file, like the C function discussed earlier, is then compiled into object format and (optionally) placed into a library.

CAUTION When the compiler tries to resolve names inside a class member function, it first looks to the member function itself, then to class scope, and finally to global scope. If all three fail, you will get a compiler error.

 Write a header file containing the class and only the member function declarations, and a definition file containing the member function definitions. Don't forget to use the scope resolution operator to associate the member functions with the class.

What the Users Do Now

Finally, the users include the class's header file in their own implementation file, such as **main()**:

```
// File main.cpp

#include "circle.h"

int main()
{
  // Do something with the Circle class
}
```

The end result is that the users of the class have access only to the header file, include this header file in the program, and thereby provide the compiler with all of the requisite member declarations. That's all the compiler needs in order to be kept happy. Eventually the linker will run, find the member definitions, and produce an executable file to run.

SUMMARY Anyone using the class needs only to include the class's header file. The linker will take care of finding the appropriate definitions.

In Summary . . .

By separating the member function definitions from their respective declarations, the implementation of the functions themselves is *hidden* from the users of the class. This makes perfect sense with respect to the object-oriented programming paradigm because *how* a member function carries out its work is really not the user's concern. This is similar to C. Do you *really* need to know how, for example, **printf()** and **scanf()** work? Of course not. It's the same for class member functions. Also, if the implementation of a member function changes, then the users merely have to relink their saved object files, not recompile them.

SUMMARY Strive to keep member function definitions hidden from the users of your class by modularizing your class and compiling it into object format.

CAUTION It should now be obvious that it's usually a poor idea to declare a local variable within a member function that has the same name as that of a member at class scope. Such code can be very confusing to read and can produce the wrong results.

How to Access Class Members via Instances

You access the members of a class in a similar manner to the way you do it for structures in C. That is, you write the object's name followed by the dot (direct member) operator, followed by the member you want. But also recall that under the principle of data hiding, the only members of a class that you can legally access are those that have been declared public. This normally implies that only the public member functions of the class (the public interface) will be available for your use, because a class will rarely have any public data.

Let's put it all together and write a complete program, using the **Circle** class, that includes member functions to store the radius, retrieve the radius, and retrieve the circle's area. (The center point of the circle is deliberately being ignored.) First, here is the **Circle** header file:

```
// File circle.h

#ifndef CIRCLE_H
#define CIRCLE_H

class Circle
{
    public:
    void storeRadius(int newRadius);
    int getRadius() const;
```

```
    double getArea() const;
      private:
    int radius;
};

#endif
```

Next is the **Circle** implementation file:

```
// File circle.cpp

#include "circle.h"

void Circle::storeRadius(int newRadius)
{
  if(newRadius > 0)
    radius = newRadius;
}

int Circle::getRadius() const
{
  return radius;
}

double Circle::getArea() const
{
  double const pi = 3.1416;
  return pi * radius * radius;
}
```

Finally, here is a program to test the **Circle** class:

```
// File main.cpp

#include <iostream>
#include "circle.h"

int main()
{
  Circle circleInstance;
  circleInstance.storeRadius(2);
  std::cout << "With a radius of "
            << circleInstance.getRadius()
            << " the area is "
            << circleInstance.getArea() << '\n';
  Circle *ptrCircle = new Circle;
```

```
    ptrCircle->storeRadius(3);
    std::cout << "With a radius of "
            << ptrCircle->getRadius()
            << " the area is "
            << ptrCircle->getArea() << '\n';
    delete ptrCircle;
}


/* Output:

With a radius of 2 the area is 12.5664
With a radius of 3 the area is 28.2744


*/
```

 Don't forget that whenever you have a *pointer* to an instance of a class, you must use the arrow operator to access the member functions.

Use the direct member operator (the dot) with an instance of a class to access the public interface of that class. Use the arrow operator when you have a pointer to an instance.

EXERCISE 6.1

Write a header file that contains a class called **Double** that encapsulates the primitive type **double** as its private data member. In the public interface, include two functions that set and get the value of this member. In the class's definition file, define the two member functions. Then write a **main()** function to test your class.

Inline Functions

If you look at the program to test the **Circle** class very closely, you should be able to discern a potential problem with it in terms of efficiency. Whenever you invoke the member functions **storeRadius()** or **getArea()**, the compiler will generate an assembly language "call" instruction and all of the overhead that goes along with it, such as pushing and popping arguments onto and off the stack. For the simple tasks of storing a new radius into **circleInstance** via the member function **storeRadius()**, and then computing the area via the member function **getArea()**, the time and space involved might be too big a price to pay. Only a profiler will give you an accurate measurement.

Of course, the C language does not have this problem because, as the user of a structure, you can simply access its data members directly with the dot operator and not think twice about it. In C++, however, under the principle of data hiding, this is not allowed;

instead, you must always work through the public interface, which, in this case, consists of the member functions **storeRadius**() and **getArea**(). Does this mean that the efficiency of the C language must be sacrificed to the great goddess of C++ called the principle of data hiding? Fortunately, the answer is no, because the concept of an inline function neatly solves this dilemma.

SUMMARY ▶   Working through a class's public interface, while adhering to the principle of data hiding, is sometimes too big a price to pay in terms of efficiency.

What Is an Inline Function?

An inline function is, by definition, a function whose code gets substituted instead of the actual call to that function. That is, whenever the compiler encounters a call to that function, it merely replaces the call with the code itself, thereby saving you all of the overhead of pushing and popping. This inline function can be either a member function of a class, a namespace function, or a global function.

Inline functions work best when they are small, straightforward bodies of code that are not called from too many different places within your program (which could then significantly increase the size of your code). Even if you request that the compiler make a function into an inline function, the compiler might or might not honor that request. It depends on the type of code the function contains and which compiler you're using. If the inline request is not honored, your compiler should emit a warning message.

How an Inline Function Compares to a Macro

Don't get the idea that an inline function is just like a macro, because it isn't. Consider both an inline function and a macro that take the absolute value of a number. Putting aside the fact that a macro is much more difficult to debug, macros can introduce side effects. In the following code sample, for example, the parameterized macro **ABS** introduces a nasty side effect by adding 1 *twice* to its parameter of -5 to yield an absolute value of 3. The inline function **abs**(), on the other hand, adds 1 just once to its parameter of -5 to correctly yield an absolute value of 4:

```
#include <iostream>

#define ABS(a) ((a < 0) ? (-(a)) : (a))

inline int abs(int arg)
{
   return arg < 0 ? -arg : arg;
}

int main()
{
   int const value = -5;
```

```
    int x = value;
    std::cout << ABS(++x) << '\n';
    int y = value;
    std::cout << abs(++y) << '\n';
}

/* Output:

3
4

*/
```

 There's a big difference between a macro and an inline function.

Make Inline Functions Available to the Compiler

Obviously, in order for the compiler to make the code substitution that an inline function calls for, it must have access to the code of the function itself. This simply means that the source code constituting the function body must be part of the project or program you are compiling, and it must appear prior to any call to it. Of course, the disadvantage with inline functions is that, if the code itself ever needs to be modified, all programs that use the function would have to be recompiled. Furthermore, a class member function that is inlined can be viewed as a violation of implementation hiding, but whoever said you get something for nothing?

 An inline function is one whose code replaces the assembly language "call" that would normally be generated.

Where Inline Functions Are Placed

The compiler must have access to the source code itself in order to make the code substitution, so you should get into the habit of placing all inline functions in header files because they are included in every compilation.

CAUTION It's possible to place inline functions inside definition files, as long as you're aware that they cannot constitute part of the public interface of a class.

 Place inline functions in header files.

Linkage of Inline Functions

You should also be aware that inline functions, by default, have static (internal) linkage; therefore, even if the compiler does not honor the inline request, it will *not* cause the linker to generate a duplicate definition error (despite the fact that duplicate bodies of code are being passed to the linker). Instead, the code of the final executable file will be a little bigger because a copy of the (presumed) inline function must be created in each of the object files, which includes the header file containing the definition of the inline function.

 If the inline request is *not* honored by the compiler, your generated code will be bigger but the linker will not produce a duplicate definition error.

How to Write a Global Inline Function

Let's get away from class member functions for a moment and consider a global or name-space inline function. To ask the compiler to inline this function, you must (1) precede the function's name with the keyword **inline**, and (2) ensure that the function definition (not the declaration) appears before any calls to that function.

For example, in the following program, the global function **isUpperCase()** is not inlined, but **isLowerCase()** is:

```
bool isUpperCase(int ch)
{
    return ch >= 'A' && ch <= 'Z';
}

inline bool isLowerCase(int ch)
{
    return ch >= 'a' && ch <= 'z';
}

int main()
{
    char aChar = 'A';
    bool upper = isUpperCase(aChar);      // Generates a call
    bool lower = isLowerCase(aChar);      // No call generated
}
```

 For a global or namespace function, write the keyword **inline** in front of the function's name in the definition. Be sure the compiler sees this definition before any calls to the function are made.

How to Write a Class Member Inline Function

As shown in the **Circle** example we just looked at, a member function that merely stores into a private data member, or that returns the value of a private data member, is an excellent candidate for inlining (but again, I must note that only a profiler can make this determination accurately). Is this a violation of modularization and implementation hiding? Yes, it is, so use inlining judiciously. And don't forget that all such inline member functions must appear in the class's header file, so any changes in a class's implementation will have a recompile impact on all clients.

SUMMARY ▶ Don't forget to place class member inline functions into the class's header file.

Implicit Inlining

You can accomplish inlining of member functions in one of two ways. The first way is to completely define it within the class definition itself. This is called *implicit inlining*. There is no need to write the keyword **inline** in front of the definition because it is automatically implied by this scheme.

For example, here is the class **Circle** once again, but notice how the member functions are no longer defined outside the class definition. In fact, you might recall that this is how function encapsulation was shown at the beginning of this chapter:

```
// File circle.h

#ifndef CIRCLE_H
#define CIRCLE_H

class Circle
{
    public:
  void storeRadius(int newRadius)  // Implicit inline function
  {
    if(newRadius > 0)
      radius = newRadius;
  }

  int getRadius() const            // Implicit inline function
  {
    return radius;
  }

  double getArea() const           // Implicit inline function
  {
    double const pi = 3.1416;
    return pi * radius * radius;
  }
    private:
  int radius;
};

#endif
```

I know what you're thinking now. How can the member functions access the private data member **radius** if the member functions physically occur in the class definition *before* the compiler has even seen **radius**? This is not a problem because C++ guarantees that the inline functions are not evaluated until they are called, at which time the compiler substitutes the code. Then they are compiled to ensure that there are no syntax errors. By then, of course, the **radius** data member is well known to the compiler. In other words, each inline function definition "knows" about all class members automatically, even members that appear later in the class definition.

SUMMARY An implicit inline function is one whose complete definition appears within the class's definition.

Explicit Inlining

The second way to inline a class member function is to declare it within the class definition and then define it outside the class definition (but still as part of the class's header file!), preceding the member function's name with the keyword **inline**. This is called *explicit inlining*. Note that the function declaration, or definition, or both, *must* be preceded by the keyword **inline**. You have to do this to avoid the inclusion of a true member function definition inside a header file (that is, a member function that will generate a separate body of object code). And please don't forget that, because each member function definition occurs outside the friendly confines of the class definition, the scope resolution operator is required.

Here is the previous example using explicit inlining:

```
// File circle.h

#ifndef CIRCLE_H
#define CIRCLE_H

class Circle
{
    public:
    inline void storeRadius(int newRadius);
    int getRadius() const;
    inline double getArea() const;
    private:
    int radius;
};

void Circle::storeRadius(int newRadius)    // Explicit inline function
{
    if(newRadius > 0)
        radius = newRadius;
}
```

```
inline int Circle::getRadius() const      // Explicit inline function
{
    return radius;
}

inline double Circle::getArea() const     // Explicit inline function
{
    double const pi = 3.1416;
    return pi * radius * radius;
}

#endif
```

 An explicit inline function occurs outside the class's definition, but it is still inside the class's header file. The keyword **inline** must be used with either the function's declaration, definition, or both.

Implicit or Explicit Inlining?

Which of the two inlining techniques, implicit or explicit, is better? The unwritten rule is that you should define inline member functions outside the class definition (explicit inlining), on the theory that the smaller the class definition (public interface) is kept, the better off you are. However, many people say there is nothing wrong with writing the member functions inside the class definition (implicit inlining). I would only add that, if you're going to do implicit inlining, restrict the member function to no more than one line of code.

CAUTION In the interest of clarity, from now on all explicit inline member functions will use the keyword **inline** in both the declaration and the definition.

SUMMARY Prefer explicit inlining to implicit inlining in order to keep the public interface as small as possible.

mutable Keyword

Recall that a member function declared with the keyword **const** immediately following the closing parenthesis promises to support constant objects and not modify any of the class's (nonstatic) data members. That's why the member functions **getRadius()** and **getArea()** of the **Circle** class included this keyword as part of their signatures.

A problem exists when, on rare occasions, a constant function really does need to modify a nonstatic data member and still support constant objects at the same time. For example, maybe a constant member function needs to cache a piece of data, or perhaps a counter needs to be incremented.

The C++ keyword **mutable**, written as part of the declaration of a nonstatic data member, allows this member to be modified by a constant class member function. This data member can be a part of either the invoking object or an explicit object of the same class type that gets passed in to the member function.

Returning to the **Circle** class, let's assume that it's necessary to save the area whenever it is computed and returned. This allows another member function to retrieve this saved value. This is what the modified class would look like:

```cpp
// File circle.h

#ifndef CIRCLE_H
#define CIRCLE_H

class Circle
{
    public:
  double getArea() const;
  double getSavedArea() const;
  // Other member functions
    private:
  int radius;
  mutable double savedArea; // Note keyword 'mutable'
};

#endif

// File circle.cpp

#include "circle.h"

double Circle::getArea() const
{
  double const pi = 3.1416;
  return savedArea = pi * radius * radius;       // Cache area
}

double Circle::getSavedArea() const
{
  return savedArea;
}
```

 Use the keyword **mutable** whenever a constant member function needs to modify a nonstatic data member.

How to Display the Contents of a Class

A fundamental principle of object-oriented design states that a class should do just one task (sometimes called the "One Responsibility Rule"). What this "one task" encompasses is, of course, open to interpretation. A class can certainly encapsulate more than one member function and still adhere to this rule. But what the class is *not* allowed to do is "display itself." There can be many "views" of the internal representation of a class, and therefore this is not something that is logically part of the class itself. Rather, a "view" is a completely different task and, as such, must be isolated into its own individual class. Stated differently, suppose that a **Circle** class did indeed contain a member function that displayed the center and radius values on some **ostream** device. Later, someone might want to see a **Circle** object displayed on a graphics device, which has nothing whatsoever to do with class **ostream**. Nevertheless, the class still has to suffer the possible overhead that using **ostream** might incur, or any other code used to display the values.

The Model/View/Controller Pattern

This method of viewing the internal parts of a class by using a separate class is called the "Model/View/Controller" pattern. Although strictly adhering to this pattern requires more coding techniques than you have learned up to now, we'll do just the fundamental part and separate the view (the display) from the model (the internal workings of the class). (The controller part, which would be a separate class that changes the internal state of the model class, will be completely ignored.) To do this, the class must contain functions (usually constant) that merely return the values of the internal data members (by value if primitive, and by reference-to-**const** if user-defined.)

For example, here is a simple class that encapsulates the primitive type **int** with functions that set and get the value:

```
// File integer.h

#ifndef INTEGER_H
#define INTEGER_H

class Integer
{
    public:
  void setData(int d = 0);
  int getData() const;
    private:
  int data;
};

#endif
```

```
// File integer.cpp

#include "integer.h"

void Integer::setData(int d)
{
   data = d;
}

int Integer::getData() const
{
   return data;
}
```

Next, we'll create the **View** class and make it aware of the **Integer** class by encapsulating a pointer. There is a function to set this pointer and the display function itself:

```
// File view.h

#ifndef VIEW_H
#define VIEW_H

class Integer;
class View
{
   Integer *ptrInteger;
     public:
   void set(Integer *ptr);
   void display() const;
};

// File view.cpp

#include <iostream>
#include "integer.h"

void View::set(Integer *ptr)
{
   ptrInteger = ptr;
}

void View::display() const
{
   std::cout << ptrInteger->getData() << '\n';
}
```

Finally, here is a test program:

```
// File main.cpp

#include "integer.h"
#include "view.h"

int main()
{
    ADT adt;
    adt.setData(123);
    View view;
    view.set(&adt);
    view.display();
}

/* Output:

123

*/
```

EXERCISE 6.2

Modify Exercise 6.1 to include a class called **View** that is used to display the contents of a **Double** object.

Enumerated Types within Classes

As you know, writing an enumeration is a way to create a new type in order to make the code more readable and to restrict the possible values of any variables that are declared. Recall from Chapter 1 that enumerated types in C++ have stronger typing restrictions, so it is no longer possible to assign or initialize an enumerated variable with anything but a legitimate value of the enumeration type itself.

When enumerated types are encapsulated within a class, there is no possibility of conflict between enumerations with the same name or the same values:

```
class Flag
{
    enum Color { Red, White, Blue };
    // ...
};
```

```
class Crayon
{
   enum Color { Red, White, Blue };        // OK; no conflict
   // ...
};
```

 If an enumerated type is to be used by a particular class, then be sure to encapsulate the enumeration.

Why Use an Enumeration?

If a class encapsulates an enumeration, typically it also contains a data member of the enumeration type. For example, if a class wishes to abstract a **Button** object, an instance would take on only the states of "out" and "in." These two states practically beg to be enumerated. So why would you want to abstract a **Button** object using type **int**? Type **int** can have literally thousands of different values (states) and it makes no sense to do it this way. The **Button** class would look something like this:

```
class Button
{
   enum Status { out, in };
   Status state;
   // ...
};
```

CAUTION Ensure that the enumeration appears prior to its use within a class so that the compiler knows that the type is valid.

 An enumeration is useful because it provides stronger type checking and restricts the number of possible valid values.

A Private Enumeration

If the enumeration is in the private part of the class, it's up to you to provide the appropriate "setter" and "getter" member functions for each enumerated value so that the state variable can be changed and interrogated accordingly. That is, the variable that represents the state of the object itself must be able to be put into any enumerated state (the "setter" member function) and must be able to be accessed (the "getter" member function). Thus, the total number of "setter" and "getter" member functions is always twice the number of enumerated values.

For example, here is a **Button** object with four member functions to set and interrogate the states of "out" and "in":

```
// File button.h

#ifndef BUTTON_H
#define BUTTON_H
```

```
class Button
{
    public:
  void setToOut();
  void setToIn();
  bool isOut() const;
  bool isIn() const;
    private:
  enum Status { out, in };
  Status state;
};

#endif

// File button.cpp

#include "button.h"

void Button::setToOut()
{
  state = out;
}

void Button::setToIn()
{
  state = in;
}

bool Button::isOut() const
{
  return state == out;
}

bool Button::isIn() const
{
  return state == in;
}

// File main.cpp

#include <iostream>
#include "button.h"

void checkState(Button const &panic)
```

```
{
  if(panic.isOut())
    std::cout << "State is out\n";
  else if(panic.isIn())
    std::cout << "State is in\n";
}

int main()
{
  Button panic;
  panic.setToOut();
  checkState(panic);
  panic.setToIn();
  checkState(panic);
}

/* Output:

State is out
State is in

*/
```

SUMMARY A private enumerator requires a "setter" and a "getter" member function for each possible valid state.

A Public Enumeration

Do you see a potential problem when using a private enumeration? When you have to write a "setter" and a "getter" member function for each possible state, things can get out of control quite rapidly. For example, consider a **Date** class with the 12 months encapsulated as an enumeration. Do you really want to provide 24 (!) member functions? I didn't think so.

The solution is to make the enumeration public. This is not a violation of the principle of data hiding because the enumerated values themselves are nothing more than read-only constants, and there's really no danger of destroying the integrity of the object. The user gains access to the enumeration's type and values by using the binary scope resolution operator. As a result, only two accessor member functions are needed: one to set the state, and the other to retrieve the state. The user provides the appropriate enumeration value for the member function to set the state.

Here is the **Button** class again, now using a public enumeration:

```
// File button.h

#ifndef BUTTON_H
```

```
#define BUTTON_H

class Button
{
    public:
  enum Status { out, in };  // public enumeration
  void setState(Status newState);
  Status getState() const;
    private:
  Status state;
};

#endif

// File button.cpp

#include "button.h"

void Button::setState(Status newState)
{
  state = newState;
}

Button::Status Button::getState() const
{
  return state;
}

// File main.cpp

#include <iostream>
#include "button.h"

typedef Button::Status STATUS;
STATUS const out = Button::out;
STATUS const in = Button::in;

void printState(Button const &panic)
{
  STATUS state = panic.getState();
  if(state == out)
    std::cout << "State is out\n";
  else if(state == in)
    std::cout << "State is in\n";
}
```

```
int main()
{
  Button panic;
  panic.setState(out);
  printState(panic);
  panic.setState(in);
  printState(panic);
}

/* Output:

State is out
State is in

*/
```

 Note carefully how the return type of the member function **getState**() has been scoped to the **Button** class. This is required because, at this point in its parsing algorithm, the compiler has no clue that **Status** is encapsulated within the **Button** class; you must explicitly say so. But once the compiler notes that the member function itself belongs to the **Button** class, then all further references (e.g., **state**) will obey normal lookup rules, that is, local scope, then class scope, then global scope.

SUMMARY Use a public enumeration when the number of enumerated values becomes excessive.

The "Enum Hack"

"What's that?" you ask. Suppose you need to create a compile-time constant—10, for example—to be used as the dimension of an array inside a class. You could always hard-code this dimension, as shown here:

```
class ADT
{
  double array[10];          // OK
  // ...
};
```

When you start using the array, however, you're once again going to be hard-coding the number 10, for example, as the terminating value of a loop. This is always a poor programming practice because the dimension of the array could later change from 10 to something else, and then you would have to seek out all uses of the number 10 and change them accordingly. Obviously a much better plan would be to hard-code the number 10 just once as a constant, give it a name, and then use this name throughout your code. However, you must remember that this code,

```
class ADT
{
    int const dimension = 10; // Compiler error
    double array[dimension];
    // ...
};
```

does not solve the problem because you are not allowed to initialize a nonstatic data member at the point of declaration. Yes, you could always declare the constant value at global scope, or even use a **#define**, but doesn't encapsulating the constant sound like a better idea?

The "enum hack" solves the problem quite nicely because any enumerated name takes on a default value but can always be overridden. Thus, an unnamed enumeration can be created as in the following, with the name **dimension** set to the value 10:

```
class ADT
{
    enum { dimension = 10 };
    double array[dimension];  // OK
    // ...
};
```

Because the value of **dimension** is known at compilation time, the compiler has no trouble with the array data member. And another class could have its own **dimension** with no conflict occurring. Problem solved.

 In Chapter 8 you will see another way to create a compile-time (integral) constant within a class definition.

The "enum hack" can be used to create a compile-time constant inside a class definition.

EXERCISE 6.3

Write a class called **Clock** with the following abstraction:

```
class Clock
{
        public:
    void set(int h, int m, int s);
    void tick(int sec = 1);
        private:
    int hours, minutes, seconds;
};
```

The member function **set()** establishes an initial time value, and the member function **tick()** increments the time by the number of seconds provided.

A separate class called **ClockView** has the following abstraction:

```
class ClockView
{
    public:
 enum format{ military, civilian };
 void setClockPtr(Clock ptr*);
 void display(format = military) const;
    private:
 Clock *ptrClock;
};
```

The **display()** function displays the time in **hh:mm:ss** format. (Because formatting has not yet been discussed, don't worry if your output is not exact.) If the default value is taken, display the time in military format; otherwise, display it in civilian format (A.M. and P.M. notation).

Create header and definition files for both classes. Use the following **main.cpp** file to test:

```
// File main.cpp

#include "clock.h"
#include "clockview.h"

int main()
{
 Clock BigBen;
 ClockView view(&BigBen);
 int const hours = 23, minutes = 59, seconds = 45;
 BigBen.set(hours, minutes, seconds);
 for(int i = 0; i < 30; ++i)
 {
   BigBen.tick();
   view.display();
 }
 BigBen.set(hours, minutes, seconds);
 for(int i = 0; i < 30; ++i)
 {
   BigBen.tick(5);
   view.display(ClockView::civilian);
 }
}
```

Constructors and Destructors

Introduction

Folks, we've got a big problem on our hands. Consider the **Button** class from Chapter 6. In order to stabilize any **Button** object, you had to call a member function, such as **setState()**. Unfortunately, this violates a fundamental principle of good object-oriented design—namely, the one that says that when an object comes into existence, it must immediately reside in a stable condition and remain stable throughout its lifetime. In simple terms, this means that an object never contains "junk" in its instance variables. But after the program instantiates the **Button** class instance **panic**, the instance's **state** data member (i.e., **panic.state**) contains an indeterminate value. In other words, the initial value of the **state** data member is totally unknown.

In Chapter 6 we solved the part about *remaining* in a stable condition by writing appropriate "setter" member functions that check the validity of new values that the user wants to store. But what about the state of an object as soon as it's created? In other words, what are the initial values in an object's data members when the object is instantiated? So far, the answer really is junk. Yes, junk. Like C, C++ provides no automatic initialization of variables (or class instances) created on the stack. The problem is quite simple: What's going to happen if the user of your class fails to call your initialization member function (such as **setState()**), but instead immediately calls a "getter" member function (such as **getState()**) to retrieve a value or uses the result of a computation that referenced the uninitialized values? Once again, the answer is junk.

A similar problem exists if the program is expected to perform some kind of "clean up" action when an object reaches the end of its lifetime. For example, an object might have a pointer variable as a data member, and within that pointer variable is the address of a block of memory that the program has allocated from the free store. Clearly, the program must return this memory block back to the free store *before* the object ceases to exist; otherwise, the program will "leak" memory (see Chapter 5). As before, we could write a member function that performs the desired "pre-mortem" housekeeping tasks, and then the user could call this function just before an object's lifetime ends. Of course, if the program fails to call the class's housekeeping function when an instance of that class is about to be destroyed, then any resources the instance holds (e.g., a block of storage from the free store) will not get released back to the system.

Fortunately, *constructors* and *destructors* solve this problem by providing the means by which your user-defined objects will *automatically* be initialized and destroyed.

> **SUMMARY** Constructors and destructors solve the problem of providing stability to class instances as soon as they are created.

Constructor Definition

A *constructor* (also known as a *ctor* by the language lawyers) is a special nonstatic member function that gets called by the compiler whenever an object of some class type is instantiated. That statement is so important I'm going to say it again, and it's one you should burn into your brain's memory bank. *Whenever a class gets instantiated, the compiler guarantees that a constructor will get called.* It makes no difference where the instance lives, be it the stack, the data segment, or the free store. If the instance is contained within another instance, or is a subpart of some other instance (involving the process of derivation), it still implies the invocation of a constructor.

The execution of a constructor (assuming that it has been written properly) means that the instance variables of the object will be initialized properly. In addition, the constructor is responsible for the allocation of any private resources that the object might need, such as a disk file, an input/output device, or space on the free store. Because a constructor is so fundamental to good class design, it is often referred to as a *manager function*.

> **SUMMARY** When a class gets instantiated, a constructor is guaranteed to be called by the compiler.

For example, for some typical class called **ADT** (meaning Abstract Data Type), the following (individual) constructor declarations are all valid:

```
class ADT
{
    public:
ADT();
ADT(int);
ADT(double);
ADT(int, double);
```

```
    ADT(int, char);
    ADT(short, double, long = 0);
    // ...
};
```

Syntax Rules

Here are the syntax rules for writing a constructor:

▲ Its name must be the same as that of the class to which it belongs, so that the compiler knows the member function is a constructor. For example, for class **ADT**, all constructors would be named **ADT()**; for class **Circle**, all constructors would be named **Circle()**, and so on.

▲ It is declared with no return type (not even **void**).

▲ It cannot have the qualifiers **static**, **const**, or **volatile**.

▲ It cannot be declared with the **virtual** modifier (virtual functions are discussed in Chapter 11).

▲ It can have public, protected, or private access within the class, and in this regard it follows the same rules that exist for other class member functions.

▲ It can be overloaded. That is, the class can have more than one constructor.

SUMMARY ➤ The constructor has the same name as the class to which it belongs, and it can be overloaded.

When a Constructor Is *Not* Invoked

It is important to understand that the creation of a primitive type, pointer, or reference *never* invokes a constructor for the simple reason that these types are not instances of a user-defined type (meaning a structure or a class). For example, when an instance of some class is passed as an argument into a function by pointer or by reference, no constructor is called. Similarly, if a non-**auto** instance of some class is returned from a function by pointer or by reference, no constructor is called. In order for a constructor to be called, there must be an instantiation of a *structure* or *class*.

SUMMARY ➤ The creation of a primitive type, pointer, or reference (any type other than a class or structure) *never* invokes a constructor.

The Compiler-Supplied Default Constructor

"Whenever a class gets instantiated, the compiler guarantees that a constructor will get called." Does that sentence sound familiar? It should, because it's the one I asked you to commit to memory. But something should be bothering you. In the last chapter you went around happily instantiating **Circle** objects that, you have to believe, caused a constructor to get called. But since you never wrote a constructor for the **Circle** class, how did the compiler let you get away with such a sinful omission?

The answer is, if you fail to write any constructor in a class (as has been the case up to now), the compiler *automatically* supplies one for you. This is called the *compiler-supplied default constructor*. By default (pun intended?) it has public access within the class and essentially serves to satisfy the implicit call that the compiler is guaranteed to make. Note, however, that it also serves two useful purposes:

▲ The compiler-supplied default constructor initializes any nonstatic data members that themselves are user-defined types by automatically invoking *their* default constructors. If the class for the encapsulated user-defined type does not have a default constructor, or if it's there but is not accessible, then the compiler will emit an error message.

▲ If the class involved is a derived class, the compiler-supplied default constructor invokes the default constructor of the base class, if it exists (discussed in Chapter 11).

Insofar as nonstatic *primitive* data members are concerned, they remain *uninitialized.*

CAUTION   If the compiler-supplied default constructor truly has no work to perform, its code can be optimized away by the compiler.

Let's see an example by revisiting the **Circle** class:

```
// File circle.h

#ifndef CIRCLE_H
#define CIRCLE_H

#include "point.h"

class Circle
{
    public:
  void storeRadius(int newRadius);
  int getRadius() const;
    private:
  Point center;
  int radius;
};

#endif

// File main.cpp
```

```
#include "circle.h"

int main()
{
    Circle circleInstance;
    // ...
}
```

In this case, the creation of the instance **circleInstance** will invoke the compiler-supplied default constructor for the **Circle** class. This constructor will invoke the compiler-supplied default constructor for the **Point** class.

SUMMARY

The compiler-supplied default constructor satisfies the requirement that a constructor be called whenever an instantiation of a class occurs. This particular constructor exists only if no other constructor in the class is present.

The Default Constructor: A General Definition

The compiler-supplied default constructor is only an *example* of a default constructor, and it does not constitute the complete definition of the term itself. The term *default constructor* refers to *any* constructor that can be invoked with no arguments, whether it is supplied automatically by the compiler or is written by you. Such a constructor can have either of two formats: (1) its parameter list is empty, that is, **void**; or (2) its parameter list consists of all default arguments, that is, a default argument is defined for every parameter in the function's parameter list. Of course, you cannot have more than one default constructor in a class because the compiler would then get confused as to which one it should invoke.

For example, in the **Circle** class either one of the two default constructors shown here would be valid, because both are callable with no arguments:

```
// File circle.h

#ifndef CIRCLE_H
#define CIRCLE_H

class Circle
{
    public:
    Circle();                    // Default constructor, or
    Circle(int radius = 10);  // Default constructor
    // ...
};

#endif
```

You should also be aware that a class **X** *must* have a callable default constructor when: (1) you want to create an array of **X** objects on the free store, or (2) some other class **Y** contains an array of **X** objects. For example:

```
class X
{
   // ...
};
X *ptrX = new X[5];   // Default constructor for X required
// ...
class Y
{
   X array[5]; // Default constructor for X required
   // ...
};
```

The instantiation of these **X** objects demands that a constructor be called for each object, and it is impossible to explicitly tell the compiler which (of possibly many) constructor to call, so the compiler has no choice except to call the default constructor.

 A default constructor is one that can be called with no arguments. Either its formal parameter list is empty (meaning **void**), or it takes all default parameters.

Initializing Constant Objects

Because C++ insists that all constant primitive types be initialized, the rule extends to user-defined types in the sense that the compiler will look for an explicitly defined constructor to do the job. Thus, in the following example, the only constructor in the class is the one supplied by the compiler, so the instantiation of the constant object is an error:

```
class ADT
{
   // ...
};

void func()
{
   ADT const object;   // Error here
}
```

CAUTION It's possible that your compiler might not enforce this restriction.

SUMMARY Be sure to supply an explicitly declared default constructor if there are no other constructors and you want to let the user create constant objects.

Constructor Overloading

As mentioned earlier, a class can have more than one constructor for the simple reason that there can be more than one way to construct an instance of that particular class. To illustrate, let's shift gears and talk about a string class, that is, a class that encapsulates an array of zero or more characters, terminated by the null character ('\0'). As you know, this is the definition of a string literal in C, but you will soon see the advantage of using a C++ class for its representation. Just to illustrate, C strings aren't strings, they are arrays of characters where you hope and pray that the last character is a null. Unfortunately, they are unsafe and error prone.

First, we must decide on the data representation. To be as flexible as possible, we must stay away from a fixed-size array of characters. After all, what dimension would suffice? 5? 10? 500? It's impossible to know, because only the user of the class knows how many characters need to be represented. Therefore, this decision must be deferred from compilation time until execution time, and it can easily be implemented by using a pointer-to-character type that will eventually point to space on the free store where the characters themselves will be held (and thereby enable you to use the free store management techniques you learned in Chapter 5).

The start of the class called **String** looks like this:

```
// File string.h

#ifndef STRING_H
#define STRING_H

class String
{
    public:
  // public interface
    private:
  char *ptrChars;
};

#endif
```

Next, we must decide on how a **String** object can be constructed. Does it make sense to construct an instance given no information whatsoever? The answer is yes, because this case is simply an empty **String** object. How about a single character as input? Again, the answer is yes. How about a **String** object from a C language array of characters? Once again, this makes perfect sense. Let's now add these three constructor declarations to our class, and we get the following:

```
// File string.h

#ifndef STRING_H
```

```
#define STRING_H

class String
{
    public:
  String();
  String(char ch);
  String(char const *chars);
  // ...
    private:
  char *ptrChars;
};
```

```
#endif
```

We can simplify matters by combining the default constructor with the array-of-characters constructor by using an empty string literal as the default value:

```
// File string.h

#ifndef STRING_H
#define STRING_H

class String
{
    public:
  String(char ch);
  String(char const *chars = "");
  // ...
    private:
  char *ptrChars;
};
```

```
#endif
```

CAUTION If you choose not to write a formal argument name for the second constructor declaration, for example, **char const** *=" "*, be sure to leave at least one space between the *
and the =. Otherwise, you will be writing the "multiply-and-assign" operator (*=), and
the compiler will scold you mercilessly.

Next, we'll write the definition file for these two constructor declarations. For the constructor accommodating a single character, it's just a matter of allocating the required space on the free store (exactly two characters) and then plugging this raw space with the input character and a null character (since that's how all C strings are terminated). For the constructor accommodating an array of characters, the required amount of space is allocated, and a copy of the characters is made:

```cpp
// File string.cpp

#include <cstring>
#include "string.h"

String::String(char ch)
{
  ptrChars = new char[2];
  ptrChars[0] = ch;
  ptrChars[1] = '\0';
}

String::String(char const *chars)
{
  chars = chars ? chars : "";
  ptrChars = new char[std::strlen(chars) + 1];
  std::strcpy(ptrChars, chars);
}
```

If a user maliciously decides to instantiate the **String** class using a constant of 0 that is cast to a **char const *** type, as in the following,

```cpp
String danger(static_cast<char const *>(0));
```

then the second constructor would be using 0 as a memory address and is in danger of either aborting or yielding disastrous results at run time. Notice how the constructor guards against this situation by testing the value of **chars**. In the case of 0 (Boolean **false**), the empty string literal will be used instead. (Of course, if it's possible for a **String** object to legitimately exist at address 0 in your particular system, then this validity check should be removed.)

 For the **String** class, it makes perfect sense to overload the constructor because there are several different ways in which a **String** object can be constructed.

A Constructor Cannot Be Called Directly

Note that a constructor can *never* be called directly by the user of the class because it's simply invalid syntax to try to do so. Only the compiler itself can make this call as a result of an instantiation of the class:

```cpp
void someFunction(String &arg)
{
  arg.String();       // Error; won't compile
}
```

 Only the compiler can call the constructor as the result of an instantiation.

EXERCISE 7.1

Modify Exercise 6.2 to include a constructor in the **Double** class that is callable with either no argument or one argument. If it's called with no argument, the value should default to zero. Be sure to test your modified class.

Destructor Definition

A *destructor* (also known as a *dtor*) is a special member function that is guaranteed to get executed whenever an instance of the class to which it belongs goes out of scope. An instance on the stack goes out of scope when the program reaches the closing brace of the code block that created the instance; an instance on the free store goes out of scope when a **delete** is issued for the pointer that points to the instance. So you can see that a destructor is somewhat the opposite of a constructor in the sense that it helps to "destroy" an instance by releasing the private resources that the constructor might have allocated, by closing a disk file, and so on. (Of course, such resources could be allocated after the constructor has long since completed executing, but the destructor is still responsible for releasing them.) In addition, like a constructor, the destructor is another example of a manager function.

SUMMARY ➤ A destructor is guaranteed to get called whenever an instance of a class goes out of scope.

The Compiler-Supplied Destructor

Because a destructor is guaranteed to get called by the compiler when an instance goes out of scope, the compiler automatically supplies its own default destructor with every class you write if you do not explicitly write the destructor yourself.

What the Destructor Does

For some class **ADT**, whether you write your own destructor or let the compiler supply one for you, the destructor always performs these three steps in this order:

1. The body of the destructor is executed;
2. All nonstatic data members of a user-defined type (subobjects) are automatically destroyed in reverse order of their construction;
3. If class ADT has an immediate base class, then the destructor for this base class is automatically called.

Of course, in all cases the destructors must be accessible.

CAUTION
If you terminate your program abnormally—for example, with an **exit()** call—then the destructor will be called only for global instances, not for stack-based instances. So although the **exit()** function is commonly used to abort a C program, a C++ program rarely (if ever!) calls **exit()** because this prevents the C++ program from calling those destructors (of stack-based objects) that are responsible for releasing allocated system resources. The "proper" way to abort a C++ program is by throwing an exception (see Chapter 9).

SUMMARY
If you do not write your own destructor, the compiler will supply one for you in order to satisfy the guarantee that a destructor must get called when an instance goes out of scope.

Writing Your Own Destructor

Of course, you are always free to write your own destructor. In this case the compiler-supplied destructor is suppressed. Therefore, a class is guaranteed to always have exactly one destructor. As mentioned, the destructor that you provide will automatically execute the three tasks listed earlier that the compiler-supplied default constructor performs.

In the case of the **String** class, the destructor is responsible for releasing the space on the free store that the constructor allocated. The following is the enhanced class definition with the destructor defined:

```
// File string.h

#ifndef STRING_H
#define STRING_H

class String
{
    public:
  ~String();
  // ...
    private:
  char *ptrChars;
};

#endif

// File string.cpp

#include "string.h"

String::~String()
```

```
    {
        delete [] ptrChars;
    }
```

Syntax Rules

Here are the syntax rules for writing a destructor:

- ▲ Its name is the same as that of the class to which it belongs, except that the name is preceded by a tilde (~).That is, for class **ADT**, the destructor would be named ~**ADT**(); for class **Circle**, it would be named ~**Circle**(), and so on.
- ▲ It is declared with no return type (not even **void**) because it cannot return a value.
- ▲ It cannot have the modifiers **const**, **static**, or **volatile**.
- ▲ It can be declared **virtual** (virtual functions are discussed in Chapter 11).
- ▲ It takes no input arguments and therefore cannot be overloaded.
- ▲ Unlike the constructor, it can be called directly; this is hardly ever done, however.

The compiler recognizes the destructor as having the same name as the class to which it belongs, preceded by a tilde.

How to Instantiate a Class and Invoke the Default Constructor

The process of creating objects (or instances) from a class or structure is called *instantiation*. Just as a cookie cutter creates (instantiates) cookies, a class instantiates objects, or instances. The C++ syntax to do this is really quite intuitive because it's the same syntax that the C language uses to create its variables.

For example, to create a **String** object and invoke the default constructor, you would write the following:

```
String stringName;
```

In the **String** class that we've been writing, this line of code causes the compiler to generate a call to the default constructor, which was declared as:

```
String(char const *chars = "");
```

No parameter was provided during the process of instantiation, so the formal argument's value will default to the empty string literal.

To instantiate a class and invoke the default constructor, simply write the class name followed by the instance name.

How to Instantiate a Class
and Pass Arguments to the Constructor

Most of the time, however, you will want to instantiate the **String** class using a constructor that takes at least one argument. To do this, you write the object name followed by a list of arguments within parentheses; each argument is separated by a comma. A suitable constructor must exist that can accommodate these arguments, and it must be accessible. For example, this is how you would invoke the two constructors in the **String** class while passing appropriate values:

```
String stringName('A');      // Character passed
String stringName("C++");    // String literal passed
```

This particular syntax is called "C++ style initialization," as opposed to "C style initialization," which resembles the way you would write C code. In other words, using C style initialization, the previous two lines would appear as:

```
String stringName = 'A';     // Character passed
String stringName = "C++";   // String literal passed
```

Although technically correct, the C style initialization should not be used because (1) it does not extend itself easily when more than one argument is needed; (2) it might not be quite as efficient as C++ style initialization; and (3) it will fail to compile if the constructor has been qualified with the **explicit** keyword (discussed later in this chapter under the heading "How to Suppress Implicit Type Conversion"). The moral of the story is this: Use C++ style initialization, and you can't go wrong.

For the sake of consistency, a variable of some primitive type can also be initialized using C++ style initialization, but there's no particular reason why you would write it this way:

```
int data(6);              // OK; same as: int data = 6;
```

SUMMARY▶ Use C++ style initialization when you need to pass arguments to a constructor. This consists of following the object's name with a parenthesized list of arguments.

Where You Could Go Wrong

Be very careful that you don't do the following:

```
String stringName(); // This is a function declaration!
```

This statement declares a global function called **stringName** that takes no arguments (same as **void**) and returns a **String** object by value. This is not good, if your intent was to perform an instantiation. Therefore, be sure that you do *not* write parentheses after the object's name when you wish to invoke the default constructor. All other times, when using C++ style initialization, you *must* use parentheses.

When performing an instantiation, always write parentheses after the object's name unless you wish to invoke the class's default constructor.

How to Prevent Instantiations with the Default Constructor

Two ways exist for preventing users of your class from instantiating it with an implicit call to the default constructor. The first way is easy—just declare a default constructor in the private part of the class definition. Because it is private, the compiler will not be able to generate a call to it from a nonmember function.

For example, this is how our **String** class would then be written:

```
// File string.h

#ifndef STRING_H
#define STRING_H

class String
{
    public:
    String(char ch);
    String(char const *chars);        // Not a default constructor
    // ...
    private:
    String();               // Private default constructor
    char *ptrChars;
};

#endif

// File main.cpp

#include "string.h"

int main()
{
    String stringName; // Compiler error
    // ...
}
```

Recall, however, that the member functions of the **String** class can call any other **String** class member function. This implies the following: A **String** class member function *can* use the **String** class's private default constructor to instantiate and default-construct another **String** class instance. So the "moral" of this code sample is this: Functions that are not members of the **String** class cannot default construct instances of the **String** class.

The second way to suppress instantiation with the default constructor is to write any (non-default) constructor of your choosing. When you do this, *the compiler-supplied default constructor is suppressed.* This is as it should be, because now the compiler has no idea if you really want to have a default constructor in the first place. It probably is not necessary to go so far as to declare a private default constructor. The revised class definition would look like this:

```
// File string.h

#ifndef STRING_H
#define STRING_H

class String
{
    public:
  String(char ch);
  String(char const *chars);
  // ...
    private:
  char *ptrChars;
};

#endif

// File main.cpp

#include "string.h"

int main()
{
  String stringName; // Compiler error
  // ...
}
```

This version of the **String** class does not have a default constructor. Therefore, the program cannot default construct instances of the **String** class—not even within the **String** class's own member functions.

Consider making the default constructor private, or even eliminating entirely, if that's what the class design calls for.

EXERCISE 7.2

Modify the **Clock** class from Chapter 6 by adding a constructor that is callable with three arguments:

```
class Clock
{
    public:
  Clock(int h = 12, int m = 0, int s = 0);
  void tick(int sec = 1);
    private:
  int hours, minutes, seconds;
};
```

Change the **main.cpp** file accordingly.

```
// File main.cpp

#include "clock.h"
#include "clockview.h"

int main()
{
  int const hours = 23, minutes = 59;
  Clock BigBen(hour, minutes);
  ClockView view(&BigBen);
  for(int i = 0; i < 30; ++i)
  {
    BigBen.tick(3);
    view.display();
  }
}
```

Implicit Type Conversion

Implicit type conversion in the C language is the process by which the compiler is allowed to implicitly convert one type into another type without the user's needing to write a cast. For example, the conversion of an **int** value into a **double** value is done implicitly, as is the conversion from type **double** into type **short**. In fact, any C language primitive type (excluding pointers) can always be implicitly converted into any other primitive type.

Because C++ introduces user-defined types, implicit type conversion now means that the compiler "knows" how to implicitly convert a primitive type into a user-defined type, and the user still does not need to write a cast. How does the compiler do this? By silently looking for a *converting constructor* in the class definition. This is a constructor that is callable with exactly one argument. For example, in our generic **ADT** class, all of the following constructors are converting constructors (and it's possible that they might also be default constructors as well):

```
class ADT
{
    public:
  ADT(char);
  ADT(int);
  ADT(double = 0.0);
  ADT(short, long = 0L);
  ADT(int = 0, double = 0.0);
};
```

Having the compiler' call a converting constructor results in the creation of a temporary, unnamed instance of the class on the stack.

CAUTION   The **ADT** class shown above is actually ill formed. Recall that a class cannot have more than one default constructor defined for it. In this case, the class has *two* default constructors defined (i.e., the third and fifth ctors).

The following constructors are *not* converting constructors because each one is *not* callable with exactly one argument:

```
class ADT
{
    public:
  ADT();
  ADT(double, short);
  ADT(short, long, int = 0);
};
```

The following is an example using our **String** class. Notice that both constructors are converting constructors. I've added a member function called **search**() that receives a reference to a const-qualified **String** object, and whose purpose is to see if the string pattern in the referenced **String** object matches the same string pattern in the **String** object to which the **search**() message is sent. In addition, note the support for constant objects:

```
// File string.h

#ifndef STRING_H
#define STRING_H
```

```
class String
{
    public:
  String(char ch);
  String(char const *chars = "");
  bool search(String const &) const;
  // ...
    private:
  char *ptrChars;
};

#endif

// File main.cpp

#include "string.h"

int main()
{
  String const masterString("C++");
  if(masterString.search("+"))      // String literal passed
     // Found a match
  if(masterString.search('C'))      // Character passed
     // Found a match
  // ...
}
```

The first call to **search**() uses a string literal, and the second uses a character. Because the **search**() member function expects to receive a **String** object by reference-to-**const** as its one explicit parameter, the compiler will implicitly visit the appropriate converting constructor in order to instantiate a **String** object. The resulting stack instance is then aliased by this **String** reference in **search**(). When the function ends, the reference goes out of scope, and the temporary **String** object is then popped off the stack (and its destructor gets called).

We'll see many more examples of implicit type conversion throughout this book, and I'll point them out as they occur.

SUMMARY ▶ Implicit type conversion allows a primitive type to be implicitly converted to a user-defined type as the compiler silently visits a converting constructor in the class. This is a constructor that is callable with exactly one argument.

How to Suppress Implicit Type Conversion

You also have the option to suppress implicit type conversion for a class. This is accomplished by writing the keyword **explicit** (meaning "not implicit") as a modifier for a converting constructor. Typically, vector and array classes declare their converting constructors to be explicit.

Here is an example showing what does and does not work for the **String** class when dealing with the converting constructor that takes a **char** type as its one argument:

```cpp
// File string.h

#ifndef STRING_H
#define STRING_H

class String
{
    public:
  explicit String(char ch); // Note 'explicit' keyword
  // ...
    private:
  char *ptrChars;
};

#endif

// File main.cpp

#include "string.h"

int main()
{
  // These instantiations work
  String stringName('A');
  String stringName = String('A');
  String stringName = (String)'A';
  String stringName = static_cast<String>('A');
  String *ptrString = new String('A');
  String stringArray[] = { String('A') };
  String stringArray[] = { (String)'A' };
  String stringArray[] = { static_cast<String>('A') };

  // These instantiations are erroneous
  String stringName = 'A';  // Note C style initialization
  String stringArray[] = { 'A' };
}
```

In all of the erroneous cases, the class name **String** does not appear to the right of the equal sign. In all of the cases in which the instantiations work, the class name does indeed appear to the right of the equal sign.

Use the C++ keyword **explicit** as a modifier to a converting constructor to suppress the use of implicit type conversion

EXERCISE 7.3

Modify Exercise 7.1 so that the **Double** class contains a function called **add()** declared as:

```
void add(Double const &val) const;
```

Its purpose is to add the input value **val** to the encapsulated **double** value. Modify the **main()** function to call **add()** with a primitive type to illustrate the implicit type conversion that will occur.

Copy Constructor

All C++ classes have another constructor with which you must be familiar. This is called the *copy constructor*. To get an understanding of what it is all about, consider the following C language program:

```
/* A C language program */

typedef struct
{
  int data;           // Just some typical data
} T;

T someFunction(T arg)
{
  return arg;
}

int main(void)
{
  T instance1 = { 1 };
  T instance2 = instance1;
  T instance3 = someFunction(instance2);
  return 0;
}
```

After the object **instance1** has been created, the following items should be apparent:

▲ When **instance2** is instantiated, the value in **instance1** is copied into **instance2**;

▲ When the formal argument **arg** is instantiated (as a consequence of the call to function **someFunction()**), the value in **instance2** is copied into the formal argument **arg**;

▲ When **someFunction()** executes its **return** statement, a temporary, unnamed type **T** object is instantiated and **arg**'s value is copied into temporary (and popped off the stack);

▲ When **instance3** is instantiated, the value in the unnamed, temporary **T** object (that **someFunction()** returns) is copied into **instance3**;

▲ The unnamed, temporary **T** object goes out of scope and is automatically destroyed by the program.

Now let's run that same code through a C++ compiler. The instantiation of any user-defined type in C++ (including a structure) *always* invokes a constructor (sound familiar?), so a constructor that can accommodate all of this copying must exist in the class. This constructor does indeed exist and is called the *copy constructor*. The purpose of a class's copy constructor is to take an existing instance (of that class) and instantiate a new instance that is a "copy" of the existing instance. To be more precise, the copy constructor copies the values from an existing instance's nonstatic data members into the corresponding data members of the instance that is currently under construction.

Based on the example above, you can see that the copy constructor will be invoked automatically by the compiler under these three conditions:

▲ An instance of a class is made directly from some existing instance of that same class,

▲ An instance of a class is passed into a function *by value,*

▲ An instance of a class is returned from a function *by value.*

As a general rule, you should almost never pass an instance of a class into a function by value. Instead, pass it in by reference-to-**const** to avoid the wasteful call to the copy constructor (and destructor when the object goes out of scope). This has virtually the same effect as a pass-by-value, but is much more efficient. Of course, as mentioned in Chapter 1, you must never return an auto (stack-based) object from a function by reference or by pointer, because the resultant reference or pointer would then be referring or pointing to space you no longer own. Sometimes you have to "pay the penalty" of returning an object by value from a function. (As we'll soon see, however, this call to the copy constructor can be optimized out of existence by the compiler.)

CAUTION The copy constructor could get called in a fourth situation involving exception handling. This is covered in Chapter 9.

SUMMARY The copy constructor gets called whenever a copy of an existing class instance needs to be made.

Default Copy Constructor

If you fail to declare a copy constructor, as was the case in that simple C language program we just looked at, then the compiler will implicitly supply one for you that does a *memberwise (or shallow) copy* of the instance variables. What's a memberwise copy? For a C language primitive type, it simply copies the bits from the existing object into the object under construction. For a C++ user-defined type, however, it involves calling the copy constructor for that particular type, because only that class knows how it should be copied. This, in turn, might call another copy constructor, which might call yet more copies, until only primitive types are copied.

 If you fail to declare your own copy constructor, the compiler will always supply one that does a memberwise copy of the nonstatic data.

Syntax of the Copy Constructor

The copy constructor, whether supplied implicitly by the compiler or written by you, takes as its one mandatory parameter a reference to an instance of its own class, which is usually implemented as a reference-to-**const** in order to support constant objects. For example, in the **String** class, the copy constructor would be declared as the following:

```
String(String const &);
```

Note that the reference is required:

```
String(String const);        // Illegal; won't compile
```

 The copy constructor takes as its one mandatory parameter a reference to an instance of its own class; it is usually implemented as a reference-to-**const**.

How Many Copy Constructors Are There?

A class always has at least one copy constructor; in fact, it could have more, but this is extremely unlikely. For example, in the **String** class, the following constructors are all valid copy constructor declarations:

```
class String
{
    public:
  String(String &);
  String(String const &);
  String(String const &, int = 0);
};
```

Unlike the default constructor, the copy constructor is guaranteed to exist regardless of whether you write no other constructors or a hundred of them.

A class has at least one copy constructor, but it can have more, even though this is highly unlikely.

Shallow versus Deep Copy

Before proceeding to the topic of writing your own copy constructor, let's examine closely the differences between performing a shallow and performing a deep copy of an object. Using a primitive type, the following is how a shallow copy is done:

```
int *ptr1 = new int(1);
int *ptr2 = ptr1;           // Shallow copy
// ...
delete ptr1;
*ptr2 = 2;                  // Oops...undefined behavior
delete ptr2;                // Also undefined
```

The copy is shallow because only the bits comprising the pointer value **ptr1** are being copied into **ptr2**. As a result, two pointers are now pointing at the same space on the free store. Consequently, after the first **delete** is issued, the pointer **ptr2** cannot be dereferenced and cannot be **delete**d because it now points to space that has already been released.

Alternatively, a deep copy entails copying the actual object being pointed at, so now each pointer points to its own unique space on the free store and all **delete**s can be issued with complete safety:

```
int *ptr1 = new int(1);
int *ptr2 = new int(*ptr1);     // Deep copy
// ...
delete ptr1;            // OK
*ptr2 = 2;              // OK
delete ptr2;            // OK
```

A shallow copy copies only the bits of an object. A deep copy copies the entire object itself.

Writing Your Own Copy Constructor

As a general rule (and the nice thing about generalizations is that they're generally true), except for the most trivial classes, you should plan on writing your own copy constructor. This is especially important when the class contains a pointer that manages space on the free store, as is the case for the **String** class. So what if you don't? Then the compiler will supply the class with its own default copy constructor, and the pointer member that we've called **ptrChars** will merely be copied into any new instance. Thus, there will be at least two pointers containing the same address on the free store. When the destructors

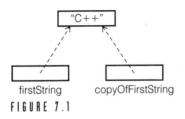

firstString   copyOfFirstString

FIGURE 7.1

for these **String** objects execute, however, all calls after the first will then attempt to release space *that has already been released and is no longer owned.* This, my friends, is like playing with fire and can be illustrated by Figure 7.1 and the following code example:

```
// File string.h

#ifndef STRING_H
#define STRING_H

class String
{
    public:
  String(char const *chars = "");
  ~String();
    private:
  char *ptrChars;
};

#endif

// File string.cpp

#include <cstring>
#include "string.h"

String::String(char const *chars)
{
  chars = chars ? chars : "";
  ptrChars = new char[std::strlen(chars) + 1];
  std::strcpy(ptrChars, chars);
}

String::~String()
{
  delete [] ptrChars;
}
```

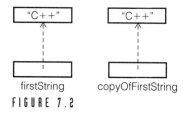

firstString   copyOfFirstString

FIGURE 7.2

```cpp
// File main.cpp

#include "string.h"

int main()
{
    String firstString("C++");
    String copyOfFirstString(firstString);
} // Danger here when both String objects go out of scope
```

Therefore, you must write your own copy constructor, and you must perform what's called a *deep*, or *intelligent*, copy. To do this, you must ensure that each **String** object holds its own internal representation of a string literal. Therefore, you must allocate space on the free store each time a **String** object is instantiated and copy the existing string literal into this space. Then, when the destructors for these objects run, there will be no problem because each internal pointer points only to its own privately held space on the free store, as illustrated in Figure 7.2 and the following code:

```cpp
// File string.h

#ifndef STRING_H
#define STRING_H

class String
{
    public:
    String(String const &);
    ~String();
    // ...
    private:
    char *ptrChars;
};

#endif
```

```
// File string.cpp

#include <cstring>
#include "string.h"

String::String(String const &str)
{
   // What the default would do:
   // ptrChars = str.ptrChars;
   ptrChars = new char[std::strlen(str.ptrChars) + 1];
   std::strcpy(ptrChars, str.ptrChars);
}

String::~String()
{
   delete [] ptrChars;
}

// File main.cpp

#include "string.h"

int main()
{
   String firstString("C++");
   String copyOfFirstString(firstString);
   // or...
   String copyOfFirstString = firstString;
}
```

Note that the call to the copy constructor in **main**() can use either C or C++ style initialization syntax.

![SUMMARY] Plan on writing your own copy constructor, especially when the class contains a pointer that manages space on the free store.

How to Suppress Object Copying

If for any reason you do not want to allow the users of your class to make copies of existing objects, then it is up to you to declare a *private* copy constructor in your class definition:

```
// File string.h

#ifndef STRING_H
```

```
#define STRING_H

class String
{
    public:
  String(char const *chars = "");
  // ...
    private:
  String(String const &);   // Private copy constructor
  char *ptrChars;
};

#endif

// File main.cpp

#include "string.h"

int main()
{
  String firstString("C++");
  String copyOfFirstString(firstString);     // Compiler error
  // or...
  String copyOfFirstString = firstString;    // Compiler error
}
```

It might not make sense to do this for the **String** class, but there are plenty of other classes for which it makes perfect sense to have a private copy constructor. In addition, there is no need to *define* the copy constructor, because it will never (successfully) be called. (Note, however, that it can still be called by a member function of the **String** class. When the linker fails to find a definition, you will get a link error.)

SUMMARY Declare a private copy constructor if you want to prevent the users of your class from making copies of existing objects.

EXERCISE 7.4

Modify the **Double** class to include a user-defined copy constructor.

Function Style Cast

Consider a complex number class that encapsulates both real and imaginary parts as type **int**, with a good-looking default/converting constructor and copy constructor, such as the following:

```
class Complex
{
    public:
  Complex(int r = 0, int i = 0);
  Complex(Complex const &);
    private:
  int real, imag;
};
```

Now suppose that a nonmember function called **getComplexNumber**() is designed to prompt the user for two **int** values to be used to instantiate a **Complex** number. This number is then returned out of the function (by value, of course, because it lives on the stack). Your first instinct might be to write the function like this:

```
Complex getComplexNumber()
{
  std::cout << "Enter two integer values: ";
  int real, imag;
  std::cin >> real >> imag;
  Complex number(real, imag);
  return number;
}
```

Then you might call the function like this:

```
int main()
{
  Complex comp(getComplexNumber());
  // ...
}
```

Of course, the creation of **number** will most certainly cause a constructor to get invoked; when the function terminates, **number** will go out of scope and the destructor will get called. In addition, because **number** is being returned by value, you should recall that this is one of those situations that calls for the invocation of the copy constructor. Finally, the creation of the object **comp** most certainly demands that a constructor be called again. That's a total of three constructor calls! Must we really pay such a high price in terms of constructor calls for such a simple task?

Happily, the answer is no. The key to solving this little efficiency dilemma is have the function use a *function style cast*. By definition, this cast creates an unnamed, temporary instance of a class on the stack. The syntax of this cast is the class name followed by a parenthetical list of arguments (if any) to be passed to the constructor. That's all there is to it. Because a function style cast is so important, and you will be seeing it so often, I'm going to describe its syntax again: A class name followed by a parenthetical list of arguments (if any) to be passed to the constructor.

Let's revisit the **getComplexNumber()** function again, but this time we'll use a function style cast instead of a named object:

```
Complex getComplexNumber()
{
   std::cout << "Enter two integer values: ";
   int real, imag;
   std::cin >> real >> imag;
   return Complex(real, imag);      // Function style cast
}
```

So what's the big deal, you ask? Aren't three constructors still being called? In all probability, the answer is that, in fact, only *one* constructor will be called to create the object called **comp**. By employing a function style cast, you give the compiler a much better chance of performing optimization in which it can combine all three theoretical constructor calls into one. This process is called *return value optimization*. However, the return of a named object will almost surely invoke the overhead of a call to the copy constructor and subsequent destructor, resulting in a minimum of two constructor calls. (Would this be called return value pessimization?)

By the way, in case you're wondering why you can't use a **static_cast** here, consider this code:

```
Complex getComplexNumber()
{
   std::cout << "Enter two integer values: ";
   int real, imag;
   std::cin >> real >> imag;
   return static_cast<Complex>(real, imag);
}
```

In this case, the compiler treats the comma between **real** and **imag** on the last line as the comma operator. Thus, it will ignore the **real** value, and effectively reduce the line to this:

```
return static_cast<Complex>(imag);
```

This produces a **Complex** number with **imag** as the real part and 0 (the default value) as the imaginary part. Oops. That's why a function style cast must be used.

Let's enhance the **Complex** class with the capability of adding two complex numbers together using a nonmember function called **add()**:

```
// File complex.h

#ifndef COMPLEX_H
#define COMPLEX_H
```

```
class Complex
{
    public:
  Complex(int r = 0, int i = 0);
  Complex(Complex const &);
  int getReal() const;
  int getImag() const;
  // ...
    private:
  int real, imag;
};

Complex const add (Complex const &first, Complex const &second);

#endif

// File complex.cpp

#include "complex.h"

Complex::Complex(int r, int i)
{
  real = r;
  imag = i;
}

Complex::Complex(Complex const &arg)
{
  real = arg.real;
  imag = arg.imag;
}

int Complex::getReal() const
{
  return real;
}

int Complex::getImag() const
{
  return imag;
}

Complex const add (Complex const &first, Complex const &second)
{
```

```
    // Note function style cast to create the sum of 'first'
    // and 'second'
    return Complex(first.getReal() + second.getReal(),
                     first.getImag() + second.getImag());
}


// File main.cpp

#include "complex.h"

int main()
{
    Complex c1(1, 2), c2(3), sum(add(c1, c2));
}
```

As a result of our excellent style of coding in the function **add**(), the compiler will most likely generate only three constructor calls for the three objects **c1**, **c2**, and **sum** (although the exact number is always compiler dependent). All other calls will be discarded. What more could you ask for?

 The reason why **add**() was written as a nonmember function instead of a member function will be explained in Chapter 8. In addition, its return type is **const**-qualified to guarantee that the object being created is nonmodifiable.

 When possible, consider using a function style cast instead of creating a name object, especially when returning an object from a function by value. This gives the compiler the chance to optimize one or more constructor calls out of existence.

Initialization versus Assignment

Does anyone remember the PITA rule from Chapter 1? Of course you do! That's the rule that says to Prefer (declaration and) Initialization To Assignment. Now take another look at the previous example, in particular the constructor definitions of the **Complex** class. Are the two lines of code in each body performing initialization or assignment? Of course they're good old-fashioned C language assignment statements, thereby violating the PITA rule. After all, shouldn't our goal be to *initialize* the data members?

 Get ready to start *initializing* nonstatic data members of a class instead of assigning into them.

Base/Member Initialization List

The base/member initialization list (also known as the constructor initialization list, or simply the member initializer list) is used to *initialize* (rather than assign into) the non-static data members of a class, and thus it adheres to the PITA rule. This list is valid only in the context of a constructor definition. It must appear immediately after the closing parenthesis of the formal argument list.

Here is a simple example in which a **Person** class contains both a **String** object (for the name) and a **long** variable (for the Social Security Number) and properly *initializes* both members:

```
// File person.h

#ifndef PERSON_H
#define PERSON_H

#include "string.h"

class Person
{
    public:
    Person(char const *n, long s);
    private:
    String name;
    long ssn;
};

#endif

// File person.cpp

#include "person.h"

Person::Person(char const *n, long s) : name(n), ssn(s) { }
```

Now let's have a look at the syntax that is used for initialization. To repeat, this syntax appears after the closing parenthesis in the constructor definition and consists of the following items:

▲ A single colon,

▲ The name of a nonstatic data member to be initialized,

▲ A parenthetical list of initializing values for the nonstatic data member. For a primitive type, only one such value can appear. For a user-defined type, any number of values can appear, assuming that a suitable constructor exists and is callable. Each initializing value can be any valid C++ expression, including a function call,

▲ A comma; repeat the previous two steps if another nonstatic data member is to be initialized.

Notice how the first argument of the **Person** constructor receives a pointer-to-**const char** (i.e., the address of a **const**-qualified string literal), and uses it to initialize the data member **name** whose type is **String**. How can this be, you ask, since the two types are different? Implicit type conversion solves the problem quite nicely as the converting constructor in the **String** class is visited to produce a temporary **String** object. (In fact, a C++ compiler is allowed to optimize away this temporary object. That is, it can use the converting constructor to directly construct the data member **name** "in place.") Of course, don't forget to write the body of the constructor, starting and ending with curly braces, even if there's nothing else to do.

Admittedly, you could have assigned the formal arguments **n** and **s** into the members **name** and **ssn**, respectively, and gotten the correct result; as noted earlier, however, it's still better style to prefer initialization to assignment. For the **name** field, it now becomes a matter of efficiency, as you will soon see.

SUMMARY ▶ Use the base/member initialization list to perform true initialization of the class's non-static data members.

Default Initialization

What happens if you fail to initialize a nonstatic member of a class? In the case of a primitive type, its value will be unknown. If its name in the base/member initialization list is followed by *empty parentheses,* however, then it will be initialized with the type's default static value, that is, zero.

Here's a simple example in which the value of **data1** will be zero and the value of **data2** will be unknown after construction:

```
class ADT
{
    public:
  ADT() : data1() { }
    private:
  int data1, data2;
};
```

In the case where a user-defined type is used as a data member (called a *subobject member*) of another class (e.g., the **name** member in the **Person** class), if the data member's name is followed by a pair of empty parentheses in the member initialization list—for example, **name()**—this specifies that the default constructor will be used to initialize that data member (assuming the default constructor is present and accessible). But unlike a primitive type, if you fail to say anything one way or the other about the subobject member, then the default constructor will still be invoked because the compiler guarantees that a constructor *must* be called whenever a user-defined type gets instantiated. Remember: Whenever a class needs to be instantiated and you've given the compiler no direction whatsoever, the compiler will always try to invoke the default constructor.

Thus, in the following example it makes no difference if the commented code is present or absent. If it is absent, the **String** class's default constructor will automatically get called to initialize the data member **name**:

```
class Person
{
    public:
    Person(char const *n) /* : name() */ { }
    private:
    String name;
};
```

SUMMARY For a primitive type, use empty parentheses to achieve default initialization. For a user-defined type, empty parentheses are optional.

EXERCISE 7.5

Modify the **Clock** class so that all constructors perform *initialization* on the data members, not assignment.

Mandatory Use of the Base/Member Initialization List

Do you remember from Chapter 1 that *all* constants and *all* reference variables in C++ must be *initialized*? The rule hasn't gone away, and it holds true for nonstatic data members of a class. In this case, the base/member initialization list *must* be used to perform the initialization of constants and references. What if you don't? The answer is quite simple — you'll get a nasty compiler error.

Consider the following trivial class. Because only the compiler's default constructor is present, and it will leave the data members untouched, no one is taking responsibility for performing the requisite initialization of the members **constant** and **reference**. Therefore, you will get two error messages:

```
class ADT
{
    int const constant;
    int &reference;
};
```

Let's enhance the class by providing a constructor that properly initializes the data members using values that are passed in:

```
class ADT
{
    public:
    ADT(int c, int &r) : constant(c), reference(r) { }
```

```
    private:
  int const constant;
  int &reference;
};
```

 If the class has more than one constructor, then each constructor must initialize all constants and references.

SUMMARY You have no choice but to initialize all constants and references by using the base/member initialization list.

EXERCISE 7.6

Modify Exercise 7.4 so that the **View** class takes a reference to an instance of the **Double** class.

Another Case Calling for Initialization

In addition, the base/member initialization list *should* be used to initialize any nonstatic data members that are user-defined types and that need to be constructed with something other than the default constructor.

For example, once again here is the **Person** class containing an instance of the **String** class to represent the **name** field:

```
// File person.h

#ifndef PERSON_H
#define PERSON_H

#include "string.h"

class Person
{
    public:
  Person(char const *n, long s);
    private:
  String name;
  long ssn;
};

#endif

// File person.cpp

#include "person.h"
```

```
Person::Person(char const *n, long s)
{
  name = n;
  ssn = s;
}
```

The big difference now, however, is that the PITA rule is being abandoned in favor of using *assignment* for the two data members (the PATI rule?). The problem is that, by definition, no assignment into an object can occur until that object has been created, so the compiler must first instantiate the **name** object using the **String** class's default constructor (what else could it possibly do?). Next, it will call the appropriate converting constructor (in the **String** class) to convert the argument **n** from pointer-to-**const char** into an unnamed, temporary instance of the **String** class. Finally, the unnamed, temporary **String** class instance is assigned into the data member **name** using the **String** class's overloaded assignment operator (discussed in Chapter 10). Now, a lot of free store management is occurring needlessly, and why would you want to invoke *three* member functions in the **String** class (the default constructor call that initially constructs the data member **name**, then the converting constructor call that converts **n** into a **String** instance, and finally the **String** class's overloaded assignment operator call) as opposed to one? The answer, of course, is that you wouldn't, which is why you should always prefer to *initialize* the nonstatic data instead of assigning to them, especially for user-defined types.

Even in the case of the Social Security Number, where the efficiency is about the same, you should still prefer initialization because at some point in the future the data member might be declared **const** (in which case your code will still work). Besides, it looks better and it shows the rest of the world that you know you're doing (always a good idea).

Here is the way it should be done:

```
// File person.h

#ifndef PERSON_H
#define PERSON_H

#include "string.h"

class Person
{
    public:
  Person(char const *n, long s);
    private:
  String name;
  long ssn;
};

#endif
```

```
// File person.cpp

#include "person.h"

Person::Person(char const *n, long s) : name(n), ssn(s) { }
```

 Even if a class's data member is neither constant nor a reference, you should still prefer to initialize it.

What About Pointers?

Pointers as class data members that point to space on the free store require special handling. They involve issues dealing with the concept of *exception handling*, and this topic is not discussed until Chapter 9. For now, just be aware that you should *not* attempt to initialize pointers to point to the free store in the base/member initialization list, but instead you should *assign* to them in the body of the constructor. Is this a violation of the PITA rule? Not really; in Chapter 9 you will learn how pointers should be initialized and managed properly.

 Continue to assign into pointers in the body of the constructor.

Formal Argument Names versus Class Member Names

C++ allows a formal argument name to be identical to that of a class's nonstatic data member. There is no ambiguity in the base/member initialization list because the member to be initialized will always be resolved at class scope, so it's not as though the formal argument is being "initialized" with itself. Of course, within the body of the constructor, where only assignment can occur, it's a different story. For example:

```
class ADT
{
    public:
  ADT(int data) : data(data) { }   // OK; no ambiguity
    private:
  int data;
};
```

 It's OK to initialize a nonstatic data member with a formal argument having the same name.

Initialization Order of Nonstatic Data Members

The order of initialization of the nonstatic data members is completely dependent on their order of declaration inside the class, and it has absolutely nothing to do with the order of these members in the base/member initialization list itself. Because there is always exactly one destructor in every class, this destructor must call the destructors of the respective members (assuming that they're user-defined types) in some prescribed order (LIFO, meaning Last-In-First-Out). Therefore, all constructors must construct these data members in exactly the opposite order, even if their base/member initialization lists are all different. Nevertheless, a good programming practice is to write the members in the base/member initialization list in the same order in which they are declared in the class.

To prove that data members are initialized in declaration order, note that **x** in the following is still being initialized before **y** even though the initialization of **y** appears first in the base/member initialization list:

```
// File adt.h

#ifndef ADT_H
#define ADT_H

class ADT
{
    public:
  ADT();
    private:
  int x, y;
  int initializeX();
  int initializeY();
};

#endif

// File adt.cpp

#include <iostream>
#include "adt.h"

ADT::ADT() : y(initializeY()), x(initializeX()) { }

int ADT::initializeX()
{
  std::cout << "Initializing x\n";
  return 0;
}
```

```
int ADT::initializeY()
{
  std::cout << "Initializing y\n";
  return 0;
}



// File main.cpp

#include "adt.h"

int main()
{
  ADT();         // Note function style cast
}

/* Output:

Initializing x
Initializing y

*/
```

SUMMARY Nonstatic data members will get initialized in the same order in which they are declared in the class.

A Primitive Type Array as a Nonstatic Data Member

The C++ language does not allow you to use the base/member initialization list to initialize the individual elements of a nonstatic array that is declared as part of a class. The best you can do is: (1) default initialize all of the array's elements, and then (2) assign the desired initial values to the array's elements within the body of the constructor. Is this a violation of the PITA rule? Well, yes, which just proves the old adage that we live in an imperfect world:

```
// File adt.h

#ifndef ADT_H
#define ADT_H

class ADT
{
    public:
  ADT();
```

```
      private:
   enum { dimension = 5 };
   int array[dimension];
};


#endif


// File adt.cpp


#include "adt.h"


ADT::ADT()      // The data member 'array' cannot be
                // initialized here
{
   // The best you can do is assign into each element
   // of the array
   for(int i = 0; i < dimension; ++i)
     array[i] = i;
}
```

 An array of a primitive type inside a class cannot be initialized in the base/member initialization list. The best you can do is assign into each element.

An Array of User-Defined Types as a Nonstatic Data Member

If some user-defined class **X** has an array data member whose elements are objects of some other user-defined class **Y**, then the class **Y** objects that comprise the array's elements must be fully constructed before the program enters the body of any class **X** constructor call. Because class **X**'s constructors cannot use a base/member initialization list to specify initial values for each of the **Y** objects in the member array, the only possible construction for these **Y** objects is default construction. If the member array has 'n' elements, there will be 'n' calls to class **Y**'s default constructor, that is, one default constructor call for each class **Y** object (element) in the array. Of course, if class **Y**'s default constructor does not initialize each **Y** object with the initial values that class **X** requires, the program will need to perform some extra work within the body of the class **X** constructor to correct this situation. Specifically, class **X**'s constructor must now use (for example) class **Y**'s converting constructors and class **Y**'s overloaded assignment operator(s) to assign the desired initial values into the class **Y** objects that comprise the member array's elements. You've got to believe this is a poor class design!

We'll use our **String** class in the following example to illustrate this:

```
// File adt.h

#ifndef ADT_H
#define ADT_H

#include "string.h"

class ADT
{
    public:
  ADT();
    private:
  enum { dimension = 5 };
  String array[dimension];
};

#endif

// File adt.cpp

#include "adt.h"
#include "string.h"

ADT::ADT()
// String default constructor called 'dimension' times
{
  for(int i = 0; i < dimension; ++i)
    array[i] = "C++";
}
```

SUMMARY ► An array consisting of a user-defined type is guaranteed to have the type's default constructor called for each array element.

How to Create an Array of User-Defined Instances

We just saw that when an array consisting of a user-defined type is declared *inside* a class, the type's default constructor will get called for each array element. Happily, this restriction does not apply when that same array is defined *outside* a class. As with an array of fundamental types, you can specify initializers between braces, and those initializers will determine which constructor will get called.

As a quick review, let's see how it's done with a primitive type. The actual values are listed between braces and separated by commas. Remember that the dimension of the array does not need to be written if you let the compiler do the counting for you. In addition, if you specify the dimension and if the number of initializing values is less than this dimension, then all remaining elements are automatically set to binary zero. That is, under ANSI C it is not possible to partially initialize an array; it's an all-or-nothing situation. For example, using an array of **int**s:

```
// 3 elements: unknown values
int array[3];

// 3 elements: 0, 0, 0 (see caution)
int array[3] = { };

// 3 elements: 0, 0, 0
int array[3] = { 0 };

// 3 elements: 1, 2, 3
int array[3] = { 1, 2, 3 };

// 3 elements: 1, 2, 0
int array[3] = { 1, 2 };

// 3 elements: 1, 2, 3
int array[]  = { 1, 2, 3 };

// Error; too many initializers
int array[3] = { 1, 2, 3, 4 };

// Error; no dimension and no initializers
int array[];
```

CAUTION   From Chapter 1, specifying a dimension and an empty initializer list is valid code, but this might not yet be supported by your favorite compiler.

When the array consists of instances of some user-defined type, it should be obvious that, if you provide initial values, a constructor that accepts these values as formal arguments must be written. In addition, for any uninitialized array element, the compiler will attempt to invoke the default constructor and therefore the class's default constructor must be implemented and accessible.

Note that when you write the values that each array element will take on, you should use a *function style cast* unless the constructor expects only one value; in this case, the cast is optional because implicit type conversion will apply (assuming a suitable converting constructor exists). To have the compiler invoke the default constructor, write a function style cast with empty parentheses:

```
String array1[3];              // 3 elements using the default ctor
String array2[5] =
{
  String(),                    // Default constructor used
  "C++",                       // Converting constructor used
  String("C++")                // Converting constructor used
}; // Last 2 elements will use the default constructor
```

It's possible to provide true initialization of an array that is not a member of a class and that does not exist on the free store.

How to Declare an Array of Constant Data Members

If you ever need to declare an array of constant data members in some class, you come face to face with a real dilemma. On the one hand, C++ insists that *all* constants be initialized using, of course, the base/member initialization list. On the other hand, an array as a nonstatic class member *cannot* be initialized in the base/member initialization list. Given this tug of war, what's a poor C++ programmer to do? For example:

```
class ADT
{
  enum { dimension = 10 };
  int const array[dimension];      // No way!
};
```

Different compilers are likely to yield different results from this example. Just thought you'd like to know.

In C++ it's impossible to create an array of constant elements as a nonstatic member of a class.

How to Create a Single
User-Defined Type on the Free Store

Like a primitive type, a single instance of a user-defined type created on the free store can also be initialized by specifying some value or values between parentheses. Of course, the compiler will then call the appropriate constructor, in this case the **String** constructor that accepts a **char const ***:

```
String *ptrString = new String("C++");
// ...
delete ptrString;
```

If you wish to invoke the default constructor, you can write empty parentheses after the class name, or you can eliminate the parentheses entirely:

```
String *ptrString = new String;          // or...
String *ptrString = new String();
// ...
delete ptrString;
```

 Do not confuse this choice with the case in which the object is created on the stack. Here, parentheses after the object's name cannot be written.

 A user-defined type can be instantiated on the free store just like a primitive type. Any arguments to be passed to the constructor can be written between parentheses.

How to Create an Array of a User-Defined Type on the Free Store

If you want to allocate an array of user-defined objects on the free store, you might be tempted to write this:

```
int const dimension = 10;
String *ptrString = new String[dimension];
// ...
delete [] ptrString;
```

You have no choice here but to invoke the default constructor **dimension** times. Then you will have to iterate across the array and perform an assignment into each **String** object. Does this sound like a violation of the PITA rule to you? It sure does to me.

The solution is to first allocate an array of pointers (storing the output into a pointer-to-pointer type) and then iterate across this array while allocating the individual objects on the free store and passing whatever you want to the appropriate constructor. In this fashion, whatever the default constructor would do is bypassed, and the PITA rule is followed:

```
int const dimension = 10;
// First, allocate the array of pointers
```

```
String **ptrString = new String*[dimension];
// Second, loop and allocate each object
for(int i = 0; i < dimension; ++i)
{
  // Get the value for the String to be allocated
  ptrString[i] = new String( /* value */ );
}
// Do your processing
// ...
// Loop and delete all objects
for(int i = 0; i < dimension; ++i)
  delete ptrString[i];
// Finally, delete the array of pointers
delete [] ptrString;
```

 The topic of allocating dynamic memory will be revisited in Chapter 9 when we discuss exception handling.

 An array of user-defined types can be created on the free store by first allocating an array of pointers, then the objects themselves.

Placement Syntax When Calling **new**

Although the keyword **new** is used to allocate dynamic space on the free store, it can also be used to allocate memory on the stack or in the global space. This is useful for allocating an object at a specific hardware location. It can also be used to (literally) reinitialize an instance.

To do this, you must use the *placement syntax*. It looks like this:

```
T *ptr = new (/* address */) T(/* optional args here */);
```

In particular, the syntax consists of writing the following items:

▲ The keyword **new**,
▲ The stack or global memory address within parentheses,
▲ The type of the object,
▲ A parenthesized list of initializing values, if any.

Note very carefully that when you use the placement syntax, you must *not* issue a **delete** using the pointer returned by **new**. Instead, in order to have the object's destructor called, you must call it directly. In addition, the header file **new** must be included.

In the following example, an **ADT** object is allocated in the global space:

```cpp
// File adt.h

#ifndef ADT_H
#define ADT_H

class ADT
{
  double const data;
    public:
  ADT(double d = 0.0);
  ~ADT();
};

#endif

// File adt.cpp

#include <iostream>
#include "adt.h"

ADT::ADT(double d) : data(d)
{
   std::cout << "Constructing " << data << '\n';
}

ADT::~ADT()
{
   std::cout << "Destructing " << data << '\n';
}

// Global space
char globalMemory[sizeof(ADT)];

// File main.cpp

#include <new>
#include "adt.h"

int main()
{
   // Place an ADT object in the global space
```

```
ADT *ptr = new (globalMemory) ADT(1.23);
// Call its destructor
ptr->~ADT();
// Let's do it again!
ptr = new (globalMemory) ADT(-76.49);
// Call its destructor
ptr->~ADT();

}


/* Output:

Constructing 1.23
Destructing 1.23
Constructing -76.49
Destructing -76.49


*/
```

SUMMARY ▶ Use the placement syntax of **new** when you want to allocate an object somewhere in memory other than the free store.

EXERCISE 7.7

A container of type **Array** is designed to hold **double** values in an array on the free store. Write a program that first obtains the array dimension from the terminal operator, then reads **double** values interactively and calls the **addValue**() member function for each one. When the **Array** object has been completely filled, display all of its values by calling the function **at**(). In addition, be sure to write a copy constructor that does a deep copy.

```
// File array.h

#ifndef ARRAY_H
#define ARRAY_H

class Array
{
   public:
 Array(int dim);
 Array(Array const &);
 ~Array();
```

```
    void addValue(double);
    double at(int index) const;
        private:
    double *ptr;
    int dimension;
    int top;
};

#endif

// File array.cpp

#include <iostream>
#include "array.h"

// All Array definitions

// File main.cpp

#include <iostream>
#include "array.h"
using std::cout;
using std::cin;

int main()
{
 cout << "Enter the dimension: ";
 int dim;
 cin >> dim;
 if(dim < 1)
  return 1;
 Array container(dim);
 for(int i = 0; i < dim; ++i)
 {
  cout << "Enter a double value: ";
  double value;
  cin >> value;
  container.addValue(value);
 }
 Array anotherContainer(container);
 for(int i = 0; i < dim; ++i)
  cout << anotherContainer.at(i) << '\n';
}
```

EXERCISE 7.8

Define and implement a class called **Int** that encapsulates and emulates the primitive type **int**. Be sure to write all of the manager functions, an accessor member function for **data**, and a nonmember function called **add**() that adds two **Int** objects together:

```
// File int.h

#ifndef INT_H
#define INT_H

class Int
{
   public:
 // public interface
   private:
 int const data;
};

#endif
```

Did you test your **Int** class before proceeding? Good. Next, define and implement a class called **Complex** that abstracts a complex number consisting of constant real and imaginary parts, each of which is type **Int**. Be sure to write all of the manager functions, accessor member functions for **real** and **imag**, a **display**() member function, and a nonmember function called **add**() that adds two **Complex** numbers together:

```
// File complex.h

#ifndef COMPLEX_H
#define COMPLEX_H

#include "int.h"

class Complex
{
  Int const real, imag;
    public:
  // public interface
};

#endif
```

Test your classes using the following **main**():

```
// File main.cpp

#include "complex.h"

int main()
{
    Complex const c1(-1, 2), c2(3, -4), c3(c1), c4(c2);
    Complex sum(add(c3, c4));
    sum.display();
}
```

8

More Class Features

Introduction

In Chapters 6 and 7 you learned how to write a class definition, encapsulate member data and functions, specify access categories, create instances of the class, and write constructors and destructors. However, you should be familiar with many more features of C++ classes, such as the **this** pointer, static members, friends, operator conversion functions, and pointers to class members.

 We will now continue with other features of a class with which you should be familiar.

The **this** Pointer

Let's return to those thrilling days of yesteryear when you were still programming in the C language. According to the discussion in Chapter 6, in order to have a (global) function manipulate the contents of a structure object, you had to pass a pointer to that object into the function, and then the function could apply the arrow operator to the pointer in order to grab the data. For example, look at the following:

```
#include <stdio.h>

typedef struct
{
   char *ptrChars;
```

```
} String;

void displayString(String const *const ptrString)
{
   puts(ptrString->ptrChars);
}

void changeString(String *const ptrString, int idx, char ch)
{
   ptrString->ptrChars[idx] = ch;
}

int main(void)
{
   String str = { "B++" };
   changeString(&str, 0, 'C');
   displayString(&str);
   return 0;
}
```

Notice how the **displayString()** and **changeString()** functions receive a constant pointer to a **String** object and then use the arrow operator to access **ptrChars**. In addition, the **displayString()** function supports any constant **String** objects that might be passed to it.

Now let's translate this same program into C++ code:

```
// File string.h

#ifndef STRING_H
#define STRING_H

class String
{
    public:
   String(char const *chars = "");
   void displayString();
   void changeString(int idx, char ch);
    private:
   char *ptrChars;
};

#endif

// File string.cpp

#include <cstring>
```

```
#include <cstdio>
#include "string.h"

String::String(char const *chars)
{
  ptrChars = new char[std::strlen(chars) + 1];
  std::strcpy(ptrChars, chars);
}

void String::displayString()
{
  std::puts(ptrChars);
}

void String::changeString(int idx, char ch)
{
  ptrChars[idx] = ch;
}

// File main.cpp

#include "string.h"

int main()
{
  String str("B++");
  str.changeString(0, 'C');
  str.displayString();
}
```

As advertised, the pointer to the **String** object has disappeared from each of the functions. Or has it? Actually, it's still there, just hidden. Recall from Chapter 6 that member functions and member data are encapsulated within the class definition, thereby giving the functions direct access to the data without the need to have a pointer to some instance explicitly passed in to the function. This is true, but only in a logical sense. Physically speaking, encapsulation does not really exist, which means that the member functions and member data are not literally kept "together" in the computer's memory in something we've been calling a "class."

Think about this: Does it make sense to duplicate the class's member functions for all of the instances that you might want to create (and this doesn't even take into consideration the fact that hardware architecture would probably prohibit it anyway)? Of course not, so there is only one copy of each class member function kept by the compiler; this copy is therefore shared by all instances of the class.

To solve the problem of which instance a given member function is operating on, the compiler generates code that looks very much like a C language program. That is, the compiler *automatically* generates the address of the invoking instance and passes this address to each nonstatic member function as a hidden first argument. This parameter is given a predetermined name of **this**. If you mentally substitute **this** instead of **ptrString** in the C language program above, you will have a good idea of how C++ passes the invoking object into each and every nonstatic member function.

Let's summarize by giving a formal definition: The **this** pointer is a hidden first parameter that is generated by the compiler in *every* nonstatic member function of a class; when this member function is called, this (!) pointer is initialized with the address of the invoking object.

Even though the **this** pointer is implicitly declared, you can use it anywhere you deem appropriate; for example, to be quite clear that you're referring to the data members of the invoking object as opposed to an explicit object of the same type. Remember: As with any other formal argument, the **this** pointer has absolutely no meaning outside the scope of a nonstatic member function.

The implicit declaration of the **this** pointer varies slightly, depending on whether the member function has been declared **const** (meaning a constant member function). For our **String** class, it would be declared as the following:

```
String *const this            // Mutator member function
String const *const this       // Constant member function
```

Recall that the **const** immediately to the left of **this** means that the pointer itself cannot be modified, and the **const** to the left of the asterisk allows the member function to support constant **String** objects.

SUMMARY The **this** pointer is a hidden first argument to *every* nonstatic member function. When the function is called, the pointer is initialized to point to the invoking object.

Dereferencing the **this** Pointer to Make a Copy of the Invoking Object

The **this** pointer always points to the invoking instance of a nonstatic member function call, which means that if you were to write the expression ***this**, you would obtain the invoking object itself. What good does this do for you? For one thing, sometimes a nonstatic member function needs to make a copy of the invoking instance so that it can modify the copy without affecting the original instance.

For example, suppose that the **String** class has a member function called **toUpper()** that returns a new copy of the invoking object with all letters in upper case. We will call upon a private function in the class called **upperCase()** to help us:

```
// File string.h

#ifndef STRING_H
#define STRING_H
```

```cpp
class String
{
    public:
  String(String const &);
  String toUpper() const;
  // ...
    private:
  char *ptrChars;
  void upperCase(char *) const;
};

#endif

// File string.cpp

#include <cstring>
#include <cctype>
#include <cstddef>
#include "string.h"

String String::toUpper() const
{
  String newInstance(*this);
  upperCase(newInstance.ptrChars);
  return newInstance;
}

void String::upperCase(char *str) const
{
  for(std::size_t i = 0; i < std::strlen(str); ++i)
    str[i] = static_cast<char>(std::toupper(str[i]));
}
```

Within a member function, write *this to obtain the invoking object itself. You can then make a copy of the invoking object by passing *this to the copy constructor.

Dereferencing the this Pointer to Allow Function Chaining

Calls to member functions can be chained together. This means that more than one message can be sent to an instance of a class in just one statement. Generically speaking, it looks like this:

```cpp
instanceName.firstMessage().secondMessage();
```

To allow the user to write such code, the member function must return the value **this.*
The return type of the function should be its own class type by reference. Because **this*
really represents the object to which the message is being sent, and it's being returned
from the function by reference, we're all set up to send a subsequent message to this same
object.

Here is an illustration in which the function **refresh()** is chained to the function
toUpper():

```
// File string.h

#ifndef STRING_H
#define STRING_H

class String
{
    public:
    String(char const * = "");
    String toUpper() const;
    String &refresh(char const *chars);
    // ...
    private:
    char *ptrChars;
    void upperCase(char *) const;
};

#endif

// File string.cpp

#include <cstring>
#include <cctype>
#include <cstddef>
#include "string.h"

String String::toUpper() const
{
    String newInstance(*this);
    upperCase(newInstance.ptrChars);
    return newInstance;
}

void String::upperCase(char *str) const
{
    for(std::size_t i = 0; i < std::strlen(str); ++i)
```

```
      str[i] = static_cast<char>(std::toupper(str[i]));
}


String &String::refresh(char const *chars)
{
   std::size_t newLength = std::strlen(chars);
   if(std::strlen(ptrChars) != newLength)
   {
      delete [] ptrChars;
      ptrChars = new char[newLength + 1];
   }
   std::strcpy(ptrChars, chars);
   return *this;
}


// File main.cpp

#include "string.h"

int main()
{
   String str("C");
   String language(str.refresh("c++").toUpper());
}
```

After the message **refresh()** has been sent to the **String** object **str**, the message **toUpper()** can also be sent because the output of the call to **refresh()** really is **str** itself.

By the way, this is exactly how the insertion operator (<<) and extraction operator (>>) member functions work when a program chains together a sequence of output operations using the output stream object **cout**, or when it chains together a sequence of input operations using the input stream object **cin**. The return types of the insertion and extraction operator functions are **ostream &** and **istream &**, respectively, and each function returns a reference to *this; in this particular case, that would be a reference to either **cout** or **cin**:

```
cout << a << b;        // cout.operator<<(a).operator<<(b);
// ...
cin >> a >> b;         // cin.operator>>(a).operator>>(b);
```

In Chapter 10, you will see other reasons to use *this in a nonstatic member function.

 In order to chain a constant member function, the return type must be **const**-qualified.

 A member function can be chained to another function if it returns *this, and specifies its own class name by reference as the return type.

Static Class Data Members

Static class data members were mentioned back at the start of Chapter 6. They were also called *class variables*. What purpose do they serve, and how do you create them?

Let's continue with our **String** class and add a data member whose purpose is to keep count of the number of instantiations currently in existence. Naturally, each constructor must add 1 to this counter, and the destructor must subtract 1. The counter should be encapsulated inside the class itself (*not* inside each class instance), and at the same time it should be obvious that only *one* such counter is needed regardless of the number of **String** instantiations. In other words, this counter is *instance independent,* which is a good way to describe a static data member logically.

To create this counter, precede its declaration with the keyword **static**. It's a data member, so you will probably want it declared in the private part of the class. Incidentally, there's nothing wrong with declaring a static data member to be **const** if it will never be modified. Just don't forget that, like all constants, it must be explicitly initialized in the definition file (*not* in the base/member initialization list). For example, the value for the terminating null character called **null** just begs to be declared both **static** and **const**:

```
// File string.h

#ifndef STRING_H
#define STRING_H

class String
{
    public:
  String(char ch);
  String(char const *chars = "");
  String(String const &other);
  ~String();
  // ...
    private:
  char *ptrChars;
  static unsigned instanceCounter;
  static char const null;
  // ...
};

#endif
```

Because this data member, which we have called **instanceCounter**, is *instance independent,* it really has nothing to do with any instantiations that the user might or might not perform. In this sense, it's more like a member function declaration in that, if the program uses this member, the linker will require an explicit definition.

And where are definitions *always* written? In the class's definition file, of course. The easiest way to accomplish this is to copy and paste the declaration of the static member into the definition file, and then (1) delete the word **static**, (2) use the scope resolution operator (::) to scope the data member to its class name, and (3) optionally provide an initial value for the data member. If you don't provide a value, the type's default value will be used (since all static definitions are physically kept in the global space while retaining their class scope).

Thus, the class's definition file containing the definition of our counter might look like this:

```cpp
// File string.cpp

#include <cstring>
#include "string.h"

unsigned String::instanceCounter = 0;       // Static definition
char const String::null = '\0';             // Static definition

String::String(char ch)
{
  ptrChars = new char[2];
  ptrChars[0] = ch;
  ptrChars[1] = null;
  ++instanceCounter;
}

String::String(char const *chars)
{
  chars = chars ? chars : "";
  ptrChars = new char[std::strlen(chars) + 1];
  std::strcpy(ptrChars, chars);
  ++instanceCounter;
}

String::String(String const &other)
{
  ptrChars = new char[std::strlen(other.ptrChars) + 1];
  std::strcpy(ptrChars, other.ptrChars);
  ++instanceCounter;
}

String::~String()
```

```
{
  delete [] ptrChars;
  --instanceCounter;
}
```

Can a static data member be a user-defined type? Of course! It's defined in the same manner in the definition file, and it's optionally initialized. If no initialization is provided, then naturally the default constructor of its class will be called.

One more point: While a class instance cannot have a *nonstatic* data member that is an instance of the class itself (because constructing such a beast would be impossible!), there's nothing wrong with a class that defines a *static* data member that is an instance of the class itself, as shown in the following example:

```
// File string.h

#ifndef STRING_H
#define STRING_H

class String
{
    public:
  // ...
    private:
  String oops;            // Error; 'oops' is nonstatic
  static String message;  // OK; 'message' is static
  // ...
};

#endif

// File string.cpp

#include "string.h"

String String::message("This is the String class");
```

A static data member of a class is one that is *instance independent.* It is declared using the keyword **static**, and it must be defined in the class's definition file.

Initializing Static Class Data Members within the Class Definition

C++ supports another way of initializing a static data member. This can be done *within the class definition itself* at the point of declaration if (1) the data member is declared **const**, and (2) it is an integral type (i.e., not floating-point and not user-defined). To do this, simply write the static data member declaration as before, and then append an equal sign and an initialization constant. These values are known to the compiler and therefore can be used in any program construct that requires a compile-time constant expression, such as to dimension an array. (Actually, this is just a replacement for the "enum hack" shown in Chapter 6.) Here's an example:

```
// File string.h

#ifndef STRING_H
#define STRING_H

class String
{
    public:
  // ...
    private:
  static char const firstLetter = 'A';
  static char const lastLetter = 'Z';
  static char arrayOfLetters[lastLetter - firstLetter + 1];
  // ...
};

#endif

// File string.cpp

#include "string.h"

char const String::firstLetter;    // No initial value allowed
char const String::lastLetter;
char String::arrayOfLetters[lastLetter - firstLetter + 1] =
{
  'A', 'B', 'C', /* etc. */, 'Y', 'Z'
};
```

CAUTION Does the static member still need to be defined? You can certainly do so, but in this case you are not allowed to specify any initial value. Even if you fail to provide a definition, however, your program will probably still link successfully. If not, just provide one. When the definition of a static data member is and is not required is still an unresolved issue.

SUMMARY A static data member can be given an initial value at its point of declaration if it's both **const** and integral. Nevertheless, don't forget to define it in the class's definition file.

Static Member Functions

A static data member allows you to create some data inside a class that is instance independent, that is, the data lives and dies independently of any instantiations of the class. In a similar manner, a static member function is also instance independent, thereby allowing the user of a class to call it without having first to perform an instantiation of the class. The primary purpose of a static member function is to access the static data members of the class.

For example, going back to the **String** class, to prove that the initial value of **instanceCounter** is zero a member function must be written to either retrieve it or display it. If you were to write a *nonstatic* member function, however, then you would have to perform an instantiation of the class in order to invoke this member function, and the counter would then be incremented by one when the constructor runs. However, a *static* member function solves the problem quite nicely because no instantiation needs to be done, and the counter remains at zero.

A static member function, like a nonstatic member function, can be declared implicit inline, explicit inline, or defined in the definition file. For the latter two cases, be sure to eliminate the word **static** before scoping the member function name to the class name:

```
// File string.h

#ifndef STRING_H
#define STRING_H

class String
{
    public:
    static unsigned getInstanceCounter();
    // ...
    private:
    char *ptrChars;
    static unsigned instanceCounter;
    // ...
};

#endif

// File string.cpp

#include "string.h"

unsigned String::instanceCounter = 0;     // Static definition
```

```
unsigned String::getInstanceCounter()
{
  return instanceCounter;
}
```

A static member function is called by prepending the member function name with the class name using the scope resolution operator:

```
// File main.cpp

#include <iostream>
#include "string.h"

int main()
{
  std::cout << String::getInstanceCounter()
               << " instances " << '\n';
}
```

Incidentally, because a static member function is instance independent, it should be apparent that there is no **this** pointer passed to a static member function (because there is no instance involved to which **this** can point). And because a static member function does not have a **this** pointer, it cannot refer to any nonstatic members (data or functions) of its own class. Finally, a static member function cannot be declared "constant" because the word **const** after the formal argument list directly affects the **this** pointer, which in this case is nonexistent.

Let's look at an example that illustrates these errors:

```
// File string.h

#ifndef STRING_H
#define STRING_H

class String
{
    public:
  void foo();
  static String &func() const      // Error; cannot be const
  {
    String s;          // OK
    s.foo();           // OK
    s.value = 2;       // OK
    foo();             // Error; tries to call ::foo()
    value = 2;         // Error; tries to modify ::value()
    return *this;      // Error; no 'this' pointer
  }
```

```
    // ...
       private:
    int value;
};

#endif
```

In the definition of the **String** class's static member function **func()**, the compiler treats the identifier **foo** as the name of a function with global scope—that is, **::foo()**—and not as the name of the nonstatic class member function **String::foo()**. In other words, the compiler does not treat the call to function **foo()** as a nonstatic member function call (i.e., **this–>foo()**). Likewise, the compiler treats the identifier **value** as the name of a variable with global scope—that is, **::value**—and not as the name of the nonstatic, class data member **String::value** (i.e., **this–>value**).

A static member function (like static data) is instance independent and used primarily to access the static data members of a class. It is called by prepending the name with the class name and scope resolution operator.

A Random Number Generator Class

OK, it's show time. Let's start by writing a class called **Random** whose job is to seed the system's random number generator just once and to provide a member function that returns a random number in the range 0 to **limit – 1**, where the value of **limit** is specified by the user. Note that there are no data members in this class, so it is "stateless":

```
// File random.h

#ifndef RANDOM_H
#define RANDOM_H

class Random
{
    public:
   Random();
   unsigned getRandomNumber(int limit) const;
};

#endif

// File random.cpp

#include <cstdlib>
#include <ctime>
#include "random.h"
```

```
Random::Random()
{
   std::srand(static_cast<unsigned>(std::time(0)));
}

unsigned Random::getRandomNumber(int limit) const
{
   return std::rand() % limit;
}
```

A Class to "Die" For

Next, we'll create a class called **Die** that emulates a die object that you would use in games such as Monopoly, Parcheesi, Yatzhee, or even Dungeons and Dragons, if that's your preference. It is also used to play the popular casino game C Raps. (Think about it.) To allow the **Die** object to take on random values, we'll encapsulate an instance of our **Random** class and make it **static** because only one such instance is needed regardless of the number of **Die** objects that will be created:

```
// File die.h

#ifndef DIE_H
#define DIE_H

#include "random.h"

class Die
{
    public:
  Die(int sides = defaultNumberOfSides);
  Die(Die const &);
  Die &toss(); // Allow function chaining
  int getNumberOfSides() const;
  unsigned getFaceValue() const;
  static int getDefaultNumberOfSides();
    private:
  int const numberOfSides;
  unsigned faceValue;
  unsigned generateFaceValue() const;
  static int const defaultNumberOfSides;
  static int const minimumNumberOfSides;
  static Random rand;
};

#endif
```

```cpp
// File die.cpp

#include "die.h"
#include "random.h"

Die::Die(int sides) : numberOfSides
     (sides < minimumNumberOfSides  // If less than minimum,
       ? defaultNumberOfSides        // take the default
       : sides)                      // else take what's provided
{
  faceValue = generateFaceValue();
}

unsigned Die::generateFaceValue() const
{
  return rand.getRandomNumber(numberOfSides) + 1;
}

Die::Die(Die const &other) :
        numberOfSides(other.numberOfSides),
        faceValue(other.faceValue) { }

Die& Die::toss()
{
  faceValue = generateFaceValue();
  return *this;
}

int Die::getNumberOfSides() const
{
  return numberOfSides;
}

unsigned Die::getFaceValue() const
{
  return faceValue;
}

int Die::getDefaultNumberOfSides()
{
  return defaultNumberOfSides;
}

// All static definitions
```

```
int const Die::defaultNumberOfSides = 6;
int const Die::minimumNumberOfSides = 2;
Random Die::rand; // Invoke Random's default constructor
```

Note the following items in the **Die** class:

- ▲ The static constants designate the default number of sides and the minimum number of sides. (There is no maximum number of sides, per se.) In the **die.cpp** file, all of the static data members are defined. Naturally, 6 is the default number of sides, and I arbitrarily decided to make 2 the minimum number of sides.

- ▲ The **Die** default/converting constructor assigns (instead of initializes) into the **faceValue** data member to ensure that the **numberOfSides** data member has been initialized first. Because **faceValue** needs to use **numberOfSides**, if the order of declaration of these two members were to be reversed, and if **faceValue** were also to be initialized, the class would be broken (because **faceValue** would then be initialized before **numberOfSides**, and the value of **numberOfSides** would therefore be unknown).

- ▲ When the **rand** object gets created, the default constructor in the **Random** class will run, and the random number generator will already have been seeded by the time the user is ready to roll the first die object. Are the benefits of using classes for data and function encapsulation now becoming clearer?

A Dice Class

Let's face it: You typically don't play with a single die, but instead you use at least two of them in a game of chance. So rather than dealing with **Die** objects individually, it makes more sense to encapsulate them into another class that we'll call **Dice**:

```
// File dice.h

#ifndef DICE_H
#define DICE_H

#include "die.h"

class Dice
{
    public:
  Dice(int number = defaultNumberOfDice,
      int sides = Die::getDefaultNumberOfSides());
  ~Dice();
  Dice const &roll() const;
  unsigned getDieValue(int index) const;
  int getNumberOfSides() const;
  int getNumberOfDice() const;
```

```cpp
    unsigned getTotalOfDice() const;
      private:
    Die **ptrDice;
    int const numberOfDice;
    Dice(Dice const &); // Private copy constructor
    static int const defaultNumberOfDice;
    static int const minimumNumberOfDice;
};

#endif

// File dice.cpp

#include <iostream>
#include "dice.h"

Dice::Dice(int number, int sides) :
            numberOfDice(number < minimumNumberOfDice
            ? defaultNumberOfDice : number)
{
  ptrDice = new Die *[numberOfDice];
  for(int i = 0; i < numberOfDice; ++i)
    ptrDice[i] = new Die(sides);
}

Dice::~Dice()
{
  for(int i = 0; i < numberOfDice; ++i)
    delete ptrDice[i];
  delete [] ptrDice;
}

Dice const &Dice::roll() const
{
  for(int i = 0; i < numberOfDice; ++i)
    ptrDice[i]->toss();
  return *this;
}

unsigned Dice::getDieValue(int index) const
{
  return ptrDice[index]->getFaceValue();
}
```

```
int Dice::getNumberOfSides() const
{
   return ptrDice[0]->getNumberOfSides();
}

int Dice::getNumberOfDice() const
{
   return numberOfDice;
}

unsigned Dice::getTotalOfDice() const
{
   unsigned total = 0;
   for(int i = 0; i < getNumberOfDice(); ++i)
     total += ptrDice[i]->getFaceValue();
   return total;
}

// Static definitions
int const Dice::defaultNumberOfDice = 2;
int const Dice::minimumNumberOfDice = 1;
```

Several items in this class are worth noting:

▲ The **Dice** constructor is callable in three different ways because of the two default parameters. The second default that specifies the number of sides is extracted directly from the **Die** class via a static member function call because that's where its value belongs.

▲ The **roll()** member function allows for member function chaining, so that the user could then immediately call another member function, such as **getTotalOfDice()**.

▲ The copy constructor has been declared private so that no one can make a copy of a **Dice** object.

▲ The abstraction of pointer-to-pointer-to-**Die** allows us to avoid invoking the default constructor of the **Die** class (according to the discussion in Chapter 7).

Next, we'll create a class called **DiceView** to be used for viewing the **Dice** class:

```
// File diceview.h

#ifndef DICEVIEW_H
#define DICEVIEW_H

class Dice;
class DiceView
```

```
{
   public:
  DiceView(Dice &ref) : refDice(ref) { }
  void displayDice() const;
   private:
  Dice &refDice;
};

#endif

// File diceview.cpp

#include <iostream>
#include "dice.h"
#include "diceview.h"

void DiceView::displayDice() const
{
  for(int i = 0; i < refDice.getNumberOfDice(); ++i)
    std::cout << refDice.getDieValue(i) << ' ';
  std::cout << ": Total = " << refDice.getTotalOfDice()
             << '\n';
}
```

The **Dice** class might be used in the following way:

```
// File main.cpp

#include <iostream>
#include "dice.h"
#include "diceview.h"

void display(Dice const &dice, DiceView const &view)
{
  std::cout << "Using " << dice.getNumberOfDice()
             << " die objects, each of which has "
             << dice.getNumberOfSides() << " sides:\n";
  view.displayDice();
  dice.roll();
  view.displayDice();
}

int main()
{
  Dice dice1;
```

```
        DiceView view1(dice1);
        display(dice1, view1);
        Dice dice2(3);
        DiceView view2(dice2);
        display(dice2, view2);
        Dice dice3(5, 10);
        DiceView view3(dice3);
        display(dice3, view3);
    }


    /* Typical output:  .

    Using 2 die objects, each of which has 6 sides:
    4 4 : Total = 8
    4 1 : Total = 5
    Using 3 die objects, each of which has 6 sides:
    4 4 2 : Total = 10
    5 5 1 : Total = 11
    Using 5 die objects, each of which has 10 sides:
    4 8 2 8 5 : Total = 27
    7 4 2 1 1 : Total = 15


    */
```

The Size of a Class

If you ever need to compute the size of a class, you can use the **sizeof** operator. This will tell you how much space any instance of the class is occupying. Just be aware that only *nonstatic* data members are counted. The following items (which occupy storage) are *not* counted when the **sizeof** operator is applied to the name of a class or one of its instances: (1) functions (both nonstatic and static) and *static* data members are not counted for the simple reason that they are not replicated for each instantiation, and (2) the size of the dynamically allocated storage region is not counted when a class instance has a pointer variable as a data member, and the pointer variable holds the address of a storage region that was dynamically allocated from the free store.

In addition, the size of a class is guaranteed to be greater than zero. In other words, all instantiated objects will have a size of at least one byte, even if there is no nonstatic data in the class.

CAUTION The use of a virtual function (discussed in Chapter 11) might affect the size of a class instance.

You can use the **sizeof** operator to determine the amount of storage a class instance occupies. Only nonstatic data members are counted.

EXERCISE 8.1

Write a class called **SavingsAccount** that encapsulates a **double** balance and a static member that represents the yearly interest rate. The constructor initializes the balance with $100.00 unless specified otherwise. Provide member functions to add to the balance, retrieve the balance, and compute interest earned (the yearly interest rate divided by 12 times the balance).

Test using the following **main.cpp** file:

```cpp
// File main.cpp

#include <iostream>
using std::cout;

int main()
{
  SavingsAccount account(100.00);
  cout << account.getBalance() << '\n';
  account.add(10.00);
  cout << account.getBalance() << '\n';
  account.computeInterest();
  cout << account.getBalance() << '\n';
}
```

Friend Functions

As you know, because of encapsulation and the principle of data hiding, the only functions that have unrestricted access to a class's nonpublic members are the member functions of that particular class. Any attempt by a nonmember function to directly access these nonpublic data members will result in a compilation error.

Several circumstances exist, however, in which a nonmember function must have access to these nonpublic members. The easy way to do this would be to change the access category from **private** to **public**, but then this completely violates the whole concept of encapsulation and data hiding. So what can you do?

This dilemma can be solved by declaring the function in question to be a *friend* of the class in which the nonpublic data members are located. That is, the class in which the nonpublic members are located bestows friendship on the function (not the other way around). In this fashion, the friend function then has access to all of the class's members, including the nonpublic ones. Remember, the function itself cannot choose to become a friend of a class ("I choose to be your friend; therefore, I now have complete and unlimited access to your private members"), because this would make no sense and it would violate the principle of data hiding.

Although a class can also grant friendship to a member function of another class, this situation is rarely done, it is more easily handled by friend classes; it will be shown in the next section.

SUMMARY ▶ A friend function is one that has access to the nonpublic members of a class. The class grants friendship to the function.

How a Class Grants Friendship to a Function

A class grants friendship to a nonmember function by including the function's declaration inside the class definition and then preceding this declaration with the keyword **friend**. The **friend** keyword cannot ever be written outside a class definition. The nonmember function, by default, will reside in the global space.

For example, in the following the class **String** is granting friendship to the global function called **join**() whose job is to create a new **String** object consisting of the concatenation of two existing **String** objects:

```cpp
// File string.h

#ifndef STRING_H
#define STRING_H

class String
{
   friend String const join
               (String const &left, String const &right);
     public:
   String(char const *chars = "");
   // ...
     private:
   char *ptrChars;
};

#endif

// File string.cpp

#include <cstring>
#include "string.h"

String const join(String const &left, String const &right)
{
   int lengthLeft = std::strlen(left.ptrChars);
```

```
      int lengthRight = std::strlen(right.ptrChars);
      char *buffer = new char[lengthLeft + lengthRight + 1];
      std::strcpy(buffer, left.ptrChars);
      std::strcat(buffer, right.ptrChars);
      String newString(buffer);
      delete [] buffer;
      return newString;
}


// File main.cpp

#include "string.h"

int main()
{
   char const *pLeft = "This is a test";
   char const *pRight = " of concatenation";
   String str1(pLeft);
   String str2(pRight);
   String str3(join(str1, str2));        // OK
   String str4(join(pLeft, str2));       // OK
   String str5(join(str1, pRight));      // OK
   String str6(join(pLeft, pRight));     // OK
}
```

Technically, you may place a friend declaration anywhere in the class definition you want. Because this declaration now refers to a *nonmember* function, the access specifiers (**public**, **private**, **protected**) are completely irrelevant. However, since a lot of folks (including me) like to list members in order of decreasing accessibility, I will be listing all friend declarations first.

Note that for the instantiations of **str4**, **str5**, and **str6**, implicit type conversions are being done on the C language string literals to transform them into C++ **String** objects.

SUMMARY Use the keyword **friend** to declare a function to be a friend of the class. This declaration can be placed anywhere within the class definition.

Member versus Nonmember Functions

Do I hear someone in the audience asking "If you were to make **join()** a member function of the class instead of a nonmember friend function, then of course it would have access to the nonpublic parts, and the whole issue of friendship becomes moot"? This is a good point, and it deserves some consideration. If **join()** were implemented as a non-static class member function, the first argument of each call to **join()** *must* be an existing **String** class instance, that is, the **String** instance whose address is passed to the **join()**

function via the implicit **this** pointer. The **join()** function's second argument can continue to be any value whose type is **String** or a type that is convertible to **String**. This second argument is passed into the **join()** function via its only formal argument, whose type is **const**-reference to **String**. Even so, notice how the **join()** function still continues to support constant (**String**) objects:

```cpp
// File string.h

#ifndef STRING_H
#define STRING_H

class String
{
    public:
  String(char const *chars = "");
  String const join(String const &right) const;
  // ...
    private:
  char *ptrChars;
  // ...
};

#endif

// File string.cpp

#include <cstring>
#include "string.h"

String const String::join(String const &right) const
{
  int lengthLeft = std::strlen(this->ptrChars);
  int lengthRight = std::strlen(right.ptrChars);
  char *buffer = new char[lengthLeft + lengthRight + 1];
  std::strcpy(buffer, this->ptrChars);
  std::strcat(buffer, right.ptrChars);
  String newString(buffer);
  delete [] buffer;
  return newString;
}

// File main.cpp

#include "string.h"
```

```
int main()
{
    char const *pLeft = "This is a test";
    char const *pRight = " of concatenation";
    String str1(pLeft);
    String str2(pRight);
    String str3(str1.join(str2));           // OK
    String str4(pLeft->join(str2));         // Error
    String str5(str1.join(pRight));         // OK
}
```

The problem with the implementation is this: Because **join**() is a member function of the **String** class, the message to invoke it must be sent to an *explicit existing instance* of the class. For the instantiation of **str4**, this has not been done because the object to the left of the arrow operator is simply a plain C language string literal. In other words, implicit type conversion does *not* apply in this situation, and the string literal will *not* automatically be converted into a **String** object. (If a C language string literal is passed in as the explicit parameter, as is the case for the instantiation of **str5**, then the implicit type conversion will indeed occur.) Therefore, because of this lack of symmetry when passing arguments into the function, you would have to agree that making **join**() a nonstatic member function is not a good idea. Instead, making it a nonmember function (possibly with friendship) is a much better design decision.

In summary, you should make a function a friend of a class if (1) you need to perform implicit type conversion on the left-hand argument, and (2) there is no suitable public interface through which the function can work.

CAUTION   This topic will be discussed further in Chapter 10.

SUMMARY   Use a friend function if you need to perform implicit type conversion on the left-hand argument being passed in to the function.

If You Really Don't Like Having Friends . . .

An alternative to granting friendship to a nonmember function, while still being able to retain the benefit of having the compiler perform implicit type conversion on the left-hand argument, is to declare a nonmember nonfriend function and then have this function merely call a public member that does all the work. This is shown in the following example in which the **join**() function is declared as a nonmember nonfriend (yet is still inside the header file!), and calls the public member function **joinStrings**():

```
// File string.h

#ifndef STRING_H
#define STRING_H
```

```
class String
{
    public:
  String(char const *chars = "");
  String const joinStrings(String const &right) const;
  // ...
    private:
  char *ptrChars;
};


// join() now as a non-member non-friend function
String const join(String const &left, String const &right);


#endif


// File string.cpp


#include <cstring>
#include "string.h"


String const join(String const &left, String const &right)
{
  // Call member function joinStrings()
  return left.joinStrings(right);
}


String const String::joinStrings(String const &right) const
{
  int lengthLeft = std::strlen(this->ptrChars);
  int lengthRight = std::strlen(right.ptrChars);
  char *buffer = new char[lengthLeft + lengthRight + 1];
  std::strcpy(buffer, this->ptrChars);
  std::strcat(buffer, right.ptrChars);
  String newString(buffer);
  delete [] buffer;
  return newString;
}


// File main.cpp


#include "string.h"


int main()
{
  char const *pLeft = "This is a test";
```

```
        char const *pRight = " of concatenation";
        String str1(pLeft);
        String str2(pRight);
        String str3(join(str1, str2));        // OK
        String str4(join(pLeft, str2));        // OK
        String str5(join(str1, pRight));       // OK
        String str6(join(pLeft, pRight));      // OK
    }
```

SUMMARY ▶ Instead of granting friendship to a nonmember function, the function can simply pass control to a public member function to get the work done.

Friend Declarations for Classes in a Namespace

If the class that is granting friendship to a function resides within a namespace, the friend function must be forward-declared to force it to have namespace (not global) scope. Note also how the definition of **join()** must be scoped within the namespace:

```
// File string.h

#ifndef STRING_H
#define STRING_H

namespace NS
{
  // Forward declaration needed to force join() to have
  // scope in this namespace
  class String;
  String const join (String const &left, String const &right);

  class String
  {
    friend String const join
                  (String const &left, String const &right);
      public:
    String(char const *ptr = "");
      private:
    char *ptrChars;
  };
}

#endif
```

```cpp
// File string.cpp

#include <cstring>
#include "string.h"
using NS::String;

String::String(char const *ptr)
{
  ptr = ptr ? ptr : "";
  ptrChars = new char[std::strlen(ptr) + 1];
  std::strcpy(ptrChars, ptr);
}

String const NS::join          // Note scoping of function name
                    (String const &left, String const &right)
{
  int lengthLeft = std::strlen(left.ptrChars);
  int lengthRight = std::strlen(right.ptrChars);
  char *buffer = new char[lengthLeft + lengthRight + 1];
  std::strcpy(buffer, left.ptrChars);
  std::strcat(buffer, right.ptrChars);
  String newString(buffer);
  delete [] buffer;
  return newString;
}

// File main.cpp

#include "string.h"
using NS::String;

int main()
{
  char const *pLeft = "This is a test";
  char const *pRight = " of concatenation";
  String str1(pLeft);
  String str2(pRight);
  String str3(join(str1, str2));          // OK
  String str4(join(pLeft, str2));         // OK
  String str5(join(str1, pRight));        // OK
  String str6(join(pLeft, pRight));       // Error
  String str7(NS::join(pLeft, pRight));   // OK
}
```

Note that the Koenig lookup rule (from Chapter 2) does not apply to the **join()** call that's made during the instantiation of **str6** (because no **String** instance appears in the call). In this case, you *must* use the fully qualified name **NS::join()** to call the **join()** function, as shown for the instantiation of **str7**.

Friend Classes

Rather than having a class grant friendship to just one nonmember function, it's sometimes necessary to grant this friendship to one or more member functions of another class. This could be done by granting friendship to each individual member function of the other class, but it's usually much easier to grant friendship to the entire class, which imparts friendship to all the member functions.

This blanket friendship is easily accomplished by forward-declaring the class name preceded by the keyword **friend**. For example, here is a class called **StringRep** granting friendship to all member functions of the **String** class:

```
class StringRep
{
    friend class String;
    // ...
};
```

Now, why would you ever want to do this? The situation typically occurs when you want to hide the interface of class and allow access to only one client. That is, the class receiving the friendship (**String**) needs to access the services (member functions) of the class granting the friendship (**StringRep**), and it is the only class that needs these services. Usually the class granting the friendship is merely an implementation detail of the class receiving the friendship (which will be shown shortly).

Let's look at an example by using these two classes to implement a simple reference counting idiom. In this idiom, different **String** objects will be able to share any underlying representations that are the same. In other words, if one **String** object is created and it encapsulates the literal "C++", and it is then copied to a new **String** object, this second object will *not* have to create a brand new literal consisting of the same characters. Instead, it will share the one and only literal containing "C++". To the user, the code doesn't change:

```
String one("C++");
String two(one);      // No new literal is created
```

What this idiom *cannot* accommodate is the case in which two disjointed **String** objects are created that happen to encapsulate the same literal, as in the following:

```
String one("C++");
String two("C++");    // No reference counting here
```

It should be obvious that a potential problem exists with reference counting when the two **String** destructors run, because they are not allowed to release the same dynamic space. Not to worry; we'll neatly program around this.

First, we'll create a class called **StringRep** whose job is to encapsulate the array of characters for the underlying **String** representation, as well as a counter that indicates how many **String** objects are currently sharing (pointing to) this particular **StringRep** object. This is illustrated in the following figure:

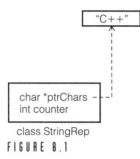

class StringRep

FIGURE 8.1

We'll create a constructor for the class as well as member functions that increment, decrement, and retrieve the value of the reference counter:

```cpp
// File stringrep.h

#ifndef STRINGREP_H
#define STRINGREP_H

class StringRep
{
   friend class String;
   // All data and member functions are private
   StringRep(char const *chars);
   ~StringRep();
   void incrementCounter();
   void decrementCounter();
   int getCounter() const;
   char *getPtrChars() const;
   int getCounter() const;
   char *ptrChars;
   int counter;
};

#endif

// File stringrep.cpp

#include <iostream>
```

```cpp
#include <cstring>
#include "stringrep.h"

StringRep::StringRep(char const *chars)
                        : ptrChars(0), counter(1)
{
  ptrChars = new char[std::strlen(chars) + 1];
  std::strcpy(ptrChars, chars);
}

StringRep::~StringRep()
{
  delete [] ptrChars;
}

void StringRep::incrementCounter()
{
  ++counter;
}

void StringRep::decrementCounter()
{
  --counter;
}

char *StringRep::getPtrChars() const
{
  return ptrChars;
}

int StringRep::getCounter() const
{
  return counter;
}
```

There is an important concept to note here: *Every* member of the **StringPtr** class is private; the **StringPtr** class does not provide a public interface. Also note that the **StringPtr** class declares the **String** class as its friend. Consequently, the **String** class has full access to the members of the **StringPtr** class, including its constructor functions. (Do you see where this is going?) In other words, our "friendly" **String** class is the only program entity that is allowed to instantiate and use **StringRep** objects.

The **String** class will now be changed to encapsulate only a pointer (called **ptrStringRep**) to a **StringRep** object. The reference counting comes into existence when more than one **String** object points to a single **StringRep** object, as shown in the following figure:

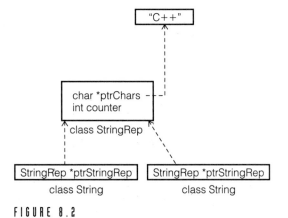

FIGURE 8.2

Notice how the copy constructor of the **String** class does *not* allocate space on the free store, but instead merely (1) initializes the pointer to point to the existing **StringRep** object, and (2) increments the counter. The destructor decrements the counter; if the counter is equal to zero, the destructor deletes the **StringRep** object:

```
// File string.h

#ifndef STRING_H
#define STRING_H

class StringRep;      // Only a forward-declaration is needed
class String
{
    public:
  String(char const *chars = "");
  String(String const &);
  ~String();
  char const *getString() const;
  int getCounter() const;
    private:
  StringRep *ptrStringRep;
};

#endif

// File string.cpp

#include "string.h"
#include "stringrep.h"
```

```cpp
String::String(char const *chars)
{
  chars = chars ? chars : "";
  ptrStringRep = new StringRep(chars);
}

String::String(String const &str)
                       : ptrStringRep(str.ptrStringRep)
{
  ptrStringRep->incrementCounter();
}

String::~String()
{
  ptrStringRep->decrementCounter();
  if(ptrStringRep->getCounter() == 0)
    delete ptrStringRep;
}

char const *String::getString() const
{
  return ptrStringRep->getPtrChars();
}

int String::getCounter() const
{
  return ptrStringRep->getCounter();
}
```

Now we're ready to run a test:

```cpp
// File main.cpp

#include <iostream>
#include "string.h"

void display(String const &str)
{
  char const quote = '\"';
  int counter = str.getCounter();
  std::cout << quote << str.getString() << quote
            << " is used " << counter
            << " time" << ((counter == 1) ? "\n" : "s\n");
}
```

```
int main()
{
  String const one("C++");
  display(one);
  {
    String const two(one);
    display(one);
  } // 'two' goes out of scope here
  display(one);
}

/* Output:

"C++" is used 1 time
"C++" is used 2 times
"C++" is used 1 time

*/
```

CAUTION   It's possible for the **String** class to directly access the **counter** and **ptrChars** data members of the **StringRep** class, but it's still preferable to work through a member function instead in order to create a looser coupling between the two classes. Note also that a friend of a friend is not automatically a friend. That is, if the **String** class were to grant friendship to a nonmember function, then that function is *not* a friend of the **StringRep** class.

SUMMARY   Use a friend class when you want to hide the interface of class and allow access to only one client.

Encapsulating a Class

To prove that the **StringRep** is just an implementation detail of the **String** class, it's possible to do away with the friendship altogether and literally encapsulate the **StringRep** class inside the **String** class. To make this change, first move the forward-declaration of the **StringRep** class into the private part of the **String** class:

```
// File string.h

#ifndef STRING_H
#define STRING_H

class String
{
```

```
    public:
  String(char const *chars = "");
  String(String const &);
  ~String();
  char const *getString() const;
  int getCounter() const;
    private:
  class StringRep;
  StringRep *ptrStringRep;
};
```

```
#endif
```

Then define the **StringRep** class, making sure to scope the class itself and its members as part of the **String** class (because that's where it now lives). Remove the friend declaration from the class and make the member functions public (because there's no longer any friendship). It's still impossible for anyone other than the **String** class to instantiate a **StringRep** object because it was declared in the private part of the **String** class:

```
// File stringrep.h

#ifndef STRINGREP_H
#define STRINGREP_H

#include "string.h"

class String::StringRep
{
    public:
  StringRep(char const *chars);
  ~StringRep();
  void incrementCounter();
  void decrementCounter();
  char *getPtrChars() const;
  int getCounter() const;
    private:
  char *ptrChars;
  int counter;
};

#endif

// File stringrep.cpp

#include <iostream>
#include <cstring>
```

```
#include "stringrep.h"

String::StringRep::StringRep(char const *chars) : counter(1)
{
  ptrChars = new char[std::strlen(chars) + 1];
  std::strcpy(ptrChars, chars);
}

String::StringRep::~StringRep()
{
  delete [] ptrChars;
}

void String::StringRep::incrementCounter()
{
  ++counter;
}

void String::StringRep::decrementCounter()
{
  --counter;
}

char *String::StringRep::getPtrChars() const
{
  return ptrChars;
}

int String::StringRep::getCounter() const
{
  return counter;
}
```

Rather than have a class granting friendship, its declaration can literally be encapsulated in the private part of the other class and then defined with a public interface. No other class or function can gain access to any part of it because its declaration is private.

EXERCISE 8.2

Copy the following **Card** class and define the member functions in the file **card.cpp**. Assume that two cards are equal if their suits and ranks are the same:

```
// File card.h

#ifndef CARD_H
#define CARD_H
```

```cpp
class Card
{
    public:
 enum Suit
 {
    Clubs, Diamonds, Hearts, Spades
 };
 enum Rank
 {
    Ace, Deuce, Trey, Four, Five, Six, Seven,
    Eight, Nine, Ten, Jack, Queen, King
 };
 Card(Suit, Rank);
 Suit getSuit() const;
 Rank getRank() const;
 bool equals(Card const &) const;
    private:
 Suit const suit;
 Rank const rank;
 Card(Card const &); // Do not define
};

#endif
```

Test the **Card** class with the following **main.cpp** file:

```cpp
// File main.cpp

#include <iostream>
#include "card.h"

int main()
{
 for(int s = 0; s < 4; ++s)
 {
    for(int r = 0; r < 13; ++r)
    {
      Card::Suit suit = static_cast<Card::Suit>(s);
      Card::Rank rank = static_cast<Card::Rank>(r);
      Card card(suit, rank);
      std::cout << "The " << card.getRank() << " of "
              << card.getSuit() << '\n';
    }
 }
}
```

EXERCISE 8.3

Enhance Exercise 8.2 by adding a viewing class called **CardView** that will be used to display a **Card** object in a more friendly format. A **Card** object should be displayed as text, such as "The Ace of Hearts," "The Queen of Clubs," and so on. Write the definitions for the **CardView** class.

```cpp
// File cardview.h

#ifndef CARDVIEW_H
#define CARDVIEW_H

class Card;
class CardView
{
  public:
 CardView(Card const &ref) : refCard(ref) { }
 void display() const;
  private:
 Card const &refCard;
 static char const *suitDesc[];
 static char const *rankDesc[];
};

#endif
```

Test your classes using the following **main.cpp** file:

```cpp
// File main.cpp

#include "card.h"
#include "cardview.h"

int main()
{
 for(int s = 0; s < 4; ++s)
 {
  for(int r = 0; r < 13; ++r)
  {
   Card::Suit suit = static_cast<Card::Suit>(s);
   Card::Rank rank = static_cast<Card::Rank>(r);
   Card card(suit, rank);
   CardView view(card);
   view.display();
  }
 }
}
```

EXERCISE 8.4

Continue Exercise 8.3 by copying the following **Deck** class, which encapsulates 52 cards, and write the member function and static definitions in the file **deck.cpp**. Use the **Random** class shown earlier in this chapter:

```
// File deck.h

#ifndef DECK_H
#define DECK_H

#include "random.h"
class Card;

class Deck
{
  public:
 Deck();
 ~Deck();
 void shuffle() const;
 Card const *getNextCard() const;
 static int const numberOfSuits = 4;
 static int const numberOfRanks = 13;
 static int const numberOfCards =
                          numberOfSuits * numberOfRanks;
  private:
 Card **array;
 mutable int index;        // Next card to be fetched
 static Random rand;
 Deck(Deck const &);       // Do not define
};

#endif
```

Test the **Deck** class using the following **main.cpp** file:

```
// File main.cpp

#include "deck.h"
#include "cardview.h"

int main()
{
 Deck deck;
 for(int i = 0; i < Deck::numberOfCards; ++i)
```

```
{
 Card const &refCard = *deck.getNextCard();
 CardView view(refCard);
 view.display();
 }
}
```

EXERCISE 8.5

Continue Exercise 8.4 by adding a **DeckView** class that displays the contents of a **Deck** object. (To display a **Deck** object means displaying all of the encapsulated **Card** objects using the **CardView** class.) Write the **deckview.cpp** file:

```
// File deckview.h

#ifndef DECKVIEW_H
#define DECKVIEW_H

class Deck;
class DeckView
{
    public:
 DeckView(Deck &ref);
 void display() const;
    private:
 Deck &refDeck;
};

#endif
```

Test the **Deck** class using the following **main()**:

```
// File main.cpp

#include "deck.h"
#include "deckview.h"

int main()
{
 Deck deck;
 DeckView view(deck);
 view.display();
 deck.shuffle();
 view.display();
}
```

EXERCISE 8.6

Finally, you are ready to use your **Deck** class to play a little game. In this game, you shuffle two decks of cards, draw all 52 cards from each deck one at a time, and compare each pair of cards as they are drawn to see if they are identical. In theory, then, for the two decks you could have anywhere from zero to 52 matches. If a match occurs, display one of the cards. If no match occurs for this one game, then say so. Play any number of such games; when done, display the probability of obtaining 0 matches, 1 match, and so forth, up to 52 matches — each of which is the number of times a match occurred divided by the number of games played.

Use the following **game.h** header file, and write the file **game.cpp**:

```
// File game.h

#ifndef GAME_H
#define GAME_H

#include "deck.h"

class Game
{
   public:
 Game(long g = 10000L);       // Default to 10,000 games
 void play();
 void display() const;
   private:
 Deck deck1, deck2;
 long const games;
 int answers[Deck::numberOfCards + 1];
};

#endif
```

Test using the following **main.cpp** file:

```
// File main.cpp

#include "game.h"

int main()
{
 Game statistics;
 statistics.play();
 statistics.display();
}
```

Operator Conversion Functions

You know that a constructor is (typically) designed to take one or more primitive types and convert them into a user-defined type. For example, we've seen how a C language string literal can easily be converted into a **String** object using a constructor in the **String** class.

An *operator conversion function* is somewhat the opposite of a constructor in the sense that its purpose is to start with a user-defined type and convert it into a primitive type. (It can also convert into a different user-defined type, but this is not done too often.) This conversion can be done *implicitly*, hence extending the kinds of implicit type conversions that are possible in C++.

SUMMARY ▶ An operator conversion function can implicitly convert from a user-defined type into a primitive type.

Purpose

One purpose of an operator conversion function is to provide a friendly interface to the user of a class by allowing the user to write an instance name where the compiler would normally expect to find the name of a fundamental type. For example, our **String** class might provide an operator conversion function to allow the user to write an instance in conjunction with the insertion operator (<<):

```
// File string.h

#ifndef STRING_H
#define STRING_H

class String
{
    public:
  String(char const *chars = "");
  operator char const *() const;
  // ...
    private:
  char *ptrChars;
};

#endif

// File string.h

#include "string.h"
```

```
String::operator char const *() const
{
    return ptrChars;
}


// File main.cpp

#include <iostream>
#include "string.h"

int main()
{
    String str("C++");
    // Call operator conversion function implicitly
    std::cout << str << '\n';
    // Call operator conversion function explicitly
    std::cout << str.operator char const *() << '\n';
}
```

 An operator conversion function can be used to provide a more friendly interface for the user.

Syntax

The name of an operator conversion function consists of the keyword **operator** followed by the type to which the conversion is to be made. For example, if the resultant type is **int**, then the function name is **operator int()**. Note that no formal arguments are allowed and, as with a constructor and destructor, no explicit return type can be written. It should typically be declared **const** to support constant and temporary invoking objects.

 To create an operator conversion function, specify no return type, write the keyword **operator** followed by the type to which the conversion is to be made, and write empty parentheses. Don't forget to support constant objects, where appropriate.

Of course, in the previous code example there is no insertion operator in the **iostream** library that "knows" how to accommodate a **String** object. However, the compiler is smart enough to *implicitly convert* the **String** object **str** into a **char const*** type (via a "behind-the-scenes" call to the operator conversion function), after which the insertion operator displays the characters to which **ptrChars** points.

You must be very careful if you decide to write an operator conversion function for your class, however. Consider the following piece of code:

```
String str("C++");
char const *ptr = str - 100;
```

Do you really want the user to be able to take a **String** object and subtract 100 from it? Or add 13? That's probably meaningless code, so the answer is no! Yet, with an operator conversion function, the code compiles just fine because the compiler is quite content to convert the **String** object **str** into type **char const *** and then perform normal pointer arithmetic on the resultant pointer. As a matter of fact, the C++ library's **std::string** class (note the lowercase **s**) does not contain an operator conversion function, but instead provides the same functionality with a member function called **c_str()**. This solves the problem because now there is no implicit type conversion occurring.

 Instead of overloading the insertion operator for a class, an operator conversion function can be used.

Introduction to Pointers to Class Members

Suppose you have a class that contains various public functions to do a variety of tasks. Instead of executing these tasks as they are encountered, you need to queue them up in an array or linked list for execution at a later time. One way to "remember" which member function is to be called would be to store the address of that function in an array or linked list. Then, later in the program, the array or linked list would be traversed and the appropriate function executed.

Obviously, what is needed in this scenario is the ability to create a pointer to a class member function. Just as you can declare pointers to nonclass variables and functions, you can declare pointers to the individual function members of a class.

 Pointers to class member functions can be created to hold addresses of those functions.

Pointers to Global Functions

Ignoring classes for the moment, let's do a quick review of pointers to global functions. Assume we have a function named **func()** that takes a **float** as its only argument and returns an **int**. If you wanted to store the address of function **func()** in a pointer variable, you would create an appropriately typed function pointer and store **func()**'s address into it:

```
int (*ptrFunction)(float) = func;
```

Give yourself a break, though, and use a **typedef** to simplify the code:

```
typedef int (*PointerFunction)(float);
PointerFunction ptrFunction = func;
```

The name of a function without parentheses always yields the address of that function, so the address-of (**&**) operator is optional. When it's time to invoke the function using the pointer, you can use the pre-ANSI style of enclosing the pointer variable within parentheses, preceded by the dereferencing operator, or you can use the ANSI style of just writing the pointer variable. Of course, both styles then specify the actual arguments, if any:

```
typedef int (*PointerFunction)(float);
int func(float);
// ...
PointerFunction ptrFunction = func;
float f = 53.7F;
int x = (*ptrFunction)(f);  // Call func() pre-ANSI style
int y = ptrFunction(f);     // Call func() ANSI style
```

The name of a global function without parentheses yields the address of that function. This address can be stored into a pointer, which can subsequently be dereferenced to call the function.

Pointers to Nonstatic Class Member Functions

Now let's do the same thing for a *nonstatic* class member function. First, in order to create a pointer-to-member-function variable of some class **ADT**, you must qualify the pointer name with the class name and scope resolution operator:

```
class ADT
{
    public:
    int func(float);
};
// ...
typedef int (ADT::*PointerMemberFunction)(float);
PointerMemberFunction ptrMemberFunction;
```

To take the address of the class member function called **ADT::func()**, you must qualify the function's name with the class name and scope resolution operator. Unlike the case with a global function, the use of the address-of operator **&** is mandatory. In addition, the member function must have public access if its address is being taken by a function that is not a member of the **ADT** class:

```
ptrMemberFunction = &ADT::func;
```

To take the address of a nonstatic member function, you must scope its name to the class to which it belongs. Also, you must use the **&** operator.

Invoking Functions Using Pointers to Nonstatic Member Functions

Creating a pointer to a nonstatic, class member function is only half the story. Recall that a nonstatic member function is *always* passed (implicitly) a pointer named **this** that holds the address of a specific class instance. Assuming we have an **ADT** class instance—or, perhaps, a pointer to an **ADT** class instance—and a member function pointer variable that points at a nonstatic member function of the **ADT** class, we now need a C++ operator that "knows" how to operate on these two entities, that is, an operator that knows how to pass the **ADT** instance's address (i.e., the implicit **this** pointer) to the "pointed at" nonstatic member function via the member function pointer variable. This sounds like a job for C++'s pointer-to-member operators, dot-star (.*) and arrow-star (–>*).

If you want to use a class instance to call a nonstatic member function via a nonstatic member function pointer, write the instance name, the pointer-to-member operator (.*), and then the name of the nonstatic member function pointer. Be sure to enclose the instance name, the pointer-to-member operator, and the name of the nonstatic member function pointer within parentheses. This expression is then followed by the member function's argument list:

```
ADT instance;
float f = 53.7F;
int x = (instance.*ptrMemberFunction)(f);
```

If you want to use a pointer to a class instance to call a nonstatic member function via a nonstatic member function pointer, write the instance pointer name, the pointer-to-member operator (–>*), and then the name of the nonstatic member function pointer. Be sure to enclose the instance pointer name, the pointer-to-member operator, and the name of the nonstatic member function pointer within parentheses. This expression is then followed by the member function's argument list:

```
ADT pointer = new ADT;
float f = 53.7F;
int x = (pointer->*ptrMemberFunction)(f);
delete pointer;
```

SUMMARY ▶ Use the .* and –>* operators to invoke nonstatic member functions whose addresses have been stored into pointers.

Pointers to Static Class Member Functions

As mentioned earlier in this chapter, a static member function is never passed an implicit **this** pointer. Consequently, a program can call a static member function directly, without first instantiating a class instance. In this respect, a static member function is similar to an ordinary (non-class-member) function. It should come as no surprise, then, that a pointer to a static member function has the exact same type syntax as for an ordinary function with the same parameter list and return type. For the purpose of creating a pointer to a static member function, you treat the static member function "as if" it were an ordinary function with class scope. Specifically, you use the address-of operator **&** to take the address of the static member function in exactly the same way as for a nonstatic member function. The resulting address is then stored in an *ordinary* function pointer and not in a nonstatic member function pointer. At this point, the program can use the ordinary pointer-to-function call syntax to call the static member function (no special operators are required):

```
class ADT
{
    public:
  static int func(float);   // static member function
};
// ...

int someFunction(float) { ... }            // ordinary function

typedef int (*PointerFunction)(float);
PointerFunction ptrFunction;
float f = 53.7F;

ptrFunction = &ADT::func;
int x = ptrFunction(f);                    // calls ADT::func

ptrFunction = someFunction;
int y = ptrFunction(f);                    // calls someFunction
```

When taking the address of a static member function, the pointer is declared just like that of a global function. It is not scoped to its class name.

9

Exception Handling

Introduction

Exception handling in C++ provides a means by which a function can "raise" or "throw" an exception (an error condition) and pass that exception to a completely different part of the program so that it can then be "caught."

Why do you need exception handling? Sometimes the "normal" method of indicating that an error condition has occurred, such as a function returning a special value, can prove to be inadequate because of the semantics of the language itself. For example, suppose that a function promises to return type **double**, and yet no **double** value exists to indicate that an error occurred. Or perhaps the function is not able to return anything—for example, a constructor. Now you've got a big problem on your hands.

SUMMARY ▶ Exception handling allows an error condition to be "raised" or "thrown" by one function to a completely different function so that it can be "caught."

How to Throw an Exception

An exception is thrown from a function by writing the keyword **throw** followed by any valid C++ expression. When this happens, a copy of the expression is made and is passed out (propagated) to the function that called the one currently executing. The return type of the function (or lack thereof) is completely ignored when this occurs, and no more statements in the function are executed.

For example, the following **throw** statements are all valid:

```
throw 0;
int x = 1;
throw x;
throw x + 4;
throw String("Out of range");       // Note function style cast
```

Of course, if a user-defined object is thrown, a copy is made by calling the class's copy constructor.

SUMMARY Write the keyword **throw** followed by any valid C++ expression to throw an exception.

How to Catch an Exception

So an exception has been thrown, and it's now sailing from the function that launched it back to the calling function. The calling function must now decide if this exception should be caught and handled, or if it should simply be ignored. If it is to be caught, the function must write a *try/catch handler*. The first part of this handler consists of the keyword **try** followed by a pair of braces. This is called a *try block*:

```
try
{
   // Your code here
}
```

The second part consists of one or more *catch blocks,* which must immediately follow the try block. All such catch blocks must be contiguous, that is, they must have no intervening code. A catch block is written with the keyword **catch** followed by exactly one argument between parentheses:

```
catch( / * one argument here */ )
{
   // Your code here
}
// Possibly another catch block follows
catch ( /* one argument here */ )
{
   // Your code here
}
```

If the catch handler consists of the ellipsis punctuator (. . .), then it designates a handler that is capable of catching any exception that has not yet been handled by a previous catch block. Obviously, if you choose to write such a handler, it must be the last one in a series of handlers:

```
catch(...)
{
    // Your code here
}
```

 Write a try/catch handler if you want to catch exceptions that are thrown from within the context of the try block.

How Exception Handling Works

In order to catch an exception that a called function might throw, the call to this function must occur within a try block. If this is done, and an exception is subsequently thrown, the type of thrown exception is compared to the type of argument in each successive catch block, in order, top to bottom. If a match occurs, the code in that catch block is executed and all remaining catch blocks are bypassed. If no match occurs, the exception automatically propagates up the stack to the next enclosing try/catch handler, which might be in the same function but is usually located in the function that called this one, and once again all catch blocks are examined. Of course, if a function doesn't even bother specifying a try/catch handler, the exception automatically propagates up to the next higher function.

 A thrown exception is compared to the single argument that is specified in each catch block. If a match is found, the code in the catch block is executed, and all remaining blocks are skipped. If no match is found, the exception propagates to the next higher try/catch handler.

Matching Process for Catch Blocks

What constitutes a match if an exception is thrown? Suppose an object of type **T** is thrown. Any catch block that takes an argument of type **C** provides an acceptable match if:

▲ **T** and **C** are the same type (e.g., **int** can be caught by **int**),

▲ **C** adds a **const** qualifier (e.g., **int** can be caught by **int const** and **int** * can be caught by **int const** *),

▲ **C** adds a reference qualifier (e.g., **int** can be caught by **int &**),

▲ **C** is an accessible base class of the publicly derived class **T** (discussed in Chapter 11),

▲ **T** and **C** are data pointer types, and a standard conversion exists from **T** to **C** (e.g., **int** * can be caught by **void** *).

Promotions and all other standard conversions are *not* done. For example, neither a **char** nor an **enum** object can be caught by type **int**, and an **int** object cannot be caught by type **double**. Of course, a user-defined object should be caught by reference-to-**const** to avoid a needless call to the class's copy constructor.

The matching process for catch blocks is more restrictive than the matching process for function calls.

A Simple Example of Exception Handling

Let's look at a program in which you should use exception handling:

```
#include <iostream>
using std::cout;
using std::cerr;
using std::cin;

double getQuotient(int numerator, int denominator)
{
  if(denominator == 0)
    throw "Zero denominator";
  return static_cast<double>(numerator) / denominator;
}

int main()
{
  cout << "Enter a numerator and denominator: ";
  int num, den;
  while(!(cin >> num >> den).eof())
  {
    try
    {
      cout << "Quotient is " << getQuotient(num, den)
            << '\n';
    }
    catch(char const *error)
    {
      cerr << error << '\n';
    }
    cout << "Next numerator and denominator: ";
  }
}

/* Sample output:

Enter a numerator and denominator: 123 5
Quotient is 24.6
```

```
Next numerator and denominator: 44 0
Zero denominator
Next numerator and denominator: ^Z
```

```
*/
```

The function **getQuotient**() is designed to return the quotient of its two input **int** arguments as a type **double**. If, however, the denominator is zero, no division can occur (lest the program abort), so an exception must be thrown instead. The **main**() function, ever vigilant that the user might input a zero for the denominator value, correctly uses a try/catch handler in case an exception does indeed get thrown. Consequently, the program can continue to execute normally regardless of what the user inputs.

Now you could, I suppose, make the argument that **main**() should be checking for a denominator of zero before calling the function, thereby negating the need to use a try/catch handler. The problem is that the **getQuotient**() function could be used by many different functions, and who is to say that all of these functions will remember to perform this check? By localizing this validity check in **getQuotient**(), a divide-by-zero error will never occur. If the caller neglects to write a try/catch handler, the exception will propagate out and the program will terminate abnormally, but whose fault is that? Not yours, if you're the author of **getQuotient**(). If you failed to make this check, and the user also failed to make it, the error would occur in the **getQuotient**() function, and you would be held responsible. You don't really want to be held responsible for a program's abnormal termination, do you?

Unwinding the Stack

If you haven't already done so, you should be thinking about the problem of having a number of user-defined objects on the stack when an exception is thrown. Because no more processing will occur in the function, and its closing brace will never be reached (at which point all stack objects will get popped), don't we have the potential of having an unpopped stack, not to mention the disastrous situation of destructors failing to get called? Fortunately, the answer is no, because the compiler guarantees that all stack objects will be destroyed when an exception gets thrown.

SUMMARY ▶ Even if an exception gets thrown, all stack objects will get popped, thereby guaranteeing that all destructors will get called.

What If the Call to **new** Fails?

Believe it or not, even with tons of memory and sophisticated operating systems, only a finite amount of space can be allocated on the free store. Consequently, it's possible that your program can exceed this limit whenever you use the keyword **new**. If this should ever happen, the generated call to **operator new**() will throw an exception of type **std::bad_alloc**, which is a class defined in the header file **new**. Of course, you have the option to either catch this exception or ignore it. For example, here is a simple program that requests space on the free store and checks for an out-of-memory condition:

```cpp
#include <iostream>
#include <new>

int main()
{
  try
  {
    int *ptr = new int(1234);
    // Continue processing
    delete ptr;
  }
  catch(std::bad_alloc const &)
  {
    std::cerr << "Out of memory\n";
  }
}
```

As noted earlier, the exception is caught by reference-to-**const** to support a possible constant (and temporary) object and to avoid a needless call to the copy constructor. Of course, you could have avoided using the class **std::bad_alloc** altogether by using ellipses (. . .) if you simply wanted to catch anything that **operator new**() might throw:

```cpp
#include <iostream>

int main()
{
  try
  {
    int *ptr = new int(1);
    // Continue processing
    delete ptr;
  }
  catch(...)
  {
    std::cout << "Out of memory\n";
  }
}
```

 Be aware that **new** could throw an out-of-memory exception of type **std::bad_alloc**.

How to Prevent **new** from Throwing an Exception

Instead of allowing **operator new**() to throw an exception, it's possible to emulate how the C language handles an out-of-memory condition when **malloc**() is called—by having **operator new**() return a null pointer rather than throwing a **std::bad_alloc** exception. You can do this by writing the expression **std::nothrow** between parentheses immediately following the keyword **new**, as in the following:

```
#include <iostream>
#include <new>

int main()
{
    int *ptr = new (std::nothrow) int(1);
    if(ptr)
    {
        // Continue processing
        delete ptr;
    }
    else
        std::cout << "Out of memory\n";
}
```

 The object **std::nothrow** is an instance of the class **std::nothrow_t**. Both are declared in the header file **new**.

SUMMARY ▶ Write the expression (**std::nothrow**) after the keyword **new** to force **operator new**() to return a zero if an out-of-memory condition occurs. No exception will be thrown.

Propagating an Exception

If a function decides to write a try/catch handler, it very well might want to propagate the exception (or even throw a different exception) after it's been caught. For example, if a constructor calls **new**, and a **std::bad_alloc** exception gets thrown because there is not enough space available on the free store, the constructor should catch this exception, perhaps do some cleanup, and then rethrow the current **std::bad_alloc** exception (or perhaps throw some other kind of exception) to the code block that called the constructor.

The following program demonstrates this by having the **String** constructor catch an exception and then propagate its own string literal. To simulate the throwing of an exception by the call to **new**, we'll just hard-code a **throw** statement in the **try** block in the constructor:

```cpp
// File string.h

#ifndef STRING_H
#define STRING_H

class String
{
    public:
  String(char const *chars = "");
  ~String();
    private:
  char *ptrChars;
};

#endif

// File string.cpp

#include <cstring>
#include <new>
#include "string.h"

String::String(char const *chars) : ptrChars(0)
{
  try
  {
    ptrChars = new char[std::strlen(chars) + 1];
    // Pretend we're out of memory
    throw std::bad_alloc();
    std::strcpy(ptrChars, chars);
  }
  catch(...)
  {
    throw "Object cannot be constructed";
  }
}

String::~String()
{
  delete [] ptrChars;
}
```

```
// File main.cpp

#include <iostream>
#include "string.h"

int main()
{
  try
  {
    String str("C++");
  }
  catch(char const *error)
  {
    std::cerr << error << '\n';
  }
}

/* Output:

Object cannot be constructed

*/
```

 After catching an object, a function can propagate it to the next higher try/catch handler, or it can emit a completely different exception.

How to Manage Pointers to the Free Space

Even though the class in the previous example contained a pointer to the free store, it required no special management (even though it was initialized to 0) and it did not matter whether or not an exception got thrown. Now let's look at a case where you do need to manage your pointers and catch an exception before propagating it.

We'll modify the **String** class so that it now encapsulates two pointers—one that will point to a lowercase version of the string literal, and the other that will point to an uppercase version:

```
// File string.h

#ifndef STRING_H
#define STRING_H

class String
```

```cpp
{
    public:
  String(char const *chars = "");
  ~String();
    private:
  char *ptrLowercaseChars;
  char *ptrUppercaseChars;
  void cleanup();
  void toLower(char *) const;
  void toUpper(char *) const;
};

#endif

// File string.cpp

#include <cstring>
#include <cctype>
#include <cstddef>
#include "string.h"

String::String(char const *chars)
                : ptrLowercaseChars(0), ptrUppercaseChars(0)
{
  try
  {
    // Mangage the first pointer
    ptrLowercaseChars = new char[std::strlen(chars) + 1];
    std::strcpy(ptrLowercaseChars, chars);
    toLower(ptrLowercaseChars);
    // Manage the second pointer
    ptrUppercaseChars = new char[std::strlen(chars) + 1];
    std::strcpy(ptrUppercaseChars, chars);
    toUpper(ptrUppercaseChars);
  }
  catch(...)
  {
    cleanup();
    throw "Object cannot be constructed";
  }
}

String::~String()
```

```
{
  cleanup();
}

void String::cleanup()
{
  delete [] ptrLowercaseChars;
  delete [] ptrUppercaseChars;
}

void String::toLower(char *ptr) const
{
  for(std::size_t i = 0; i < std::strlen(ptr); ++i)
    ptr[i] = static_cast<char>(std::tolower(ptr[i]));
}

void String::toUpper(char *ptr) const
{
  for(std::size_t i = 0; i < std::strlen(ptr); ++i)
    ptr[i] = static_cast<char>(std::toupper(ptr[i]));
}

// File main.cpp

#include <iostream>
#include "string.h"

int main()
{
  try
  {
    String str("C++");
  }
  catch(char const *error)
  {
    std::cerr << error << '\n';
  }
}
```

Notice carefully that both pointers are being initialized to zero in the constructor's base/member initialization list. As a result, no matter which call to **new** might fail, the private function **cleanup()** is called when the exception is caught, and both pointers are deleted. The deletion of either (1) space on the free store that we own or (2) a zero-based pointer (which does no harm) is guaranteed, so there will never be a memory leak. Also, to save on code repetition, the destructor itself calls **cleanup()**.

In case you are wondering why the previous example performs its calls to **new** within the constructor's try block and not within the constructor's base/member initialization list, here's the explanation. Recall that during the base/member initialization phase, control has not yet entered the body of the constructor. Also recall that a catch block can catch only exceptions that are thrown by code that resides within the catch block's corresponding try block. Because the constructor's base/member initialization list does not reside within the constructor's try block, the corresponding catch block cannot catch exceptions that are thrown during the base/member initialization phase. Here is the erroneous code:

```
String::String(char const *chars)
    : ptrLowercaseChars(new char[std::strlen(chars) + 1]),
      ptrUppercaseChars(new char[std::strlen(chars) + 1])
{
  try
  {
    // Mangage the first pointer
    std::strcpy(ptrLowercaseChars, chars);
    toLower(ptrLowercaseChars);
    // Manage the second pointer
    std::strcpy(ptrUppercaseChars, chars);
    toUpper(ptrUppercaseChars);
  }
  catch(...)
  {
    cleanup();
    throw "Object cannot be constructed";
  }
}
```

Now consider the following scenario. Assume a successful initialization of **ptrLowercaseChars**, that is, the call to **new** allocates the specified amount of storage from the free store, and the starting address of that storage region is stored in the data member **ptrLowercaseChars**. Now assume a failed initialization of **ptrUppercaseChars**, that is, the call to **new** fails to allocate the requested amount of storage from the free store and consequently throws a **std::bad_alloc** exception. The **try-catch** implementation shown in the previous code sample is useless in this case, because (1) control has not yet entered the try block when the exception is thrown, and therefore (2) the catch block cannot catch the exception and perform cleanup on the partially constructed **String** object. This code sample has no way to deallocate the storage region that **ptrLowercaseChars** currently points at before control exits the constructor call as a consequence of the **std::bad_alloc** exception. Therefore, this code sample has a potential memory leak if an exception is thrown during the base/member initialization phase. Not a good programming idea.

If a class contains one or more pointers to the free store, be sure to initialize all such pointers to zero before managing them in the body of the constructor.

You Can't Destroy What You Haven't Created

You should note that whenever a constructor fails to run to completion, the compiler guarantees that the destructor for that incomplete object will *not* be executed. By "completion," I mean that the closing brace of the constructor's body has been reached, or that the body has terminated via a **return** statement. This makes perfect sense because the destructor wouldn't know what to do anyway with a partially constructed object.

 A class's destructor will run only if the complete object has successfully been built by the constructor.

Rethrowing an Object

A catch block can rethrow the current exception so that a **catch** block in an enclosing scope can also try to handle the exception. To rethrow the current exception, write the keyword **throw** by itself (i.e., without any arguments) in the body of the **catch** block. This is useful when you have a catch handler using ellipses (. . .), and you want to propagate the same exception that was just caught:

```
catch(...)
{
  // Your code here
  throw;        // Rethrow whatever was caught
}
```

Catching Throws from Subobject Members

A subobject member is any user-defined data member of a class. In other words, it's an object within an object. Consider the following **Person** class, which contains a **String** called **name** as a subobject member:

```
// File person.h

#ifndef PERSON_H
#define PERSON_H
```

```
#include "string.h"

class Person
{
    public:
  Person(String const &n);
    private:
  String name;
};

#endif

// File person.cpp

#include "person.h"
#include "string.h"

Person::Person(String const &n) : name(n) { }

// File main.cpp

#include <iostream>
#include "person.h"

int main()
{
  try
  {
    Person inventor("Bjarne");
    // Continue processing
  }
  catch(...)
  {
    std::cerr << "Instantiation failure\n";
  }
}
```

A **Person** must be instantiated with a name of type **String** (which **main()** is doing by having the string literal "Bjarne" visit the converting constructor of the **String** class). The initialization of the **name** field then occurs when the copy constructor of the **String** class is called. Now consider what happens if and when the **String** class's converting constructor throws an exception. Does the **Person** constructor catch it? No, so it will propagate back to **main()** where the exception is caught by the ellipses **catch** block. But what if the constructor wants to catch this exception, perhaps to propagate a different exception? How, can a try/catch handler be written in this context?

Function-Try-Blocks

To write a try/catch handler that will allow a constructor to catch an exception, you must use a *function-try-block*. This entails writing the keyword **try** just prior to the colon that starts the base/member initialization list. Thus, for some generic type **T**, if the initialization of **data** might cause an exception to be thrown, you would code:

```
class ADT
{
    public:
  ADT(T const &d) try : data(d)
  {
    // Body of constructor
  }
  catch(/* catch argument */)
  {
    // Body of catch handler
  }
    private:
  T data;
  // ..
};
```

Notice that the catch handler corresponding to the keyword **try** must appear immediately *after* the body of the constructor. In effect, the base/member initialization list and the body of the constructor together constitute the entire **try** block.

When working with function-try-blocks, you must remember two crucial points. First, the catch handler(s) for a function-try-block *cannot* access the instance's nonstatic members (data or functions). Clearly, if a function-try-block handler contains code that tries to use the nonstatic members of the unconstructed class instance, the results are undefined. Second, it is impossible to exit from the catch handler of a function-try-block without propagating an explicit exception or rethrowing the one that was just caught. In other words, insofar as C++ is concerned, once the catch handler is entered, there is no way to create an object successfully for the simple reason that a critical subobject part of that object could not be created. In effect, it's an "all or nothing" situation. Therefore, even if you fail to propagate an exception, the one that was caught will automatically be rethrown for you.

Using a function-try-block, the **Person** class would now be written like this:

```
// File person.h

#ifndef PERSON_H
#define PERSON_H
```

```cpp
#include "string.h"

class Person
{
    public:
  Person(String const &n);
    private:
  String name;
};

#endif

// File person.cpp

#include "person.h"
#include "string.h"

// Note the function-try-block
Person::Person(String const &n) try : name(n)
{
  // Constructor body
}
catch(...)
{
  // Your handler code here
  // An exception is always rethrown
  // Do NOT try to access the Person class's
  // nonstatic members in this catch block!
}

// File main.cpp

#include <iostream>
#include "person.h"

int main()
{
  try
  {
    Person inventor("Bjarne");
    // Continue processing
  }
  catch(...)
  {
```

```
        std::cerr << "Instantiation failure\n";
    }
}
```

 The handling of subobject members also applies to any exceptions that a base class constructor might throw. That is, a function-try-block can be used to catch these exceptions as well. The subject of inheritance is covered in Chapter 11.

 Use a function-try-block to catch exceptions that are thrown during the base/member initialization phase.

Mixing Subobject Members and Pointers

If a class contains at least one subobject member and at least one pointer, you've got a real headache. Consider this example in which two pointers of some generic type **T** have been added to the **Person** class:

```
// File person.h

#ifndef PERSON_H
#define PERSON_H

#include "string.h"

class Person
{
    public:
  Person(String const &n);
  ~Person();
    private:
  String name;
  T *ptr1, *ptr2;            // Two pointers added
  void cleanup();
};

#endif

// File person.cpp

#include "person.h"
#include "string.h"

// Note the function-try-block
```

```
Person::Person(String const &n) try
                                : name(n), ptr1(0), ptr2(0)
{
  ptr1 = new T( /* arguments */ );
  ptr2 = new T( /* arguments */ );
}
catch(...)
{
  cleanup();   // Warning: undefined behavior at runtime
  // Your handler code here
  // An exception is always rethrown
}

Person::~Person()
{
  cleanup();
}

void Person::cleanup()
{
  delete ptr1;
  delete ptr2;
}

// File main.cpp

#include <iostream>
#include "person.h"

int main()
{
  try
  {
    Person inventor("Bjarne");
    // Continue processing
  }
  catch(...)
  {
    std::cerr << "Instantiation failure\n";
  }
}
```

It appears that everything is coded properly in order to handle the case where either the first or second call to **operator new**() might throw an exception. That is, the exception is caught and the private **cleanup**() function is called to release whatever space may have been allocated. But wait! If the initialization of **name** via the call to the **String** class's copy constructor throws an exception, the initialization of **ptr1** and **ptr2** will never occur, and the subsequent calls to **delete** will then be using *uninitialized pointers*. And if that's not bad enough, don't forget that the behavior of the nonstatic member function **cleanup**() is undefined in the function-try-block handler! (Recall that if a function-try-block handler uses the nonstatic members of an unconstructed instance, the results are undefined.)

The solution to this dilemma is to encapsulate all such pointers into wrapper classes so that they become true subobject members and, as such, can manage themselves by using their own constructors and destructors.

SUMMARY Don't use pointers to objects on the free store in a class that contains at least one subobject member and a function-try-block.

Partial Construction of an Object

The C++ compiler has some good news for you: Class-type subobject members will always be destructed if they're successfully constructed, even if an exception is subsequently thrown. This rule also applies to arrays of user-defined types that are encapsulated inside a class. In fact, the destructor for a successfully constructed subobject member will be called before entering the catch handler of a function-try-block.

Let's enhance our **Person** class to include both a first name and a last name as subobject members of the **Person** class. Of course, the construction of either one could throw an exception. If **firstName** gets constructed successfully, and the construction of **lastName** throws, the destructor for **firstName** is guaranteed to be called. Therefore, in your catch handler, there's really nothing to do except propagate or rethrow the exception. Consequently, there is no way for the user of your class to be left with a partially initialized object.

Another way of looking at it is to ask the following question: Was an exception thrown as a result of initializing a subobject member? If so, and if it was not caught in the constructor, the exception will propagate back to the user, who won't have an object to use. And if the exception was caught in the constructor, then the same or a different exception can be rethrown. As I stated earlier, however, even if this is not done in the catch handler, the exception that was caught will be automatically rethrown back to the user, so there is still no way that this user will have a valid object:

```
// File person.h

#ifndef PERSON_H
#define PERSON_H

#include "string.h"

class Person
```

```
{
    public:
  Person(String const &first, String const &last);
    private:
  String firstName, lastName;
};

#endif

// File person.cpp

#include "person.h"
#include "string.h"

Person::Person(String const &first, String const &last)
                       try : firstName(first), lastName(last)
{
  // Constructor body
}
catch(...)
{
  // Your handler code here
  // An exception is always rethrown
}

// File main.cpp

#include "person.h"

int main()
{
  Person inventor("Bjarne", "Stroustrup");
}
```

 The C++ compiler guarantees that either an instance will be fully constructed or an exception will be thrown from a constructor.

Writing Exception-Safe Code

Let's take a look at how you can create user-defined objects on the stack and on the free store while adhering to the rules of exception- safety. That is, you will never cause a memory leak to occur and an object will never be left in a partially constructed state.

A Single Object on the Stack

If you want to allocate a single object on the stack and catch any exceptions that might propagate from the object's constructor call, your code should look something like this:

```
#include "string.h"

int main()
{
  try
  {
    String str("C++");
    // Process normally
  }
  catch(...)
  {
    Your handler code here
  }
}
```

If the **String** constructor throws an exception, your catch handler gets control; you can then do whatever you please, such as display an error message. The **String** class itself is responsible for cleaning up whatever resources it might have allocated. Of course, there's no law that says you have to catch the exception, but it's certainly better than having the program abort for no apparent reason.

An Array of Objects on the Stack

This is the same for an array of user-defined objects on the stack. Here is an array of 10 **String** objects. Your code should be something like the following:

```
#include "string.h"

int main()
{
  try
  {
    String array[10];
    // Process normally
  }
  catch(...)
  {
    // Your handler code here
  }
}
```

Now suppose that the first nine **String** objects are constructed successfully, but the construction of the last **String** object fails. Do you have a problem? The answer is no, because the compiler guarantees that the destructors for all of the previously created nine objects will be called (in last-in-first-out [LIFO] order). After this happens, the exception will be propagated back to you. In any event, no memory leak occurs, and the array is not usable. Your catch handler can then do whatever it wishes.

A Single Object on the Free Store

Now, writing exception-safe code gets more interesting. If your object is to live on the free store, there are two places where an exception could be thrown. First, there might not be enough space on the free store to hold the object itself, and second, even if there is, the constructor might throw. Therefore, you must write your code as follows:

```
#include "string.h"

int main()
{
  String *ptr = 0;
  try
  {
    ptr = new String("C++");
    // Process normally...
  }
  catch(...)
  {
    // Your handler code here
  }
  delete ptr;
}
```

Here are the various outcomes:

▲ If space on the free store for the **String** object cannot be allocated, your catch handler gets control and does whatever it wishes, after which the delete occurs. Because the pointer was carefully initialized to zero, however, it's just a case of "no harm, no foul." (Recall that a delete of a zero-based pointer is perfectly safe.)

▲ If space on the free store is allocated successfully but the **String** constructor throws, the compiler: (1) destroys any class-type subobjects that have already been constructed (in reverse order of their creation), (2) automatically deallocates the storage that it allocated from the free store, and (3) transfers control to your catch handler, which does whatever it wishes. In this scenario, the exception occurs "in the middle of" the call to **new**, so it never returns. Therefore, the value in **ptr** is not modified (its value is still zero), which means the subsequent **delete** call acts upon a zero-based pointer, which is perfectly safe. The **String** destructor is never called because the constructor did not run to completion.

▲ If everything works successfully (no exception is thrown), the **delete** causes the **String** destructor to be called, after which the space on the free store is released.

A Single Object on the Free Store (Revisited)

One problem with using a pointer to point to an object on the free store is that there is no automatic destruction of that object. In other words, when a pointer variable reaches the end of its lifetime, the object that the pointer variable is pointing at is *not* automatically destroyed when the pointer variable itself is destroyed. Therefore, it's up to you to issue a call to **delete** in order to have the object's destructor called and the space released. If this call does not happen, you can be sure that a memory leak will occur. Stack objects, of course, are not subject to this danger because they are automatically popped, which causes their destructors to be called.

A solution to the free-store problem is to bury the pointer inside a class type object and write a destructor for the class that explicitly deletes the region on the free store that the object's pointer is pointing at. Then, when this object goes out of scope, its destructor will be called; this will release the space occupied by the object being pointed at, and, like magic, no memory leak can ever occur.

Happily, a wonderful class for such objects already exists in the C++ Standard Library. Its name is **std::auto_ptr** and it's defined in the header file **memory**. Because it is a *template* (discussed in detail in Chapter 12), its type must be specialized by writing the specific type in which you're interested between angle brackets right after the class name. To use an **std::auto_ptr** object, initialize it with the address of the space on the free store that **new** has returned, *using C++ style initialization*:

```
#include <memory>
#include "string.h"
// ...
std::auto_ptr<int> api(new int(1));
std::auto_ptr<double> apd(new double(76.483));
std::auto_ptr<String> aps(new String("C++"));
```

Now the code for an object on the free store looks the same as if the object lived on the stack:

```
#include <memory>
#include "string.h"

typedef std::auto_ptr<String> AUTO_PTR_STRING;
int main()
{
  try
  {
```

```
            AUTO_PTR_STRING aps(new String("C++"));
            // Process normally...
        }
        catch(...)
        {
            // Your handler code here
        }
    }
```

Let's once again explore the three possible outcomes:

▲ If space on the free store for the **String** object cannot be allocated, your catch handler gets control and does whatever it wishes. The object **aps** is not created.

▲ If the space on the free store is allocated successfully, but the **String** constructor throws, once again your catch handler gets called and does whatever it wishes. The **String** destructor is never called because the **String** constructor did not run to completion, but the compiler guarantees that the space on the free store is automatically released. The object **aps** is not created.

▲ If everything works successfully (no exception is thrown), then, when the **aps** object goes out of scope at the end of the try block, its destructor will be called; this will then cause the **String** destructor to be called, after which the space on the free store is automatically released.

An Array of Objects on the Free Store

If the array of **String** objects must exist on the free store, you should code it like this:

```
#include "string.h"

int main()
{
    String *ptr = 0;
    try
    {
        ptr = new String[10];
    }
    catch(...)
    {
        // Your handler code here
    }
    delete [] ptr;
}
```

Once again, here are all of the possible scenarios:

▲ If the space for the array itself cannot be allocated, **operator new**[]() will throw an exception for you to catch and do whatever you wish in the handler, after which the delete is executed. Because the pointer was initialized to 0, it's just a case of "no harm, no foul" again.

▲ If the space for the array itself is successfully allocated but the **String** default constructor should happen to throw during the construction of any of the 10 objects, then all currently constructed String objects will be destructed (in LIFO order), and the space on the free store is automatically released. Note that the value of the pointer variable **ptr** is not changed from its initial value of 0. You catch the exception and again delete a pointer that contains a 0.

▲ If everything works properly, space for the array is allocated, and the 10 **String** objects will be successfully created. Of course, the default constructor will run 10 times. The pointer **ptr** will then point to the array's first element. When the call to **delete**[] executes, the **String** destructor gets called 10 times (in LIFO order), after which the space for the array itself will be released.

That was fun, but not as much fun as trying to adhere to the PITA rule when creating user-defined types on the free store. In Chapter 7 we saw how this could be done by using a pointer to an array of pointers, each of which then points to the object itself. In this fashion, arguments can be passed to the object's constructor, thereby avoiding whatever values the default constructor provides. But that code wasn't exception safe. Here is how to do it:

```
#include "string.h"

int main()
{
  int const size = 10;
  String **ptr = 0;
  try
  {
    ptr = new String *[size];
    for(int i = 0; i < size; ++i)
      ptr[i] = 0;
    try
    {
      for(int i = 0; i < size; ++i)
        ptr[i] = new String( /* arguments */ );
      // Process normally
    }
    catch(...)
    {
      // Your handler code here
    }
```

```
      for(int i = 0; i < size; ++i)
        delete ptr[i];
    }
    catch(...)
    {
      // Your handler code here
    }
    delete [] ptr;
  }
```

Notice how a try/catch handler for the individual **String** objects is completely contained within an existing try/catch handler for the array of pointers, and how each pointer must be zeroed before being assigned into. Do you really want to walk through the various scenarios? I didn't think so.

An Array of Objects on the Free Store (Revisited)

Let's be honest. That previous code example was far too messy. Once again, the library's **std::auto_ptr** class can help simplify the code by eliminating the second try/catch handler:

```
// File main.cpp

#include <memory>
#include "string.h"

typedef std::auto_ptr<String> AUTO_PTR_STRING;
int main()
{
  AUTO_PTR_STRING *array = 0;
  try
  {
    array = new AUTO_PTR_STRING[10];
    for(int i = 0; i < 10; ++i)
    {
      AUTO_PTR_STRING ptr(new String( /* arguments */ ));
      // Ownership of the free store is transferred when
      // an auto_ptr is assigned
      array[i] = ptr;
      // Process normally
    }
  }
  catch(...)
```

```
{
   // Your handling code here
}
delete [] array;
}
```

The possibilities here are the same as for any array of user-defined types on the free store, and yet we're still able to initialize each **String** object with its proper value instead of being forced to invoke the **String** default constructor 10 times. Actually, it's the **auto_ptr** default constructor that's being called 10 times, but all it does is initialize its internal pointer to 0, so we're not paying too much of a penalty here.

EXERCISE 9.1

The quadratic equation $AX^2 + BX + C = 0$ has as its two solutions:
$(-B \pm sqrt(B^2 - 4AC))/(2A)$

Write a function called **Quadratic()** whose arguments are the three coefficients **A**, **B**, and **C**, and a fourth argument of type **bool** indicating which root is to be returned. The function must return the proper root as a type **double**. If the coefficient **A** is equal to zero, then throw an exception of type **int**. If the discriminant ($B^2 - 4AC$) is less than zero, throw an exception of type **char ***.

Write a **main()** function that prompts for the three coefficients, displays the two roots, and loops until end-of-file is entered. If an exception is thrown, be sure to catch it and display an appropriate message. Otherwise, display the two roots and prove that they are correct.

Destructors and Exception Handling

The rule regarding destructors and exception handling is quite simple: Destructors must never throw exceptions. If a destructor should ever throw, the global function **terminate()** will get called (discussed shortly), and there is no way that you can ever write exception-safe code. And the C++ Standard forbids it anyway.

 Never have a destructor throw an exception.

Exception Specifications

A function (definition or declaration) can choose to explicitly document the exceptions it could possibly throw by writing an *exception specification* after (not part of) its signature. This entails writing the keyword **throw** followed by a list of formal argument types in parentheses.

Exception specifications do not participate in overloading resolution. This means that a function can be compiled with a different exception specification than what is found in the function declaration. Therefore, always make sure that a function declaration and its definition are consistent in their use of an exception specification. For example:

```
// func1 could throw anything
void func1( /* Arguments here */ )

// func2 promises not to throw anything
void func2( /* Arguments here */ ) throw()

// func3 may throw an 'int'
void func3( /* Arguments here */ ) throw(int)

// func4 may throw an 'int' or a 'double'
void func4( /* Arguments here */ ) throw(int, double)

// func5 may throw a 'String' or any class derived from
// 'String'
void func5( /* Arguments here */ ) throw(String)
```

SUMMARY ▶ Exception specifications tell the user what a function can legitimately throw.

Exception Specification Violations

A function violates the promise made by its exception specification if (1) that specification is **throw**() and the function throws any exception; (2) the function throws any exception that is not in the exception specification list; or (3) the function lets an exception propagate through itself that violates its own exception specification list. Although the compiler is under no obligation to do so, it can catch (pun intended?) this violation at compilation time and issue either a fatal or a warning message. For example, one popular compiler gives a warning message when it sees the **throw** statement, as in the following:

```
void func() throw()
{
   throw 0;     // Violation of exception specification
}

int main()
{
   func();
}
```

On the other hand, given this slightly more complicated program, the exception coming from **func1**() violates the specification in **func2**(), but the compiler is unable to detect this:

```
void func1() throw(char)
{
    throw 'A';
}

void func2() throw()
{
    func1();
}

int main()
{
    func2();
}
```

 The compiler might or might not be able to detect a violation of an exception specification.

Error Conditions

If the compiler is not able to emit a fatal message about an exception specification violation, the error must be deferred until execution time. Two kinds of runtime errors can occur with respect to exception specification violations.

Unexpected Error

The first error is called *unexpected,* and it occurs when a function throws (or lets propagate through it) an exception object whose type is not specified in the function's exception specification list. In this case, the function **std::unexpected**() will be called, which will then call the function **std::terminate**() (discussed next). So the users are protected from having something, well, unexpected thrown at them.

 An unexpected error occurs when a function violates its exception specification.

Terminate Error

The second error is called *terminate,* and it occurs when an exception is thrown and no one ever catches it. In effect, it propagates right out of your program. In this case, the function **std::terminate**() gets called, which then calls the global function **abort**().

A terminate error occurs when an exception is never caught and propagates out of a program.

How the Compiler Treats Exception Specifications

It's quite possible that using an exception specification might cause the compiler to generate a significant amount of code, so be careful. For example, in the following, **func2**(), which could throw a **double** or a **char**, calls upon **func1**(), which could throw anything:

```
void func1()
{
    // ...
}

void func2() throw(double, char);
{
    func1();
    // ...
}
```

To ensure that a **double** or a **char** does not propagate from **func2**(), the compiler must generate code similar to this:

```
void func2()
{
    try
    {
        func1();
    }
    catch(double)
    {
        throw;
    }
    catch(char)
    {
        throw;
    }
    catch(...)
    {
        std::unexpected();
    }
}
```

Be aware of the code that an exception specification could generate.

Defining **operator new()** for a Class

Whenever you write the keyword **new** followed by a class name, the global function **operator new**() gets called. It tries to allocate the required amount of space and, if successful, returns a pointer to the space so that the compiler can then call the appropriate constructor. Suppose, however, that you need to perform some specialized behavior whenever an instance of your class gets allocated on the free store. In this case, a class can have its own **operator new**() member function that behaves the way you want.

To do this, the first argument to the class's **operator new**() member function is always a parameter of type **std::size_t** that represents the size (in bytes) of the object being instantiated. Any additional formal arguments that the program should be allowed to pass into the **operator new**() function are specified next. The function's return type must be specified as **void ***. Within the body of the **operator new**() member function, the program allocates the required amount of space and returns a pointer of type **void *** to that space. As is the case with the standard library's **operator new**() functions, when a call to the class's **operator new**() member function returns, the class's constructor is automatically called to construct the specified class instance within the allocated space.

A class can also have an **operator delete**() member function. This member function always takes two arguments: a **void *** pointer that points at the object that's to be deleted, and a **std::size_t** argument that specifies the size (in bytes) of the object that's being deleted. When the user issues a **delete**, the destructor for the object gets called, followed by a call to the class's **operator delete**() member function.

Note that both of these member functions are presumed to be declared **static**, even if you don't explicitly say so.

If you need to pass in additional arguments to a class's **operator new**() member function, you can write them between parentheses after the keyword **new** and before the type name. For example, suppose you want to log exceptions to the **std::clog** output stream if **operator new**() should fail. In the class **std::bad_alloc** the member function **what**() indicates the reason for the failure. The **std::clog** object must therefore be passed to the class's **operator new**() function. You might write the class like this:

```
// File adt.h

#ifndef ADT_H
#define ADT_H

#include <memory>
#include <iosfwd>
#include <cstddef>
```

```cpp
class ADT
{
    public:
  static void *operator new
                      (std::size_t size, std::ostream &logFile)
                      throw(std::bad_alloc);
  static void operator delete(void *ptr, std::size_t size);
  ADT();
  ~ADT();
};

#endif

// File adt.cpp

#include <iostream>
#include <memory>
#include <cstddef>
#include "adt.h"
using std::cout;

void *ADT::operator new(std::size_t size,
                        std::ostream &logFile)
                        throw(std::bad_alloc)
{
  cout << "operator new called\n";
  try
  {
    return ::operator new(size);
  }
  catch(std::bad_alloc const &err)
  {
    // Log all allocation failures
    char const *whoami = "ADT::operator new(), ";
    logFile << whoami << "size: " << size << '\n'
            << whoami << "what: " << err.what() << '\n';
    throw err;
  }
}

void ADT::operator delete(void *ptr, std::size_t size)
{
  ::operator delete(ptr);
  cout << "operator delete called\n";
}
```

```
ADT::ADT()
{
   cout << "constructor\n";
}

ADT::~ADT()
{
   cout << "destructor\n";
}

// File main.cpp

#include <iostream>
#include "adt.h"

int main()
{
   ADT *ptr = new (std::clog) ADT;
   delete ptr;
}

/* Output:

operator new called
constructor
destructor
operator delete called

*/
```

If an array of **ADT** objects is to be allocated, you can also define **operator new**[]() and **operator delete**[]() member functions for the **ADT** class to handle this case.

EXERCISE 9.2

Given a typical stack class that holds type **int**,

```
#include <cstddef>
template <class T>
class Stack
{
    public:
 Stack();
 ~Stack();
 Stack(Stack const &);
```

```
Stack &operator=(Stack const &);
std::size_t size() const;
void push(int);
int pop();                      // If empty, throws an exception
      private:
int *ptr;
std::size_t size;               // Physical size
std::size_t inUse;              // Number of elements in use
};
```

write all the functions in an exception-safe manner. Use the following function to avoid code repetition:

```
int *copyHelper(int const *source, std::size_t sourceSize,
                std::size_t destSize)
{
 int *dest = new int[destSize];
 try
 {
   for(std::size_t i = 0; i < sourceSize; ++i)
       dest[i] = source[i];
 }
 catch(. . .)
 {
   delete [] dest;    // This can never throw
   throw;
 }
 return dest;
}
```

Function Overloading

Introduction

Because the concept of function overloading is so fundamental to the C++ language, it has been impossible to avoid. The first real use of it came in Chapter 3 where you saw that the insertion and extraction operators are overloaded in order to accommodate a variety of different types. Also, in Chapter 7 you saw how it was possible to write more than one constructor in a class; this, too, constitutes overloading.

The term *function overloading* itself means the ability to declare more than one function in the same scope with the same name. This frees the user from having to remember many different function names that essentially do the same task. The compiler differentiates one function from another by examining the formal argument lists and by noting differences in the number of arguments and their types.

SUMMARY ▶ Function overloading is the declaration of more than one function in the same scope with the same name.

Some Examples of Overloading

For example, at the global scope, at namespace scope, and at class scope, all of the following functions have the same name, **func**(), and they all constitute valid overloading within that single scope:

```
// Global scope
void func();
int func(double);
char func(long);
short func(double, long);
long func(char, int = 0);

// Namespace scope
namespace NS
{
   void func();
   int func(double);
   char func(long);
   short func(double, long);
   long func(char, int = 0);
}

// Class scope
class ADT
{
   void func();
   int func(double);
   char func(long);
   short func(double, long);
   long func(char, int = 0);
};
```

 Function overloading can occur within a single scope. When the same signature of a function occurs in a different scope, no conflict exists.

The Return Type Is Ignored

The return type of a function is always ignored when the compiler does overload resolution. As stated earlier, in order to successfully overload a function you must create another function in the same scope whose argument list differs in the type(s), the number of arguments, or both. See, for example, the following:

```
int func();
double func();        // Error; not valid overloading
```

 You cannot perform function overloading based solely upon the return type.

const-Qualifying an Argument Passed by Value

If a function receives a parameter passed in by value (as opposed to pointer or reference), then adding a **const** (or **volatile**) qualifier does *not* constitute function overloading. Instead, it's merely a function redeclaration (which is valid but redundant). See the following:

```
void func(int);
void func(int const);          // Function redeclaration
```

 const-qualifying an argument when passing by value does *not* constitute function overloading.

const-Qualifying an Argument Passed by Pointer

It's a different story, however, if the parameter is passed by pointer. In this case this *does* constitute valid overloading because the **const** qualifier applies not to the parameter itself but to the object being pointed at. A call to the function using a pointer to a nonconstant object will call the function expecting that type (even though both functions are callable). The same is true for a call to the function using a pointer to a constant object (which is the only one that is callable because it's the only one supporting constant objects):

```
void func(int *);          // #1
void func(int const *);    // #2
// ...
void test(int *ptrInt, int const *ptrConstInt)
{
   func(ptrInt);      // Calls #1
   func(ptrConstInt); // Calls #2
}
```

 const-qualifying an argument passed into a function by pointer *does* constitute valid function overloading.

const-Qualifying an Argument Passed by Reference

References work in the same way as pointers insofar as overloading is concerned, as shown in the following example:

```
void func(int &);          // #1
void func(int const &);    // #2
```

```
// ...
void test(int &refInt, int const &refConstInt)
{
   func(refInt);      // Calls #1
   func(refConstInt); // Calls #2
}
```

 const-qualifying an argument passed into a function by reference also constitutes valid function overloading.

Mutator versus Constant Member Functions

A mutator member function of a class can be differentiated from a constant member function with the same name and same formal argument list. A constant object will invoke the constant member function, whereas a nonconstant object will invoke the mutator member function:

```
class ADT
{
    public:
   void func();            // #1
   void func() const;      // #2
};
// ...
void test(ADT &refADT, ADT const &refConstADT)
{
   refADT.func();          // Calls #1
   refConstADT.func();     // Calls #2
}
```

A mutator member function can be overloaded with a constant member function even if both have the same formal argument list.

Overload Resolution

In order to determine unambiguously which overloaded function to call, the compiler goes through a process known as *overload resolution,* in which an algorithm matches the actual arguments in the function call against the argument list of all the functions with that same name. The order of the declarations of all functions participating in this process is irrelevant.

More specifically, for each actual argument in a function the compiler determines the set of functions that could possibly be called for that argument, according to the rules listed below, and selects those function(s) that constitute the "best match." As soon as at least one function has been found for a particular argument, the searching stops.

 The compiler performs overload resolution one argument at a time in an attempt to find the "best match" for that argument.

The Rules of Overload Resolution

In order to determine which of possibly many functions with the same name to call, the compiler performs a five-category matching process for each argument, in order. As soon as it finds at least one match in any category, it stops processing that argument and moves on to the next one. A list of these five categories follows:

1. Exact match, including the adding of **const** qualifiers and array-to-pointer conversions.

2. Promotions:
   - ▲ **char** to **int**
   - ▲ **unsigned char** to **int**
   - ▲ **signed char** to **int**
   - ▲ **enum** to **int**
   - ▲ **short** to **int**
   - ▲ **unsigned short** to **int**
   - ▲ **int** bit field to **int**
   - ▲ **wchar_t** to **int**
   - ▲ **bool** to **int**
   - ▲ **float** to **double**

3. Standard conversions:
   - ▲ Integral conversions
   - ▲ Floating-point conversions
   - ▲ Floating-integral conversions
   - ▲ Pointer conversions
   - ▲ Pointer-to-member conversions
   - ▲ Base class conversions (discussed in Chapter 11)

4. User-defined conversions:
   - ▲ Constructors
   - ▲ Operator conversion functions

5. Ellipsis conversion sequence; this consists of any function whose formal argument list is an ellipsis (3 dots). This constitutes an acceptable match for any actual argument.

All of the candidate functions for each argument, if any, are put into a set. If there are three arguments, then three sets are created. Each set could consist of any number of functions, even none at all. From all of the sets, the compiler looks to see which functions are common to all. If there is exactly one function in common, that is the one chosen to be called. If no function is common to all sets, or if there is more than one function common to all sets, the compiler yields a fatal error message because it has no idea of which one to call.

To perform overload resolution, the compiler goes through a five-step matching process for each argument, putting candidate functions into sets. There must be exactly one common function in all these sets to constitute an unambiguous match.

Overloading on a Pointer Type

Notice that the following code works because the constant zero is type **int**, which is an exact match for the function expecting an **int** (see the first rule, above), whereas the conversion of zero to a pointer is not as good a match (see the third rule):

```
void func(int);
void func(char const *);
// ...
func(0);        // Calls func(int)
```

The following code does not work because an **int** to a **long** and an **int** to a **char const ***
are both standard conversions (see Rule #3 above), and the compiler will not choose one function over the other:

```
void func(long);
void func(char const *);
// ...
func(0);        // Error
```

Be very careful when overloading a pointer type with an integral type.

Name Mangling

The concept of function overloading presents a potential problem to the linker because it must be able to associate any particular function call with its corresponding library code. In other words, many functions in the library could have the same name, so it is not enough for the linker to identify a function simply by using only its name. Instead, the number and types of function arguments must also be factored in.

The compiler solves this problem by a process known as *name mangling* in which the unique identity of each function is, in fact, some combination of the function name and its arguments.

Thus, given the function declaration,

```
void func(char, int, char const *);
```

a call to **func()** that selects this declaration will produce (from one popular compiler) the following assembly language code:

```
call @@func$qcipxc
```

Now that's a mangled name! The **@@func** part refers to a global function called **func**, the **$q** separates the function name from the start of the formal argument list, **c** means **char**, **i** means **int**, **p** means pointer, and **x** means **const**. Thus, the function takes a **char**, an **int**, and a pointer to a **const**ant **char**. Amazing!

Because that was so much fun, let's do another one involving the **String** class we've used in previous chapters:

```cpp
// File string.h

#ifndef STRING_H
#define STRING_H

class String
{
    public:
  String(char const * = "");
  String(String const &);
  void display() const;
    private:
  char *ptrChars;
};

#endif

// File main.cpp

#include "string.h"

int main()
{
  String str1("C++");      // call @@String@$bctr$qpxc
```

```
    String str2(str1);      // call @@String@$bctr$qrx6String
    str2.display();         // call @@String@display$qv
}
```

Note that the abbreviation **bctr** represents the name for the constructor. See if you can deduce how the name-mangling scheme works in this situation.

CAUTION   The C++ Standard says nothing about how a compiler should perform name mangling, so it's quite likely that different compilers will incorporate different name-mangling schemes. This becomes very important if and when you ever purchase a third-party library of object modules involving a scheme that is different from the scheme your compiler is using to make calls to these modules.

SUMMARY   The compiler performs name mangling to translate a declaration into a unique function name.

How to Avoid Name Mangling

Hello C++, we've got a problem. This name-mangling scheme does not work with any C style library functions. Recall that the C programming language does not allow function name overloading, which implies that function names in a C module (or in a C library) are never mangled. Therefore, a C++ code module that contains a call to, say, the **cstdio** function **puts()** must generate a call to a C library function named **puts**; it must not generate a call to an (undefined!) C++ function whose mangled name is something like **@@std@puts$qpxc**.

To resolve this dilemma, you can tell the compiler to "escape" from using the C++ name-mangling scheme by writing the keyword **extern** followed by the string literal **"C"**. This declaration tells the compiler *not* to perform name mangling on the specified functions. You can declare more than one function by enclosing them within a scope, or you can declare just one function without the braces:

```
extern "C" functionDeclaration;
// Or...
extern "C"
{
   functionDeclaration1;
   functionDeclaration2;
   functionDeclaration3;
   // Etc.
}
```

For example, the header file **cstdio** contains code similar to this:

```
extern "C"
{
   int printf(char const *, ...);
```

```
    int puts(char const *);
    // Etc.
}
```

Typically such declarations are found in all C library header files already provided for you. But because a C program cannot recognize such a special **extern "C"** declaration, a test for the macro **__cplusplus** (two leading underscores) must be made. (Do you remember this from Chapter 1?) Therefore, the code in the **cstdio** header file must be similar to the following:

```
#ifdef __cplusplus
extern "C" {
#endif
int printf(char const *, ...);
int puts(char const *);
// Etc.
#ifdef __cplusplus
}
#endif
```

Now we're in business because this header file can be used for both a C and C++ compilation. For C, the macro **__cplusplus** evaluates to false, and you are left with just the function declarations. For C++, the macro evaluates to true; although the function declarations are still processed, they've now been "escaped."

SUMMARY   All C language header files provide code to avoid name mangling because it's valid only in C++.

Type-safe Linkage

As a benefit of name mangling, all C++ compilers will perform *type-safe linkage*. To understand what this is all about, consider the following code:

```
// File #1

void doSomething(double, char, int);
void testIt()
{
    doSomething(35.64, 'A', 78);
}

// File #2
void doSomething(char c, int i, double d)
{
    // Do something
}
```

In the C language, the call to **doSomething**() within **testIt**() compiles successfully, and the linker is happy to use the definition of **doSomething**() regardless of its argument list, which just happens to be wrongly coded. (After all, function names in any C library know nothing about formal arguments.) The definition converts the actual arguments into types that are totally unexpected, however, so an incorrect result is quite likely to be the outcome.

C++ does not have this problem because the name-mangling scheme ensures a name mismatch between the function call in File #1 and the function definition in File #2. For example, as the compiler translates the source code in File #1, it emits an assembly language call to a function whose mangled name is **@@doSomething$qdci**. During the translation of File #2—which contains the definition of function **doSomething**()— the compiler emits assembly language code for a function whose mangled name is **@@doSomething$qcid**. These two mangled names are not identical, which means that the linker cannot associate the function call in File #1 with the function definition in File #2. Consequently, the linker emits an "unresolved external" message for the function call in File #1 (Hey, I can't find a definition for a function named **@@doSomething$qdci**) and aborts the link process.

 As a benefit of name mangling, C++ performs type-safe linkage to prevent errors that might occur in C.

Operator Function Overloading

Operator function overloading provides a more intuitive interface to the user by allowing the designer to write classes making use of the native operators that C++ provides for the fundamental types.

For example, our **String** class would be much easier to use if the **cstring** library functions such as **strcpy**(), **strcmp**(), and **strcat**() were replaced by C++ operators such as **=**, **==**, and **+=**, respectively. Of course, whichever operators you choose to overload for a given class, those operators should be implemented in such a way that they have "inherent meaning" with respect to the objects of that class. In other words, the implementation of a given operator should be such that its use is easily and clearly understood. For example, you should not overload the **+** operator to mean subtraction (that is, not if you want to keep your job).

 Operator overloading can sometimes provide a more intuitive interface to the users of a class.

Start with the Precedence Chart

The only operators you can overload are the ones from the C++ precedence chart shown in Table 10.1 (and not all of those are available). You cannot arbitrarily choose a new symbol (such as @ or **) and attempt to give it meaning by "overloading" it.

TABLE 10.1

Prec	Symbol	Name	Unary/Binary	Overload?
1	::	Scope resolution	Unary	No
	::	Scope resolution	Binary	No
2	.	Direct member access	Binary	No
	->	Indirect member access	Unary	Yes
	[]	Subscripting	Binary	Yes
	()	Function call	N/A	Yes
	()	Function style cast	N/A	No
	++	Postfix increment	Unary	Yes
	--	Postfix decrement	Unary	Yes
	typeid	Type identification	Unary	No
	static_cast	Compile-time checked conversion	Unary	No
	reinterpret_cast	Unchecked conversion	Unary	No
	const_cast	**const** conversion	Unary	No
	dynamic_cast	Run-time checked conversion	Unary	No
3	sizeof	Size of	Unary	No
	++	Prefix increment	Unary	Yes
	--	Prefix decrement	Unary	Yes
	~	One's complement	Unary	Yes
	!	Not	Unary	Yes
	−	Unary minus	Unary	Yes
	+	Unary plus	Unary	Yes
	&	Address of	Unary	Yes
	*	Dereference	Unary	Yes
	new	Allocate single instance	Binary	Yes
	new []	Allocate array of instances	Binary	Yes

(*continued*)

TABLE 10.1 (*continued*)

Prec	Symbol	Unary/Name	Binary	Overload?
	delete	Delete single instance	Binary	Yes
	delete []	Delete array of instances	Binary	Yes
	()	C style cast	Unary	No
4	.*	Direct pointer-to-member	Unary	No
	–>*	Indirect pointer-to-member	Unary	Yes
5	*	Multiply	Binary	Yes
	/	Divide	Binary	Yes
	%	Modulus	Binary	Yes
6	+	Binary add	Binary	Yes
	–	Binary subtract	Binary	Yes
7	<<	Bitwise left shift	Binary	Yes
	>>	Bitwise right shift	Binary	Yes
8	<	Less than	Binary	Yes
	<=	Less than or equal to	Binary	Yes
	>	Greater than	Binary	Yes
	>=	Greater than or equal to	Binary	Yes
9	==	Equal to	Binary	Yes
	!=	Not equal to	Binary	Yes
10	&	Bitwise AND	Binary	Yes
11	^	Bitwise exclusive OR	Binary	Yes
12	|	Bitwise inclusive OR	Binary	Yes
13	&&	Logical AND	Binary	Yes
14	||	Logical OR	Binary	Yes
15	? :	Conditional	Ternary	No
16	=	Assignment	Binary	Yes

(*continued*)

TABLE 10.1 (*continued*)

Prec	Symbol	Name	Unary/Binary	Overload?
	*=	Multiply and assign	Binary	Yes
	/=	Divide and assign	Binary	Yes
	%=	Modulus and assign	Binary	Yes
	+=	Add and assign	Binary	Yes
	– =	Subtract and assign	Binary	Yes
	<<=	Shift left and assign	Binary	Yes
	>>=	Shift right and assign	Binary	Yes
	&=	Bitwise AND and assign	Binary	Yes
	|=	Bitwise inclusive OR and assign	Binary	Yes
	^=	Bitwise exclusive OR and assign	Binary	Yes
17	,	Comma	Binary	Yes

Giving the Operator a Name

You start the process of operator overloading by declaring a function in the normal fashion, but its name must be the expression **operator@**, in which the symbol @ generically represents the operator itself that is to be overloaded. You can leave one or more spaces before the @, but this is typically not done.

The name of an overloaded operator is always **operator@**, where @ represents the operator you're overloading.

Default Arguments

Unlike "normal" global and class member functions that you declare, no default arguments can be specified in overloaded operator functions. However, there is one exception to this rule in regard to the function call operator, which will be explained later in this chapter.

Overloaded operator functions cannot accommodate default function arguments, with one exception to this rule.

Inherently Supplied Operators

Who says there's no such thing as a free lunch? In C++ there is, because every class has operators that the compiler will define and make available automatically. For some generic class **ADT**, these operators are: (1) assignment, (2) address-of (mutator), and (3) address-of (constant). Why? To be backward-compatible with C, of course. Note that the compiler-supplied assignment operator does a recursive memberwise assignment in the same fashion that the compiler-supplied copy constructor does recursive memberwise initialization.

The following is what these operators do in a typical class:

```
// File adt.h

#ifndef ADT_H
#define ADT_H

class ADT
{
    public:
  ADT &operator= (ADT const &);    // #1
  ADT *operator&();                // #2
  ADT const *operator&() const;    // #3
};

#endif

// File main.cpp

#include "adt.h"

int main()
{
  ADT adt1;
  ADT const adt2;
  adt1 = adt2;                        // Call #1
  ADT *ptrADT = &adt1;                // Call #2
  ADT const *ptrConstADT = &adt2;    // Call #3
};
```

SUMMARY ▶ C++ provides three free built-in operators for every class you write.

Precedence Cannot Be Changed

The predefined operator precedence rules cannot be changed. You cannot, for example, make binary **+** have a higher precedence than binary *. Thank goodness for that!

Operator precedence cannot be changed when an operator is overloaded.

The "Narity" Cannot Be Changed

What's that, you ask? It means simply that the unary/binary characteristics of the operator cannot be changed. If an operator is unary, that is, the operator operates on a single argument, you must overload it as a unary operator. If the operator is binary, that is, the operator operates on two arguments, you must overload it as a binary operator. If the operator is either unary or binary, you can overload it either way or both ways. (The operators +, −, * and & are both unary and binary.)

When overloading, a unary operator must remain unary, and a binary operator must remain binary.

Associativity Cannot Be Changed

Associativity is retained because, if an operator normally binds right-to-left, such as an assignment operator, then an overloaded assignment operator for a class will also bind right-to-left. Similarly, binary add and subtract bind left-to-right, and that cannot be changed.

The associativity of an operator cannot be changed.

Member versus Nonmember

An overloaded operator function for a class can be either a nonstatic member function or a nonmember function (with some exceptions to be noted). Remember that a nonstatic member function *always* has one argument implicitly declared (the **this** pointer). A nonmember function has no **this** pointer, so it needs to have all of its arguments explicitly declared. For example, if a class wishes to overload the unary negation operator, it could do so in either of two ways:

```
// Overload unary -
class ADT
{
    public:
  ADT operator-() const;          // One argument: this pointer
};
// or...
ADT operator-(ADT const &arg);    // One argument: arg
```

There is no one "catch-all" rule that dictates whether an operator should be overloaded as a member or as a nonmember. Sometimes the decision is a toss-up. However,

TABLE 10.2

Symbol	Name	Unary/Binary
=	Assignment	Binary
()	Function call	N/A
[]	Subscript	Binary
–>	Indirect member	Unary

you will probably want to opt for a nonmember function under the following circumstances:

▲ The function is "symmetrical" in the sense that its arguments can be specified in either order. Typically, these functions are binary, and they include all six relational operators and add, subtract, multiply, divide, and modulus. Note also that you will probably want to perform implicit type conversion on the left-hand argument. A nonmember function will accommodate this.

▲ The function needs to be invoked by some instance that is not of the class type in which the operator is located. Typically this implies the overloaded insertion and extraction operators whose messages are sent to input/output stream objects such as **cout** and **cin**. You might also want to grant friendship to your stream insertion/extraction operator functions.

Otherwise, opt for a member function. Nevertheless, the four operators shown in Table 10.2 *must* be overloaded as *member* functions.

 Follow the stated guidelines for choosing between a member and a nonmember function.

Supply at Least One Class Instance

At least one of the arguments (implicit or explicit) to an overloaded function must be an instance of the class to which the operator belongs. This is done automatically in a non-static member function via the **this** pointer. You must do it explicitly for a nonmember function. This makes sense because otherwise you would be attempting to declare a function whose arguments consist of only primitive types, and this infringes upon the territory belonging to a couple of guys named Kernighan and Ritchie. (Remember them from your C language days?)

 You must supply at least one instance of your class to an overloaded operator function.

Infix versus Functional Notation

In all probability, the users of your overloaded operator functions will be calling them using *infix notation*. This means that the operator is used in the same way it's used in C. However, your users might choose to call them using *functional notation*. This means that they're called just like old-fashioned named functions. For a nonmember function, the users would write the function name (**operator@**) followed by a list of arguments; for a member function, they would write an instance name followed by a dot and the function name, as in the following:

```
class ADT
{
  friend ADT const operator+(ADT const &, ADT const &);
    public:
  ADT &operator= (ADT const &);
  ADT &operator!();
};
// ...
ADT adt1, adt2;
ADT sum(adt1 + adt2);// Same as:
                     // ADT sum(operator+(adt1, adt2));
adt1 = adt2;         // Same as: adt1.operator=(adt2);
!adt1;               // Same as: adt1.operator!();
```

By the way, notice that for the call to the overloaded assignment operator, the invoking instance is always assumed to be the one written on the left-hand side of the operator.

 Note how an overloaded operator function can be called using either infix or functional notation.

Binary Members and Implicit Type Conversion

The topic of implicit type conversion when calling functions was mentioned in Chapter 8 during the discussion of friend functions. The main concept to understand is that, if you want the compiler to perform implicit type conversion on the left-hand argument, then (1) the class must have an accessible converting constructor, and (2) the overloaded operator function *must* be nonmember (with or without friendship). Here is a quick review using the example from Chapter 8, but now we've replaced the name **join**() with the more intuitive **operator+**():

```
// File string.h

#ifndef STRING_H
#define STRING_H
```

```
class String
{
    friend String const operator+
                (String const &left, String const &right);
      public:
    String(char const *chars = "");
    // ...
      private:
    char *ptrChars;
    // ...
};

#endif

// File main.cpp

#include "string.h"

int main()
{
    char const *pLeft = "This is a test";
    char const *pRight = " of concatenation";
    String str1(pLeft);
    String str2(pRight);
    String str3(str1 + str2);               // OK
    String str4(pLeft + str2);              // OK
    String str5(str1 + pRight);             // OK
}
```

CAUTION Although a named function (such as **join**() that was used in Chapter 8) can be called with two string literals, these literals cannot be "added" using **+** because such code violates the rule that at least one argument must be a user-defined type.

Because **operator+**() is overloaded as a nonmember function, all of the implicit type conversions from the C language string literal into **String** objects occur successfully. If you made **operator+**() a member function, however, you're in trouble, as shown in the following:

```
// File string.h

#ifndef STRING_H
#define STRING_H

class String
```

```
{
    public:
    String(char const *chars = "");
    String const operator+(String const &right) const;
    // ...
    private:
    char *ptrChars;
    // ...
};

#endif

// File main.cpp

#include "string.h"

int main()
{
    char const *pLeft = "This is a test";
    char const *pRight = " of concatenation";
    String str1(pLeft);
    String str2(pRight);
    String str3(str1 + str2);        // OK
    String str4(pLeft + str2);       // Error
    String str5(str1 + pRight);      // OK
}
```

The instantiation of **str4** fails because the compiler will *not* implicitly convert the literal **"This is a test"** into a **String** object.

 Use a nonmember function when you want to allow implicit type conversion on the left-hand argument.

Repeated Overloading or Allowance of Implicit Type Conversion

If you don't want to visit the converting constructor when you want to concatenate a string literal, you must overload the **+** operator as many times as necessary to accommodate all possible calls. For example, in the following program three **+** operators are defined to handle a **String** and a **String**, a **char** * and a **String**, and a **String** and a **char** *. (As just mentioned, you cannot add a **char** * and a **char** * as this would constitute invalid pointer arithmetic.) If you want to handle a single character in conjunction with a **String**, that's two more functions to write. Is it worth the trouble? You decide.

This is what the code might look like should you become enamored with the concept of function overloading:

```
// File string.h

#ifndef STRING_H
#define STRING_H

class String
{
  friend String const operator+
              (String const &left, String const &right);
  friend String const operator+
              (char const *left, String const &right);
  friend String const operator+
              (String const &left, char const *right);
    public:
  String(char const *chars = "");
  // ...
    private:
  char *ptrChars;
  // ...
};

#endif

// File string.cpp

#include <cstring>
#include <cstddef>
#include "string.h"

String const operator+
              (String const &left, String const &right)
{
  std::size_t lengthLeft = std::strlen(left.ptrChars);
  std::size_t lengthRight = std::strlen(right.ptrChars);
  char *buffer = new char[lengthLeft + lengthRight + 1];
  std::strcpy(buffer, left.ptrChars);
  std::strcat(buffer, right.ptrChars);
  String newString(buffer);
  delete [] buffer;
  return newString;
}

String const operator+
                (char const *left, String const &right)
```

```
{
  std::size_t lengthLeft = std::strlen(left);
  std::size_t lengthRight = std::strlen(right.ptrChars);
  char *buffer = new char[lengthLeft + lengthRight + 1];
  std::strcpy(buffer, left);
  std::strcat(buffer, right.ptrChars);
  String newString(buffer);
  delete [] buffer;
  return newString;
}


String const operator+
                    (String const &left, char const *right)
{
  return right + left;
}


// File main.cpp

#include "string.h"

int main()
{
  char const *pLeft = "This is a test";
  char const *pRight = " of concatenation";
  String str1(pLeft);
  String str2(pRight);
  String str3(str1 + str2);       // OK
  String str4(pLeft + str2);      // OK
  String str5(str1 + pRight);     // OK
}
```

 In place of implicit type conversion, you can provide more than one version of an overloaded operator.

EXERCISE 10.1

For the **String** class, write all six relational operators and overload the logical NOT (!) operator to return true if the **String** object is empty.

Overload the Family of Operators

It makes sense that if you decide to overload the binary **+** operator, for example, then the users of your class can reasonably assume that the unary **+**, unary **++** (both prefix and postfix), and binary **+=** are also available. So it's probably a good idea to overload these operators as well for the sake of completeness. The same applies for all – (subtract) operators.

SUMMARY When overloading one member of a family of operators, consider overloading the whole family of operators.

Assignment Operator

As noted above, if you fail to write an assignment operator, the compiler supplies one for you that automatically does a memberwise recursive assignment of the nonstatic data members. For simple classes, this should suffice. However, you are responsible for assigning each individual nonstatic data member if you decide to write your own classes. By the way, the assignment operator is the last of the manager functions that were introduced in Chapter 7 (the constructor and destructor were the other two manager functions).

However, you must overload the assignment operator whenever the class contains a pointer that points to space on the free store and whenever you want the user to have the capability to assign one instance to another instance. The reason is the same as the one in Chapter 7 in the discussion of the compiler-supplied copy constructor (that is, two **String** objects have their internal pointers pointing to the same space on the free store). In other words, this is how the compiler will generate (sometimes called *synthesize*) an assignment operator for the **String** class:

```
// File string.h

#ifndef STRING_H
#define STRING_H

class String
{
    public:
    String(char const *chars = "");
    String &operator= (String const &);
    // ...
    private:
    char *ptrChars;
};

#endif

// File string.cpp

#include "string.h"
```

```
String &String::operator= (String const &str)
{
  ptrChars = str.ptrChars;
  return *this;
}


// File main.cpp

#include "string.h"

int main()
{
  String str1, str2("C++");
  str1 = str2;
}
```

It's quite apparent that when the destructor runs for both objects created in **main()**, an attempt will be made to release the same space twice. (Crash!) The moral is that you had better write your own assignment operator to avoid this problem. And—in the same vein as the copy constructor—declare the assignment operator to be private if you do not want the user of your class to be able to assign one object to another.

What follows is one possible implementation of an assignment operator for the **String** class. Note that the lengths of the string literals are compared; if they are the same, the existing space on the free store is simply written over. Otherwise, fresh heap space will be allocated. Because the call to **operator new()** (via the keyword **new**) could throw an exception, it is not safe to release the old space on the free store before ensuring that there is enough fresh space available to hold the string literal. (If the space were to be released, and not enough fresh space was available, the invoking object would be left in a very unstable condition.) As the code is written, if **operator new()** throws, the exception propagates out to the caller and the invoking object is unmodified. In addition, the function returns *this to emulate the chaining effect that occurs with the primitive types:

```
// File string.h

#ifndef STRING_H
#define STRING_H

class String
{
    public:
  String(char const *chars = "");
  String(String const &);
  String &operator= (String const &);
  // ...
```

```
    private:
  char *ptrChars;
};


#endif


// File string.cpp


#include <cstring>
#include "string.h"
using std::strlen;


String &String::operator= (String const &str)
{
  if(strlen(ptrChars) != strlen(str.ptrChars))
  {
    char *ptrHold = new char[strlen(str.ptrChars) + 1];
    delete [] ptrChars;
    ptrChars = ptrHold;
  }
  std::strcpy(ptrChars, str.ptrChars);
  return *this;
}


// File main.cpp


#include "string.h"


int main()
{
  String str1, str2("C++");
  str1 = str2;
}
```

This implementation is exception safe because, if **new** happens to throw, the invoking object (**str1** in **main()**) will not have been modified.

Let's look at a different approach to solving the same problem that is also exception safe:

```
// File string.h


#ifndef STRING_H
#define STRING_H


class String
```

```
{
    public:
  String(char const *chars = "");
  String(String const &);
  String &operator= (String str);
  // ...
    private:
  char *ptrChars;
};

#endif

// File string.cpp

#include "string.h"

String &String::operator= (String str)
{
  char *ptrHold = ptrChars;
  ptrChars = str.ptrChars;
  str.ptrChars = ptrHold;
  return *this;
}

// File main.cpp

#include "string.h"

int main()
{
  String str1, str2("C++");
  str1 = str2;
}
```

Here the existing **String** object is passed in to the assignment operator *by value* in order to invoke the class's copy constructor so that the object **str** is identical to the object on the right-hand side of the assignment. Then the two **ptrChars** pointers from the invoking object and **str** are swapped. When the **str** object goes out of scope, its destructor call will release the space that was pointed at by the invoking object, but now the pointer in the invoking object points to space that contains a copy of the literal that is encapsulated in the explicit **String** object. Task accomplished. If the copy constructor happens to throw, once again the object **str1** will not have been modified.

SUMMARY ▶ Make sure that any assignment operator you write is exception safe.

Checking for Self-Assignment

By the way, although it won't buy you very much (because it's so unlikely to happen), you might want to first check for the possibility of self-assignment by the user. That is, the user decides to assign an instance of the **String** class to itself:

```
// File main.cpp

#include "string.h"

int main()
{
   String str1;
   str1 = str1;        // Self-assignment
}
```

Instead of executing all of the code to do essentially nothing, you can guard against this possibility by writing:

```
String &String::operator=(String const &str)
{
   if(this != &str)
   {
     // Your code here
   }
   return *this;
}
```

SUMMARY ▶ You might want to check for the possibility of self-assignment.

Function Call Operator

The overloaded function call operator **operator**()() is unique because it can take any number of explicit arguments and it can even take one or more default arguments. When the operator (which is just a pair of parentheses) is applied to an instance of a class, it appears as though the instance itself is the name of a function. In addition, recall that the function call operator must be implemented as a *member* function.

For example, let's add an overloaded function call operator to the **String** class that accepts one argument of type **char const*** and returns the number of times this string literal occurs within the invoking **String** object. If the function is called with no argument, then the default search string is "**+**":

```
// File string.h

#ifndef STRING_H
#define STRING_H
```

```cpp
#include <cstddef>

class String
{
    public:
  String(char const *chars = "");
  std::size_t operator()(char const *chars = "+") const;
  // ...
    private:
  char *ptrChars;
};

#endif

// File string.cpp

#include <cstring>
#include <cstddef>
#include "string.h"
using std::size_t;

size_t String::operator()(char const *chars) const
{
  size_t counter = 0;
  size_t size = std::strlen(chars);
  size_t tests = std::strlen(ptrChars) - size + 1;
  for(size_t i = 0; i < tests; ++i)
    if(!std::strncmp(ptrChars + i, chars, size))
       ++counter;
  return counter;
}

// File main.cpp

#include <cstddef>
#include "string.h"
using std::size_t;

int main()
{
  String const str("C++");
  size_t answer1 = str();                      // 2
  size_t answer2 = str("C+");                   // 1
  size_t answer3 = str("+");                    // 2
```

```
        size_t answer4 = str("++");              // 1
        size_t answer5 = str("D");               // 0
    }
```

CAUTION   The function call operator is used extensively in C++'s standard library, and objects
that overload this function are referred to as *function objects* or *functors*.

    The function call operator takes any number of arguments, including defaults, and
it can make an object behave like a function.

Subscript Operator

The subscript operator is useful whenever the class encapsulates an array (e.g., the **String**
class contains an array of characters) and you want to give the user the ability to access
and/or modify the individual elements of that array. This operator is binary and must be
a member function with the **this** pointer as the first argument and the subscript value as
the second (explicit) argument.

To properly overload the subscript operator, you must define it twice — once as a
mutator member function and once as a constant member function. The mutator member function must return a single array element by "reference-to-nonconst" (in order to
create a modifiable lvalue), and the constant member function must return the element
either by reference-to-**const** or by value. In general, user-defined types are returned by
reference-to-**const**, and primitive types are returned by value.

Recall that earlier in this chapter I noted the rule the compiler uses to determine
which subscript operator gets called. If the class instance is *mutable,* the mutator member function will be invoked. If the class instance is *constant,* the constant member function will be invoked.

Here the **String** class has been overloaded to exhibit both overloaded subscript operators. To keep things interesting, we'll have the operators throw an exception if the subscript value they receive is outside the bounds of the array of characters. Note that the
last line in **main()** fails to compile because the constant member function returns an
rvalue; this is not allowed on the left-hand side of an assignment:

```
// File string.h

#ifndef STRING_H
#define STRING_H

#include <cstddef>

class String
{
    public:
  String(char const *chars = "");
  char &operator[](std::size_t index) throw(String);
```

```
      char operator[](std::size_t index) const throw(String);
      // ...
        private:
      char *ptrChars;
      static String errorMessage;
};

#endif

// File string.cpp

#include <cstring>
#include <cstddef>
#include "string.h"

char &String::operator[](std::size_t index) throw(String)
{
  if(index >= std::strlen(ptrChars))
    throw errorMessage;
  return ptrChars[index];
}

char String::operator[](std::size_t index) const
                                              throw(String)
{
  if(index >= std::strlen(ptrChars))
    throw errorMessage;
  return ptrChars[index];
}

String String::errorMessage("Subscript out of range");

// File main.cpp

#include "string.h"

int main()
{
  String str1("Mutable string");
  String const str2("Constant string");
  str1[0] = 'A';      // OK
  str1[0] = str2[0]; // OK
  str2[0] = 'A';      // Compiler error
}
```

SUMMARY ▶ The subscript operator is used to fetch an individual element from an encapsulated array. It must be overloaded as both a mutator and a constant member function.

Indirect Member Operator

The indirect member operator –> (also known as the arrow operator) is useful for implementing what is known as a "smart pointer" class. In its native form this operator must be applied to a pointer, so any class that overloads it typically encapsulates a pointer to some other class, and the definition of the operator merely returns this pointer. The advantage of this class is that it's impossible for the user to use an instance of the class in an errant way, such as dereferencing it if it contains an unknown value or zero. The class ensures that nothing unknown will ever occupy the encapsulated pointer, and the value zero is used to indicate that the instance has not been "initialized" to point to an instance of the underlying class. If the user ever tries to apply the arrow operator, an exception will be thrown.

In the following example, the **Pointer** class contains a pointer to a **String** object and overloads the arrow operator to return a **String *** type:

```
// File string.h

#ifndef STRING_H
#define STRING_H

class String
{
    public:
    String(char const *chars = "");
    String(String const &str);
    ~String();
    void display() const;
    // ...
    private:
    char *ptrChars;
};

#endif

// File string.cpp

#include <iostream>
#include <cstring>
#include "string.h"
```

```cpp
String::String(char const *chars)
{
  chars = chars ? chars : "";
  ptrChars = new char[std::strlen(chars) + 1];
  std::strcpy(ptrChars, chars);
}

String::String(String const &str)
{
  ptrChars = new char[std::strlen(str.ptrChars) + 1];
  std::strcpy(ptrChars, str.ptrChars);
}

String::~String()
{
  delete [] ptrChars;
}

void String::display() const
{
  std::cout << ptrChars << '\n';
}

// File pointer.h

#ifndef POINTER_H
#define POINTER_H

class String;
class Pointer
{
    public:
  Pointer();
  Pointer(String const &n);
  ~Pointer();
  String *operator->() const;
    private:
  String *ptr;
  static String errorMessage;
};

#endif
```

```
// File pointer.cpp

#include "pointer.h"
#include "string.h"

Pointer::Pointer() : ptr(0) { }

Pointer::Pointer(String const &n)
{
  ptr = new String(n);
}

Pointer::~Pointer()
{
  delete ptr;
}

String *Pointer::operator->() const
{
  if(!ptr)
    throw errorMessage;
  return ptr;
}

String Pointer::errorMessage("Uninitialized pointer");

// File main.cpp

#include "pointer.h"

int main()
{
  try
  {
    Pointer ptr1("C++");
    ptr1->display();                // Infix notation
    ptr1.operator->()->display(); // Functional notation
    Pointer ptr2;
    ptr2->display();
  }
  catch(String const &error)
  {
    error.display();
  }
}
```

```
/* Output:

C++
C++
Uninitialized pointer

*/
```

SUMMARY   The overloaded arrow operator is used to implement a smart pointer class.

Compound Assignment Operators

Although not strictly mandatory, you should overload all compound assignment operators (+=, -=, *=, etc.) as member functions (because the assignment operator itself must be a member function). One easy way to overload these operators is to implement them in terms of their C language definitions. For example, += adds the left-hand argument to the right-hand argument and stores the sum back into the left-hand argument.

In the following example, the **String** class has overloaded the binary + operator to concatenate two **String** objects. This allows the overloaded += operator to be written in just one line of code:

```
// File string.h

#ifndef STRING_H
#define STRING_H

class String
{
   friend String const operator+
                       (String const &left, String const &right);
     public:
   String(char const *chars = "");
   String &operator=(String const &);
   String &operator+=(String const &);
   // ...
     private:
   char *ptrChars;
};

#endif

// File string.cpp

#include <cstring>
#include <cstddef>
```

```
#include "string.h"

String const operator+
              (String const &left, String const &right)
{
  std::size_t lengthLeft = std::strlen(left.ptrChars);
  std::size_t lengthRight = std::strlen(right.ptrChars);
  char *buffer = new char[lengthLeft + lengthRight + 1];
  std::strcpy(buffer, left.ptrChars);
  std::strcat(buffer, right.ptrChars);
  String newString(buffer);
  delete [] buffer;
  return newString;
}

String &String::operator+=(String const &other)
{
  return *this= *this + other;
}
```

Some people like to take the opposite approach, however, and write the overloaded **operator+()** in terms of **operator+=()**. By doing this, **operator+()** never has to be a friend function (although it must still be a nonmember function):

```
// File string.h

#ifndef STRING_H
#define STRING_H

class String
{
    public:
  String(char const *chars = "");
  String &operator= (String const &);
  String &operator+= (String const &);
  // ...
    private:
  char *ptrChars;
};

// Nonmember nonfriend function
String const operator+
              (String const &left, String const &right);

#endif
```

```
// File string.cpp

#include <cstring>
#include <cstddef>
#include "string.h"

String &String::operator+=(String const &other)
{
   std::size_t lengthThis = std::strlen(ptrChars);
   std::size_t lengthOther = std::strlen(other.ptrChars);
   char *buffer = new char[lengthThis + lengthOther + 1];
   std::strcpy(buffer, ptrChars);
   std::strcat(buffer, other.ptrChars);
   delete [] ptrChars;
   ptrChars = buffer;
   return *this;
}


String const operator+
             (String const &left, String const &right)
{
   return String(left) += right;
}
```

 Write the **operator+=()** by calling **operator+()** and **operator=()**, or write
operator+() by calling **operator+=()**.

Increment and Decrement Operators

You can choose to overload the operators **++** and **−−** as either prefix or postfix, but you
should probably choose to do both for the sake of completeness. If you overload both as
unary member functions, then in theory both of them receive just a **this** pointer and no
explicit arguments. But how can you then provide distinct declarations so that one member function can be differentiated from the other? Here's the answer:

```
class ADT
{
    public:
  ADT &operator++(); // prefix
  ADT const operator++(int); // postfix
  // ...
};
// ...
ADT object;
```

```
++object; // Call prefix operator
object++; // Call postfix operator
```

You should note the following items:

▲ For the postfix version, the compiler will automatically push an extra argument of type **int** onto the stack when it detects a postfix call. This extra argument then must be declared in the postfix operator, thereby creating a different declaration from the prefix operator. The actual value of this **int**, of course, is meaningless, so a formal argument name need not be written when the function is defined.

▲ The postfix version must return its answer *by value,* which means the **ADT** class must also have a properly implemented copy constructor. The **const** qualifier is used to ensure that chaining of postfix calls cannot occur (which is similar to the way primitive types behave).

▲ It's also an excellent idea to write the postfix form so that it merely calls upon the prefix form in order to save on redundant coding and to ensure consistency between the two functions. (After all, they really should be doing essentially the same task.)

▲ A variable that uses a prefix or postfix operator should *never* be used in the same statement more than once because the order of evaluation of subexpressions is undefined.

For example, here is the **String** class again in which the operator ++ has been overloaded in both prefix and postfix forms to add one to each character:

```
// File string.h

#ifndef STRING_H
#define STRING_H

class String
{
    public:
    String(char const *chars = "");
    String(String const &);
    String &operator++();          // Prefix
    String const operator++(int);  // Postfix
    // ...
    private:
    char *ptrChars;
};

#endif
```

```cpp
// File string.cpp

#include <cstring>
#include <cstddef>
#include "string.h"

String &String::operator++()          // Prefix
{
  // Increment the value of each character in the String
  for(std::size_t i = 0; i < std::strlen(ptrChars); ++i)
    ++ptrChars[i];
  return *this;
}


String const String::operator++(int)       // Postfix
{
  String copy(*this);
  ++(*this);             // Call prefix member function
  return copy;
}


// File main.cpp

#include "string.h"

int main()
{
  String str1("ABC");
  String str2(++str1);       // str1 and str2 become "BCD"
  String str3(str1++);       // str3 becomes "BCD"
                             // str1 becomes "CDE"
}
```

Note how the postfix operator saves a copy of the invoking object (***this**) into a new **String** object called **copy**, calls the prefix operator to do all the work on the invoking object, and finally returns **copy** by *constant value* (because **copy** is on the stack and no chaining of postfix calls should be allowed). This is exactly how a postfix operator behaves for a primitive type.

 When appropriate, overload both the prefix and postfix increment/decrement operators. The postfix version takes an extra argument to differentiate it from the prefix version.

Overloading the Comma Operator

It's really quite simple: Don't overload the comma operator! Because it lives at the bottom of the precedence chart, ask yourself if you really want the user to be able to write the following code in which the assignment into **str3** will occur *before* the comma operator takes its effect on the operands **str1** and **str2**:

```
int main()
{
   String str1, str2, str3;
   str3 = str1, str2;          // Parsed as: (str3 = str1), str2;
}
```

SUMMARY Don't even think about overloading the comma operator.

Overloading Logical AND and OR

Again, this is something you should stay away from. These operators imply left-to-right behavior, but overloading them for a class does not preserve this behavior. In other words, in the following code if **ptr** is not zero, then the evaluation continues onward to calling **std::strlen()** (because **true** AND *somethingElse* requires that *somethingElse* be evaluated). If **ptr** is equal to zero, however, then the evaluation stops because **false** AND *somethingElse* is always **false**):

```
#include <cstring>

void func(char const *ptr)
{
   if(ptr && std::strlen(ptr) > 20)
      // ...
}
```

If **ptr** is a user-defined type, both sides of the **&&** (or **‖**) operator are evaluated in no specified order, thereby not mimicking how the primitive type behave. Not good.

SUMMARY Don't overload the **&&** and **‖** operators.

Overloading the Insertion Operator

Although it's a violation of the Model/View/Controller pattern first discussed in Chapter 6, you might want to have your user-defined types behave as much as possible like primitive types by overloading the insertion operator to accommodate a particular type. As a result, the syntax for displaying an instance of your class appears exactly like the syntax for displaying a primitive type.

Recall that this overload must be done as a *nonmember* function, with or without friendship. Bitwise left-shift (<<) is a binary operator and both arguments are explicit, which means that the first one is always a reference to the output stream object to which the data should be sent (usually **cout**), and the second is an instance of the class to be displayed, which is typically passed to the function by reference-to-**const**.

For example, let's overload the insertion operator for the **String** class to display the encapsulated array of characters within double quotation marks:

```
// File string.h

#ifndef STRING_H
#define STRING_H

#include <iosfwd>

class String
{
  friend std::ostream &operator<<
                (std::ostream &stream, String const &str);
    public:
  String(char const *chars = "");
  // ...
    private:
  char *ptrChars;
};

#endif

// File string.cpp

#include <iostream>
#include "string.h"

std::ostream &operator<<
                (std::ostream &stream, String const &str)
{
  char const quote = '\"';
  return stream << quote << str.ptrChars << quote;
}

// File main.cpp

#include <iostream>
#include "string.h"

int main()
```

```
{
    String language("C++");
    std::cout << "The language is " << language << '\n';
}
```

 Overload the insertion operator so that instances of the class can be displayed exactly like the primitive types.

Summary of the Operators

Table 10.3 provides an overview of how to overload the various operators.

TABLE 10.3

Unary Operator	Binary Operator	Member?	You should return:	Support Constant Objects (SCO) rule for:
+		Yes	Result by value	**this**
−		Yes	Result by value	**this**
!		Yes	Result by value	**this**
−>		Yes	Underlying pointer	**this**
++ −− (prefix)		Yes	**this** by reference	N/A
++ −− (postfix)		Yes	Result by **const** value	N/A
	& | && | | ,	Bad idea		
	+ − * / %	No	Result by **const** value	Both explicit arguments
	= += −= etc	Yes	**this** by reference	Explicit argument
	<<	No	Stream by reference	Second argument
	>>	No	Stream by reference	N/A
	< > <= >= == !=	No	Type **bool**	Both arguments
	[] (constant func)	Yes	Type by ref-to-**const**	**this**
	[] (mutator func)	Yes	Type by reference	N/A
	()	Yes	Varies	Varies

EXERCISE 10.2

Given the following abstraction of a floating-point number and a test program,

```
// File real.h

#ifndef REAL_H
```

```
#define REAL_H

class Real
{
 static int const exp;   // Defined to be 4
 static double const factor;   // Defined to be 10.0 to the
                               // power 'exp'
 int whole;
 int fraction;        // 'positions' accuracy at most
 // public interface
};

#endif

// File main.cpp

#include <iostream>
#include "real.h"

int main()
{
 Real r1(12.3456789), r2(r1);
 r1 = r2;
 std::cout << -(-(+(r1 + r2))) << '\n';
}
```

write the file **real.cpp** that contains the class definitions. Be sure to include:

1. A default constructor that accepts one argument of type **double** defaulting to 0.00. Example: 12.345678 would initialize **whole** to 12 and **fraction** to 3456,

2. A copy constructor,

3. An overloaded assignment operator that checks for self-assignment and allows for chaining,

4. An overloaded nonmember addition operator (written in just one line of code) that adds two **Real** numbers together,

5. An overloaded nonmember insertion operator (written in just one line of code) that displays a **Real** number in its original **double** format,

6. An overloaded unary + operator (and be sure to SCO),

7. An overloaded unary – operator (and be sure to SCO).

EXERCISE 10.3

Write a **Fraction** class with an abstraction of a numerator and denominator of type **int**. Include the following member functions:

Default constructor

Converting constructor

Copy constructor

Destructor

operator−() to negate the number

operator+() to leave the number unchanged

operator!() to invert the number

operator conversion function to return the floating-point representation

And the following nonmember functions:

operator+() to add two **Fraction** objects

operator*() to multiply two **Fraction** objects

operator<<() to display a **Fraction** object

EXERCISE 10.4

Recall that you cannot allocate a two-dimensional array from the free store at execution time because the compiler needs to know the number of columns. You can solve this dilemma by creating a class called **TwoDimensionalArray**. This class contains an array of pointers to integers (the length of which is equal to the number of rows). Each element will point to an array of integers (the length of which is equal to the number of columns).

The outline for the class is:

```
class TwoDimensionalArray
{
    public:
TwoDimensionalArray(int rows, int cols);
~TwoDimensionalArray();
// This overloaded operator[]() function will return the
// address
// contained in element 'index' of the array of pointers
int *operator[](int index) const;
    private:
int **ptrArray;
int rows, cols;
};
```

11

Inheritance

Introduction

Inheritance is the process by which a class is created as the result of extending, or enhancing, an existing class. This saves you from having to "reinvent the wheel"; if a new class greatly resembles an existing class, all of the properties of the existing class can be inherited by the new class and any new features can then be added. The term *base class* is typically used to describe the class from which inheritance occurs. The term *derived class* is typically used to describe the new class being defined. Other terms you might come across are *parent class/child class* and *super class/sub class*.

 With inheritance, you can create a class by using an existing class as a starting point.

A Derived Class Instance in Memory

A derived instance in memory consists of two logical pieces: an inherited base piece and a newly created derived piece. The inherited base piece is commonly referred to as the "base class subobject." All members of the base class are inherited into every derived class object (with several exceptions noted later). Consequently, you can assume that a derived class instance is at least as big as its base class instance. This is what a derived class instance looks like in memory:

 A derived instance consists of an inherited base part plus a newly created derived part.

287

```
┌─────────────────────────┐
│  Inherited base instance │
│ ─ ─ ─ ─ ─ ─ ─ ─ ─ ─ ─ ─ │
│  New derived members     │
└─────────────────────────┘
```
Derived instance

FIGURE 11.1

Using Inheritance to Create an *is-a* Relationship

Inheritance allows you to collect related classes into a hierarchy, with the base classes at the top serving as abstractions for the derived classes below. This implies that a derived class *is a* specialization of its base class. In other words, the derived class *is a* type of base class, but with more detail added. Inheritance allows you to take a general software component and specialize it for use in a specific project. Bear in mind, however, that not all inheritance creates an *is-a* relationship.

 Inheritance is usually used to create an *is-a* relationship between the derived class and the base class.

How to Define a Derived Class

A singly inherited derived class is defined by writing the following items:

▲ The keyword **class** or **struct**,

▲ The name of the derived class,

▲ A single colon (:),

▲ Optionally, the type of derivation you want to perform (private, protected, or public),

▲ The keyword **virtual** if you want the base class to be virtual (discussed during multiple inheritance),

▲ The name of the base class,

▲ The remainder of the class definition, starting with an open brace and ending with a closing brace and a semicolon.

For example, the following is a class called **DerivedString** that is inherited from the **String** class used in previous chapters:

```
class String
{
    // All class members (private by default)
};
```

```
class DerivedString : String              // Private derivation
{
   // All class members (private by default)
};

class DerivedString : public String       // Public derivation
{
   // All class members (private by default)
};

struct DerivedString : String             // Public derivation
{
   // All class members (pubic by default)
};

struct DerivedString : private String     // Private derivation
{
   // All class members (public by default)
};
```

Because the only way to create an *is-a* relationship is to perform a public derivation, and because it's typical to use classes instead of structures, the form of derivation you will see used most often is the following:

```
class DerivedString : public String       // Public derivation
{
   // All class members (private by default)
};
```

A Structure versus a Class (Revisited)

Recall from Chapter 6 that a structure is identical to a class, with two small exceptions in the area of accessibility. The first of these two differences is that a class's members are private by default, whereas a structure's members are public by default. The second major difference between class and structure types is their default derivation type. When you derive a new class from an existing class type (i.e., from an existing class or structure), the compiler uses *private* derivation by default. Therefore, if you want to perform a *public* derivation when deriving a new class from an existing class type, you must explicitly say so. On the other hand, when you derive a new structure from an existing class type (i.e., from an existing class or structure), the compiler uses *public* derivation by default.

There is a general consensus within the C++ community that a structure in a C++ program should have essentially the same "look and feel" as a structure in a C program.

This being the case, you typically do not derive a new class from an existing structure, or vice versa, even though such derivations are allowed.

The Keyword **protected**

Recall that under the principle of data hiding, the only functions that have access to the private members of a class are the class member functions themselves and friend functions. Because every derived instance contains within it a base class subobject, and that base class subobject contains within it the base class data members, the problem should be obvious: How can the member functions of a derived class gain access to the private members of the base class subobject that is within each instance of the derived class?

One possible solution to this dilemma is to redesign the base class by changing its private members to *protected*. This means that member functions in a derived class and friends of the derived class can access these protected members. For the member functions, this is true only for the **this** pointer and for an explicit instance of the same derived class. For a friend function, it is true only for an explicit instance of the same derived class. In other words, what is *not* allowed is for a member function of the derived class, or friend function of the derived class, to gain access to the nonpublic (i.e., protected or private) members of an explicitly declared instance of the base class:

```
class String
{
  // Public interface
    protected:
  int data;
};

class DerivedString : public String
{
  friend void func(String &baseInstance, DerivedString
            &derivedInstance)
  {
    derivedInstance.data = 0;       // OK
    baseInstance.data = 0;          // Error
  }
  void func(String &baseInstance, DerivedString
          &derivedInstance)
  {
    data = 0;                       // OK
    derivedInstance.data = 0;       // OK
    baseInstance.data = 0;          // Error
  }
};
```

SUMMARY   A protected member allows new member functions of a derived class to have access to the member.

Access Privileges

Think of access in terms of this example: Just because you inherit your parents' wealth does not necessarily mean that you have access to it. Similarly, just because a base class member gets inherited does not necessarily mean that nonstatic member functions in the derived class have access to it.

To be more precise:

▲ In a public derivation:

    ▲ *The base class's public members are inherited as public members in the derived class.* They are available to member functions of the derived class and clients of the derived class.

    ▲ *The base class's protected members are inherited as protected members in the derived class.* They are available to member functions of the derived class but not to clients of the derived class.

    ▲ *The base class's private members are inaccessible to the derived class.* They cannot be accessed by member functions of the derived class or by clients of the derived class.

▲ In a protected derivation:

    ▲ *The base class's public and protected members are inherited as protected members in the derived class.* They are available to member functions of the derived class but not to clients of the derived class.

    ▲ *The base class's private members are inaccessible to the derived class.* They cannot be accessed by member functions of the derived class or by clients of the derived class.

▲ In a private derivation:

    ▲ *The base class's public and protected members are inherited as private members within the derived class.* They are available to member functions of the derived class but not to clients of the derived class.

    ▲ *The base class's private members are inaccessible to the derived class.* They cannot be accessed by member functions of the derived class or by clients of the derived class.

Here are all of the possibilities shown in code:

```
class B
{
    public:
    int a;
    protected:
```

```
    int b;
      private:
    int c;
};

class D1 : public B
{
  // D1::a is public
  // D1::b is protected
  // D1::c is inaccessible to D1
};

class D2 : protected B
{
  // D2::a is protected
  // D2::b is protected
  // D2::c is inaccessible to D2
};

class D3 : private B
{
  // D3::a is private
  // D3::b is private
  // D3::c is inaccessible to D3
};
```

CAUTION   Because you will probably go to your grave having never encountered a protected derivation, much less have the need to write one, it will not be discussed any further here.

    When you create a derived class, a private derivation is assumed. When you create a structure, a public derivation is assumed. Use a public derivation to create an *is-a* relationship.

Base Class "Accessor" Functions

What if a member function in a derived class wants (or *needs*) to interact with a private member of its base class? How can this be accomplished? One way would be to redeclare the base class members as protected, rather than as private (as previously discussed). This is not always a desirable option, however, so here's another way: Within the base class, provide some so-called accessor member functions that provide controlled access to the base class's nonpublic members (in this case, to its private data members). The derived class inherits these member functions from the base class, so the derived class can use them to access—albeit indirectly—the private members of its base class subobject.

Of course, the base class's accessor functions must not be declared as private; if they are, they too will be inaccessible to the member functions of the derived class:

```
class Base
{
    public:
  // accessor function
  int get_n() const
  {
    return n;
  }
  void set_n(int value)
  {
    n = value;
  }
    private:
  bool test_n() const
  {
    return(n > 0);
  }
  int n;
};

class Derived : public Base
{
  void func()
  {
    int i = n;          // ERROR - n is inaccessible
    int j = get_n(); // OK
    n = 1234;           // ERROR - n is inaccessible
    set_n(1234);        // OK
    if (test_n())       // ERROR - test_n() is inaccessible
      // ...
  }
};
```

 A derived class can use its base class's nonprivate accessor functions to gain controlled access to the private members of the base class subobject within a derived class instance.

Changing the Inherited Access

Suppose you decide to do a private derivation, so that all of the public member functions in the base class are inherited as private in the derived class. You have therefore prevented users of the derived class from accessing these member functions. But suppose also that you want to make available to the users a particular inherited member function; its access in the derived class has to be public. How can you do this?

The access privilege of the member function in the base class can be restored to its original value by writing a *using declaration* in the public region of the derived class, thereby bringing all such members with the specified name into this region.

In the following example, a private derivation is being performed; because of the using declaration, all of the **func()** member functions are deemed to be public in the derived class, while **anotherFunc()** remains private:

```cpp
class String
{
  // Public interface
    public:
  void func();
  void func(int);
  void func(double);
  void anotherFunc();
};

class DerivedString : String              // Private derivation
{
    public:
  using String::func;
  // ...
};

int main()
{
  DerivedString derivedInstance;
  derivedInstance.func();                 // OK
  derivedInstance.func(0);                // OK
  derivedInstance.func(95.57);            // OK
  derivedInstance.anotherFunc(95.57);     // Error
}
```

 Use a using declaration to restore public access to certain functions when using a private derivation.

Private or Public Inheritance?

Unless you have a good reason for doing otherwise, be sure that you always perform a *public* derivation. As mentioned earlier, the default derivation type for classes is *private*, and with structures it's *public*. Only a public derivation can create an *is-a* relationship.

To prove this point, consider the following example. The **String** class has declared a member function called **func()** that does some interesting work. Class **DerivedString** publicly inherits the **String** class, which means the inherited member function **func()** is automatically public in **DerivedString**. Therefore, since **DerivedString** *is-a* kind of **String**, the user has no problem sending the **func()** message to any instance of **DerivedString**:

```
class String
{
    public:
  void func();
};

class DerivedString : public String       // Public derivation
{
  // ...
};

int main()
{
  DerivedString derivedInstance;
  derivedInstance.func();                  // OK
}
```

If a *private* derivation were to occur, however, then **func()** becomes a *private* member of **DerivedString**, and the user is unable to access it:

```
class String
{
    public:
  void func();
};

class DerivedString : String               // Private derivation
{
  // ...
};

int main()
{
  DerivedString derivedInstance;
  derivedInstance.func();                  // Error
}
```

The conclusion is that if you're willing to bring the public interface of a base class into a derived class, thereby implying that you want to create an *is-a* relationship, you must perform a *public* derivation.

SUMMARY ▶ Unless there is a good reason to do otherwise, always perform a public derivation.

Function Hiding

Assume for the moment that you have a class named **B** that declares one or more member functions named **func**, and that class **B** is an immediate base class for a derived class named **D1**. If the definition of class **D1** also contains a declaration for a member function named **func**, this declaration *hides* all of the member functions named **func** that **D1** inherited from class **B**. In other words, the inherited member functions named **func** are *hidden* from consideration by the compiler when it tries to resolve a call to a member function named **func** in class **D1**. This is called *function hiding*. It is *not* function overloading for the simple reason that a base class and a derived class each define a unique scope, and overloading must occur within the same scope.

For example, let's return to our **String** class and include a member function called **append**() that appends its character input argument onto the end of the invoking object:

```
// File string.h

#ifndef STRING_H
#define STRING_H

class String
{
    public:
  // ...
  String &append(char ch);
    protected:
  char *ptrChars;
};

#endif

// File string.cpp

#include <cstring>
#include <cstddef>
#include "string.h"

String &String::append(char ch)
{
  std::size_t length = std::strlen(ptrChars);
```

```
    char *buffer = new char[length + 2];
    std::strcpy(buffer, ptrChars);
    buffer[length] = ch;
    buffer[length + 1] = '\0';
    delete [] ptrChars;
    ptrChars = buffer;
    return *this;
}

// File main.cpp

#include "string.h"

int main()
{
    String language("C+");
    language.append('+');
}
```

After this class has been tested and placed into a library, you decide that it would be a good idea to let the users have the option to append a string literal as well. So you derive a new class and add the new **append**() member function, but you still want to retain the capability of appending just a single character:

```
// File derivedstring.h

#ifndef DERIVED_STRING_H
#define DERIVED_STRING_H

#include "string.h"

class DerivedString : public String
{
    public:
    // ...
    DerivedString &append(char const *chars);
};

#endif

// File string.cpp

#include <cstring>
#include <cstddef>
#include "derivedstring.h"
```

```
DerivedString &DerivedString::append(char const *chars)
{
  std::size_t length = std::strlen(ptrChars);
  char *buffer = new char[length + std::strlen(chars) + 1];
  std::strcpy(buffer, ptrChars);
  std::strcat(buffer, chars);
  delete [] ptrChars;
  ptrChars = buffer;
  return *this;
}

// File main.cpp

#include "derivedstring.h"

int main()
{
  DerivedString language("C");
  language.append("+");    // OK
  language.append('+');    // Error!!
}
```

Oops. While the call to **append**() with a string literal works just fine, the call with a single character no longer compiles. The reason, as stated earlier, is that the declaration of a member function named **append**() in the derived class **DerivedString** has totally hidden the member function **append**() that was inherited from the **String** class. (Note that the inherited **append**() function is still present in the derived class; it is simply hidden from the compiler during the name lookup process.) Therefore, the compiler tries in vain to convert the character into a pointer-to-character, and of course it fails to do so. Remember that this is *function hiding*, not function overloading.

Before you get too upset over this design decision, just remember that all you have to do to accomplish your goal is bring all **String** declarations into the scope of **DerivedString** with a using declaration:

```
// File derivedstring.h

#ifndef DERIVED_STRING_H
#define DERIVED_STRING_H

#include "string.h"

class DerivedString : public String
{
    public:
  // ...
```

```
    DerivedString &append(char const *chars);
    using String::append;
};
```

```
#endif
```

Of course, if you no longer want the user to be able to call **append**() with a single character, then a *private* derivation does the job perfectly. In this situation, the derived class
DerivedString is said to be implemented in terms of the base class **String**. Note that an
is-a relationship no longer exists. It's almost identical to having an instance of the **String**
class as a data member of the **DerivedString** class, which is simpler and much easier to
understand.

SUMMARY A member function declaration in a derived class hides all inherited functions with
the same name. A using declaration can be used to bring the hidden names into the
scope of the derived class.

How a Derived Class Member Function Calls a Base Class Member Function

Assuming that the member function is accessible, a derived class can call a hidden base
class member function by simply scoping its name. For example, we'll change the definition of the **append**() member function in the **DerivedString** class to call upon the
append() member function in the **String** class to process one character at a time:

```
// File derivedstring.h

#ifndef DERIVED_STRING_H
#define DERIVED_STRING_H

#include "string.h"

class DerivedString : public String
{
    public:
    // ...
    DerivedString &append(char const *chars);
};

#endif

// File derivedstring.cpp
```

```
#include <cstring>
#include <cstddef>
#include "derivedstring.h"

DerivedString &DerivedString::append(char const *chars)
{
  for(std::size_t i = 0; i < std::strlen(chars); ++i)
    String::append(chars[i]);
  return *this;
}
```

Of course, without the scoping on the call to **append**(), the compiler would tell you that it could not find an **append**() member function accommodating a single character. It should be obvious that if no hiding is occurring, then scoping to the base class name is optional.

By the way, the member function **String::append**() is a nonstatic member function, which means that it *must* be invoked on behalf of a specific **String** class instance. In the definition of the **DerivedString::append**() member function, the inherited **String::append**() member function is being invoked on behalf of "this" **DerivedString** instance:

```
DerivedString &DerivedString::append(char const *chars)
{
  for(std::size_t i = 0; i < std::strlen(chars); ++i)
    this->String::append(chars[i]);
  return *this;
}
```

For now, ignore the fact that "this" happens to point at a **DerivedString** instance and not a **String** instance; all will be explained shortly. The explicit "this" pointer syntax shown above hints at the fact that the scoping syntax can also be used as follows:

```
void f1(DerivedString &ds)
{
  ds.String::append('?');          // OK
  // ...
}

void f2(DerivedString *pds)
{
  pds->String::append('\n');       // OK
  // ...
}
```

Recall that **String::append**() is inherited as a public member function in class **DerivedString**. Granted, the inherited **String::append**() member function is hidden by the member function **DerivedString::append**(), but it is there nevertheless, and it is public with respect to the **DerivedString** class. The inherited **String::append**() member function, which is public in the **DerivedString** class, can be invoked (using some scoping magic) on behalf of the **DerivedString** instance **ds**, as was just shown.

If an inherited member function has been hidden, it can be called by explicitly scoping its name.

Manager Functions

Recall that the manager functions of a class are its constructor(s), destructor, and assignment operator. These member functions are *never* inherited by a derived class. For example, each class must declare its own constructors because it's impossible for a base class to know anything about a derived class. How could an "inherited" constructor do any initializing of derived class data members? Also, each class has exactly one destructor and one assignment operator that takes an instance of its own class by reference-to-**const**. If you don't write your own versions, the compiler will provide them for you.

CAUTION Of course, you can always overload the assignment operator to take any argument type you want. If you declare one or more **operator=**() class member functions that take arguments other than an instance of the same class, the compiler will still synthesize its default assignment operator member function for your class; this default **operator=**() member function will participate in overload resolution with the **operator=**() member functions that you have declared.

How to Write the Manager Functions

For any manager function that you write in a derived class, you are responsible for ensuring that it interacts properly with the corresponding manager function of the base class. Sometimes this is done automatically (e.g., to invoke a base class default constructor or destructor), and sometimes you must write the appropriate syntax (e.g., to invoke a base class copy constructor or assignment operator).

SUMMARY A manager function in a derived class must interact properly with its corresponding function in the base class.

Constructors

Let's start with constructors. Recall that when a derived class instance comes into existence, it consists of two parts: the inherited instance variables from the base class and any new instance variables that might have been added in the derived class. A base class constructor is still responsible for initializing the base class instance variables (i.e., the base class subobject within the derived class instance), and a derived class constructor is responsible for initializing the derived class instance variables. It should be obvious, therefore, that the instantiation of a derived class must implicitly invoke a constructor in *both* the base class and the derived class. Fortunately, the compiler guarantees this.

SUMMARY ▶

Whenever a derived class gets instantiated, the compiler guarantees that both a derived class and a base class constructor will get called.

Order of Initialization

The compiler also guarantees that the base class portion of the object will be initialized *before* the derived class portion. Thus, assuming that the compiler, at the point of instantiation, can find a suitable unambiguous derived class constructor, the invocation of this constructor immediately generates a call to some base class constructor in order to construct the base class subobject within the derived class instance. After the immediate base class constructor finishes executing, the program resumes execution of the derived class constructor. This sequence of events corresponds to the layout of the instance variables in memory, in which the base class variables always come before the derived class variables. Isn't that nice?

SUMMARY ▶

The base class constructor will always execute before the derived class constructor.

But Which Base Class constructor to Call?

Yes, this is all very nice, except for one small item: The compiler needs to know *which* base class constructor to invoke. If you give it no guidance whatsoever, it has no choice but to invoke the base class's default constructor. Of course, if this default constructor is missing or inaccessible, you will get a compilation error. But to have any other base class constructor invoked, you *must* use the base/member initialization list in the derived class constructor definition. (You should recall that this syntax was first discussed in Chapter 7.) Now you know why it's called the *base*/member initialization list—because, in addition to providing for the initialization of nonstatic data members, it's also used to guide the compiler as to which *base* class constructor to invoke.

To guide the compiler to a particular base class constructor, simply write the base class name followed by a parenthetical list of arguments to be passed to the constructor. Note that this syntax is the same as that of a function style cast. Of course, the base class name followed by an empty set of parentheses invokes the default constructor. Then continue in the base/member initialization list by initializing any derived class data members. As noted in Chapter 7, the order of items in the base/member initialization list is irrelevant, but it's probably best to specify the base class name first followed by the derived class data members in declaration order.

Let's look at an example to see how the derived class **DerivedString** uses its various constructors to interface with the corresponding constructors in the base class **String**:

```
// File string.h

#ifndef STRING_H
#define STRING_H
```

```
class String
{
    public:
  String(const char *chars = "");
  String(String const &str);
    protected:
  char *ptrChars;
};
```

```
#endif
```

```
// File derivedstring.h
```

```
#ifndef DERIVED_STRING_H
#define DERIVED_STRING_H
```

```
#include "string.h"
```

```
class DerivedString : public String
{
    public:
  DerivedString();
  DerivedString(char const *chars);
  DerivedString(DerivedString const &str);
  DerivedString(String const &str);
};
```

```
#endif
```

```
// File derivedstring.cpp
```

```
#include "derivedstring.h"
#include "string.h"
```

```
DerivedString::DerivedString() /* : String() */ { }
DerivedString::DerivedString(char const *chars)
                           : String(chars) { }
DerivedString::DerivedString(DerivedString const &str)
                           : String(str) { }
DerivedString::DerivedString(String const &str)
                           : String(str) { }
```

Be sure to note how the derived class must *not* repeat the default argument that appears in the base class (the empty string literal), and therefore it must create separate constructors to handle the default case and a pointer-to-constant-characters. The C style comment that is sandwiched in between the declaration and the definition of the **DerivedString** class's default constructor indicates that the code is optional. Specifically, if you delete this comment altogether, the compiler will (by default) call the **String** class's default constructor in response to an invocation of the **DerivedString** class's default constructor. If you uncomment this base/member initialization list, however, the compiler explicitly calls the **String** class's default constructor in response to an invocation of the **DerivedString** class's default constructor. Either way, the end result is exactly the same. Also, note the derived class constructor that takes a base class object as its one parameter, as this is a perfectly reasonable event.

SUMMARY ▶ Use a function style cast in the base/member initialization list to guide the compiler to the appropriate base class constructor.

Destructor

Now let's turn to the destructor. This is a no-brainer. Because the base portion of the object is initialized before the derived portion, the derived portion must be destroyed first, followed by the base portion (think LIFO—last in, first out). So when the program invokes the derived class's destructor on behalf of a derived class instance, the body of the derived class's destructor is executed first. Then the compiler automatically invokes the destructor of the immediate base class, whereupon the body of that destructor is executed. Of course, if the immediate base class is itself a derived class, then the compiler now invokes *its* base class's destructor, and so on, all the way up the class hierarchy:

```
// File string.h

#ifndef STRING_H
#define STRING_H

class String
{
    public:
  ~String();
  // ...
    protected:
  char *ptrChars;
};

#endif

// File string.cpp

#include "string.h"

String::~String()
```

```
{
   delete [] ptrChars;
}

// File derivedstring.h

#ifndef DERIVED_STRING_H
#define DERIVED_STRING_H

#include "string.h"

class DerivedString : public String
{
    public:
  ~DerivedString()
  {
    //       This code is executed first...
    // ...
  } //       Implied call to String destructor
};

#endif
```

The derived class destructor will always execute first, and it will automatically call the base class destructor.

Assignment Operator

The final manager function is the assignment operator. It's guaranteed to exist in the derived class, so it always hides the base class assignment operator. Common sense should tell you that when a derived class object is assigned to another derived class object, the nonstatic data members in the base class subobject should be assigned first. The easiest way to do this, of course, is to explicitly invoke one of the base class's assignment operators with respect to the base class subobjects within the source and destination instances. To make sure that this happens, you must explicitly call the base class assignment operator within the derived class assignment operator:

```
// File string.h

#ifndef STRING_H
#define STRING_H

class String
{
    public:
  // ...
```

```
      String &operator= (String const &str);
        protected:
      char *ptrChars;
};

#endif

// File derivedstring.h

#ifndef DERIVED_STRING_H
#define DERIVED_STRING_H

#include "string.h"

class DerivedString : public String
{
    public:
    // ...
    DerivedString &operator= (DerivedString const &str);
};

#endif

// File derivedstring.cpp

#include "derivedstring.h"
#include "string.h"

DerivedString &DerivedString::operator=
                                    (DerivedString const &str)
{
  // str is the source
  // *this is the destination

  // Use the base class's assignment operator to perform
  // the assignment from the String subobject in 'str' to
  // the String subobject in 'this'
  this->String::operator= (str);

  // Now perform any DerivedString-specific assignments
  // from 'str' to 'this'
  // ...

  return *this;
}
```

By the way, if you do *not* explicitly write an assignment operator for the derived class, the compiler will generate one for you that will (1) call the base class assignment operator, (2) perform a memberwise copy of the derived class's nonstatic data members, and (3) return ***this** to allow for function chaining. If you want something different to happen, you had better write your own.

Have the derived class assignment operator explicitly call the base class assignment operator and then assign the derived class nonstatic data members. If you fail to write a derived class assignment operator, the compiler will generate an assignment operator for you that will "do the right thing" with respect to calling the immediate base class's assignment operator.

Derived-to-Base Standard Conversion

In the previous code sample, several calls from the derived class passed a derived class instance to member functions in the base class that apparently do not expect to receive a derived class instance. Because the actual argument is a derived type, it would appear that you are asking the compiler to find a base class member function whose one formal argument receives a derived class object. There's just one small problem with this scenario: A base class knows *nothing* about *any* derived class. So how can it possibly contain a member function that accepts a derived class argument? The answer is it can't, and it really doesn't need to.

C++ solves this dilemma by adding a *standard conversion* that allows a base class pointer (or reference) to point to (or refer to) a base class subobject within a derived class object. In addition, a base class object can be instantiated by invoking the base class's copy constructor and passing into it a base class subobject that is part of a derived class object. (In other words, the program instantiates a base class instance that is a copy of a base class subobject.) This process is sometimes called an *upcast* because you are traversing *up* the inheritance hierarchy as you go from derived to base. A related term is *object slicing*. In this case, the derived class portion of the object is being "sliced off" during the copy process, leaving you with only the base class portion of the derived class instance.

The derived class must be *publicly* inherited from the base class for this standard conversion to occur.

For example, the following code shows various ways in which to perform an upcast or an object slice:

```
DerivedString dstr;
String *ptr = &dstr; // upcast
String &ref = dstr;  // upcast
String str(dstr);    // slice
str = dstr;          // slice
```

Interestingly, the same standard conversion occurs on the **this** pointer because in the **DerivedString** copy constructor and assignment operator it points to the entire

DerivedString object; in the **String** class copy constructor and assignment operator, the **this** pointer points only to the **String** subobject within the **DerivedString** object.

 The implicit conversion of derived-to-base is a standard conversion, called an upcast or "object slicing."

Hiding Nonmember Functions

It's quite possible for a derived class header file to declare a nonmember function that overloads a nonmember function of the same name that is declared in a base class header file. A typical example of this kind of nonmember function overloading is the stream insertion operator (<<). One could conceivably write a function that overloads the stream insertion operator for use with base class instances (this function would be declared in the base class's header file), and another function that overloads the stream insertion operator for use with derived class instances (this function would be declared in the derived class's header file). Thus, to do its work, the nonmember function that works with derived class objects might want to call upon its base class counterpart to let it handle the workload that's specifically related to base class processing and then proceed with any additional work to process derived class data. It can call the base class function by forcing an upcast using a **static_cast** on the derived class parameter.

For example, suppose the **String** class declares two nonmember (and friend) functions that overload the insertion and equality operators. Then the **DerivedString** class does the same. To invoke the corresponding **String** class functions, **static_cast**s are used in the **DerivedString** definitions:

```
// File string.h

#ifndef STRING_H
#define STRING_H

#include <iosfwd>

class String
{
   friend std::ostream &operator<<
               (std::ostream &stream, String const &str);
   friend bool operator==(String const &left, String const
                          &right);
   // ...
     protected:
   char *ptrChars;
};

#endif
```

```cpp
// File string.cpp

#include <iostream>
#include <cstring>
#include "string.h"

std::ostream &operator<<
            (std::ostream &stream, String const &str)
{
  return stream << str.ptrChars;
}

bool operator==(String const &left, String const &right)
{
  return !std::strcmp(left.ptrChars, right.ptrChars);
}

// File derivedstring.h

#ifndef DERIVED_STRING_H
#define DERIVED_STRING_H

#include <iosfwd>
#include "string.h"

class DerivedString : public String
{
  friend std::ostream &operator<<
            (std::ostream &stream, DerivedString const &str);
  friend bool operator==(DerivedString const &left,
                         DerivedString const &right);
  // ...
};

#endif

// File derivedstring.cpp

#include <iostream>
#include "derivedstring.h"
#include "string.h"

std::ostream &operator<<
            (std::ostream &stream, DerivedString const &str)
```

```
{
   return stream << static_cast<String const &>(str);
}

bool operator==
      (DerivedString const &left, DerivedString const &right)
{
   return static_cast<String const &>(left) ==
               static_cast<String const &>(right);
}
```

SUMMARY ▶ A nonmember function taking derived class parameters can invoke its corresponding base class function by performing a **static_cast** on the parameters.

Don't Use an Upcast with Arrays

Sure, an upcast allows a base class pointer to point to a derived class object. And this pointer can indeed point to the first element, because the name of an array of derived class objects (usually) mutates into a pointer to the first element. Don't do it! If you subsequently perform pointer arithmetic on the pointer, you're in nowheresville. Why? Take a look at the following example:

```
class String
{
   // ...
};

class DerivedString : public String
{
   // ...
};

String *ptr = new DerivedString[10];      // OK
++ptr;            // But where are we?
```

Every time you add 1 to the pointer called **ptr**, the actual number of bytes in memory goes up by **sizeof(*ptr)**; *ptr is type **String** (regardless of what it's pointing at), so you're incrementing by **sizeof(String)** bytes. But because you're really pointing to **DerivedString** objects, each of which could be larger than a **String** object, the pointer is not guaranteed to point to the start of the next **DerivedString** object. So where are you?

SUMMARY ▶ Never allow a base class pointer to point to an array of derived class objects.

Introduction to Polymorphism

Let's go back to the topic of using an upcast with our **String** and **DerivedString** classes, such as this:

```
String *ptr = new DerivedString;
// ...
delete ptr;
```

This is perfectly legal code, but you might be wondering what its purpose is. After all, remember the principle that a base class knows nothing about any of its derived classes. Therefore, **ptr** can *never* be used to gain access to anything in the *derived* portion of the object being pointed at. In fact, **ptr** can be used only to gain access to the nonprivate members of the *base* subobject within the derived object that **ptr** is pointing at. Why would you ever want to have a base class pointer pointing to a derived class object?

To answer that question, consider the following three loan classes. The first, called **GenericLoan** is just that. It holds the abstraction of a loan that you might get from your friendly banker or mortgage broker. The class knows how to display itself (using an overloaded insertion operator), and it can calculate and return the monthly payment. Or can it? By definition, a generic loan doesn't know what specific type it is, so the best that the member function can do is something neutral, such as return 0.00:

```
// File genericloan.h

#ifndef GENERIC_LOAN_H
#define GENERIC_LOAN_H

#include <iosfwd>

class GenericLoan
{
    friend std::ostream &operator<<
        (std::ostream &stream, GenericLoan const &loan);
    public:
    GenericLoan(double principal, int length, double rate);
    ~GenericLoan() { }
    double getMonthlyPayment() const;
      protected:
    double const principal;
    int const length;
    double const rate;
};

#endif
```

```
// File genericloan.cpp

#include <iostream>
#include "genericloan.h"

std::ostream &operator<<
              (std::ostream &stream, GenericLoan const &loan)
{
  return stream << loan.getMonthlyPayment();
}

GenericLoan::GenericLoan
                (double principal, int length, double rate)
                : principal(principal),
                      length(length),
                      rate(rate) { }

double GenericLoan::getMonthlyPayment() const
{
  return 0.00; // For lack of anything better to do
}
```

Next, we'll derive from **GenericLoan** to create a specific type of loan called **Simple-InterestLoan**. In this case, the starting principal is paid back in equal monthly payments. It too has a nonstatic member function named **getMonthlyPayment()**, so this member function *hides* the inherited member function named **getMonthlyPayment()** in the base class:

```
// File simpleinterestloan.h

#ifndef SIMPLE_INTEREST_LOAN_H
#define SIMPLE_INTEREST_LOAN_H

#include "genericloan.h"

class SimpleInterestLoan : public GenericLoan
{
    public:
  SimpleInterestLoan
            (double principal, int length, double rate);
  double getMonthlyPayment() const;
};

#endif
```

```
// File simpleinterestloan.cpp

#include "simpleinterestloan.h"

SimpleInterestLoan::SimpleInterestLoan
            (double principal, int length, double rate)
              : GenericLoan(principal, length, rate) { }

double SimpleInterestLoan::getMonthlyPayment() const
{
  double monthlyRate = rate / 12;
  int lengthInMonths = length * 12;
  return (principal * (monthlyRate * lengthInMonths + 1))
            / lengthInMonths;
}
```

Next, we'll derive from **GenericLoan** again to create another specific type of loan called **AmortizedLoan**. In this case, equal monthly payments are made, but the amount of interest varies according to the principal balance. After the interest has been paid, anything left over reduces the principal amount for the following month:

```
// File amortizedloan.h

#ifndef AMORTIZED_LOAN_H
#define AMORTIZED_LOAN_H

#include "genericloan.h"

class AmortizedLoan : public GenericLoan
{
    public:
  AmortizedLoan(double principal, int length, double rate);
  double getMonthlyPayment() const;
};

#endif

// File amortizedloan.cpp

#include <cmath>
#include "amortizedloan.h"

AmortizedLoan::AmortizedLoan
            (double principal, int length, double rate)
                : GenericLoan(principal, length, rate) { }
```

```
double AmortizedLoan::getMonthlyPayment() const
{
  double monthlyRate = rate / 12;
  int lengthInMonths = length * 12;
  double power = std::pow(1 + monthlyRate, lengthInMonths);
  return (principal * monthlyRate * power) / (power - 1);
}
```

Finally, we'll write a test program to see if we're better off taking out a **SimpleInterest-Loan** or an **AmortizedLoan** in the amount of $300,000.00 for 30 years at 8.00% interest:

```
// File main.cpp

#include <iostream>
#include <cstddef>
#include "simpleinterestloan.h"
#include "amortizedloan.h"

int main()
{
  double const principal = 300000.00;
  int const length = 30;
  double const rate = 0.08;
  GenericLoan *allLoans[] =
  {
    new SimpleInterestLoan(principal, length, rate),
    new AmortizedLoan(principal, length, rate)
  };
  std::size_t const dimension =
                    sizeof(allLoans) / sizeof(*allLoans);
  for(std::size_t i = 0; i < dimension; ++i)
  {
    std::cout << *allLoans[i] << '\n';
    delete allLoans[i];
  }
}


/* Output:

0
0

*/
```

Note the array of pointers to **GenericLoan** objects called **allLoans**. Do you see the up-casts here? Two base class pointers (the array's elements) are pointing to derived class objects. The **for** loop iterates across all of the objects and displays each one. The insertion operator then uses the **GenericLoan** object it receives to call the **getMonthlyPayment**() member function. This, of course, is the member function in the **GenericLoan** class itself, which simply returns 0. Boring, right?

Not exactly. If (and it's a big "if"), instead of always calling the **getMonthlyPayment**() member function of the base class, we could automatically call the corresponding member function of whatever class the pointer is pointing at (or a reference referring to), the boredom would soon disappear. This, in fact, is exactly what we want to happen. In other words, if the expression *allLoans[i] is a **SimpleInterestLoan** object, then we want the program to call **SimpleInterestLoan::getMonthlyPayment**() and not **GenericLoan::getMonthlyPayment**(). Same story for the **AmortizedLoan** class. What magic do we need to make this happen?

SUMMARY ▶ Until a solution can be found using a pointer (or reference) to a base class that points (or refers) to a derived class object, we're locked in to calling base class 'member functions.'

Polymorphism to the Rescue

The magic we need in order to call the correct member function in the preceding example involves the concept of *polymorphism* (meaning "many forms"). In other words, the same message can be sent to different objects, and that message will take on different "forms" as it is carried out by the different member functions that could be invoked. In standard function-calling behavior, the caller decides which function gets called. In polymorphic behavior, the receiving object decides which function gets called. In the previous example, if the message **getMonthlyPayment**() is sent to a **SimpleInterestLoan** object, the member function **SimpleInterestLoan::getMonthlyPayment**() should get called. Similarly, if the message is sent to an **AmortizedLoan** object, then the member function **AmortizedLoan::getMonthlyPayment**() should get called. This is also called *late-time binding, dynamic binding,* or *run-time binding.* Without polymorphism, the message would *always* get sent to **GenericLoan::getMonthlyPayment**(). This is also called *early-time binding, static binding,* or *compile-time binding.*

SUMMARY ▶ Polymorphism allows the correct member function to be called.

Polymorphism and Virtual Functions

C++ implements polymorphism with the use of a *virtual function.* (In other object-oriented languages, such as Smalltalk, Lisp, and Java, polymorphism is done automatically.) The mechanics of a virtual function can be summarized as follows: If a nonstatic member function in a base class definition is declared with the keyword **virtual**, and it is overridden in one or more derived classes, all calls to that member function using either pointers or references of the base class type will invoke the member function that has been overridden by the object being pointed at or referred to.

The keyword **virtual** is written as a modifier of the declaration of the member function; it can only appear inside a class definition, never outside. It needs to be written only in the base class definition because, if a member function is virtual in the base class, it is automatically virtual in all derived classes.

As with a nonvirtual member function, a virtual function's implementation is inherited into all derived classes. Of course, a derived class can accept this inherited implementation or it can choose to define a different implementation.

Therefore, the solution to the earlier loan problem is to add the **virtual** modifier to the **getMonthlyPayment**() member function in the definition of the base class **GenericLoan**:

```
class GenericLoan
{
  // ...
  virtual double getMonthlyPayment() const;
  // ...
};
```

Now the correct member function is guaranteed to get called because, in the definition of the insertion operator,

```
std::ostream &operator<<
              (std::ostream &stream, GenericLoan const &loan)
{
  return stream << loan.getMonthlyPayment();
}
```

the call to **getMonthlyPayment**() is a polymorphic call to the member function of the class to which the base class reference **loan** refers. That is, the argument **loan** could be referring to a **SimpleInterestLoan** object or to an **AmortizedLoan** object, or even to a type of loan that has yet to be invented!

With this change in place, the program now produces its answer:

```
2833.33
2201.29
```

Conclusion: You're much better off with an amortized loan.

SUMMARY Polymorphism in C++ is implemented with the use of a virtual function.

Programmer-Friendly versus Programmer-Hostile Code

The previous section mentioned the following: If a member function is declared virtual in a base class, that member function will automatically be virtual in all derived classes. This has the following implication: If a derived class declares a member function that overrides a virtual member function in one of its base classes, the overriding member function in the derived class is automatically virtual, even if it is not explicitly declared as such. Even though you are not strictly required to use the **virtual** keyword when declaring an overriding virtual member function in a derived class, you might still want to do so for documentation purposes:

```
// File y.h

#ifndef Y_H
#define Y_H

#include "x.h"

class Y : public X
{
    public:
  void f1();
  virtual void f2();
};

#endif
```

Looking at the contents of the header file **y.h**, you can see that class **Y** is derived from class **X**. What you *cannot* tell is whether the member function **Y::f1()** is virtual or not. Recall that if *any* of class Y's base classes declares a virtual member function whose signature exactly matches the declaration of **Y::f1()**, then **Y::f1()** is automatically virtual, even if **Y::f1()** is not explicitly declared as such. The only way to know for sure whether **Y::f1()** is virtual or not is to open the header file **x.h** and look to see if class **X** declares a virtual member function **X::f1()** whose signature matches the signature of **Y::f1()** exactly. If so, then **Y::f1()** is virtual. If not, then the fun doesn't stop there. If class **X** is derived from a base class **W**, you must now open the header file for class **W** and look to see if it declares a virtual member function **W::f1()** whose signature exactly matches the signature of **Y::f1()**, and so on. This must be done for *every* base class in the hierarchy of classes that defines class **Y**. Talk about programmer-hostile code!

Now consider the declaration of the virtual member function **Y::f2()** and note the following: By explicitly applying the keyword **virtual** to the declaration of **Y::f2()**, you can immediately see that **f2()** presumably overrides a virtual member function named **f2()** in one of the base classes of class **Y**. There's no need to go digging through the header files in class **Y**'s hierarchy to find out if one of the base classes declares **f2()** as virtual or not. So even though it is not strictly required, it's generally considered a "programmer-friendly" practice to explicitly declare a virtual member function as such by applying the **virtual** keyword to the member function's declaration.

SUMMARY Write programmer-friendly code by explicitly applying the **virtual** keyword to the declaration of each virtual member function.

Overriding a Virtual Function

Don't forget that when a derived class wants to override an inherited virtual function, the signatures must match exactly. In other words, if you attempt to *hide* rather than *override,* no polymorphism is really occurring, and you might produce a compiler error. For example:

```
class Base
{
    public:
  virtual void func();
};

class Derived : public Base
{
    public:
  virtual void func(int);   // Hiding, not overriding
};
// ...
Base *ptr = new Derived;
ptr->func(0);                 // Compiler error
```

Note that the **Base** class does not have a virtual member function whose signature is **func(int)**. Consequently, when the **Derived** class declares a member function whose signature is **func(int)**, this declaration *hides* the inherited member function **Base::func()**; it does not override it.

The previous code sample brings up another important concept regarding polymorphism in C++ programs: You cannot use a **Base** class pointer to call a **Derived** class member function whose signature is **func(int)**, even if this member function is explicitly declared **virtual** in the **Derived** class. Why? Because (1) the **Base** class does not have a function whose signature is **func(int)**, and (2) the **Base** class knows *nothing* about "added features" in a derived class. In other words, if the **Base** class does not declare a (possibly virtual) member function whose signature is **func(int)**, you cannot invoke such a member function on behalf of a **Base** class instance, or a **Base** class pointer, or a **Base** class reference.

Insofar as the return type of a virtual member function is concerned, C++ allows a little leniency in that the member function can return a pointer or reference of its own class type. This would allow, for example, a unary operator such as ++ to be overloaded as a virtual function and to accommodate function chaining by returning its own class type by reference, as in the following:

```
class Base
{
    public:
  virtual Base &operator++();
  // ...
};

class Derived : public Base
{
    public:
```

```
    virtual Derived &operator++();   // OK; valid overriding
};
// ...
Base *ptr = new Derived;
++(*ptr);       // Calls Derived::operator++()
delete ptr;
// ...
ptr = new Base;
++(*ptr);       // Calls Base::operator++()
delete ptr;
```

SUMMARY   Make sure that you override, not hide, virtual functions in a derived class.

Virtual Destructor

Take another look at the **main()** function that was used to test the loan classes, especially this line:

```
delete allLoans[i];
```

This statement generates a call to the destructor of the class corresponding to the type of **allLoans[i]**. That is, it's a pointer to a **GenericLoan**, so the **GenericLoan** destructor always gets called. But you know this can't be correct behavior because, if the pointer is pointing to either a **SimpleInterestLoan** or a **AmortizedLoan** object, that particular object's destructor must get called, followed by the implicit call to the **GenericLoan** destructor. As a matter of fact, the call to **delete** is actually ill-formed code and is likely to result in undefined behavior.

Fortunately, the solution (as we now know) is quite simple: Just make the destructor in the **GenericLoan** class virtual:

```
class GenericLoan
{
    public:
    virtual ~GenericLoan();
    // ...
};
```

Polymorphic behavior can now take place with respect to object destruction, regardless of which type of concrete loan object **allLoans[i]** points to. If you intend to have people derive from your class, and you expect them to delete polymorphically through a base class pointer, you had better make the destructor virtual.

Alternatively, if you ever want to create a class from which it is fine to derive, but that should never be deleted polymorphically, all you have to do is make the destructor protected and nonvirtual. The derived class can still destruct its base class subobject by invoking the base class's protected destructor function. (Recall that a derived class has direct access to all of the *nonprivate,* i.e., public and protected, members of its immediate base class). However, functions that do not have access to the nonpublic members of the **Base** class cannot directly invoke the **Base** class's destructor:

```
class Base
{
    public:
  // ...
    protected:
  ~Base();
};

class Derived : public Base
{
  ~Derived()
  {
    // Derived-specific destructor code
    // ...
  } // Base::~Base() invoked OK
  // ...
};

// ...
void func(Base *ptr)
{
    delete ptr; // Compiler error
}
```

Make base class destructors virtual if you want users to be able to delete objects poly-morphically through a base class pointer or reference. Otherwise, make them protected and nonvirtual.

Trying to Invoke a Virtual Function from a Base Class Constructor

In short, it can't be done. That is, in the following code,

```
class Base
{
    public:
  Base()
  {
    func();   // Calls Base::func()
  }
  virtual void func();
};
```

```
class Derived : public Base
{
    public:
  virtual void func();
};
```

```
// ...
Derived derivedObject;
```

the call to **func**() from the base class constructor will always call **Base::func**(), never **Derived::func**(), even though the **this** pointer really does point to a derived class object. Conceptually, when the base class constructor is running, the derived portion of the complete object has not yet been constructed; therefore, there is no **func**() in the derived class to call.

SUMMARY ▶ Polymorphism does not apply from a base class constructor.

Abstract Base Classes

An *abstract base class* (ABC) is a class that is used when you want to describe the abstraction of an object—that is, its "polymorphic interface—" without (necessarily) specifying the implementation. Instead of being designated explicitly by a C++ keyword, an abstract base class is created implicitly whenever you declare at least one of the class's virtual member functions as a *pure virtual function*. This is done by appending the special syntax = **0** to its declaration. A derived class inherits the interface (declaration) of the pure virtual function, and it must provide the implementation (definition). Otherwise, the derived class itself becomes another abstract base class.

SUMMARY ▶ An abstract base class contains at least one pure virtual function, and as a result it cannot be instantiated.

The Loan Example (Revisited)

Once again let's pay a visit to our loan example and take another look at the **GenericLoan** class. It's impossible to compute the monthly payment on a generic loan, and this calculation can be made only by the derived classes, so the **GenericLoan** class should really be an abstract base class. This can easily be done by making the **getMonthlyPayment**() member function a pure virtual function:

```
// File genericloan.h

#ifndef GENERIC_LOAN_H
#define GENERIC_LOAN_H
```

```
#include <iosfwd>

class GenericLoan
{
    friend std::ostream &operator<<
                   (std::ostream &stream, GenericLoan const &loan);
      public:
    GenericLoan(double principal, int length, double rate);
    virtual ~GenericLoan();
    virtual double getMonthlyPayment() const = 0;
      protected:
    double const principal;
    int const length;
    double const rate;
};


#endif
```

There is no reason to provide a definition of our pure virtual function in this example, but there is also nothing to stop you from writing one. Of course, it can be invoked only from a derived class member function because it's impossible to instantiate the abstract base class. In addition, note that it's illegal to make such a definition implicit inline. That is, if present, it must be defined outside the class definition.

Exception Specifications with Virtual Functions

If a virtual function in a base class specifies an exception specification, then a function in a derived class that overrides the base class function is allowed only to make this specification more restrictive. For example, **Base::func1**() promises to throw only an **int**; **Derived::func1**(), however, can throw anything, so it is less restrictive and an error. **Base::func2**() is allowed to throw anything, but **Derived::func2**() can throw only an **int**; the latter is more restrictive and thus OK:

```
class Base
{
    virtual void func1() throw(int);
    virtual void func2();
};

class Derived : public Base
{
    virtual void func1();            // Error; less restrictive
    virtual void func2() throw(int); // OK; more restrictive
};
```

When overriding a virtual function, any exception specification can only be more restrictive.

Liskov Substitution Principle

There's one other important point about doing a public derivation that you should know. Not all public derivations create an *is-a* relationship. The "acid test" of whether such a relationship exists is the *Liskov Substitution Principle*. This principle states that wherever an instance of a base class pointer or reference occurs in a program, you can freely substitute an instance of a derived class *and expect to observe the same behavior*. For example, suppose a base class called **Telephone** has a function called **ring**(), which plays a ringing sound. You derive from this class to create a new class called **CellPhone**. Sending the **ring**() message to a **CellPhone** is identical to sending a **ring**() message to a **Telephone**. The caller can't tell, nor should he or she care, if the **ring**() message goes to a **Telephone** or to a **Cellphone**.

This might seem obvious at first sight, but there are pitfalls. The quintessential example is having a base class of a rectangle and then deciding that a square, which is just a rectangle whose four sides are identical, *is-a* specialized kind of rectangle. We'll start by including the usual complement of "setter" and "getter" functions for the **Rectangle** class. Of course, it doesn't quite make sense to make the "setter" functions virtual because there's no reasonable expectation that this functionality would ever change, but we'll do it anyway. If the user then writes a **changeDimensions**() function that receives a reference to a **Rectangle**, and a new width and height, notice how a **Square** object cannot be passed in because the assertion will fail. Thus, the Liskov Substitution Principle has been violated, and we are forced to conclude that a square fails the test of being "a kind of" rectangle:

```
// File rectangle.h

#ifndef RECTANGLE_H
#define RECTANGLE_H

class Rectangle
{
    public:
    Rectangle(double w, double h);
    virtual void setWidth(double w);
    virtual void setHeight(double h);
    double getWidth() const;
    double getHeight() const;
    double getArea() const;
```

```
      private:
   double width, height;
};

#endif

// File rectangle.cpp

Rectangle::Rectangle(double w, double h)
                          : width(w), height(h) {}

void Rectangle::setWidth(double w)
{
   width = w;
}

void Rectangle::setHeight(double h)
{
   height = h;
}

double Rectangle::getWidth() const
{
   return width;
}

double Rectangle::getHeight() const
{
   return height;
}

double Rectangle::getArea() const
{
   return width * height;
}

// File square.h

#ifndef SQUARE_H
#define SQUARE_H

#include "rectangle.h"

class Square : public Rectangle
```

```cpp
{
    public:
  Square(double len);
  virtual void setWidth(double w);
  virtual void setHeight(double h);
};

#endif

// File square.cpp

#include "square.h"

Square::Square(double len) : Rectangle(len, len) { }

void Square::setWidth(double w)
{
  Rectangle::setWidth(w);
  Rectangle::setHeight(w);
}

void Square::setHeight(double h)
{
  Rectangle::setWidth(h);
  Rectangle::setHeight(h);
}

// File main.cpp

#include <cassert>
#include "rectangle.h"
#include "square.h"

void changeDimensions(Rectangle &rec, double w, double h)
{
  rec.setWidth(w);
  rec.setHeight(h);
  assert(rec.getWidth() * rec.getHeight() == w * h);
}

int main()
{
  Square sq(5);
  changeDimensions(sq, 9, 10);
}
```

```
/* Output:

Assertion failed: rec.getWidth() * rec.getHeight() == w * h

Abnormal program termination

*/
```

Multiple Inheritance

Multiple inheritance occurs when a derived class is inherited from more than one base class. (Some people say that it occurs when more than one rich aunt or uncle dies on the same day, but that's another story.) This is not a feature that you will be using every day, but it's something with which you should be familiar just in case that special day arrives.

For example, let's start with a class called **Appliance** that contains a cost (among other members):

```
// File appliance.h

#ifndef APPLIANCE_H
#define APPLIANCE_H

class Appliance
{
    public:
  Appliance(double cost);
  double get_cost() const;
    protected:
  double cost;
};

#endif
```

You would certainly have to agree that a radio *is a* kind of appliance, so let's publicly derive a class called **Radio** with some representative data and a public interface:

```
// File radio.h

#ifndef RADIO_H
#define RADIO_H

#include "appliance.h"
```

```
class Radio : virtual public Appliance
{
  enum band { AM, FM };
    public:
  Radio(double cost, band amFm = AM, double station = 810)
        : Appliance(cost), amFm(amFm), station(station) { }
  void setStation(double);
  double getStation() const;
  void setBand(band);
    protected:
  band amFm;
  double station;
};
```

```
#endif
```

Note carefully the use of the keyword **virtual** as part of the derivation process. This will be explained shortly.

Next, let's create a class called **Time** that encapsulates the current time:

```
// File time.h

#ifndef TIME_H
#define TIME_H

#include <iosfwd>

class Time
{
  friend std::ostream &operator<<
                (std::ostream &stream, Time const &);
    public:
  Tme(int hours, int minutes, int seconds);
  // ...
    private:
  int hours, minutes, seconds;
};
```

```
#endif
```

An alarm clock contains a clock time and an alarm time, and it also is a kind of appliance:

```
// File alarmclock.h

#ifndef ALARM_CLOCK_H
```

```
#define ALARM_CLOCK_H

#include "applicance.h"
#include "time.h"
class AlarmClock : virtual public Appliance
{
    public:
  AlarmClock(double cost,
                      Time const &clockTime = defaultTime,
                      Time const &alarmTime = defaultTime)
                      : Appliance(cost),
         clockTime(clockTime), alarmTime(alarmTime) { }
  Time const &getClockTime() const;
  Time const &getAlarmTime() const;
  // ...
    private:
  Time clockTime, alarmTime;
  static Time defaultTme;
};

#endif
```

Now the stage is set. From both the alarm clock and the radio, we can perform multiple inheritance and derive a new class called a radio-clock with . . . no, wait, let's call it a clock-radio with the added capability of waking someone up to either music or a buzzing noise. The syntax to write a derived class that is created as the result of multiple inheritance is the same as single inheritance, except that you keep specifying base classes, all of which are separated by commas:

```
// File clockradio.h

#ifndef CLOCK_RADIO_H
#define CLOCK_RADIO_H

#include "alarmclock.h"
#include "radio.h"

class ClockRadio : public AlarmClock, public Radio
{
  enum sound { radio, buzz };
    public:
  Clock_radio(double cost, sound soundType = buzz)
              : Appliance(cost),  // Note this call
                soundType(soundType) { }
  void set_wakeup(sound = buzz);
```

```
      private:
    sound soundType;
  };


  #endif
```

A test of all of these classes might look as follows:

```cpp
// File main.cpp

#include <iostream>
#include "clockradio.h"
using std::cout;

int main()
{
  ClockRadio GE(49.95);
  cout << GE.getCost() << '\n';
  cout << GE.getStation() << '\n';
  cout << GE.getClock_time() << '\n';
  cout << GE.getAlarm_time() << '\n';
}
```

 Multiple inheritance occurs when more than one base class is used to create a derived class.

Virtual Base Classes

In the previous example, there could have been a problem with the call to the **Appliance::getCost()** member function because both the **Radio** and **AlarmClock** classes inherently contain an **Appliance** class subobject. Therefore, the **ClockRadio** class has inherited *two* **Appliance** subobjects—and therefore two **cost** data members—and the compiler wouldn't know which **getCost()** member function to invoke because conceptually there are two of them.

The solution is to make the **Appliance** class a *virtual base class* of the **Radio** and **AlarmClock** classes by adding the keyword **virtual** in the derivation of the **Radio** and **AlarmClock** classes. This keyword can appear before or after the derivation type, and both derived classes must specify it. The net result is that when the class **ClockRadio** is declared, it will contain only *one* **Appliance** class subobject (more specifically, its **AlarmClock** and **Radio** subobjects share a common **Appliance** subobject) and thus the ambiguity issue is resolved.

 Using the keyword **virtual** in the derivation process makes the base class virtual, and it will force only one copy of the base class to be inherited into a further derived class.

Initializing a Virtual Base Class

Note that the **Appliance** class needs an argument passed into its constructor in order to initialize the cost field, and you could reasonably inquire as to which of its derived classes should take on this responsibility—the **Radio** or the **AlarmClock** class. Surprisingly, the answer is neither one, because there really is no reason to prefer one over the other. Instead, this job becomes the responsibility of the constructor of the **ClockRadio** class (the "most derived class"). That is why the base/member initialization list in the **Clock_radio** constructor specifies the **Appliance** class and an argument to be passed to its constructor. This base class constructor call occurs before the immediate base classes of **ClockRadio** are constructed. Furthermore, the subsequent construction of the **Radio** and **AlarmClock** subobjects does not (re)invoke any base class constructor calls to the **Appliance** class.

Note that if the **ClockRadio** class's base/member initializer list does not specify which **Appliance** class constructor should be called, then the compiler will (as usual) try to invoke the Appliance class's default constructor. In this particular case, however, the program would fail to compile because the **Appliance** class does not have a default constructor.

SUMMARY

The "most derived class" is responsible for the proper construction of a virtual base class.

EXERCISE 11.1

Given the abstract base class **Employee**,

```
// File employee.h

#ifndef EMPLOYEE_H
#define EMPLOYEE_H

#include <iosfwd>

class Employee
{
   public:
 virtual ~Employee();
 char const *getName() const;
 virtual double getMonthlyEarnings() const = 0;
   protected:
 Employee(char const *name);
   private:
 char *name;
};
```

```
std::ostream &operator<<(std::ostream &, Employee const &);

#endif
```

write all of the member functions in the definition file **employee.cpp**.

Next, create a derived class called **SalariedEmployee** that includes a yearly salary, and a derived class called **HourlyEmployee** that includes an hourly wage (assume 160 hours in a month). Be sure to define the appropriate member functions for both classes.

```
// File salaried.h

#ifndef SALARIED_H
#define SALARIED_H

#include "employee.h"

class SalariedEmployee : public Employee
{
 double yearlySalary;
 // ...
};

#endif

// File hourly.h

#ifndef HOURLY_H
#define HOURLY_H

#include "employee.h"

class HourlyEmployee : public Employee
{
 double hourlyWage;
 // ...
};

#endif
```

Test your classes using the following main() function:

```
// File main.cpp

#include <iostream>
#include <cstddef>
#include "salaried.h"
```

```
#include "hourly.h"

int main()
{
 Employee *array[] =
 {
  new SalariedEmployee("Peter", 48000.0),
  new HourlyEmployee("Paul", 10.00)
 };
 std::size_t const size = sizeof(array) / sizeof(*array);
 for(std::size_t i = 0; i < size; ++i)
 {
  std::cout << *array[i] << '\n';
  delete array[i];
 }
}

/* Output:

Peter will earn $4000 this month
Paul will earn $1600 this month

*/
```

EXERCISE 11.2

Given the abstract base class **FiniteStateMachine** and the two concrete classes **ON** and **OFF**,

```
// File finitestatemachine.h

#ifndef FINITE_STATE_MACHINE_H
#define FINITE_STATE_MACHINE_H

#include <iosfwd>

class FiniteStateMachine
{
 friend std::ostream &operator<<
                    (std::ostream &, FiniteStateMachine const &);
  public:
 virtual FiniteStateMachine *changeState() const = 0;
 virtual char const *toString() const = 0;
 virtual ~FiniteStateMachine() { }
};
```

```
class ON : public FiniteStateMachine
{
    public:
 FiniteStateMachine *changeState() const;
 char const *toString() const;
};

class OFF : public FiniteStateMachine
{
    public:
  FiniteStateMachine *changeState() const;
  char const *toString() const;
};

#endif

// File FiniteStateMachine.cpp

#include "FiniteStateMachine.h"
// All member function definitions here
```

write all member functions so that the state of **OFF** transitions to the state of **ON**, and vice versa.

Next, given a **Light** class that has a pointer to a **FiniteStateMachine** object called **state**,

```
// File light.h

#ifndef LIGHT_H
#define LIGHT_H

#include <iosfwd>

class Light
{
 friend std::ostream &operator<<(std::ostream &, Light const &);
   public:
 Light(FiniteStateMachine *state = new OFF);
 ~Light();
 Light &turnKnob();
   private:
 FiniteStateMachine *state;
 Light(Light const&);            // Do not define
 void operator=(Light const&);   // Do not define
};
```

```
#endif

// File light.cpp
#include <iostream>
#include "light.h"
```

write all member functions so that each call to **turnKnob**() changes the state of the object.

Test with the following **main**():

```
#include <iostream>
#include "light.h"

int main()
{
  Light GE;
  int const turns = 5;
  for(int i = 0; i < turns; ++i)
    std::cout << GE.turnKnob() << '\n';
}

/* Output:

State is ON
State is OFF
State is ON
State is OFF
State is ON

*/
```

12

Templates

Introduction

A *template* in C++ is just what the name implies — a skeleton, framework, or outline for creating functions and classes. A function or class template differs from a nontemplate function or class because one or more types are *generic* with a template. That is, instead of writing a specific type, such as **int**, **double**, **String**, and so on, you write just an identifier that is generic and that will eventually be replaced by some specific type decided by the programmer at compilation time.

 A template creates a skeleton for a family of related functions or classes. One or more types are generic, to be replaced by specific types at compilation time.

Function Templates

Let's start with *function templates* and see what kinds of problem they are designed to solve. In the following example, a function called **greater**() returns the greater of its two input arguments. Not too exciting, but useful. Through the miracle of function overloading, the **greater**() function can accommodate various types of arguments that can conceivably be used to invoke it:

```
// File greater.h

#ifndef GREATER_H
#define GREATER_H
```

```cpp
int greater(int x, int y)
{
  return (x > y) ? x : y;
}

long greater(long x, long y)
{
  return (x > y) ? x : y;
}

double greater(double x, double y)
{
  return (x > y) ? x : y;
}

char greater(char x, char y)
{
  return (x > y) ? x : y;
}

#endif

// File main.cpp

#include <iostream>
#include "greater.h"
using std::cout;

int main()
{
  int a = 1, b = 2;
  cout << greater(a, b) << '\n';
  long c = 4L, d = 3L;
  cout << greater(c, d) << '\n';
  double e = 5.62, f = 3.48;
  cout << greater(e, f) << '\n';
  char g = 'A', h = 'a';
  cout << greater(g, h) << '\n';
}

/* Output:

2
4
```

```
5.62
a

*/
```

Even though the correct answers are obtained, there is still too much repetitious coding. In other words, each function is doing essentially the same thing — returning the greater of its two input arguments. In general, we want to remove as much duplicate code as possible. The "holy grail" would be to have no duplication whatsoever. The problem with duplicate code is that, when a change has to be made, how are you going to find all of the places that are copies of the original? It's unlikely that the algorithm of our **greater**() functions will ever change, but it doesn't take much imagination to extrapolate this idea to a more complex function, such as one with a nontrivial algorithm. If the algorithm changes, you will have a secure job while tracking down all the duplicates.

SUMMARY ▶ Function overloading is good, but it can lead to a lot of repetitious code.

Why Not Use a Macro?

You can certainly write a macro to "solve" this problem. The trouble is:

▲ Macros do not have the ability to ensure that you are not comparing arguments of different but compatible types,

▲ Macros are handled by the preprocessor, which makes debugging more difficult,

▲ Macros are very prone to error, such as forgetting a set of parentheses,

▲ Macros can have nasty side effects, such as applying an increment or decrement operator more than once.

Leave macros to the folks still writing in C. We want to pick the right tool for the job. When choosing between the compiler and the preprocessor, choose the compiler.

SUMMARY ▶ Macros can lead to all kinds of trouble, so try to avoid them.

How to Write a Function Template

The answer to the problem of duplicate coding, as I'm sure you suspected is a *function template*. Instead of writing a lot of overloaded functions, the function template acts as a "blueprint," and the compiler then creates the functions for you at compile time. Doesn't that sound like a good idea?

All function templates start with a *template parameter list,* which has the following syntax:

▲ The C++ keyword **template**

▲ A left angle bracket (<)

▲ A list of one or more *generic types*. If there is more than one type, each one is separated by a comma. A generic type consists of two parts:

  ▲ The keyword **class** or **typename**

  ▲ An identifier of your choosing that represents the generic type. Typically the name **T** or **Type** is used, but any valid C++ name will work

▲ A right angle bracket (>)

CAUTION   In the early days of C++, the keyword **class** was used in this context to indicate that a generic type followed. Later the keyword **typename** was added to the language, primarily to solve a different problem but valid in this context. This book will use **typename**.

After the template parameter list, you continue with the function declaration or definition itself. The formal argument list for a function template might or might not use each of the parameterized types that were specified in the template parameter list.

Now let's revise the **greater()** function by turning it into a function template that takes two arguments of some generic type and returns the greater of the two. We'll call this generic type **T**:

```cpp
// File greater.h

#ifndef GREATER_H
#define GREATER_H

template <typename T>
T greater(T x, T y)
{
   return (x > y) ? x : y;
}

#endif

// File main.cpp

#include <iostream>
#include "greater.h"
using std::cout;

int main()
{
   int a = 1, b = 2;
   cout << greater(a, b) << '\n';
   long c = 4L, d = 3L;
```

```
    cout << greater(c, d) << '\n';
    double e = 5.62, f = 3.48;
    cout << greater(e, f) << '\n';
    char g = 'A', h = 'a';
    cout << greater(g, h) << '\n';
}

/* Output

2
4
5.62
a

*/
```

When the function template is called, the compiler deduces the type of the actual argument and substitutes it for the generic type of **T**, thereby instantiating what is called a *generated function.* In the previous example, the compiler will instantiate generated functions with types **int**, **long**, **double**, and **char**, respectively. If a subsequent call is made using a type that has already been deduced, then the existing generated function will be used (as opposed to instantiating another generated function).

SUMMARY ▶ When the function template is called, the compiler deduces the actual type(s) and makes the substitution to create a generated function.

Optimizing the Code

In the previous example, the formal arguments to the **greater()** function are being received by value, and the result is being returned by value. This produces the correct answer, but you might want to consider using reference-to-**const** instead. Although passing arguments by value will make little or no difference in terms of efficiency for the primitive types, in the case of a user-defined type you will needlessly be invoking the class's copy constructor. This is a poor idea because the function should be finding the greater of the two original objects, *not* the greater of *copies* of those two objects.

Let's rewrite the function to use reference-to-**const** for the generic type **T**:

```
// File greater.h

#ifndef GREATER_H
#define GREATER_H

template <typename T>
T const &greater(T const &x, T const &y)
```

```
{
   return (x > y) ? x : y;
}

#endif

// File main.cpp

#include <iostream>
#include "greater.h"
using std::cout;

int main()
{
   int a = 1, b = 2;
   cout << greater(a, b) << '\n';
   long c = 4L, d = 3L;
   cout << greater(c, d) << '\n';
   double e = 5.62, f = 3.48;
   cout << greater(e, f) << '\n';
   char g = 'A', h = 'a';
   cout << greater(g, h) << '\n';
}

/* Output

2
4
5.62
a

*/
```

Of course, if **T** represents a user-defined type, it is the responsibility of the designer of class **T** to ensure either that both **operator>**() and **operator<<**() have been properly overloaded, or that a suitable user-defined conversion function exists.

CAUTION   If you want to give the user of **greater**() the capability of modifying whichever argument is greater, the function must return its answer *by value* instead of reference-to-**const**. This would apply only to user-defined types, not primitive types.

   Consider receiving and returning generic types by reference-to-**const** instead of by value.

Where Do Function Templates Go?

Until the *separate compilation model* of templates is discussed later in this chapter, we will be using the *inclusion model*. This simply means that you place *all* of the code for the function template definition in a header file (remembering that a function definition implies its declaration). What you must *not* do (for now) is to treat function templates like nontemplate functions in which you declare the functions in a header file and define them in definition files (which can then be compiled into object format). The compiler must have access to the template's entire definition when the function is actually called in order to (1) deem the code valid or invalid, and then (2) instantiate a generated function from the template.

Now, perhaps you're wondering what would happen in the case in which two definition files included the same header file and instantiated a noninlined function template with the same type. See the following:

```
// File one.cpp

#include <iostream>
#include "greater.h"

void one()
{
   int a = 1, b = 2;
   std::cout << greater(a, b) << '\n';
}

// File two.cpp

#include <iostream>
#include "greater.h"

void two()
{
   int a = 1, b = 2;
   std::cout << greater(a, b) << '\n';
}
```

Now both the object files contain a generated function with this signature and definition:

```
int const &greater<int>(int const &x, int const &y)
{
   return (x > y) ? x : y;
}
```

Doesn't this cause the linker to emit a duplicate definition error? Happily, the answer is no, because the linker is smart enough to know that these particular functions came from function templates and will not punish you for doing something that is perfectly reasonable.

Be sure to include all function template definitions in a header file. Do not create a separate definition file.

Instantiating with Different Types

You cannot instantiate a generated function from the function template **greater**() where the formal arguments of the generated function have different types (e.g., the first argument has type **int** and the second argument has type **double**). This is for the following reasons: (1) the generic type **T** cannot represent two different types at the same time, and (2) no conversions will be done on the actual arguments to try to make them "the same." For example:

```
// File main.cpp

#include <iostream>
#include "greater.h"

int main()
{
   int a = 5;
   double b = 6.1;
   std::cout << greater(a, b) << '\n';     // Compiler error
}
```

 A generic type cannot represent two different values at the same time.

EXERCISE 12.1

Write a function template called **swap**() that swaps the contents of its two input arguments. Test this function by using several different instantiations of primitive types.

EXERCISE 12.2

Write a function template that searches an array for the highest value and then returns this value.

```
// File highest.h

#ifndef HIGHEST_H
#define HIGHEST_H

template <typename T>
T const &highest(T const *ptrArray, int dim)
{
  // Your code here
}
```

```
#endif

// File main.cpp
#include <iostream>
#include "highest.h"

int main()
{
  int const array1[] = {4, 56, 0, -6, 11};
  int const dim1 = sizeof(array1) / sizeof(*array1);
  std::cout << "highest int is" << highest(array1, dim1) << '\n';
  double const array2[] = {5.78, -8.37, 6.123, -54.794};
  int const dim2 = sizeof(array2) / sizeof(*array2);
  std::cout << "highest double is" << highest(array2, dim2)
                                    << '\n';

}
```

Explicitly Specifying the Type

Common sense tells you that, in order to allow the compiler to deduce and substitute concrete types for the generic types, each generic type must appear in the function's formal argument list. In other words, consider the following function template that receives an object of type **U** and converts it into an object of type **T** using a **static_cast**:

```
template <typename T, typename U>
T convert(U const &arg)
{
   return static_cast<T>(arg);
}
// ...
double d = 1.23;
convert(d);    // Error; U is type double, but what is type T?
```

Because **T** is not specified in the function's formal argument list, how is the compiler supposed to deduce its type at compile time? The answer, of course, is that the compiler cannot do so. Consequently, there must be a way for the user to *explicitly* specify what the actual type is.

This is done by writing the actual type between angle brackets immediately following the function name when the function is called. If all of the types are not explicitly specified, the function will still work if any remaining types can be deduced from the actual arguments. Of course, there must be a valid conversion between the actual arguments and this explicit type for the **static_cast** to work. For example:

```
// File convert.h

#ifndef CONVERT_H
#define CONVERT_H
```

```
template <typename T, typename U>
T convert(U const &arg)
{
  return static_cast<T>(arg);
}

#endif

// File main.cpp

#include "convert.h"

int main()
{
  double d = 1.23;
  convert(d);                  // Error; what is T?
  convert<int>(d);             // OK; T == int, U == double
  convert<int, char>(d);       // OK; T == int, U == char
  convert<int, char *>(d);     // Error; no conversion possible
}
```

In addition to having the compiler deduce the actual types, you can specify them between angle brackets when the function is called.

Default Function Arguments

Remember default function arguments? It is certainly possible to specify them in a function template. But because you really don't know the "real" type that the user will eventually want, the best you can do is to use the expression **T()** as the default value (assuming that you have used **T** as the generic type). This expression is nothing more than a function-style cast, the value of which will evaluate to 0 if **T** is a primitive type, or whatever the default constructor of **T** produces if **T** is a user-defined type (assuming that class **T** really does have a default constructor and that it is accessible).

The only problem is figuring out what the compiler is supposed to deduce if the user calls the function and wants to use the default value. Remember, however, that you can explicitly specify the type by writing it between angle brackets immediately after the function name and before the formal argument list:

```
// File display.h

#ifndef DISPLAY_H
#define DISPLAY_H

#include <iostream>
```

```
template <typename T>
void display(T const &value = T())
{
   std::cout << "value = " << value << '\n';
}

#endif

// File main.cpp

#include "display.h"

int main()
{
   // display();                 // Error
   display<int>();
   display(56.73);
   display<char>(65);
}

/* Output:

value = 0
value = 56.73
value = A

*/
```

A function template can be written with a default argument of **T**(), where the generic type is **T**.

Fully Specializing a Function Template

Sometimes a function template cannot accommodate all of the possible types of input arguments that the user might want to provide. In this case you have two choices: (1) overload the function template, or (2) *fully specialize* the function template.

Function templates can only be *fully* specialized. Class templates, discussed later, can be either fully or partially specialized.

Here is an example of specialization:

```
// Function base template
template <typename T>
T const &greater(T const &x, T const &y)
```

```
{
   return (x > y) ? x : y;
}

// Specialize for type 'int'
template <>
int const &greater<int>(int const &x, int const &y)
{
   // Do something special for type 'int'
}

// Specialize for type 'double'
template <>
double const &greater<double>
                          (double const &x, double const &y)
{
   // Do something special for type 'double '
}

// Specialize for type 'char'
// (with an error in the return type because & is missing)
template <>
char const greater<char>(char const &x, char const &y)
{
   // Do something special for type 'char'
}
```

The original function template is called the *function base template*. To specialize it, perform the following steps:

1. Choose a type for which the function base template is to be specialized,
2. Write a template parameter list with absolutely nothing between the angle brackets, such as **template <>**,
3. Repeat the return type (including any modifiers) and, if necessary, substitute the chosen type for the generic type,
4. Repeat the name of the function,
5. Write the chosen type between angle brackets,
6. Repeat the function base template's formal argument list, and substitute the chosen type for the generic type wherever it appears. All modifiers in the formal argument list (e.g., **const**, *, **&**, etc.) must be preserved.

CAUTION   Writing the chosen type(s) between angle brackets immediately after the function name might not be necessary if the type(s) can be deduced from the parameter(s) being passed into the function.

A function template can be fully specialized to create a specific function to be examined before instantiating the template.

How a Specialized Function Gets Called

A specialized function can be called in one of two ways. In the first case, you let the compiler deduce the type of the arguments and go through the normal overloading resolution process. *The specialized functions do not participate in this process.* They are considered only if the base template class has been selected as the "best match." Only then will the compiler check to see if a specialized function exists that matches the calling arguments exactly. That is, no promotions or conversions are allowed in order to call a specialized function. For example, **char** to **int** or **double** to **short** will not work. If no specialized function exists, the selected function base template will be called.

For example:

```cpp
#include <iostream>
using std::cout;

template <typename T>
void func(T const &)
{
   cout << "T const &\n";
}

template <>
void func<int>(int const &)
{
   cout << "int const &\n";
}

int main()
{
   func(1.2);
   func(0);
   func(2.5);
}

/* Output:

T const &
int const &
T const &

*/
```

In function **main()**, the first call to function **func** (the call with a **double** argument **1.2**) tries to invoke a call to

```
void func<double>(double const &) { /* ... */ }
```

which does not yet exist. Consequently, the compiler implicitly instantiates this specialization to create a generated function from the base template, and then it invokes this specialization. Note that the compiler uses the type **double** argument **1.2** to deduce the type of the template parameter **T** to a **double**, so the compiler does *not* (and indeed *cannot*) try to convert the **double** argument into some other argument type (e.g., **int**) during the function template specialization lookup process. Consequently, the compiler does not regard the **func<int>** specialization as a valid candidate for this call.

The second call to function **func** (the call with an **int** argument) matches the user-defined **func<int>** specialization. The compiler simply invokes this specialization.

The third call to function **func** (the call with the **double** argument **2.5**) invokes a call to the same **func<double>** specialization that was previously instantiated by the compiler in response to the original **func<double>** call. In other words, once a specialization has been generated within the current translation unit, whether it is a user-defined explicit specialization (e.g., **func<int>**), or a compiler-generated specialization (e.g., **func<double>**), the compiler does not regenerate that specialization; it simply reinvokes the existing specialization.

The second way to call a specialized function is to dictate the specific type between angle brackets, as shown earlier. In this case, *only* a function base template or a specialized function will be called. That is, a nontemplate function will never be called as the result of explicitly determining the type. For example:

```
#include <iostream>
using std::cout;

template <typename T>
void func(T const &)
{
   cout << "T const &\n";
}

template <>
void func<int>(int const &)
{
   cout << "int const &\n";
}

void func(double const &)
{
   cout << "double const &\n";
}
```

```
int main()
{
   func<int>(1.2);
   func<char>(1.2);
   func(1.2);
   func('A');
}

/* Output:

int const &
T const &
double const &
T const &

*/
```

For the first call, the template argument list <**int**> explicitly specifies the type of the template parameter **T**. Because the compiler is told explicitly that **T**'s type is **int**, the compiler knows it must invoke a template specialization whose signature is:

```
void func<int>(int const &)
```

In this case, the function argument (e.g., the **double** value **1.2**) does *not* play a role in determining the type of the template parameter **T**. Therefore, the compiler *can* perform a conversion on the function argument, as needed, prior to invoking the **func<int>** specialization. The program has specified a **double** value as the function's argument, the compiler knows the **func<int>** specialization must be passed an **int**, so the compiler implicitly performs a **double**-to-**int** conversion on the argument and then invokes the (user-defined) **func<int>** specialization, passing it the **int** value from the conversion.

For the second call, the program again provides a template argument list <**char**> that explicitly defines the type of the template parameter **T**. The compiler knows it must invoke a template specialization whose signature is:

```
void func<char>(char const &)
```

This specialization does not yet exist, so the compiler implicitly instantiates it from the base template. Next, the compiler performs a **double**-to-**char** conversion on the argument **1.2**, and finally it invokes the **func<char>** specialization, passing it the **char** value from the conversion.

For the third call, we've *overloaded* (not specialized) the function base template with another function that accepts a type **double**. When an overloaded function exists with a function base template, promotions and conversions are *not* performed on the actual argument(s) in an attempt to find a match with this overloaded function. Instead, exact matches must occur for the overloaded function to get called. Since the actual argument is type **double**, and the nontemplate function expects type **double**, it will be chosen because this constitutes an exact match.

For the fourth call, the compiler is not allowed to invoke the specialized function **func<int>**, and it is not allowed to convert from **char** to **double** to call **func (double const &)**. But it can (and does!) invoke the **func<char>** specialization.

Don't forget that in order for a specialized template function to be called when the specific type is not dictated, the arguments will *not* undergo any promotions or conversions, so there must be an exact match:

```cpp
#include <iostream>
using std::cout;

template <typename T>
void func(T const &, T const &)
{
  cout << "T const &, T const &\n";
}

template <>
void func<int>(int const &, int const &)
{
  cout << "int const &, int const &\n";
}

int main()
{
  func(1.2, 1.2);
  func<char>(1, 1);
  func<char>(1, 1.2);
  func(1, 1);
  func<int>(1, 1);
  func<int>(1, 1.2);
  // func(1, 1.2);                      // Error
}

/* Output:

T const &, T const &
T const &, T const &
T const &, T const &
int const &, int const &
int const &, int const &
int const &, int const &

*/
```

For the first three calls, the function base template gets called and the specialized version is ignored. For the next three calls, the function base template again gets chosen but the specialized version is a better choice. For the last call, the function base template cannot be chosen (because of the different argument types) and therefore the specialized version is never even considered. Thus, it's a compiler error.

CAUTION   Caution! Unless inlined, fully specialized function templates are considered to be definitions in the true sense of the word, and therefore they must be placed inside definition files.

Specialize or Overload?

When a function base template receives just one parameter, there's not much difference between specializing it and overloading it. For example, in the following the template is specialized:

```
#include <iostream>
using std::cout;

template <typename T>
void func(T const &)
{
   cout << "T const &\n";
}

template <>
void func<int>(int const &)
{
   cout << "int const &\n";
}

int main()
{
   func('A');
   func(0);
}

/* Output:

T const &
int const &

*/
```

Here it is overloaded:

```
#include <iostream>
using std::cout;
```

```
template <typename T>
void func(T const &)
{
   cout << "T const &\n";
}

void func(int const &)
{
   cout << "int const &\n";
}

int main()
{
   func('A');
   func(0);
}

/* Output:

T const &
int const &

*/
```

As you can see, the results are the same. Of course, in the case of overloading, the signature of the function does not have to match that of the function base template, but the results will still be the same:

```
#include <iostream>
using std::cout;

template <typename T>
void func(T const &)
{
   cout << "T const &\n";
}

void func(int) // No longer 'int const &'
{
   cout << "int\n";
}

int main()
{
   func('A');
```

```
      func(0);
}

/* Output:

T const &
int

*/
```

However, consider this example, which uses specialization:

```
#include <iostream>
using std::cout;

template <typename T>
void func(T const &, T const &)
{
   cout << "T const &, T const &\n";
}

template <>
void func<int>(int const &, int const &)
{
   cout << "int const &, int const &\n";
}

int main()
{
   func('A', 1); // Compiler error
}
```

The call to **func()** does not compile because the function base template cannot be called with different argument types. If you use overloading instead,

```
#include <iostream>
using std::cout;

template <typename T>
void func(T const &, T const &)
{
   cout << "T const &, T const &\n";
}

void func(int const &, int const &)
```

```
{
  cout << "int const &, int const &\n";
}

int main()
{
  func('A', 1);      // OK now
}

/* Output:

int const &, int const &

*/
```

then the call works because the function base template does not provide a match; the overloaded function does provide a match via a promotion of the first argument from **char** to **int**.

Specializing the **greater()** Function Template

Let's return to the **greater()** function template and consider what happens when the program tries to use **greater()** to determine whether one string is greater than another string:

```
greater("one", "two");
```

When the compiler sees this statement, it instantiates and invokes a template function specialization whose arguments are "reference-to-constant-pointer-to-constant-character." In other words, the compiler passes to the specialization a pair of pointers that point at the two strings; it does not pass the strings themselves to the **greater()** function. Consequently, the **greater()** function compares the two pointers, that is, it compares the *addresses* that are stored in the two pointers; it does *not* compare the values of the two strings that the pointers are pointing at. It should be obvious that the function base template needs to be specialized (or overloaded) to incorporate the use of **std::strcmp()** when comparing string data. While we're at it, we'll specialize the function for both type **char *** and **char const ***. Remember that **char *** and **char const *** are distinct types, and the compiler will not do conversions to match a specialized function template:

```
// File greater.h

#ifndef GREATER_H
#define GREATER_H

#include <cstring>

// Function base template: #1
```

```
template <typename T>
T const &greater(T const &x, T const &y)
{
  return (x > y) ? x : y;
}

// Specialize for type 'char *': #2
typedef char *const &REF_CONST_PTR_CHAR;
template <>
inline REF_CONST_PTR_CHAR greater
      (REF_CONST_PTR_CHAR x, REF_CONST_PTR_CHAR y)
{
  return (std::strcmp(x, y) > 0) ? x : y;
}

// Specialize for type 'char const *': #3
typedef char const *const &REF_CONST_PTR_CONST_CHAR;
template <>
inline REF_CONST_PTR_CONST_CHAR greater
        (REF_CONST_PTR_CONST_CHAR x,
         REF_CONST_PTR_CONST_CHAR y)
{
  return (std::strcmp(x, y) > 0) ? x : y;
}

#endif

// File main.cpp

#include <iostream>
#include "greater.h"
using std::cout;

int main()
{
  double d1 = 5.6, d2 = 7.65;
  cout << greater(d1, d2) << '\n';        // Call #1

  char *s1 = "one", *s2 = "two";
  cout << greater(s1, s2) << '\n';        // Call #2

  char const *s3 = "three", *s4 = "four";
  cout << greater(s3, s4) << '\n';        // Call #3
}
```

```
/* Output:

7.65
two
three

*/
```

If you don't want to make the specializations inline functions, declare them in the header file and define them in a separate definition file. This is how it's done:

```
// File greater.h

#ifndef GREATER_H
#define GREATER_H

// Function base template: #1
template <typename T>
T const &greater(T const &x, T const &y)
{
   return (x > y) ? x : y;
}

// Specialize for type 'char *': #2
typedef char *const &REF_CONST_PTR_CHAR;
template <>
REF_CONST_PTR_CHAR greater(REF_CONST_PTR_CHAR x,
                           REF_CONST_PTR_CHAR y);

// Specialize for type 'char const *': #3
typedef char const *const &REF_CONST_PTR_CONST_CHAR;
template <>
REF_CONST_PTR_CONST_CHAR greater
                              (REF_CONST_PTR_CONST_CHAR x,
                               REF_CONST_PTR_CONST_CHAR y);

#endif

// File specialization.cpp

#include <cstring>
#include "greater.h"

// Specialize for type 'char *': #2
template <>
```

```
REF_CONST_PTR_CHAR greater
                        (REF_CONST_PTR_CHAR x,
                        REF_CONST_PTR_CHAR y)
{
  return (std::strcmp(x, y) > 0) ? x : y;
}

// Specialize for type 'char const *': #3
template <>
REF_CONST_PTR_CONST_CHAR greater
                            (REF_CONST_PTR_CONST_CHAR x,
                            REF_CONST_PTR_CONST_CHAR y)
{
  return (std::strcmp(x, y) > 0) ? x : y;
}

// File main.cpp

#include <iostream>
#include "greater.h"
using std::cout;

int main()
{
  double d1 = 5.6, d2 = 7.65;
  cout << greater(d1, d2) << '\n';        // Call #1

  char *s1 = "one", *s2 = "two";
  cout << greater(s1, s2) << '\n';        // Call #2

  char const *s3 = "three", *s4 = "four";
  cout << greater(s3, s4) << '\n';        // Call #3
}

/* Output:

7.65
two
three

*/
```

EXERCISE 12.3

Specialize the **highest**() function template in Exercise 12.2 to accommodate type
char const *.

EXERCISE 12.4

Write a function template called **count()** that accepts three arguments: a parameterized type representing a pointer to an array, the length of the array, and some value of the array type. Count the number of occurrences of the value within the array and return the resulting count. Instantiate the function using several different types.

Class Templates

A *class template* is a class that creates a "blueprint" that the compiler can use to create class definitions, just as you would do manually, except the compiler does all the work. Like a function template, the class template specifies at least one type that is parameterized. By writing such a class, you provide the user with the ability to instantiate an unbounded family of "like-minded" classes. For example, a class template representing the abstraction of some container type (array, linked list, stack, queue, etc.) can then hold objects of some user-specified type. Therefore, **array<double>** would instantiate an array class that "knows" how to store and manage values of type **double**, **stack<int>** would instantiate a stack class that "knows" how to push and pop values of type **int**, and so on. (This is the basis for the Standard Template Library, discussed in Chapter 18.)

SUMMARY ▶ A class template allows you to write a class that can be instantiated with different types.

How to Define a Class Template

A class template, like a function template, always begins with a template parameter list. You then write the class definition in the normal way, using the parameterized type(s) where appropriate.

For example, the following is the start of a complex number class whose abstraction consists of real and imaginary parts that are some generic type. For good measure, we'll also throw in a static data member:

```
// File complex.h

#ifndef COMPLEX_H
#define COMPLEX_H

template <typename T>
class Complex
{
    public:
  Complex(T const &real = T(), T const &imag = T());
  Complex(Complex const &);
```

```
      private:
   T real, imag;
   static int counter;
};
```

```
#endif
```

Note how the default constructor takes two default arguments using a function-style cast. As with a function template, if **T** is a fundamental type, the expression **T()** will produce whatever value this type would take on if an instance were defined in the global space with no explicit value (i.e., zero). If, however, **T()** is a user-defined type, the expression **T()** will invoke the default constructor for type **T**, and the temporary object that is created will be used to initialize **real** and **imag** (if the programmer does not provide overriding values).

SUMMARY ➤ A class template begins with a template parameter list. Use a function-style cast with no parameter to specify a default function argument.

Defining Members outside the Class Definition

If your class's member functions are not implicitly declared inline (i.e., if the member functions are not defined within the body of the class definition), then they must be defined outside the friendly confines of the class definition. What you have to remember is that, whenever you write the class name itself, it always needs to be *parameterized*. This entails following the class name (e.g., **Complex**) with angle brackets, between which you write the parameterized types that were specified in the template parameter list. You have the option to parameterize the class name inside the class definition.

Also, each class member function, static data member, and friend function definition that is defined outside the class definition must be preceded by its own template parameter list:

```
// File complex.h

#ifndef COMPLEX_H
#define COMPLEX_H

template <typename T>
class Complex
{
    public:
   Complex(T const &real = T(), T const &imag = T());
   Complex(Complex /* <T> */   const &);
    private:
   T real, imag;
   static int counter;
};
```

```
template <typename T>
Complex<T>::Complex(T const &real, T const &imag)
                                    : real(real), imag(imag) { }

template <typename T>
Complex<T>::Complex(Complex<T> const &arg)
                        : real(arg.real), imag(arg.imag) { }

template <typename T>
int Complex<T>::counter = 0;

#endif
```

As with function templates, for now you must use the *inclusion model* of templates, which means that all definitions, whether inlined or not, must reside in the class's header file. Do *not* write a separate definition file for the class.

When defining class members outside the class definition, you must parameterize the class name wherever it's used.

Instantiating a Class Template

The specific types of a *function template* are inferred by the compiler as a result of a call to the function (rather than having you explicitly specify the type), but in the case of a *class template* you are always responsible for explicitly specifying the types to be used. This is done when the class template is instantiated (thereby yielding a *generated class*) by following the class name with the specific type(s) written between angle brackets. This particular syntax can become quite lengthy and cumbersome, especially when it has to be written a number of times, so using a **typedef** is usually a good idea:

```
// Instantiate with type 'int' (without using a 'typedef')
Complex<int> object1(1, 2);
Complex<int> object2(3, 4);

// Instantiate with type 'double' (now using a 'typedef')
typedef Complex<double> COMPLEX_DOUBLE;
COMPLEX_DOUBLE object3(3.4, 5.6);
COMPLEX_DOUBLE object4(-67.4, 98.5);
```

You instantiate a class template by following the class name with the specific type(s) between angle brackets.

Template Instantiation of Another Template

It is possible to instantiate a class template with a type that itself is an instantiation of another class template. Thus, given the following two class templates,

```
template <typename T>
class Complex
{
  // Class members
};

template <typename T>
class Array
{
  // Class members
};
```

you would create an array of complex numbers by writing the following:

```
// Instantiate Array with type Complex<double>
// (Note the mandatory space after "<double>")
Array<Complex<double> > array;
```

Do yourself a favor, however, and use the **typedef** keyword to write it this way:

```
typedef Complex<double> ComplexDouble;
typedef Array< ComplexDouble > ArrayOfComplexDouble;
ArrayOfComplexDouble array;
```

 You can instantiate a class template with another class template that has been instantiated.

Default Template Arguments

Default template arguments are similar to the default arguments that are specified in a function's formal argument list. To write default template arguments, just follow the generic type name with the equal sign and the default type. Naturally, all such defaults must appear last in the template parameter list. When you instantiate the class, you must explicitly specify the mandatory template parameters and optionally override the defaults. If the template parameter list consists of all default values, and you want to accept all of them, simply write empty angle brackets.

In the following example, the class template **Complex** assumes that the type is **double** unless specified otherwise:

```
// File complex.h

#ifndef COMPLEX_H
```

```
#define COMPLEX_H

template <typename T = double> //Default template argument
class Complex
{
    public:
  Complex(T const &real = T(), T const &imag = T());
  Complex(Complex const &);
    private:
  T real, imag;
  static int counter;
};

#endif

// File main.cpp

#include "complex.h"

int main()
{
  // Instantiate with type 'int'
  Complex<int> c1(1, 2);
  // Instantiate with the default type.
  // Angle brackets are still required.
  Complex<> c2(3.4, 5.67);
}
```

SUMMARY The template parameter list can specify default values.

Granting Friendship to a Class from a Class Template

A class template can grant friendship to another class in three different ways. Consider the following class template called **Node** that is granting friendship to three different linked list classes, **List1**, **List2**, and **List3**:

```
// File node.h

#ifndef NODE_H
#define NODE_H

// Forward declaration of List2 as a class template
template <typename T>
class List2;
```

```
template <typename T>
class Node
{
   friend class List1;
   friend class List2<T>;
   template <typename U>
   friend class List3;
};
```

```
#endif
```

- ▲ **List1** is nontemplate class and becomes a friend to *all* instantiations of class **Node**, for example, **Node<int>**, **Node<double>**, and so on.

- ▲ **List2** is a class template of type **T** and is a friend only of instantiations of **Node** with that same type **T**. That is, **List2<int>** is a friend of **Node<int>**, but it is not a friend of **Node<double>**. To tell the compiler that **List2** really is a class template, it *must* be forward-declared as such prior to the definition of class **Node**.

- ▲ **List3** is class template of type **U** such that, when instantiated, it is a friend of *all* generated **Node** classes. That is, **List3<int>** is a friend of **Node<int>**, **Node<double>**, and so on.

Granting Friendship to a Function from a Class Template

Put your seat belts on; the ride might be a little rough. It's time now to have a class template grant friendship to a global function. There are three different scenarios, so let's take them one at a time.

Granting Friendship to a Nontemplate Function

In the following example, the class template **Complex** is granting friendship to the global nontemplate function **operator<<()**. This means that **operator<<()** must be defined for each particular specialization of **Complex** for which it is a friend. If you write the function definitions outside the class definition but within the header file, they must be explicitly inlined to avoid violating the rule that states that noninline function definitions cannot appear inside a header file:

```
// File complex.h

#ifndef COMPLEX_H
#define COMPLEX_H

#include <iostream>

template <typename T>
class Complex
```

```cpp
{
  // Friend declaration as a non-template function
  friend std::ostream &operator<<
                     (std::ostream &, Complex const &);
    public:
  Complex(T const &real = T(), T const &imag = T())
                                      : real(real), imag(imag) { }
    private:
  T real, imag;
};

inline std::ostream &operator<<
              (std::ostream &stream, Complex<int> const &arg)
{
  return stream << arg.real << " + " << arg.imag << 'i';
}

inline std::ostream &operator<<
         (std::ostream &stream, Complex<double> const &arg)
{
  return stream << arg.real << " + " << arg.imag << 'i';
}

#endif

// File main.cpp

#include <iostream>
#include "complex.h"

int main()
{
  Complex<int> complexInt(1, 2);
  std::cout << complexInt << '\n';
  Complex<double> complexDouble(3.3, 4.4);
  std::cout << complexDouble << '\n';
}

/* Output:

1 + 2i
3.3 + 4.4i

*/
```

You probably don't like the previous example very much because it presumes that you know ahead of time what specific types will be needed by the users of your class. You can get around this problem by making the friend function implicit inline:

```cpp
// File complex.h

#ifndef COMPLEX_H
#define COMPLEX_H

#include <iostream>

template <typename T>
class Complex
{
  // Friend definition as a non-template function,
  // implicit inline
  friend std::ostream &operator<<
                      (std::ostream &stream, Complex const &arg)
  {
    return stream << arg.real << " + " << arg.imag << 'i';
  }
    public:
  Complex(T const &real = T(), T const &imag = T())
                      : real(real), imag(imag) { }
    private:
  T real, imag;
};

#endif

// File main.cpp

#include <iostream>
#include "complex.h"

int main()
{
  std::cout << Complex<int>(1, 2) << '\n';
  std::cout << Complex<double>(3.3, 4.4) << '\n';
}

/* Output:

1 + 2i
```

```
3.3 + 4.4i

*/
```

SUMMARY How to grant friendship to a non-template function.

Granting Friendship to a Global Function Template

The second kind of friend declaration also has the class template **Complex** granting friendship to the overloaded insertion operator. The difference now is that the operator is a *function template* in the global space; you must explicitly tell this to the compiler by doing the following:

1. Forward-declare the class name as a class template,
2. Forward-declare the insertion operator as a function template (and don't forget to parameterize the class name),
3. Within the class definition, tell the compiler that the friend declaration is also a function template (as opposed to a nonmember function) by including the parameterized type(s) between angle brackets—**<T>**—immediately after the function name. *Make sure that you only declare the function here, not define it,*
4. Define the insertion operator outside the class definition as a function template (inlined, if you want).

See the following for an example:

```cpp
// File complex.h

#ifndef COMPLEX_H
#define COMPLEX_H

#include <iostream>

// Forward declaration of the class template
template <typename T>
class Complex;
// Forward declaration of the insertion operator
template <typename T>
std::ostream &operator<<
                    (std::ostream &, Complex<T> const &);

// Definition of the template class 'Complex'
template <typename T>
class Complex
```

```
{
    // Friend declaration as a function template
    friend std::ostream &operator<< <T>    //  Note the <T>
                            (std::ostream &, Complex const &);
      public:
    Complex(T const &real = T(), T const &imag = T())
                            : real(real), imag(imag) { }
      private:
    T real, imag;
};

// Definition of the function template
template <typename T>
std::ostream &operator<<
              (std::ostream &stream, Complex<T> const &arg)
{
    return stream << arg.real << " + " << arg.imag << 'i';
}

#endif

// File main.cpp

#include <iostream>
#include "complex.h"

int main()
{
    std::cout << Complex<int>(1, 2) << '\n';
    std::cout << Complex<double>(3.3, 4.4) << '\n';
}

/* Output:

1 + 2i
3.3 + 4.4i

*/
```

Now every instantiation of **Complex** with a specific type creates a friend insertion operator taking a **Complex** object of that type. In other words, **operator<< <int>**() is a friend of **Complex<int>**, **operator<< <double>**() is a friend of **Complex<double>**, and so forth.

SUMMARY ▶ How to grant friendship to a global function template.

Granting Friendship to a Nested Function Template

The third case also involves making the insertion operator a function template, but in a slightly different fashion. Here the friend declaration is immediately preceded by its own template parameter list (using a different type than the class's template parameter list), thereby making it totally nested within the class definition. No forward declaration of the insertion operator is needed. Also, be sure to parameterize the class name using this type in the friend declaration. The definition of the function template is the same as the previous example:

```cpp
// File complex.h

#ifndef COMPLEX_H
#define COMPLEX_H

#include <iostream>

template <typename T>
class Complex
{
  template <typename U>
  friend std::ostream &operator<<
                      (std::ostream &, Complex<U> const &);
    public:
  Complex(T const &real = T(), T const &imag = T())
                      : real(real), imag(imag) { }
    private:
  T real, imag;
};

template <typename T>
std::ostream &operator<<
              (std::ostream &stream, Complex<T> const &arg)
{
  Complex<char> c;
  c.real = 'A';              // OK
  return stream << arg.real << " + " << arg.imag << 'i';
}

#endif

// File main.cpp

#include <iostream>
#include "complex.h"
```

```
int main()
{
  std::cout << Complex<int>(1, 2) << '\n';
  std::cout << Complex<double>(3.3, 4.4) << '\n';
}

/* Output:

1 + 2i
3.3 + 4.4i

*/
```

What's different here is that the insertion operator that is instantiated with a specific type is a friend of *every* specialization of the **Complex** class template; its friendship is not restricted to the one **Complex** class specialization that has its same type. This is proven by the fact that the function definition creates its own instance of **Complex** specialized with type **char**. Sure enough, the function has no trouble gaining access to the private data member **real** of **Complex<char>**, even though the function has been instantiated first with type **int** and then with type **double**.

SUMMARY⯈ How to grant friendship to a nested function template.

Specializing a Class Template

Just like a function template, a class template can be specialized. The big difference, however, is that a class template can be either *partially* or *fully* specialized, whereas a function template can be only *fully* specialized.

SUMMARY⯈ A class template can be either partially or fully specialized.

Full Specialization

A full specialization means that all parameterized types in the primary class template are replaced with known concrete types. Here is an outline of what it looks like:

```
// Primary class template
template <typename T>
class ADT
{
  T data;
  // ...
};
// Full specialization for T=int
template <>
class ADT<int>
```

```
{
  int data;
  // ...
};
// Full specialization for T=double
template <>
class ADT<double>
{
  double data;
  // ...
};
```

To do this, make sure that the compiler has seen the primary class template. Then:

1. Write an empty template parameter list: **template <>**,
2. Start the definition of a class with the same name as the class template,
3. After the class name, list the specific type(s) between angle brackets,
4. In the class definition, replace all occurrences of the generic type(s) with the specific type(s).

Here is a simplified version of the **Complex** class template, followed by a full specialization for type **int**:

```
// File complex.h

#ifndef COMPLEX_H
#define COMPLEX_H

#include <iostream>

template <typename T>
class Complex
{
    public:
  Complex(T const &real = T(), T const &imag = T());
  Complex(Complex const &);
  ~Complex() { }
    protected:
  T real, imag;
};

template <typename T>
Complex<T>::Complex(T const &real, T const &imag)
                                : real(real), imag(imag)
```

```cpp
{
  std::cout << "Template default ctor\n";
}

template <typename T>
Complex<T>::Complex(Complex<T> const &arg)
                            : real(arg.real), imag(arg.imag)
{
  std::cout << "Template copy ctor\n";
}

// Start full specialization for T=int
template <>
class Complex<int>
{
    public:
  inline Complex(int const & = int(), int const & = int());
  inline Complex(Complex<int> const &);
  ~Complex() { }
    protected:
  int real, imag;
};

inline Complex<int>::Complex(int const &r, int const &i)
                                        : real(r), imag(i)
{
  std::cout << "Specialized default ctor\n";
}

inline Complex<int>::Complex(Complex<int> const &arg)
                            : real(arg.real), imag(arg.imag)
{
  std::cout << "Specialized copy ctor\n";
}

#endif

// File main.cpp

#include "complex.h"

int main()
{
  typedef Complex<double> CD;
```

```
    CD c1(1.11, 2.22), c2(c1);

    typedef Complex<int> CI;
    CI c3(1, 2), c4(c3);
}

/* Output:

Template default ctor
Template copy ctor
Specialized default ctor
Specialized copy ctor

*/
```

If you fail to specialize any particular function in the class template, a specialized instantiation will not be able to call it. In addition, as with the specializing of function templates, the definitions must be inlined to prevent a duplicate definition error from occurring (if more than one implementation file includes the header file). The alternative is to create a separate definition file for the member functions of the specialized **Complex** class, as done here:

```
// File complex.h

#ifndef COMPLEX_H
#define COMPLEX_H

#include <iostream>

template <typename T>
class Complex
{
    public:
  Complex(T const &real = T(), T const &imag = T());
  Complex(Complex const &);
  ~Complex() { }
    protected:
  T real, imag;
};

template <typename T>
Complex<T>::Complex(T const &real, T const &imag)
                                  : real(real), imag(imag)
{
  std::cout << "Template default ctor\n";
}
```

```cpp
template <typename T>
Complex<T>::Complex(Complex<T> const &arg)
                          : real(arg.real), imag(arg.imag)
{
  std::cout << "Template copy ctor\n";
}

template <>
class Complex<int>
{
    public:
  Complex(int const & = int(), int const & = int());
  Complex(Complex<int> const &);
  ~Complex() { }
    protected:
  int real, imag;
};

#endif

// File complex.cpp

#include <iostream>
#include "complex.h"

Complex<int>::Complex(int const &real, int const &imag)
                                : real(real), imag(imag)
{
  std::cout << "Specialized default ctor\n";
}

Complex<int>::Complex(Complex<int> const &arg)
                          : real(arg.real), imag(arg.imag)
{
  std::cout << "Specialized copy ctor\n";
}

// File main.cpp

#include "complex.h"

int main()
{
  typedef Complex<double> ComplexDouble;
  ComplexDouble c1(1.11, 2.22), c2(c1);
```

```
    typedef Complex<int> ComplexInt;
    ComplexInt c3(1, 2), c4(c3);
}


/* Output:

Template default ctor
Template copy ctor
Specialized default ctor
Specialized copy ctor


*/
```

Partial Specialization

You partially specialize a class template in somewhat the same way you did full specialization, but, rather than listing one or more specific types after the class name between angle brackets, you list generic type(s). It's even possible to list a generic pointer type. In addition, no default values are allowed in a partial specialization of a class template. For example:

```
// Primary class template: #1
template <typename T, typename U>
class ADT { }; // ( Illegal: class ADT<T, U> { }; )

// Specialize when T is any pointer: #2
template <typename T, typename U>
class ADT<T *, U> { };

// Specialize when U is a pointer of type T: #3
template <typename T>
class ADT<T, T *> { };

// Specialize when T is type 'int', and U is any pointer: #4
template <typename U>
class ADT<int, U *> { };

int main()
{
    ADT<int *, double> ();      // Call #2
    ADT<int, double *> ();      // Call #4
    ADT<int, double> ();        // Call #1
    ADT<int *, int *> ();       // Call #2
    ADT<int *, int> ();         // Call #2
```

```
    ADT<int , int> ();        // Call #1
    ADT<int, int *>();        // Error; ambiguous
}
```

Here is an explanation of all the instantiations:

- ▲ The first instantiation calls #2, making **T** type **int** and **U** type **double**. #3 and #4 are not callable because a **double** cannot be converted to a pointer type.
- ▲ The second instantiation calls #4, making **U** type **int**. #2 is not callable because an **int** cannot be converted to a pointer type, and #3 is not callable because **T** cannot represent an **int** and a **double** at the same time.
- ▲ The third instantiation calls #1 because all specializations require at least one pointer type.
- ▲ The fourth instantiation calls #2, making **T** type **int** and **U** type **int** *. #3 is not callable because **T** cannot represent an **int** * and an **int** at the same time.
- ▲ The fifth instantiation calls #2, making **T** type **int** and **U** type **int**. #3 and #4 are not callable because the second type must be a pointer.
- ▲ The sixth instantiation calls #1, making **T** type **int** and **U** type **int**. All of the specializations require at least one pointer type.
- ▲ The seventh instantiation is ambiguous because the compiler is able to invoke #3 by making **T** type **int**, and it is able to invoke #4 by making **U** type **int**.

As a more realistic example, suppose you wish to make sure that the users of the **Complex** class are not allowed to specify pointer types when instantiating specializations of the **Complex** class. In other words, users should not be allowed to specify a pointer type (e.g., **char** *) for the generic type **T** in the primary class template. To accomplish this, simply *declare* (do not also *define*) a partial specialization of the **Complex** class template for the generic pointer type **T***. If the user then tries to specify a pointer type when instantiating a specialization of the **Complex** class, the compiler will complain (via an error message) that the **T** * partial specialization is undefined (or that it is an incomplete type, or whatever). Of course, when you use this technique you should also provide (in the source code) an explanation of why this partial specialization is undefined. Otherwise, the users of the **Complex** class will be left wondering why their code fails to compile (is the compiler emitting an error message because my code has a syntax error? Or is there a bug in the **Complex** class code? Or is this a "feature" of the **Complex** class code?). Here is the code:

```
// File complex.h

#ifndef COMPLEX_H
#define COMPLEX_H

template <typename T>
class Complex
```

```
{
    public:
  Complex(T const &real = T(), T const &imag = T())
                            : real(real), imag(imag) { }
    private:
  T real, imag;
};

//The following partial specialization is intentionally
//undefined (it is only declared). Its purpose is to
//prevent the compiler from implicitly instantiating
//specializations of the Complex class for pointer
//types, e.g.,
//Complex<X*> cx;    <- Compile-time error
template <typename T>
class Complex<T *>;

#endif

// File main.cpp

#include <iostream>
#include "complex.h"

int main()
{
  Complex<double> d;
  Complex<int *> pi; // Error; incomplete type
}
```

Nesting a Class Template within a Class Template

Rather than having a class template #1 grant friendship to another class template #2, it's possible to nest #1 inside #2 and avoid the friendship. Of course, it's also possible to retain the friendship.

In the following example, the (nontemplate) **Node** class, being just an implementation detail of the **List** class, is completely defined within the **List** class. Note, however, that the template parameter list is used only with the **List** class:

```
// File list.h

#ifndef LIST_H
#define LIST_H

#include <iostream>
```

```
template <typename T>
class List;
template <typename T>
std::ostream &operator<<(std::ostream &, List<T> const &);

template <typename T>
class List
{
  friend std::ostream &operator<< <T>
                    (std::ostream &, List const &);
    public:
  List();
  List(T const &);
  List &add(T const &);
    private:
  class Node
  {
    friend std::ostream &operator<<
                    (std::ostream &stream, Node const &node)
    {
      return stream << node.data << '\n';
    }
      public:
    Node(T const &);
    Node *getNext() const;
    void setNext(Node *);
      private:
    T data;
    Node *next;
  }; // End class Node
  Node *head, *tail;
};

template <typename T>
List<T>::Node::Node(T const &arg) : data(arg), next(0) { }

template <typename T>
List<T>::Node *List<T>::Node::getNext() const
{
  return next;
}

template <typename T>
void List<T>::Node::setNext(List<T>::Node *ptrNode)
```

```cpp
{
  next = ptrNode;
}

template <typename T>
std::ostream &operator<<
                    (std::ostream &stream, List<T> const &list)
{
  typename     // Note 'typename' here
  List<T>::Node *start = list.head;
  while(start)
  {
    stream << *start;
    start = start->getNext();
  }
  return stream;
}

template <typename T>
List<T>::List() : head(0), tail(0) { }

template <typename T>
List<T>::List(T const &arg) : head(0), tail(0)
{
  add(arg);
}

template <typename T>
List<T> &List<T>::add(T const &arg)
{
  Node *newNode = new Node(arg);
  if(head = = 0)
    head = newNode;
  else
    tail->setNext(newNode);
  tail = newNode;
  return *this;
}

#endif

// File main.cpp

#include <iostream>
#include "list.h"
```

```
int main()
{
  typedef List<int> T;
  T list;
  list.add(1).add(2).add(3);
  std::cout << list;
}

/* Output

1
2
3

*/
```

CAUTION The use of the keyword **typename** in the **List** insertion operator function will be discussed later in this chapter.

Deriving from a Class Template

It's quite easy to derive from a class template, even if a new generic type is introduced into the derived class. For example, let's do exactly that for the **Complex** class in order to create a new class called **ComplexDerived** that has its own generic type; then we'll show the definitions of all of the manager functions in the derived class:

```
// File complex.h

#ifndef COMPLEX_H
#define COMPLEX_H

template <typename T>
class Complex
{
    public:
  Complex(T const &real = T(), T const &imag = T());
  Complex(Complex const &);
  Complex &operator=(Complex const &);
  ~Complex() { }
    protected:
  T real, imag;
};

#endif

// File complexderived.h
```

```
#ifndef COMPLEX_DERIVED_H
#define COMPLEX_DERIVED_H

#include "complex.h"

template <typename T>
class ComplexDerived : public Complex<T>
{
    public:
  ComplexDerived();
  ComplexDerived(ComplexDerived const &);
  ComplexDerived &operator=(ComplexDerived const &);
  ~ComplexDerived();
};

template <typename T>
ComplexDerived<T>::ComplexDerived() : Complex<T>() { }

template <typename T>
ComplexDerived<T>::ComplexDerived
        (ComplexDerived const &arg) : Complex<T>(arg) { }

template <typename T>
ComplexDerived<T> &ComplexDerived<T>::operator=
        (ComplexDerived<T> const &arg)
{
  Complex<T>::operator=(arg);
  return *this;
}

template <typename T>
ComplexDerived<T>::~ComplexDerived() { }

#endif
```

You can also derive from a class template and specialize it at the same time. Then the derived class inherits everything in the base class (except the manager functions). Simply write the normal syntax to create a derived class, but list the specific type(s) between angle brackets after the base class name.

For example, let's derive again from the **Complex** class to create a class called **ComplexInt**:

```
// File complex.h
```

```
#ifndef COMPLEX_H
#define COMPLEX_H

#include <iostream>

template <typename T>
class Complex
{
    public:
  Complex(T const &real = T(), T const &imag = T());
  Complex(Complex const &);
  Complex &operator=(Complex const &);
  ~Complex() { }
    protected:
  T real, imag;
};

#endif

// File complexint.h

#ifndef COMPLEX_INT_H
#define COMPLEX_INT_H

#include "complex.h"

class ComplexInt : public Complex<int>
{
    public:
  inline ComplexInt
      (int const &real = int(), int const &imag = int());
};

inline ComplexInt::ComplexInt
                            (int const &real, int const &imag)
                            : Complex<int>(real, imag) { }

#endif

int main()
{
  ComplexInt c1(5, 6);
}
```

Nontype Template Arguments

In addition to being instantiated with arguments of a specified *type*, a class template can be instantiated with specific *values*. The "placeholders" for these values in the template parameter list are specific types—**int**, **char**, and so forth—with the restriction that such types must be integral (as opposed to floating-point and user-defined). In addition, when the class template is instantiated, the specific integral values used must be *constant*. As a result, such values are known at compilation time. A template declaration can freely combine generic types and specific values.

The following example consists of a class that encapsulates a fixed-length array of some generic type. The dimension of this array, called **dim**, is not hard-coded within the class itself, but rather is provided at instantiation time by the user:

```
// File array.h

#ifndef ARRAY_H
#define ARRAY_H

template <typename T, int dim>
class Array
{
    public:
  Array();
    private:
  T array[dim];       // OK; dim is known at compilation time
};

template <typename T, int dim>
Array<T, dim>::Array()
{
  for(int i = 0; i < dim; ++i)
    array[i] = T();
}

#endif

// File main.cpp

#include "array.h"

int main()
{
  Array<int, 5> array1;                    // OK
  int const size = 6;
```

```
Array<double, size> array2;      // OK
int length = 7;
Array<long, length> array3;      // Error; 'length' is not
                                 // constant
Array<char, 1.2> array4;         // Error; 1.2 is not integral
}
```

Nontype template arguments can be freely combined with generic types. When replaced by the compiler, they must be integral and constant.

EXERCISE 12.5

Question: What do you have to say about the **for** loop in the constructor? What is it doing? Is it necessary? Is there any other way to achieve the same result?

Default Template Arguments and Specialization

Consider this simple example in which a nontype template argument has a default value, followed by a specialization of the primary class template:

```
#include <iostream>

template <typename T, int size = 1>
struct ADT
{
  void print() const
  {
    std::cout << "Primary class template\n";
  }
};

template <>
struct ADT<char>
{
  void print() const
  {
    std::cout << "Specialization\n";
  }
};

int main()
{
  ADT<char>().print();
  ADT<char, 1>().print();
}
```

```
/* Output:

Specialization
Specialization

*/
```

Are you surprised at the results? The primary class template is declared with two parameters (even though the second is a default), so the specialization "inherits" the default value. It's as though you had written the following:

```
template <>
struct ADT<char, 1>
{
  void print() const
  {
    std::cout << "Specialization\n";
  }
};
```

For the first call, the default value is assumed, so it's as though you had written this:

```
int main()
{
  ADT<char, 1>().print();
  ADT<char, 1>().print();
}
```

Because these two calls match the specialization exactly, the primary class template never gets invoked.

An Interesting Example Using Nontype Template Arguments

If you're wondering what else can be done with nontype template arguments, here is a way to compute a factorial (the hard way!):

```
// File factorial.h

#ifndef FACTORIAL_H
#define FACTORIAL_H

template <long n>
class Factorial : private Factorial<n - 1>
{
    public:
  Factorial() { }       // Required because an explicitly defined
                        // constructor is needed to accommodate a
                        // constant object
```

```
   long factorial() const;
};

template <long n>
inline long Factorial<n>::factorial() const
{
   return n * Factorial<n - 1>::factorial();
}

// Full class specialization
template <>
class Factorial<0L>
{
    public:
   long factorial() const;
};

inline long Factorial<0L>::factorial() const
{
   return 1L;
}

#endif

// File main.cpp

#include <iostream>
#include "factorial.h"

int main()
{
   Factorial<10> const fact;
   std::cout << fact.factorial() << '\n';
}

/* Output:

3628800

*/
```

As is the case with most programs we've seen so far, this example does most of its work at run time. The next code example, however, is vastly different from anything we've seen so far. In this example, the *compiler* computes the value of each factorial. That's right: The factorial values are computed at *compile time*. The factorial values are *not* (I repeat, *are not*) computed at run time! (Of course, the factorial values are *displayed* at run time using the **cout** output stream.) This example hints at the kinds of advanced, compile-time "meta-programming" techniques that are possible with C++ templates:

```cpp
// File factorial.h

#ifndef FACTORIAL_H
#define FACTORIAL_H

// Recursive case
template <long n>
struct factorial
{
   enum { value = n * factorial<n-1>::value };
};

// Special ending case (n == 0)
template <>
struct factorial<0>
{
   enum { value = 1 };
};

#endif

// File main.cpp
#include <iostream>
#include "factorial.h"

int main()
{
   std::cout << factorial<0>::value << '\n'
             << factorial<1>::value << '\n'
             << factorial<10>::value << '\n';
}

/* Output:

1
1
3628800

*/
```

 Use a nontype (value-based) template to compute a factorial.

Member Templates

A *member template* is a member function of a class that is also a nested function template. The enclosing class itself need not be a class template. For example, the following class encapsulates the **greater**() function template as a static, and then overloads it with one taking a **char const** * type:

```
// File greater.h

#ifndef GREATER_H
#define GREATER_H

class Greater
{
    public:
  template <typename T>
  static T const &greater(T const &first, T const &second);
  typedef char const *const &PC;
  static PC greater(PC first, PC second);
};

template <typename T>
T const &Greater::greater(T const &first, T const &second)
{
  return (first > second) ? first : second;
}

#endif

// File greater.cpp

#include <cstring>
#include "greater.h"

typedef char const *const &PC;
PC Greater::greater(PC first, PC second)
{
  return (std::strcmp(first, second) > 0) ? first : second;
}

#endif

// File main.cpp
```

```cpp
#include <iostream>
#include "greater.h"

int main()
{
  int x = 4, y = 3;
  std::cout << Greater::greater(x, y) << '\n';
  char const *one = "one", *two = "two";
  std::cout << Greater::greater(one, two) << '\n';
}


/* Output:

4
two

*/
```

CAUTION   In-class specialization of member templates is not allowed.

Now let's turn to nonstatic member templates. Why would using these be useful? Consider again the **Complex** class template. Because instantiations with different types create objects that have no relationship to each other, no conversion is allowed between these objects:

```cpp
Complex<double> c1;
Complex<int> c2;
c1 = c2;                // Error; no conversion
Complex<int> c3(c1);   // Error; no conversion
```

It might make sense to allow a **Complex** instantiated with one type to be converted to a **Complex** instantiated with a different type, so you can make it valid by writing member templates for the copy constructor and assignment operator. Instead of receiving an argument of the same class type as the one pointed at by the **this** pointer, member templates can (but do not need to) receive an argument that is a completely different type. When using member templates, a different type can be introduced and used to parameterize the argument. Note that in the definitions of the functions, both template parameter lists need to be written as the following:

```cpp
// File complex.h

#ifndef COMPLEX_H
#define COMPLEX_H

#include <iostream>
```

```cpp
template <typename T>
class Complex;
template <typename T>
std::ostream &operator<<
                    (std::ostream &, Complex<T> const &);

template <typename T>
class Complex
{
    friend std::ostream &operator<< <T>
                        (std::ostream &, Complex const &);
        public:
    T real, imag;
    Complex(T const &real = T(), T const &imag = T())
                        : real(real), imag(imag) { }

    // Copy constructor member template declaration
    template <typename U>
    Complex(Complex<U> const &);

    // Assignment operator member template declaration
    template <typename U>
    Complex& operator = (Complex<U> const &);
};

template <typename T>
std::ostream &operator<<
                (std::ostream &stream, Complex<T> const &arg)
{
    return stream << arg.real << '+' << arg.imag << 'i';
}

// Copy constructor member template definition
template <typename T>
template <typename U>
Complex<T>::Complex(Complex<U> const &arg)
                : real(arg.real), imag(arg.imag) { }

// Assignment operator member template definition
template <typename T>
template <typename U>
Complex<T>& Complex<T>::operator=(Complex<U> const &arg)
{
    real = arg.real;
```

```
        imag = arg.imag;
        return *this;
    }

    #endif

    // File main.cpp

    #include <iostream>
    #include "complex.h"
    using std::cout;

    int main()
    {
        Complex<int> c1(4, 5);
        Complex<double> c2(c1);
        cout << c1 << '\n';
        cout << c2 << '\n';
        c2 = c1;
        cout << c2 << '\n';
    }

    /* Output:

    4+5i
    4+5i
    4+5i

    */
```

SUMMARY ▶ A member function template is a member function that is declared as a nested function template. It is useful for conversions between different class template types. ·

Overloading a Member Function Template with a Nontemplate Function

Note that within a class you can overload a nontemplate function with a member function template. If the member function template is to be specialized, this must occur outside the class definition:

```
// File adt.h
#ifndef ADT_H
#define ADT_T
```

```cpp
class ADT
{
    public:
  void func(int);                          // #1

  template <typename T>
  void func(T const &);                    // #2

  template <typename T>
  static void func2(T const &);            // #3
};

// Declare an explicit specialization for T = int
template <>
void ADT::func<int>(int const &);          // #4

#endif

// File main.cpp
#include "adt.h"

void test1(ADT &object)
{
  object.func(123);                        // #1
  object.func<int>(2.5);                   // #4
  object.func(1.2);                        // #2
  object.func<double>(123);                // #2
  ADT::func2('A');                         // #3
  ADT::func2<char>(1.2);                   // #3
}

template <typename T>
void test2(T &object)
{
  object.template func<T>(object);         // #2
  object.template func<char>('A');         // #2
  object.template func<int>(123);          // #4

  T::template func2<T>(object);            // #3
  T::template func2<char>(123);            // #3
  T::template func2<int>(123);             // #3

  ADT::func2<char>('A');                   // #3
  ADT::template func2<char>('A');          // #3
```

```
        T *ptr = &object;
        ptr->template func<T>(object);          // #2
        ptr->template func<char>('A');          // #2
        ptr->template func<int>(123);           // #4
    }

int main()
{
    ADT adt;
    test1(adt);
    test2(adt);
}
```

Take a close look at the function calls in the body of template function **test2**. That weird-looking syntax involving the keyword **template** is mandatory because, in certain contexts, the compiler incorrectly views the left angle bracket < as the less-than operator and not as the start of a template parameter list. Inserting the keyword **template** in these contexts tells the compiler that the left angle bracket < is the start of a template parameter list.

So when is this special syntax required? To begin with, this syntax can *only* be used within the context of a template. Function **test1**() is not a template, so this syntax cannot be used within function **test1**(). Next, this syntax can be used only if the member template function name (e.g., **func**) is followed by a template argument list (e.g., **<char>**). And finally, this syntax *must* be used when the "thing" to the left of the member template function name (e.g., **object, ptr, T::**) explicitly depends on a template parameter. For example, you cannot know **object**'s type until the program specifies **T**'s type, so **object** explicitly depends on the template parameter **T**. If the "thing" to the left of the member template function name does not explicitly depend on a template parameter (e.g., **ADT::**), then use of the special syntax is optional.

Template Models

Until now, all template definitions have appeared in the header file so that they are known at compilation time. This makes sense because, if you were to create a separate definition file, how could it be compiled into object format? Think about it. The function contains one or more generic types, so it's impossible for the compiler to know if operations using those generic types are valid. For example, if you try to display an object of type **T** using an overloaded insertion operator, does type **T** support this operation? Beats me.

Two big problems (at least!) exist with this model. The first is that many translation units might have to include this header file, thus increasing compilation time and the sizes of the resulting object modules. Second, there is no way to prevent the user from seeing your source code (which you might like to keep secret), because all of the code is stored in a header file.

A much better approach is to treat template code just like any other C++ code, that is, provide a declaration in a header file and a definition in an implementation file. This approach is known as the *separate compilation* model of templates, and it is accomplished by writing the C++ keyword **export** in front of the template parameter list for both the declaration and the definition. This keyword instructs the compiler and linker to (somehow) provide a definition of the **greater**() function using type **int**.

Here is our old friend the **greater**() function template now modularized into a header and implementation file. The user of the function only has to include the header file:

```
// File greater.h

#ifndef GREATER_H
#define GREATER_H

export template <typename T>
T const &greater(T const &x, T const &y);

#endif

// File greater.cpp
export template <typename T>
T const &greater(T const &x, T const &y)
{
   return (x > y) ? x : y;
}

// File main.cpp

#include <iostream>
#include "greater.h"

int main()
{
   int a = 1, b = 2;
   std::cout << greater(a, b) << '\n';
}

/* Output:

2

*/
```

The separate compilation model can be applied to the **Complex** class. Once again, the user needs to include only the class's header file:

```cpp
// File complex.h

#ifndef COMPLEX_H
#define COMPLEX_H

export template <typename T>
class Complex
{
    public:
  Complex(T const &real = T(), T const &imag = T());
  Complex(Complex const &);
  ~Complex() { }
    protected:
  T real, imag;
};

#endif

// File complex.cpp

#include <iostream>
#include "complex.h"

export template <typename T>
Complex<T>::Complex(T const &real, T const &imag)
                            : real(real), imag(imag)
{
  std::cout << "Default ctor\n";
}

export template <typename T>
Complex<T>::Complex(Complex<T> const &arg)
                            : real(arg.real), imag(arg.imag)
{
  std::cout << "Copy ctor\n";
}

// File main.cpp

#include "complex.h"

int main()
```

```
{
   typedef Complex<double> ComplexDouble;
   ComplexDouble c1(1.11, 2.22), c2(c1);

   typedef Complex<int> ComplexInt;
   ComplexInt c3(1, 2), c4(c3);
}

/* Output:

Default ctor
Copy ctor
Default ctor
Copy ctor

*/
```

CAUTION   Your favorite compiler might not (yet) support the **export** keyword.

typename Keyword

A rule in the C++ Standard states: "a name used in a template is assumed not to name a type unless it has been explicitly declared to refer to a type in the context enclosing the template declaration or is qualified by the keyword **typename**." This situation can be illustrated by the following example:

```
template <typename T>
class X : public T
{
   T::Int data;        // Error
};

class Y
{
     public:
   typedef long int Int;
   // ...
};

class Z
{
     public:
   void Int() const;
};
```

When the class template **X** is parsed, the compiler has no idea if **T::Int** is or is not a valid type. After all, it could have been created as the result of a **typedef** in class **T** from which class **X** is derived, thus making it valid in the context of class **X** (consider **X<Y>**). On the other hand, **T::Int** might not be a data type at all; it might be the name of one of the member functions in class **T** (consider **X<Z>**), or it might not exist at all! In either case, the declaration of the data member named **data** in class **X** makes absolutely no sense if **T::Int** does not describe a **typedef** within the base class **T**. According to the previously mention C++ Standard rule, the compiler chooses to assume that **T::Int** does *not* name a type (because the program did not explicitly declare it as such), and it simply issues an error message on the line of code that tries to declare the data member **data** in class **X**'s definition.

The solution is to tell the compiler explicitly that **T::Int** is a valid type by preceding the declaration of **T::Int** with the keyword **typename** in class **T**'s definition:

```
template <typename T>
class X : public T
{
    typename T::Int data;      // OK
};
```

Of course, when class **X** gets instantiated, it must be with some user-defined type that does indeed provide a suitable **typedef** to replace the generic type **T::Int**:

```
template <typename T>
class X : public T
{
    typename T::Int data;      // OK
};

class Y
{
    // empty
};

class Z
{
    typedef int Int;
};

int main()
{
    X<double> x1;              // Error
    X<Y> x2;                   // Error
    X<Z> x3;                   // OK
}
```

EXERCISE 12.6

Write a generic **Array** class that can accommodate literally any type of data. Instantiate the class with the number of elements specified as a nontemplate parameter.

EXERCISE 12.7

Create a class template called **Primitive** that encapsulates a generic primitive data member, such as, **int**, **double**, and so on. Write all of the indicated class functions.

```cpp
// File primitive.h

#ifndef PRIMITIVE_H
#define PRIMITIVE_H

#include <iostream>

template <typename T>
class Primitive
{
    public:
// Default/converting constructor
// Copy constructor
// Assignment operator
// Insertion operator
// Equality operator
// Binary +
// Unary +
// Unary -
    private:
 T data;
};

// All template definitions go here

#endif

// File main.cpp

#include <iostream>
#include "primitive.h"
using std::cout;
```

```
int main()
{
 typedef Primitive<int> Pi;
 Pi obj1(1), obj2(2), obj3(obj1 + obj2);
 cout << obj3 << '\n';
 cout << ((obj1 == obj2) ? "equal" : "unequal") << '\n';
 cout << ((obj1 == obj1) ? "equal" : "unequal") << '\n';
 typedef Primitive<double> Pd;
 Pd obj4(34.639), obj5(obj4);
 obj4 = obj5;
 cout << +(-(obj4)) << '\n';
}
```

EXERCISE 12.8

Modify the **Pointer** class from Chapter 10 so that it can accommodate a pointer of any type. Test the class with both a primitive and a user-defined type.

13

Runtime Type Information

Introduction

Runtime type information (RTTI) is a mechanism by which the type of an object can be determined at execution time rather than at compilation time. It consists of two parts: dynamic casting and the **typeid** keyword.

Dynamic Casting

If you have a pointer or reference of some base class type, it might, of course, be pointing or referring to either a base class object or a derived class object:

```
Base *ptr;
// ...
ptr = new Base;      // OK
delete ptr;
ptr = new Derived;   // OK; same pointer used
delete ptr;
```

From Chapter 11, you know that if you wish to invoke a certain function with this pointer or reference, and this function has been declared virtual in the base class, then there is absolutely no problem because polymorphism will automatically take effect:

```
class Base
{
    public:
```

```
    virtual void func();
};

class Derived : public Base
{
    public:
    virtual void func();
};

void test(Base *ptr)
{
    ptr->func();        // Call Base::func or Derived::func
}
```

Suppose, however, that this function is first declared in the derived class so that the base class knows nothing about it. In this case, the compiler does not allow you to call the function using a base class pointer or reference:

```
class Base
{
  // ...
};

class Derived : public Base
{
    public:
    void func();
};

void test(Base *ptr)
{
    ptr->func();        // Compiler error; no Base::func
}
```

Instead, you must use a pointer or reference of the specific derived class type in order to invoke the function:

```
class Base
{
  // ...
};

class Derived : public Base
{
    public:
    void func();
};
```

```
void test(Derived *ptr)
{
   ptr->func();        // OK
}
```

But if all you have to work with is a base class pointer, what are you going to do? That is, how do you know if this pointer does, in fact, point to an instance of the base class or the derived class? If it's the derived class, then you can safely cast the base class pointer to a derived class pointer (called a *downcast*). To answer this critical question, you need to use the **dynamic_cast** keyword.

SUMMARY ► Given a base class pointer, you may need to know if it can safely be downcast to a derived class pointer.

How Dynamic Casting Works

The format of a **dynamic_cast** is identical to the new style of casting you learned in Chapter 1. If a base class pointer is used in the downcast, and the pointer does indeed point to a derived class object, the resultant derived class pointer will be nonzero. If the base class pointer does not point to a derived class object, the resultant derived class pointer will be zero.

In the case of a base class reference, if it does refer to a derived class object, the resultant derived class reference is created successfully. However, when the reference does not refer to a derived class object, it's impossible to create a "null" reference, so an exception of type **std::base_cast** will be thrown.

CAUTION ► Because the dynamic cast mechanism uses the compiler's table of virtual functions, the base class must contain at least one virtual function.

Here is a simple example to illustrate the use of **dynamic_cast**:

```
// File base.h

#ifndef BASE_H
#define BASE_H

class Base
{
    public:
   virtual ~Base() { }
};

#endif

// File derived.h

#ifndef DERIVED_H
```

```cpp
#define DERIVED_H

#include "base.h"

class Derived : public Base
{
  // ...
};

#endif

// File main.cpp

#include <iostream>
#include "base.h"
#include "derived.h"
using std::cout;

void func(Base *ptrBase, Base &refBase)
{
  Derived *ptrDerived = dynamic_cast<Derived *>(ptrBase);
  if(ptrDerived)
    cout << "Pointing to a Derived\n";
  else
    cout << "Pointing to a Base\n";
  try
  {
    Derived &refDerived = dynamic_cast<Derived &>(refBase);
    cout << "Referring to a Derived\n";
  }
  catch(std::bad_cast const &)
  {
    cout << "Referring to a Base\n";
  }
}

int main()
{
  Base *ptrBase1 = new Base;
  Base &refBase1 = *ptrBase1;
  func(ptrBase1, refBase1);
  delete ptrBase1;

  Base *ptrBase2 = new Derived;
```

```
    Base &refBase2 = *ptrBase2;
    func(ptrBase2, refBase2);
    delete ptrBase2;
}

/* Output:

Pointing to a Base
Referring to a Base
Pointing to a Derived
Referring to a Derived

*/
```

Use the **dynamic_cast** keyword to determine if a base class pointer or reference can safely be downcast.

The typeid Keyword

The **typeid** keyword is used to retrieve type information about an object, a type, a variable, or any valid C++ expression. Unlike the **dynamic_cast** keyword that is used to perform a safe downcast, the **typeid** keyword can be used with nonpolymorphic types (such as primitive types and classes without a virtual function).

The use of **typeid** requires that you include the header file **typeinfo**. To retrieve type-related information about something called **arg**, where **arg** is a type, object name, or any expression, you would write the following:

```
#include <typeinfo>
// ...
typeid(arg)
```

The **typeid** keyword can be used to extract run-time information about an object or a type.

The Class type_info

The use of the **typeid** keyword creates a temporary instance of the class **std::type_info**, which is defined in the header file **typeinfo**. The definition of class **type_info** follows:

```
namespace std
{
    class type_info
```

```
{
    public:
  virtual ~type_info();
  bool operator== (type_info const &) const;
  bool operator!= (type_info const &) const;
  bool before(type_info const &) const;
  char const *name() const;
    private:
  type_info(type_info const &);
  type_info &operator= (type_info const &);
};
}
```

Here is an explanation of the member functions:

▲ The two relational operators determine if two types are or are not the same.

▲ The **before**() member function returns **true** if *__this__ comes before the explicit argument in the compiler's collating sequence. This member function is rarely used because every compiler product has its own collating sequence (e.g., there is no guarantee that every compiler will say that **int** comes before **long**, or that **MyClass** comes before **Xyz**, in its collating sequence).

▲ The **name**() member function returns a compiler-specific string that represents the name of the type.

Here is a brief test of these functions:

```
// File typetest.h

#ifndef TYPETEST_H
#define TYPETEST_H

#include <iostream>
#include <typeinfo>

template <typename T, typename U>
void typeTest(T const &, U const &)
{
  std::type_info const &first = typeid(T);
  std::type_info const &second = typeid(U);

  bool test = (first = = second);
  std::cout << "Type " << first.name()
            << " is " << (test ? "equal" : "unequal")
            << " to type " << second.name() << '\n';
  if(!test)
```

```
        std::cout << "Type " << first.name() << " comes "
            << ((first.before(second)) ? "before " : "after ")
            << "type " << second.name() << '\n';
}


#endif


// File main.cpp

#include "typetest.h"

int main()
{
    char a = 'A';
    int b = 0, c = 0;
    long d = 0L;
    typeTest(b, c);
    typeTest(b, d);
    typeTest(a, b);
}


/* Output:

Type int is equal to type int
Type int is unequal to type long
Type int comes before type long
Type char is unequal to type int
Type char comes before type int


*/
```

Polymorphism is honored in the sense that if the expression to **typeid** is a dereferenced base class pointer pointing to a derived object, or a base class reference that refers to a derived object, then the derived class will be the resultant type. Of course, the base class must be polymorphic, that is, it must contain at least one virtual function; otherwise, the resultant type is always that of the base class:

```
// File typetest.h

#ifndef TYPETEST_H
#define TYPETEST_H

#include <iostream>
#include <typeinfo>
```

```cpp
template <typename T>
void typeTest(T const &arg)
{
    std::cout << typeid(arg).name() << '\n';
}

#endif

// File base.h

#ifndef BASE_H
#define BASE_H

class Base
{
    public:
    virtual ~Base() { }
};

class Derived : public Base { };

#endif

// File main.cpp

#include "typetest.h"
#include "base.h"

void test(Base *ptr)
{
    typeTest(ptr);
    typeTest(*ptr);
}

int main()
{
    Base *ptr = new Base;
    test(ptr);
    delete ptr;
    ptr = new Derived;
    test(ptr);
    delete ptr;
}
```

```
/* Output:

Base *
Base
Base *
Derived


*/
```

The following is another example in which the **typeid** keyword is used to prompt the terminal operator for the right type of object to be input. We'll test the function **input()** using both a primitive type (**int**) and a user-defined type (**ADT\<double\>**):

```
// File adt.h

#ifndef ADT_H
#define ADT_H

#include <iosfwd>

template <typename T>
class ADT;

template <typename T>
std::istream &operator>>(std::istream &, ADT<T> &);

template <typename T>
std::ostream &operator<<(std::ostream &, ADT<T> const &);

template <typename T>
class ADT
{
   friend std::istream &operator>> <T>
                            (std::istream &, ADT &);
   friend std::ostream &operator<< <T>
                            (std::ostream &, ADT const &);
     public:
   ADT(T const &d = T());
     private:
   T data;
};


#endif
```

```cpp
// File adt.cpp

#include <iostream>
#include "adt.h"

template <typename T>
ADT<T>::ADT(T const &d) : data(d) {}

template <typename T>
std::istream &operator>>(std::istream &stream, ADT<T> &adt)
{
  return stream >> adt.data;
}

template <typename T>
std::ostream &operator<<
                     (std::ostream &stream, ADT<T> const &adt)
{
  return stream << adt.data;
}

// File main.cpp

#include <iostream>
#include <typeinfo>
#include "adt.h"

template <typename T>
T const &input(T &object)
{
  std::cout << "Input data for an object of type "
            << typeid(T).name() << ": ";
  std::cin >> object;
  return object;
}

int main()
{
  int number;
  std::cout << "You entered: " << input(number) << '\n';
  ADT<double> adtObject;
  std::cout << "You entered: " << input(adtObject) << '\n';
}
```

```
/* A typical run of this program would produce:

Input data for an object of type int: 123
You entered: 123
Input data for an object of type ADT<double>: -63.581
You entered: -63.581

*/
```

14

Iostream Output

Introduction

In Chapter 3 you learned the fundamentals of how to do input and output using **iostream** member functions. Of course, there is much more to input and output (I/O) than was covered there, and in this chapter you will learn how to format your output so that it is more readable to the users of your programs.

 Prepare to start formatting your output so that it is more readable.

The Instances std::cerr and std::clog

In addition to the instance **std::cout**, C++ provides you with two other instances of the class **std::ostream**—**std::cerr** and **std::clog**. They are used for any error messages that you wish to direct to the terminal operator. The output of **std::cerr** is unbuffered, whereas the output of **std::clog** is buffered.

Although the output of both the **std::cerr** and **std::clog** instances will normally be shown on the screen, if redirection is used—say, to a printer or disk file—then the results of **std::cout** will be redirected and the results of **std::cerr** and **std::clog** will continue to be shown on the screen.

 C++ provides two other output devices for logging errors: **std::cerr** and **std::clog**.

How to Format the Output

Think about a **printf()** function call. It consists of a format string argument and, optionally, a list of expressions to be output. The format string contains literals that are output exactly as shown, and conversion specifications that indicate exactly how each expression from the list of expressions is to appear. Each conversion specification starts with a % and ends with a conversion character, such as **%d** or **%i** for decimal format, **%c** for character format, **%s** for a string, and so on. Between the start and end you can enter various flags, the field width, base formatting, justification, floating-point precision, and so forth. Each conversion specification stands on its own; there is no connection to any other one.

Now, however, you are working with the **std::cout** object that has some state, and it's this state that governs how your output data will appear on the screen. For example, if the state of **std::cout** is set to hexadecimal, then all integer output will appear in hexadecimal. If the state of **std::cout** is set to left-justify, then all fields from now on will appear left-justified.

SUMMARY ▶ The state of the **std::cout** object determines how output will be formatted.

Bit Format Flags

Within each **iostream** object (e.g., **cout**), a set of format "flags" determines how the **iostream** object formats values. Each of the format flags determines whether a particular format property is enabled for that particular **iostream** object. For example, within a given **iostream** object, the flag that controls hexadecimal formatting can be enabled or disabled for that stream. Similarly, the flag that controls left-justification formatting can be enabled or disabled for that stream. Because each **iostream** object has its own set of format flags, different **iostream** objects can potentially format the same data value in completely different ways.

At any given time, a format flag can have one of two possible states—enabled or disabled. Therefore, the flag's value can be represented using only a single bit. Each flag occupies a single bit of storage, and then the entire collection of format flag bits is aggregated together to form a value called a *bitmask,* where each bit in the bitmask corresponds to one particular format flag. Within each **iostream** object, this format flag bitmask is declared as a nonpublic nonstatic member of the **std::ios_base** class. The bitmask member's name is unspecified (this is the information-hiding principle at work), but its type is specified as **std::ios_base::fmtflags**.

CAUTION ▶ Because the name of the bitmask data member is unspecified, and because we need to refer to this member in the discussion that follows, I'll refer to this data member simply as "the **fmtflags** data member" (or something similar). Just keep in mind that the identifier **fmtflags** is the data member's *type* (i.e., **std::ios_base::fmtflags**), and not its name.

CAUTION The class **std::ios_base** is at the very top of the iostreams class hierarchy. This class encapsulates the "low level" properties and tasks that are common to all iostream-based streams (e.g., managing a stream's formatting flags).

The position of each format flag's bit within the **fmtflags** bitmask type is defined by a set of public static constant values within the class **std::ios_base**, something like this:

```
namespace std
{
  class ios_base
  {
      public:
    typedef T fmtflags;
    // where T is an implementation-defined type
    static fmtflags const boolalpha;
    static fmtflags const dec;
    static fmtflags const fixed;
    // etc.
  };
}
```

Each constant holds a unique, implementation defined value that is a nonnegative, integer power of two; for example, 1, 2, 4, 8, 16, and so on. With this scheme, it should be obvious that no two constants identify the same bit position within the **fmtflags** bitmask. Using a mutator function, these constants can be bitwise OR'ed into a specific **iostream** object's **fmtflags** data member. The bit pattern of the **fmtflags** data member within that **iostream** object thus reflects the current formatting state of that particular **iostream** object, that is, how that **iostream** object "currently" formats data values.

Because the names shown above are public, you can reference them using the scoping operator. The complete list of all such names and their meanings is shown in Table 14.1; they are discussed in more detail throughout the chapter.

SUMMARY Bit format flags are encapsulated inside the **std::cout** object and used to indicate how most (but not all) of the output is to appear.

How to Turn On the Bit Format Flags

In order to change the state of the **std::cout** object, you must be able to change the bits that represent its state. Within the class **std::ios_base**, several mutator member functions are provided to allow this to be done.

The Member Function std::ios_base::setf()

The first of these mutator member functions is called **std::ios_base::setf()**. As you can see, it is declared in the class **std::ios_base**. To call it, you must specify the instance name

TABLE 14.1

Name	Meaning
std::ios_base::skipws	Skip whitespace on input
std::ios_base::left	Left-justification of output
std::ios_base::right	Right-justification of output
std::ios_base::internal	Pad after sign or base indicator
std::ios_base::dec	Show integers in decimal
std::ios_base::oct	Show integers in octal
std::ios_base::hex	Show integers in hex
std::ios_base::showbase	Show the base for octal and hex numbers
std::ios_base::showpoint	Show the decimal point for all floating-points
std::ios_base::uppercase	Show uppercase hex numbers
std::ios_base::showpos	Show + for positive numbers
std::ios_base::scientific	Show exponential notation on floating-points
std::ios_base::fixed	Show fixed decimal output on floating-points
std::ios_base::unitbuf	Flush all streams after insertion
std::ios_base::stdio	Flush **stdout** and **stderr** after insertion
std::ios_base::boolalpha	Show **bool** values as text (true or false)

(e.g., **std::cout**), the dot operator, and then the member function name. This member function also returns the previous value of the format flags. For example, to turn on the **std::ios_base::showpos** bit, you would code:

```
std::cout.setf(std::ios_base::showpos);
```

or with some **using** declarations:

```
using std::cout;
using std::ios_base;
cout.setf(ios_base::showpos);
```

The function **std::ios_base::setf()** works by bitwise OR'ing its one argument with the existing values, thereby leaving any other bits undisturbed. This means that it's possible to turn on more than one bit with just one call to **std::ios_base::setf()** by using an expression for the first argument that contains several bits OR'ed together.

For example, to turn on the **std::ios_base::showpos** and the **std::ios_base::uppercase** bits, you would code:

```
using std::ios_base;
std::cout.setf(ios_base::showpos | ios_base::uppercase);
```

CAUTION   Do not confuse the bitwise OR (one vertical bar) with the Boolean logical OR (two vertical bars).

Unfortunately, ambiguous situations can arise. For example, from a logical perspective, you should never set the state of the **std::cout** object to specify that output should appear in decimal, hexadecimal, and octal at the same time. But there is nothing to prevent you from doing this. Of course, the results are unpredictable.

To help you guard against these ambiguous situations, **std::ios_base::setf()** has been overloaded to accept two arguments. In this case, the first argument specifies which bits are to be turned on, and the second argument specifies which bits are to be turned off first. Thus, for example, before specifying that output is to appear in octal, you can easily specify that the decimal, octal, and hexadecimal bits are to be turned off first. To do this, you would code:

```
std::cout.setf(std::ios_base::oct,
               std::ios_base::dec |      // bitwise OR
               std::ios_base::oct |      // bitwise OR
               std::ios_base::hex);
```

SUMMARY   The function **std::ios_base::setf()** is used to set the bit format flags on.

The Member Functions std::ios_base::unsetf()

In order to turn off the formatting bits, you can use the function **std::ios_base::unsetf()**. This function takes exactly one argument — the bit pattern to be turned off. Thus, to turn off the bits **std::ios_base::showpos** and **std::ios_base::uppercase**, you would code:

```
std::cout.unsetf(std::ios_base::showpos |
                 std::ios_base::uppercase);
```

SUMMARY   The function **std::ios_base::unsetf()** is used to set the bit format flags off.

The Member Functions std::ios_base::flags()

Because the **std::ios_base** class's **fmtflags** data member is nonpublic, you cannot access it directly. So the only public access to the **fmtflags** data member is through a pair of member functions named **std::ios_base::flags()**. The first is an accessor function that simply returns the current value of the **fmtflags** data member. The second is a mutator function that allows you to assign values en masse to all of the bits in the **fmtflags** data member. Specifically, the **fmtflags** value that you pass into the mutator function is stored into the stream's **fmtflags** data member, and the previous value of the stream's **fmtflags** data member is returned to you.

The **std::ios_base::flags()** member functions are useful when you want to temporarily change a stream's formatting configuration (e.g., to output a few values with a slightly different kind of formatting) and then restore the original configuration, as shown in the following example:

```
#include <iostream>
using std::cout;
using std::ios_base;

int main()
{
  // Save the current formating settings
  ios_base::fmtflags savedFmtflags = cout.flags();

  // Configure the new formatting settings
  cout.setf(ios_base::uppercase);
  ios_base::fmtflags newValue = cout.setf(ios_base::hex,
              ios_base::dec | ios_base::oct | ios_base::hex);

  // Output some values using the new settings
  cout << "Original value = " <<savedFmtflags << '\n';
  cout << "New value          = " << newValue << '\n';

  // Restore the original formating settings
  cout.flags(savedFmtflags);

  // ...
}

/* Output:

Original value  = 1008
New value       = 5008

*/
```

 The displayed values for the **fmtflags** data member can vary from one compiler to another.

 The function **std::ios_base::flags()** is used to return the entire complement of bit format flags.

How to Display Integers in the Proper Base

The ability to format your output is important because you want to have complete flexibility in the manner in which your data appears. Let's start with the base in which integers will be shown.

In a **printf()** function call, you have three choices: decimal, octal, and hex. You can get decimal output by using a format specification of **%d** or **%i**, an octal by using **%o**, and hex by using either **%x** or **%X**. (How to emulate lowercase and uppercase letters will be discussed later.) In C++, there are three bits in the enumerated values, as shown here.

Name	Meaning
std::ios_base::dec	Show integers in decimal
std::ios_base::oct	Show integers in octal
std::ios_base::hex	Show integers in hex

To guarantee that decimal output is used, you must turn on the bit **std::ios_base::dec** and ensure that the remaining two bits are turned off. The same reasoning applies to octal and hex output. If all three bits are off, the output will default to decimal. Remember that once the base has been set, it stays set for all future integers unless it is subsequently changed.

SUMMARY ▶ The format bits **std::ios::dec, std::ios::oct** and **std::ios::hex** are used to indicate the base in which an integral number is shown.

The Field std::ios_base::basefield

Recall the form of the **std::ios_base::setf()** function that you must use in order to turn on one of the three base setting bits and ensure that the other two bits are off. Because the second argument entails a lot of coding on your part, the **std::iostream** library has conveniently provided a **static const** variable that is the bitwise OR of the three base setting bits. This field is called **std::ios_base::basefield** and has the following definition:

```
const std::ios_base::fmtflags basefield =
        std::ios_base::dec |
        std::ios_base::oct |
        std::ios_base::hex;
```

The following example runs a test on all three base settings:

```
#include <iostream>
using std::cout;
using std::ios_base;

int main()
{
   int const data = 65;
```

```
    cout << "Decimal: " << data << '\n';
    cout.setf(ios_base::oct, ios_base::basefield);
    cout << "Octal: " << data << '\n';
    cout.setf(ios_base::hex, ios_base::basefield);
    cout << "Hex: " << data << '\n';
    cout.setf(ios_base::dec, ios_base::basefield);
    cout << "Decimal: " << data << '\n';
}

/* Output:

Decimal: 65
Octal: 101
Hex: 41
Decimal: 65

*/
```

SUMMARY ▶ The constant **std::ios::basefield** contains the bitwise OR of the three base setting bits.

EXERCISE 14.1

Prompt the terminal operator to enter an integer value. If end-of-file is entered, terminate the program. Otherwise, display the value in decimal, octal, and hexadecimal. Then return for a new input value.

How to Show the Base Setting of Integers

In a **printf()** function call, the use of the flag **#** causes the base of an octal or hexadecimal number to appear as 0 and 0x, respectively. The same effect can be achieved in C++ by setting on the bit **std::ios_base::showbase**. To revert back to not showing the base setting, use the **std::ios_base::unsetf()** member function.

Name	Meaning
std::ios_base::showbase	Show the base for octal and hex numbers

Here is the previous example again with the **std::ios_base::showbase** bit turned on:

```
#include <iostream>
using std::cout;
using std::ios_base;

int main()
```

```
    {
      int const data = 65;
      cout.setf(ios_base::showbase);
      cout << "Decimal: " << data << '\n';
      cout.setf(ios_base::oct, ios_base::basefield);
      cout << "Octal: " << data << '\n';
      cout.setf(ios_base::hex, ios_base::basefield);
      cout << "Hex: " << data << '\n';
      cout.setf(ios_base::dec, ios_base::basefield);
      cout << "Decimal: " << data << '\n';
    }


    /* Output:

    Decimal: 65
    Octal: 0101
    Hex: 0x41
    Decimal: 65


    */
```

 The format bit **std::ios::showbase** is used to explicitly show the base setting of a number—0 for octal and 0x for hexadecimal.

EXERCISE 14.2

Modify Exercise 14.1 so that the base for all octal and hexadecimal numbers is shown.

How to Display the Sign of an Integer

Note that on positive decimal output, a + sign is assumed and by default will not appear. In a **printf()** function call, you can force the + sign to appear if you use the flag +.

Using **iostream** member functions, if you want this sign to appear, you must turn on the bit **std::ios_base::showpos**. (Of course, if the number is negative, the − sign will always appear.) To revert back to not showing the + sign, use the **std::ios_base::unsetf()** member function.

Here is the previous example again with the **std::ios_base::showpos** bit turned on:

```
#include <iostream>
using std::cout;
using std::ios_base;

int main()
{
   int const data = 65;
```

```
    cout.setf(ios_base::showbase | ios_base::showpos);
    cout << "Decimal: " << data << '\n';
    cout.setf(ios_base::oct, ios_base::basefield);
    cout << "Octal: " << data << '\n';
    cout.setf(ios_base::hex, ios_base::basefield);
    cout << "Hex: " << data << '\n';
    cout.setf(ios_base::dec, ios_base::basefield);
    cout << "Decimal: " << data << '\n';
}


/* Output:

Decimal: +65
Octal: 0101
Hex: 0x41
Decimal: +65


*/
```

The format bit **std::ios::showpos** is used to explicitly show a + sign for a positive integral value.

EXERCISE 14.3

Modify Exercise 14.2 so that the sign of the number is explicitly shown.

How to Display Output in Uppercase Letters

You can employ one other option with hexadecimal numbers. By default, any hex digit, as well as the letter **x** in the base, appears in lowercase letters. The same rule applies to the letter **e** when printing in scientific notation. In a **printf()** function call, you would code a capital **X** to obtain hex digits in uppercase, or a capital **E** to show the E in scientific notation in uppercase.

Using **iostream**, if you want to see uppercase, turn on the bit **std::ios_base::uppercase**. To revert back to lowercase, use the **std::ios_base::unsetf()** member function.

Name	Meaning
std::ios_base::uppercase	Show uppercase hex numbers

The following example prints the hex number **abc** in hexadecimal, and shows the base setting and all hex digits in uppercase:

```
#include <iostream>
using std::cout;
```

```
using std::ios_base;

int main()
{
  cout.setf(ios_base::uppercase | ios_base::showbase);
  cout.setf(ios_base::hex, ios_base::basefield);
  cout << 0xabc << '\n';
}

/* Output:

0XABC

*/
```

SUMMARY The format bit **std::ios::uppercase** is used to display all letters of a hexadecimal number in uppercase mode.

EXERCISE 14.4

Modify Exercise 14.3 so that all letters appearing in a hexadecimal number are shown in uppercase.

How to Display a Character

If you want to display a character, there is no problem because the compiler will use argument matching to invoke the insertion operator that takes type **char** as its one explicit argument. If you want to display a character as some other type, such as an integer, then you must cast it using the **static_cast** keyword (in lieu of using a C style or function style cast):

```
#include <iostream>
using std::cout;

int main()
{
  char const ch = 'A';
  cout << "char: " << ch << '\n';
  cout << "int: " << static_cast<int>(ch) << '\n';
}

/* Output:

char: A
int: 65

*/
```

Use a **static_cast** whenever you want to display the integral representation of a character.

The Member Function std::ostream::put()

In addition to using the insertion operator to output a character, the member function **std::ostream::put()** provides a way to guarantee that any parameter gets shown in character format (think of the C function **putchar()**). This function also returns the invoking instance by reference, so it can be chained to a subsequent function call:

```
#include <iostream>
using std::cout;

int main()
{
   char const ch1 = 'A';
   int const ch2 = 66;
   double const ch3 = 67.503;
   cout.put(ch1).put(ch2).put(ch3) << '\n';
}

/* Output:

ABC

*/
```

Use the member function **std::ostream::put()** to display its argument in character format.

How to Set the Output Field Width

The field width in C++ works in a manner similar to that in C. For an output stream, the field width specifies the minimum width (in characters) of the next value's output field. If the total number of characters needed to display the next value is less than the specified field width, then any unused character positions in the output field are filled with the current fill character. (In C, the fill character in a **printf()** function call can be only a zero or a space; using **iostream** member functions, it can be any character you desire.) If the number of characters needed to display the next value exceeds the specified field width, then the output field is "expanded" to accommodate the entire value. If the program does not specify the width of the next output field, then the width defaults to zero (just as it does in C).

To specify the field width for the output stream's next value, pass the desired width value to the mutator member function **std::ios_base::width()** just before the program outputs the next value. In addition to setting the field width to the specified value, this function also returns the width value that the output stream *would* have used had you not called this function (which will typically be the default width value, zero). There is also an accessor version of the **std::ios_base::width**() that returns the current value of the output stream's field width setting.

For example, this program prints the value of a local variable named **data** in an output field that is at least five characters wide:

```cpp
#include <iostream>
using std::cout;

int main()
{
   int const data = 123;
   cout << "data: |";
   cout.width(5);
   cout << data << "|\n";
}

/* Output:

data: |  123|

*/
```

Use the member function **std::ostream::width**() to set a field width for the next integral data to be shown.

The Width Does Not "Stick"

The **std::ios_base::width**() member function is unusual in the sense that it is an exception to the "set it and forget it" rule that applies to other aspects of formatting. That is, once the width is honored, it reverts back to its default value of zero immediately. If you want to set the width for some subsequent field, you must call **std::ios_base::width**() again.

CAUTION Time out. Is something bothering you here? Does it seem like you're being forced into a lot of detailed coding just to do some simple formatting? And wouldn't it be nice to be able to perform all of the formatting in just one statement? Well, you're absolutely right—it is a lot of work, and it doesn't make the code look very pretty, either. That's the bad news. The good news is that your job will become much easier with the introduction of manipulators in Chapter 16. For now, however, you have to learn how to walk before you can learn how to run.

Once the width field is honored, it automatically reverts to its default value of 0.

EXERCISE 14.5

Modify Exercise 14.4 so that all values appear in 10-position fields.

How to Specify the Fill Character

If the total number of characters needed to display a field is less than the current field width, the extra output spaces will be filled with the current fill character. In a **printf()** function call, the default fill character is a blank; the only option you have is to change it to a zero.

Using **iostream** member functions, however, you now have the option for *any* character to serve as the fill character. As before, the default is a blank. The mutator member function **std::ios_base::fill()** is used to specify a new fill character. This function takes a single argument, the new fill character, and returns the previous fill character. Once specified, the output stream continues to use the specified fill character until the program specifies a different value for the fill character. There is also an accessor version of **std::ios_base::fill()** that retrieves the stream's current fill character.

Here is the previous example again, using a "splat" (asterisk) as the fill character:

```
#include <iostream>
using std::cout;

int main()
{
    int const data = 123;
    cout.fill('*');
    cout << "data: |";
    cout.width(5);
    cout << data << "|\n";
}

/* Output:

data: |**123|

*/
```

SUMMARY
Use the member function **std::ostream::fill()** to set a fill character that will be used for any data that is less than the specified width.

EXERCISE 14.6

Modify Exercise 14.5 so that all displayed values use a # symbol for the fill character.

How to Specify Field Justification

In a **printf()** function call, whenever a field is output, the data is always right-justified. If you want to left-justify a field, you must use the '–' formatting flag.

In the **iostream** library, three bits specify the field justification, as shown here.

Name	Meaning
std::ios_base::left	Left-justification of output
std::ios_base::right	Right-justification of output
std::ios_base::internal	Pad after sign or base indicator

SUMMARY

The format bits **std::ios::left, std::ios::right** and **std::ios::internal** are used to indicate the adjustment of an integral number.

The Field std::ios_base::adjustfield

If no bit is ever specified, the justification defaults to right. As with the integer base setting, if one of the bits is on, you must ensure that the remaining two bits are off. To this end, the field called **std::ios_base::adjustfield** has been defined with all three justification bits turned on:

```
const std::ios_base::fmtflags adjustfield =
        std::ios_base::left |
        std::ios_base::right |
        std::ios_base::internal;
```

The following example prints a number using each of these justifications. The justification **std::ios_base::internal** means that padding with the fill character, if any, will occur after the base of the number has been shown (for octal and hexadecimal numbers) and before the number itself. This is also true if a sign for the number is shown, that is, the padding will occur between the sign and the number itself.

```
#include <iostream>
using std::cout;
using std::ios_base;

int main()
{
  int const data = 65;
  cout.fill('*');
  cout.setf(ios_base::showpos);
  cout.setf(ios_base::left, ios_base::adjustfield);
  cout.width(5);
  cout << data << '\n';
```

```
    cout.setf(ios_base::right, ios_base::adjustfield);
    cout.width(5);
    cout << data << '\n';
    cout.setf(ios_base::internal, ios_base::adjustfield);
    cout.width(5);
    cout << data << '\n';
}

/* Output:

+65**
**+65
+**65

*/
```

The constant **std::ios::adjustfield** contains the bitwise OR of the three adjustment setting bits.

EXERCISE 14.7

Modify Exercise 14.6 so that all displayed values are shown both left and right justified.

How to Format Floating-Point Numbers

Floating-point numbers are output in C++ just like any other type of number. The formatting is certainly different, however, and default values are not the same as you would get from using a **printf**() function call. Your goal then is to emulate the **%f** and **%e** conversion specifications.

In the following example, some floating-point constants are output with no special formatting:

```
#include <iostream>
using std::cout;

int main()
{
    cout << 1.23456789 << '\n';              // #1
    cout << 4.00 << '\n';                    // #2
    cout << 5.678E2 << '\n';                 // #3
    cout << 666666666.78394808 << '\n';      // #4
    cout << 0.0 << '\n';                     // #5
}
```

```
/* The output of this program is:

1.23457
4
567.8
6.66667e+08
0

*/
```

Here is an explanation of each line of output:

▲ For line #1, note that no more than six digits are shown and that rounding occurs.

▲ For line #2, not only do the trailing zeroes not show, the decimal point does not appear either.

▲ For line #3, the number prints in fixed-point notation despite being keyed in scientific notation.

▲ For line #4, the number prints in scientific notation despite being keyed in fixed-point notation.

▲ For line #5, even though the value is zero, at least one significant digit will always appear.

SUMMARY   Note the default formatting that occurs for all floating-point numbers.

The Bit std::ios_base::showpoint

The first step in formatting floating-point numbers is to turn on the bit **std::ios_base::showpoint**.

Name	Meaning
std::ios_base::showpoint	Show the decimal point for all floats

This will cause a decimal point to appear, and the floating-point value will be displayed using p significant digits, where p is the output stream's current "precision" value (discussed later). The default value of p is 6. If the floating-point value has more than p significant digits, then the first p significant digits will be displayed using scientific notation:

```
#include <iostream>
using std::ios_base;
using std::cout;

int main()
{
   cout.flags(0);
```

```
    cout.setf(ios_base::showpoint);

    cout << 1.23456789 << '\n';
    cout << 4.00 << '\n';
    cout << 5.678E2 << '\n';
    cout << 666666666.78394808 << '\n';
    cout << 0.0 << '\n';
}

/* The output of this program is:

1.23457
4.00000
567.800
6.66667e+08
0.00000


*/
```

The format bit **std::ios_base::showpos** causes a decimal point to appear in a floating-point number, and 6 significant digits to appear by default.

The Bits std::ios_base::scientific and std::ios_base::fixed

To ensure that either scientific or fixed-point notation is shown, turn on either of the bits **std::ios_base::scientific** or **std::ios_base::fixed**.

Name	Meaning
std::ios_base::scientific	Show exponential notation on floating-points
std::ios_base::fixed	Show fixed decimal output on floating-points

The field **std::ios_base::floatfield** is the bitwise OR of these two bits:

```
const std::ios_base::fmtflags floatfield =
        std::ios_base::scientific |
        std::ios_base::fixed;
```

If neither bit is turned on, the compiler emulates the **%g** format specification in a **printf()** function call.

The format bits **std::ios_base::scientific** and **std::ios_base::fixed** are used to indicate the notation of a floating-point number.

Here is the previous example with the **std::ios_base::fixed** and **std::ios_base::showpoint** bits now turned on. Pay close attention to the effect that the **std::ios_base::fixed** flag has on the "meaning" of the precision setting. Specifically, when either the **std::ios_base::fixed** flag or the **std::ios_base::scientific** flag is enabled, the precision value p specifies the number of digit positions to the right of the decimal point. When neither of these two flags is enabled, the precision value p specifies the number of significant digits to be displayed.

```
#include <iostream>
using std::ios_base;
using std::cout;

int main()
{
  cout.flags(0);
  cout.setf(ios_base::showpoint);
  cout.setf(ios_base::fixed, ios_base::floatfield);

  cout << 1.23456789 << '\n';
  cout << 4.00 << '\n';
  cout << 5.678E2 << '\n';
  cout << 666666666.78394808 << '\n';
  cout << 0.0 << '\n';
}

/* The output of this program is:

1.234568
4.000000
567.800000
666666666.783948
0.000000

*/
```

SUMMARY ▶ The constant **std::ios_base::floatfield** contains the bitwise OR of the two notation setting bits.

The Member Function std::ios_base::precision()

The next step is to specify the number of digits to be displayed — either significant digits or decimal digits — depending on the states of the **std::ios_base::showpoint** and **std::ios_base::fixed** flags. To do this, use the member function **std::ios_base::precision()** and specify as its argument the number of digit positions to be shown.

If the accessor version of this function is called, the function merely returns the current value of the precision and does not alter. If the mutator version of this function is called, the precision is set using the function's argument, and the prior value for the precision is returned. If the precision is never specified, then it defaults to the value 0.

Here is the previous example again with the precision now set to 2. Notice that the **cout** stream's **std::ios_base::fixed** format flag is enabled in this example. Therefore, the precision value 2 means, "display two digits to the right of the decimal point":

```
#include <iostream>
using std::ios_base;
using std::cout;

int main()
{
   cout.flags(0);
   cout.setf(ios_base::showpoint);
   cout.setf(ios_base::fixed, ios_base::floatfield);
   cout.precision(2);

   cout << 1.23456789 << '\n';
   cout << 4.00 << '\n';
   cout << 5.678E2 << '\n';
   cout << 666666666.78394808 << '\n';
   cout << 0.0 << '\n';
}

/* The output of this program is:

1.23
4.00
567.80
666666666.78
0.00

*/
```

CAUTION   If a stream's **std::ios_base::scientific** flag or its **std::ios_base::fixed** flag is enabled, the stream's precision value specifies the number of digits to be displayed to the right of the decimal point. If neither of these flags is asserted, the precision value specifies the number of significant digits to be displayed.

SUMMARY   Use the member function **std::ios_base::precision()** to set the number of positions to be shown after the decimal point.

EXERCISE 14.8

Prompt the terminal operator for a floating-point value. If end-of-file has not been entered, prompt the operator again for an integer value that represents the number of positions to display after the decimal point. Then display the floating-point number accordingly. When done, return for another number.

How to Display a **bool** Type

Recall that a variable of type **bool** intrinsically has the value **true** or **false**. When this value is displayed, **true** will appear as a 1, and **false** will appear as a 0.

If you turn on the flag **std::ios_base::boolalpha**, the alphabetic representation of these values will appear instead of the numeric representation.

Name	Meaning
std::ios_base::boolalpha	Show **bool** values as text (**true** or **false**)

```
#include <iostream>
using std::cout;

int main()
{
  cout.setf(ios_base::boolalpha);
  bool b = false;
  cout << b << '\n';
  b = true;
  cout << b << '\n';
}

/* Output:

false
true

*/
```

The format bit **std::ios_base::boolalpha** can be set to cause a **bool** value to appear as either **true** or **false**.

How to Print an Address

The address of a variable or object can be generated by using the address operator (&). Because this operator can be applied to a wide variety of types (both primitive and user-defined), the type of the resultant address can theoretically be pointer-to-**int** or pointer-to-**float** or even pointer-to-any-class-type. To accommodate all of these various types, the class **std::ostream** contains an operator insertion function whose one explicit argument is type **void const** *. Any data pointer type can be converted to this type under Rule 3 of the argument matching rules (as specified in Chapter 10), so a match with a **void const** * is guaranteed.

For example, here is how you would print the address of a primitive type:

```
#include <iostream>

int main()
{
   int const data = 1;
   std::cout << &data << '\n';
}
```

SUMMARY ▶ To print an address, simply write the address-of operator & in front of a variable name.

Taking the Address of a String Literal

Note that in the case of a string literal (which has type **char const**[]) or a pointer-to-constant-character (which has type **char const** *), the standard library provides an insertion operator function that accepts a **char const** * as its argument type. This is fine if your intent is to print the characters of the literal to which the pointer is pointing. However, if you wish to print the content of the pointer variable itself, (i.e., the address of the first character being pointed at), then you must cast this address into a **void const** * type:

```
#include <iostream>

int main()
{
   char const *ptr = "C++";
   std::cout << ptr << '\n';
   std::cout << static_cast<void const *>(ptr) << '\n';
}

/* Output:

C++
4419804

*/
```

CAUTION ▶ The address shown will vary from one compiler to another, or even from one run to another.

To print an address coming from type **char const ***, use a **static_cast** to cast the address into type **void const ***.

How to Output to a Memory Buffer

To send output to a memory buffer (instead of directly to the **std::cout** device), you must first include the header file **sstream**. This file contains the definition of the class **std::ostringstream**, which you then instantiate. This object provides an expandable buffer that is used to receive the output of the insertion operator (or any other function you would normally use with the **std::cout** object). To retrieve the data that was placed into the object, use the member function **str()** in the class **std::ostringstream**. For example:

```cpp
#include <iostream>
#include <sstream>

int main()
{
  std::ostringstream oss;
  oss.fill('#');
  int const data = 123;
  oss << "data: |";
  oss.width(5);
  oss << data << '|';
  std::cout << oss.str() << '\n';
}

/* Output:

data: |##123|

*/
```

 Use the header file **sstream** and the class **std::ostringstream** to direct output to a memory buffer.

The Member Function ostream::flush()

If, at any time, you want to explicitly flush an output stream's buffer, you can do so by calling the member function **ostream::flush()**:

```cpp
cout.flush(); // flushes cout's internal buffer
```

For screen output, this is generally not necessary because, most of the time, screen output is flushed automatically. In the case where one disk file is being copied to another, however, you might have to flush the output buffer prior to rewinding the output file for continued use.

SUMMARY ▶ Use the member function **ostream::flush()** to flush the output stream buffer area.

Mixing the Predefined **stdio** and **iostream** Streams

By default, the operation of the predefined C++ **iostream** objects **cin**, **cout**, **cerr**, and **clog** is synchronized with the operation of the predefined C streams **stdin**, **stdout**, and **stderr**, respectively. (Note that **cerr** and **clog** are both associated with **stderr**.) Consequently, a C++ program can, by default, safely perform I/O operations using a mixture of the predefined C++ **iostream** objects and the predefined C streams:

```cpp
#include <iostream>
#include <cstdio>                // C++ version of <stdio.h>
using std::cout;
using std::printf;

int main()
{
  printf("one, ");
  cout << "two, ";
  printf("three");
  cout.flush();
}

/* Output:

one, two, three

*/
```

If your C++ program does not (in any way) invoke the standard library routines that use the predefined C streams (e.g., **printf()**, **scanf()**, **puts()**, etc.), then there is no particular need to maintain synchronization between the predefined C++ **iostream** stream objects and the predefined C streams (hereafter referred to as "the predefined C/C++ streams"). In this situation, you can disable the synchronization mechanism by passing the value **false** to the static function **std::ios_base::sync_with_stdio()**. (Note that this also eliminates the runtime overhead the program normally incurs when it uses the synchronization mechanism.) This call is typically made somewhere near the start of function **main()** for the simple reason that this function *must* be invoked before the C++ program performs any I/O operation with any of the predefined C/C++ streams. Changing the setting of the synchronization mechanism after a C++ program has begun to use the predefined C/C++ streams has undefined effects. Once the synchronization mechanism is disabled, the predefined C/C++ streams operate independently:

```cpp
#include <iostream>
#include <cstdio>                   // C++ version of <stdio.h>
using std::cout;
using std::printf;

int main()
{
  std::ios_base::sync_with_stdio(false);
  printf("one, ");
  cout << "two, ";
  printf("three");
  cout.flush();
}

/* Output:

one, threetwo,

*/
```

CAUTION   The actual output might vary from one compiler to another.

SUMMARY   Use caution when mixing **stdio** and **iostream** functions.

15

Iostream Input

Introduction

In addition to being able to control output, C++ classes also handle all input. Just as output consists of a stream of characters being sent to some device, input consists of characters coming in from some streaming device and being translated into their proper type. Unlike output, the realm of possibilities for "formatting" simply does not exist when inputting data.

 Iostream input consists of characters coming in from some streaming device.

How to Check for Errors

Unfortunately, we live in an imperfect world. People don't smile, cars crash, checks bounce, and data entry operators sometimes make mistakes. This means that, as a programmer, you are responsible for making sure your code is as robust as possible. In other words, no matter what the user might enter as "data," your program must capture it and successfully trap all error conditions to avoid such catastrophes as "garbage in, garbage out," aborts, hangs, endless loops, and others.

 Get ready to write code that checks for input errors.

Error-Reporting Flags

Within every C++ **iostream** object is a set of error-reporting flags. An **iostream** object uses its error-reporting flags to indicate whether an I/O-related operation with that particular **iostream** object was successful or not. Of course, an **iostream** object is not psychic; it cannot predict whether an upcoming I/O operation will succeed or fail. An **iostream** object's error-reporting flags therefore indicate the *outcome* of an I/O operation involving that particular **iostream** object. Specifically, the program attempts an I/O operation with an **iostream** object; then, immediately *after* the I/O attempt, the object's error reporting flags indicate whether the I/O attempt was successful or not. If an I/O attempt fails, the program can determine the specific type of failure by testing the enabled/disabled states of the **iostream** object's error-reporting flags.

The names of the error-reporting flags, as defined by the class **std::ios_base**, are shown in Table 15.1.

TABLE 15.1

Name	Meaning
std::ios_base::goodbit	Good condition, all bits off
std::ios_base::eofbit	End-of-file detected
std::ios_base::failbit	Input: The last input operation did not read the expected characters Output: The last output operation did not write the specified characters
std::ios_base::badbit	Loss of integrity in the I/O sequence

With the exception of **std::ios_base::goodbit**, each flag's state is stored as a single bit within a nonpublic bitmask data member whose type is **std::ios_base::iostate**. (Note that this is the data member's *type*, and not its name.) The position of each error flag bit within the **iostate** bitmask type is defined by a set of public static constant values within the **std::ios_base** class, something like this:

```
namespace std
{
  class ios_base
  {
     public:
    typedef T iostate;
    // T is an implementation-defined type
    static iostate const goodbit = 0;
    static iostate const failbit;
    static iostate const badbit;
```

```
    static iostate const eofbit;
    // ...
  };
}
```

The value of the data member **std::ios_base::goodbit** is always 0. This flag does not actually have its own bit, per se, within the **std::ios_base::iostate** bitmask type. Instead, it represents the state where none of the error reporting flags are enabled (all of the error-reporting bits are off), in which case the *bitmask's* value is 0.

 Every Iostream object contains a set of error reporting flags that you can interrogate to determine the state of the object.

Accessor Member Functions

The easiest way to test the error status of an **iostream** object such as **cin** is to use any of the four accessor member functions shown in Table 15.2.

TABLE 15.2

Function Name	Returns true if:
std::basic_ios::good()	No errors detected (all bits are off)
std::basic_ios::eof()	**std::ios_base::eofbit** is on
std::basic_ios::fail()	**std::ios_base::failbit** or **std::ios_base::badbit** is on
std::basic_ios::bad()	**std::ios_base::badbit** bit is on

CAUTION Class **basic_ios** is a template class that is derived directly from the **ios_base** class.

These accessor member functions have been inherited into the **std::istream** class from the class **std::basic_ios**, so you can invoke them on behalf of the **std::cin** object.

It's important to note, however, that the accessor function **std::basic_ios::fail()** indicates not only the state of the stream's **failbit** flag, but also the state of the stream's **badbit** flag. By using only the **bad()** and **fail()** accessor functions, one cannot always determine whether the stream's **failbit** flag is turned on:

```
if (cin.fail())
{
  /* Possible cases:
    1) badbit off, failbit on
    2) badbit on, failbit off
    3) badbit on, failbit on
  */
```

```
if (!cin.bad())
{
  // badbit is off, failbit is on
}
else
{
  // badbit is on
  // failbit could be on or off
}
}
```

The solution to this dilemma is the accessor member function **std::basic_ios::rdstate()**. When invoked on behalf of an **iostream** object, it returns a copy of the object's current **iostate** bitmask value. The program can then perform tests on the individual bits within this bitmask value to determine whether a specific error reporting flag is currently on or off:

```
if (cin.rdstate() & std::ios_base::failbit)
  // failbit is currently on
else
  // failbit is currently off
```

SUMMARY You may use accessor functions to determine the state of an input object.

Testing the **iostream** Object Directly

Another (and perhaps easier) way to test an **iostream** object's error state is to use the overloaded function **std::basic_ios::operator!()** (Boolean "not") on the **iostream** instance:

```
if (!std::cin)          // == fail()
  // ...
```

When invoked, this operator simply calls the accessor member function **std::basic_ios::fail()**; the result is exactly the same as if the program had called **fail()** directly. Similarly, if the program specifies the name of an **iostream** instance where a **bool** value is required, this results in a **bool** value that is the opposite of **fail()**. That is, if the instance's **badbit** and **failbit** flags are both off (e.g., a read attempt with **std::cin** successfully extracted the expected data value from the input stream), then the **iostream** instance evaluates to **true**:

```
if (std::cin) // == !fail()
  // ...
```

In this case, an operator conversion function in the class **basic_ios** will be called to convert the **iostream** instance into a value of type **void *** and then implicitly into a value of type **bool**. As you might have guessed, the **void *** operator conversion function also invokes the **fail**() accessor function. If **fail**() returns **true**, the operator conversion function returns a null pointer; otherwise, it returns a nonnull pointer.

The following program is designed to test the error state of **std::cin** instance in every possible way. Note that **std::basic_ios::good**() and **std::cin** always return the same value, as do **std::basic_ios::fail**() and **!std::cin**.

```cpp
#include <iostream>
using std::cout;
using std::cin;

void examine(std::ostream &stream = cout)
{
  stream << '\n';
  stream << "eof = " << cin.eof() << '\n';
  stream << "good = " << cin.good() << '\n';
  stream << "fail = " << cin.fail() << '\n';
  stream << "bad = " << cin.bad() << '\n';
  stream << "cin = " << static_cast<bool>(cin) << '\n';
  stream << "!cin = " << !cin << '\n';
}

int main()
{
  cout.setf(std::ios_base::boolalpha);
  cout << "Enter a number: ";
  int number;
  while(cin >> number)
  {
    examine();
    cout << "\nNext number: ";
  }
  examine();
}

/* Output:

Enter a number: ^Z

eof = true
good = false
fail = true
bad = false
cin = false
!cin = true
```

```
Enter a number: 123

eof  = false
good = true
fail = false
bad  = false
cin  = true
!cin = false

Next number: Junk

eof  = false
good = false
fail = true
bad  = false
cin  = false
!cin = true

*/
```

SUMMARY The ! (not) operator has been overloaded and may be used to test the state of an input object. A Boolean value of true means the same as **fail()**.

The Member Function std::basic_ios::clear()

If for any reason an input stream is unable to extract the next data item—for example, the input stream expects to read in an **int** but the next data item is not an **int**—the input stream turns on *at least* its **failbit** flag and then refuses to extract any more characters from the input stream. To be more specific, if *any* error-reporting flag is turned on within an **iostream** object, the **iostream** object will stop manipulating its data stream. For example:

```
cin >> n1;
cin >> n2;
```

If the input stream **cin** is unable to read the expected data item from the input stream into **n1**, **cin** will turn on *at least* its **failbit** flag to indicate that it failed to read the expected data item. Once **cin** enters this error-reporting state, **cin** refuses to manipulate its input stream any further. Therefore, **cin** makes no attempt to read data from the input stream into **n2** if the previous read into **n1** fails; the program just "skips past" the second input operation (the read into **n2**) and continues on its merry way. This behavior often comes as quite a shock to new C++ programmers the first time they encounter it.

After an **iostream** object enters its error state, the program must do two things. First, it must detect the specific type of error the object has encountered by testing the states of the object's error-reporting flags. Second, it must respond "in some appropriate way" to the detected error state. If the program intends to continue using an **iostream** object after it enters its error state, then, as part of the second step, the program must turn off *all* of the object's error-reporting flags, thereby returning the stream object to its "good" state. The program can restore the object to its "good" state by invoking the **std::basic_ ios::clear()** mutator member function with no arguments. Doing so invokes the function with its default argument, **goodbit**, which consequently assigns the value 0 to each of the stream's error-reporting flag bits.

There may be cases, however, in which the program does not want to turn off en masse all of its error-reporting flags; for example, one part of the program handles **failbit** error recovery (this part of the program is responsible for turning off the **failbit** flag), and another part of the program handles **eofbit** error recovery (this part of the program is responsible for turning off the **eofbit** flag). To turn on or off a specific flag, you invoke the **std::basic_ios::clear()** mutator function and pass it a **std::ios_base::iostate** bitmask value that specifies the on/off values for each of the error-reporting flags. In this case, the function name "clear" is a misnomer because **clear()** actually *assigns* the on/off bit values specified in the **iostate** bitmask directly to the stream's **iostate** data member.

Because the **clear()** mutator assigns the specified bitmask to the stream's **iostate** bitmask, you must be very careful when creating the **iostate** bitmask value that you pass into the **clear()** mutator function. The bitmask's value must be defined so that the following two conditions are met: (1) the specific flag bit (e.g., the **failbit** flag) within the **iostate** bitmask has the desired on/off value, and (2) the values of the remaining bits in the **iostate** bitmask reflect the current values of the stream's **iostate** bitmask.

The following three-step process describes how to turn off a particular flag bit within the **iostate** bitmask value. First, the program calls the stream's **rdstate()** accessor member function to obtain the current value of the stream's **iostate** bitmask (i.e., the current values of the stream's error-reporting flag bits). Second, the program uses an assembly-style "negate/and" bit manipulation to turn off the desired flag bit (the **failbit** flag bit, in this case) within the **iostate** bitmask value. Third, the program passes the modified **iostate** bitmask value into the **clear()** mutator function, which then assigns the bitmask value into the stream's **iostate** bitmask member.

```
using std::cin;
using std::ios_base;

ios_base::iostate flags = cin.rdstate();
flags &= ~ios_base::failbit;
cin.clear(flags);

// or...

cin.clear(cin.rdstate() & ~ios_base::failbit);
```

To turn on a specific flag bit, the program performs the same three steps, but now the program performs a bit-wise **OR** operation to turn on the desired flag bit instead of performing a bit-wise "negate/and" sequence to turn off the desired flag bit. For example, let's create a function that turns on an input stream's **failbit** flag and ensures that the remaining bits stay the same:

```
// File fail.h

#ifndef FAIL_H
#define FAIL_H

#include <iosfwd>

std::istream &Fail(std::istream &stream);

#endif


// File fail.cpp

#include <iostream>
#include "fail.h"

std::istream &Fail(std::istream &stream)
{
   stream.clear(stream.rdstate() | std::ios_base::failbit);
   return stream;
}
```

CAUTION   The **Fail()** function above was coded so that it can be used as a *manipulator*. This topic will be covered in Chapter 16.

SUMMARY   The member function **clear()** is used to set or reset any error reporting flags.

How to Flush the Input Stream Buffer

The next problem is how to eliminate any and all "garbage" characters from the input stream's internal buffer. This function is used primarily with line-buffered data sources. A line-buffered data source provides data to the **iostream** object "one line at a time," as opposed to one character at a time, or one buffer at a time, and so on. When working with a line-buffered data source (e.g., the operating system's keyboard buffer), an **iostream** object assumes that each line of data ends with (is *delimited* by) a newline character '\n'. This concept is similar to how C and C++ both assume that a character string ends with the null character '\0'; that is, '\0' identifies the end of a character string, and '\n' identifies the end of the current input line for a line-buffered data source.

The following function called **Flush**() shows how to extract and discard any unread data from an **iostream** object's internal buffer, up to and including the end-of-line delimiter character '**\n**':

```cpp
// File flush.h

#ifndef FLUSH_H
#define FLUSH_H

#include <iosfwd>

std::istream &Flush(std::istream &stream);

#endif

// File flush.cpp

#include <iostream>
#include <cstddef>
#include <numeric>

std::istream &Flush(std::istream &stream)
{
  static std::streamsize const MAX_LINE_LENGTH =
             std::numeric_limits<std::streamsize>::max();
  stream.clear(stream.rdstate() & ~std::ios_base::failbit);
  if(stream.good())
  {
    std::streambuf *ptr = stream.rdbuf();
    std::streamsize charactersToIgnore = ptr->in_avail();
    if(charactersToIgnore > 0)
      stream.ignore(MAX_LINE_LENGTH, '\n');
  }
  return stream;
}
```

Let's examine this function step by step:

▲ The static local variable **MAX_LINE_LENGTH** represents the theoretical maximum number of characters that can be transferred during an I/O operation. This value corresponds to the maximum value of the data type **std::streamsize**.

▲ The call to **std::basic_ios::clear**() turns off the stream's **failbit** state flag if it is enabled, so **Flush**() can then attempt to extract and discard any unread "garbage" characters from the input stream.

▲ The member function **std::istream::rdbuf**() returns a pointer to the stream's **std::streambuf** object, that is, the internal buffer area that holds the stream object's input characters.

▲ Using this pointer, the member function **std::streambuf::in_avail**() is called to obtain the number of available (unread) characters in the buffer.

▲ If this number is greater than 0, the member function **std::basic_ios::ignore**() is called to "ignore" (extract and discard) all unread characters in the current line, up to and including the end-of-line delimiter character '**\n**'.

Thus, a "crash-proof" program that loops while reading numbers and checking for end-of-file and garbage input might resemble the following:

```cpp
#include <iostream>
#include "flush.h"
using std::cout;
using std::cerr;
using std::cin;

int main()
{
  do
  {
    Flush(cin);
    cout << "Enter a number: ";
    int number;
    if(cin >> number)
      cout << "You entered: " << number << '\n';
    else if(!cin.eof())
      cerr << "Invalid data!\n";
  }
  while(!cin.eof() && !cin.bad());
  if(cin.bad())
    cerr << "Unrecoverable error\n";
  else if(cin.eof())
    cout << "\nEnd-of-file detected!\n";
}


/* Typical output:

Enter a number: 12
You entered: 12
Enter a number: junk
Input error!
```

```
Enter a number: 5 6
You entered: 5
Enter a number: ^Z
End-of-file

*/
```

One note about the logic of this program. If two valid numbers are entered before the operator presses <**ENTER**>, then the first number will be processed and the second will be flushed. You may or may not want this to happen, depending on your design philosophy.

SUMMARY ▶ When an input error is encountered, the input stream must be flushed of any extraneous characters. This is how it's done.

EXERCISE 15.1

Prompt the terminal operator for two numeric integral values and check for end-of-file. If either value is not valid, display an error message, flush the input buffer, and return for new input. If both values are valid, display which of the two values is greater. Then return for more input.

Character Input

As you know, you can use the extraction operator to get character input from the keyboard. Just be aware that leading whitespace is bypassed by default. Another way is provided by the **std::istream::get()** "family" of member functions. One of these **get()** functions takes a single argument, a reference to a **char**, and returns a reference to the invoking instance so that function calls can be chained together. When invoked, this version of **get()** extracts the next available character from the input stream, if one is available, and assigns its value to the **char** object that was passed into **get()** by reference. The big difference between **std::istream::operator>>()** and **std::istream::get()** is that the latter will honor any and all whitespace characters. For example:

```
#include <iostream>
#include "flush.h"
using std::cout;
using std::cin;

int main()
{
    char const quote = '\'';
    cout << "Enter 2 characters >";
```

```
      char ch1, ch2;
      while(cin.get(ch1).get(ch2))
      {
        cout << "You entered: " << quote << ch1
             << quote << " and "
             << quote << ch2 << quote << '\n';
        Flush(cin);
        cout << "Next 2 characters >";
      }
      cout << "\nEnd-of-file\n";
}

/* Output:

Enter 2 characters >A B
You entered: 'A' and ' '
Next 2 characters > C D
You entered: ' ' and 'C'
Next 2 characters >abcd
You entered: 'a' and 'b'
Next 2 characters >^Z
End-of-file

*/
```

Another version of the **std::istream::get**() member function takes no input argument (just like **getchar**() in C). This form returns a value of type **std::istream::int_type**, which represents the ordinal value of the character just read, or the constant **std::istream::traits_type::eof**() if no character could be read. Because this version of **get**() does not return a reference to its input stream object, no chaining of this form of **std::istream::get**() is possible.

   In the following example, **std::istream::get**() is used to read in a character, after which a check for end-of-file is made. Because the variable **ch** must be defined as type **std::istream::int_type**, don't forget the cast in order to display it as a character:

```
#include <iostream>
#include "flush.h"
using std::cout;
using std::cin;

int main()
{
  char const quote = '\'';
  cout << "Enter a character: ";
```

```
   std::istream::int_type ch;
   while((ch = cin.get()) !=
                std::istream::traits_type::eof())
   {
      cout << "You entered: " << quote
          << static_cast<char>(ch) << quote << '\n';
      Flush(cin);
      cout << "Next character: ";
   }
   cout << "\nEnd-of-file\n";
}

/* Output:

Enter a character: A
You entered: 'A'
Next character: ^Z
End-of-file

*/
```

SUMMARY ▶ Use the member function **get()** to read in character input.

String Literal Input Using the Extraction Operator

String literals can also be entered using the extraction operator. Don't forget that leading whitespace is bypassed (by default), and the first whitespace encountered after a sequence of nonwhitespace characters marks the end of the input field. This acts just like the function **scanf()** with the conversion specification **%s**. For example:

```
#include <iostream>
#include "flush.h"
using std::cout;
using std::cin;

int main()
{
   char const quote = '\"';
   cout << "Enter a string: ";
   int const size = 128;
   char buffer[size];
   while(cin >> buffer)
   {
      cout << "Your string: " << quote << buffer
```

```
            << quote        << '\n';
        Flush(cin);
        cout << "Next string: ";
    }
    cout << "\nEnd-of-file\n";
}

/* Output:

Enter a string: Hello world
Your string: "Hello"
Next string: C++
Your string: "C++"
Next string: ^Z
End-of-file

*/
```

 The member function **get()** has been overloaded so that it can also accommodate string input.

Limiting the Number of Input Characters

As with **scanf()**, you could have a program hang or crash if the operator enters more characters than can be accommodated by the character array that is the target for the input operation. For example, if the program specifies a 5-element char array as the target for the input operation,

```
int const BUFSIZE = 5;
char buffer[BUFSIZE]
cin >> buffer;
```

but the length of the next data item is 10 characters, then the input operation will apparently overrun the end of the 5-element char array as it reads in the 10-character data value, thereby corrupting whatever happened to be stored in memory after the array.

To guard against this disaster, you can specify the width of the next input field so as to physically limit the number of characters that the extraction operator reads from the input stream. This is done by invoking the member function **std::ios_base::width()** on behalf of the **std::cin** instance, and specifying the maximum number of characters n that the stream can store in the character array **buffer**. The result is that the extraction operator will read no more than $n - 1$ characters from the input stream into **buffer**, and then a null character will be assigned to the next available position in **buffer**; any remaining characters in the input sequence are ignored. Of course, the first whitespace character encountered at the end of a nonwhitespace sequence still terminates the input field; it could be that fewer than *n – 1* characters will be read from the input stream into **buffer**. And don't forget: Just like the **std::ios_base::width**() function used for output, the input **std::ios_base::width**() function applies only to the next item to be input; its effect is not "sticky" across multiple input operations.

For example, in the following program, the terminal operator can input any number of characters, but only the first nine will be stored into the buffer area:

```cpp
#include <iostream>
#include "flush.h"
using std::cout;
using std::cin;

int main()
{
   char const quote = '\"';
   int const size = 10;
   cout << "Enter a string no longer than " << (size - 1)
       << " characters\n";
   cin.width(size);
   char buffer[size];
   while(cin >> buffer)
   {
     cout << "Your string: " << quote << buffer
        << quote   << '\n';
     Flush(cin);
     cin.width(size);
     cout << "Next string: ";
   }
   cout << "\nEnd-of-file\n";
}

/* Output:

Enter a string no longer than 9 characters
ThisIsALongString
You entered: "ThisIsALo"
Next string: ^Z
End-of-file

*/
```

 Call the member function **width**() to limit the number of input characters.

String Input Using std::istream::getline()

Another way to read in string literals is to use the member function **std::istream:: getline()**:

```
istream &getline(char *buffer,
        istream::streamsize bufsize, char delim = '\n');
```

It takes three arguments.

▲ The first argument, **buffer**, is a pointer to the first element of a **char** array where the input characters are to be stored,

▲ The second argument, **bufsize**, specifies the maximum number of characters that can be stored into the buffer area (including the trailing null character),

▲ The third argument, **delim**, specifies the terminating character (the one that will stop the transfer of characters from the input stream into the buffer area). Its default value is the newline character '**\n**', which, of course, is produced when the user presses the <**ENTER**> key after typing in the requested data value at the keyboard. Note that if the delimiter is changed to some other character (e.g., the tab character '**\t**'), the user must still press the <**ENTER**> key when done entering data with the keyboard. (In other words, it is the *operating system* software that requires the user to press the <**ENTER**> key to signal the end of a keyboard input sequence; this is not a C++ requirement.)

Each time the **getline()** function is invoked, characters are extracted from the input stream and stored into the **buffer** area until one of the following conditions occurs (and are tested in the order shown):

▲ The input stream runs out of data, in which case the stream turns on its **eofbit** flag, or,

▲ The input stream extracts and discards the specified delimiter character (the delimiter character is *not* stored in the **buffer**), or,

▲ *bufsize – 1* characters are extracted from the input stream and stored into **buffer**, in which case **getline()** turns on the stream's **failbit** flag.

As soon as any one of these conditions occurs, **getline()** stops extracting characters from the input stream and stores a null character into the next available position in **buffer**. (In other words, when **getline()** returns, **buffer** *always* holds a null-terminated string.) If no characters are extracted from the input stream, **getline()** turns on the stream's **failbit** flag and stores a null character in **buffer[0]**.

Note that if the input stream's **failbit** flag is turned on following a **getline()** call, and if **buffer[0]** is not the null character, this indicates that the delimiter character was not found before **getline()** filled the **buffer** to its stated capacity **bufsize** (including the terminating null character). This is how one tests for the case where the current input line is too long to fit in a **buffer** whose length is **bufsize**.

Also note the similarity to the C function **fgets()**. The advantage to using **std::istream::getline()** as opposed to **std::istream::operator>>()** is that all characters up to (but not including) the specified delimiter character are retained as part of the string value. It's also possible to find out exactly how many characters the **getline()** call extracted from the input stream by invoking **std::istream::gcount()** on behalf of the input stream (whose result includes the delimiter character if it too was extracted). For example:

```
#include <iostream>
#include "flush.h"
using std::cout;
using std::cin;

int main()
{
  int const size = 256;
  cout << "Enter a string no longer than " << (size -1)
       << " characters: ";
  char buffer[size];
  while(cin.getline(buffer, size))
  {
    char const quote = '\"';
    cout << "Your string: " << quote << buffer << quote
         << " has " << (cin.gcount() - 1)
         << " characters\n";
    Flush(cin);
    cout << "Next string: ";
  }
  cout << "\nEnd-of-file\n";
}

/* Output:

Enter a string no longer than 255 characters:  Hello C++
Your string: " Hello C++" has 11 characters
Next string:
Your string "" has 0 characters
Next string: ^Z
End-of-file

*/
```

 SUMMARY Use the member function **getline()** to read in a string and honor all embedded white space characters.

16

Manipulators

Introduction

Manipulators provide you with the capability of facilitating and encapsulating the formatting that you must do with the input and output (I/O) streams. Until now, all such formatting has been painstakingly tedious and prone to error. That is about to change with the use of *manipulators*. The term itself comes from the fact that a manipulator does just what the name implies—it manipulates, or changes, the state of the I/O stream object.

 A manipulator facilitates the formatting of input and output.

The Format of a Manipulator

Because of the way in which a manipulator is called, its function signature and return type must conform to a certain pattern. For output streams, this pattern dictates that the function must take as an argument an instance of class **std::ostream** by reference, and it must return an instance of the same class by reference. To allow the chaining of manipulators with other calls to the insertion operator, the manipulator function must terminate by returning the same output stream instance that was passed into the manipulator function via its **std::ostream** reference argument. Thus, the complete definition for writing an output manipulator is:

```
std::ostream &outputManipulatorName(std::ostream &stream)
{
    // Your code here using the 'stream' object
```

```
    return stream;
}
```

In a similar fashion, all input manipulators have this format:

```
std::istream &inputManipulatorName(std::istream &stream)
{
  // Your code here using the 'stream' object
  return stream;
}
```

Focusing on the output side of the ledger for the moment, the class **std::ostream** has an overloaded insertion operator that takes as its one explicit parameter the *address* of the manipulator. That is, it takes the address of a function whose return type is **std::ostream &** and whose one argument type is **std::ostream &**. Equivalent code to define the insertion operator and to execute the manipulator would look like this:

```
using std::ostream;
typedef ostream &(*PTRF)(ostream &);
ostream &ostream::operator<<(PTRF ptr)
{
  // Execute the function to which 'ptr' points.
  // Pass the invoking object (usually 'std::cout') as the
  // argument, and return it when done
  return ptr(*this);
}
```

This implies that when you wish to use the manipulator, you do so by writing its name *without* the following parentheses, because that's what generates the address of the manipulator:

```
output_stream << outputManipulatorName
  // output_stream.operator<<(outputManipulatorName)

input_stream >> inputManipulatorName
  // input_stream.operator>>(inputManipulatorName)
```

 A manipulator takes and returns a stream object by reference. It's called by writing its name without parentheses.

Some Simple Manipulators

As an example, here is a program that creates a manipulator called **Format**() that sets the field width to 5 and the fill character to an asterisk '*'. To repeat: when **Format** is called, its name is *not* followed by parentheses:

```
// File format.h

#ifndef FORMAT_H
#define FORMAT_H

#include <iostream>

inline std::ostream &Format(std::ostream &stream)
{
    stream.width(5);
    stream.fill('*');
    return stream;
}

#endif

// File main.cpp

#include <iostream>
#include "format.h"

int main()
{
    std::cout << Format << 123 << '\n';
}

/* Output:

**123

*/
```

For an example of an input manipulator, in Chapter 15 the function **Flush**() was defined to clear the system input buffer of extraneous characters. Because the function takes an **std::istream** object by reference and returns the same object by reference, it can be used as a manipulator. Here is a repeat of the "crash-proof" program:

```
#include <iostream>
#include "flush.h"
using std::cout;
using std::cerr;
using std::cin;
```

```
int main()
{
  do
  {
    cin >> Flush;     // Flush now used as a manipulator
    cout << "Enter a number: ";
    int number;
    if(cin >> number)
      cout << "You entered: " << number << '\n';
    else if(!cin.eof())
      cerr << "Invalid data!\n";
  }
  while(!cin.eof() && !cin.bad());
  if(cin.bad())
    cerr << "Unrecoverable error\n";
  else if(cin.eof())
    cout << "\nEnd-of-file detected!\n";
}
```

Another use of a manipulator would be to ensure that all money amounts appear right-justified, 10-position field, fixed-decimal, with two decimal positions:

```
#ifndef MONEY_H
#define MONEY_H

#include <iostream>

inline std::ostream &Money(std::ostream &stream)
{
  stream.width(10);
  stream.setf(std::ios_base::right,
              std::ios_base::adjustfield);
  stream.setf(std::ios_base::fixed,
              std::ios_base::floatfield);
  stream.setf(std::ios_base::showpoint);
  stream.precision(2);
  return stream;
}

#endif

// File main.cpp

#include <iostream>
#include "money.h"
```

```
#include "flush.h"
using std::cout;
using std::cin;
using std::cerr;

int main()
{
  do
  {
    cin >> Flush;
    cout << "Enter an amount: ";
    double amount;
    if(cin >> amount)
      cout << Money << amount << '\n';
    else if(!cin.eof())
      cerr << "Invalid input!\n";
  }
  while(!cin.eof() && !cin.bad());
  if(cin.bad())
    cerr << "Unrecoverable error\n";
  else if(cin.eof())
    cout << "\nEnd-of-file detected!\n";
}

/* Output:

Enter some amount: 456.78
     456.78
Next amount: 3
       3.00
Next amount: 54.767657
      54.77
Next amount: ^Z
End-of-file detected

*/
```

 Some simple manipulator examples.

Built-In Manipulators Called with No Arguments

Because some output (and input) stream operations are done so often, the **iostream** library includes some predefined manipulators to handle these operations; they are shown in Table 16.1. They are included with all C++ compilers on the market today. Assume all manipulators are in the **std** namespace.

TABLE 16.1

Name	I, O, I/O	Description
endl	O	End-of-line (insert '\n' and flush the buffer)
ends	O	End-of-string (insert '\0')
dec	I/O	Input/output integers in decimal
oct	I/O	Input/output integers in octal
hex	I/O	Input/output integers in hexadecimal
flush	O	Flush the output stream buffer
boolalpha	I/O	Input/output **bool** values in alpha
noboolalpha	I/O	Reset **boolalpha**
showbase	O	Show the base for integers
noshowbase	O	Reset **showbase**
showpoint	O	Show the decimal point for floating-point values
noshowpoint	O	Reset **showpoint**
showpos	O	Show + sign for nonnegative integers
noshowpos	O	Reset **showpos**
ws	I	Extract whitespace
skipws	I	Skip leading whitespace
noskipws	I	Reset **skipws** (i.e., do not skip leading whitespace)
uppercase	O	Show uppercase letters
nouppercase	O	Reset **uppercase** (i.e., show lowercase letters)
internal	O	Show the field internally justified
left	O	Show the field left justified
right	O	Show the field right justified
fixed	O	Show floating-point values in fixed-point notation
scientific	O	Show floating-point values in scientific notation
unitbuf	O	Set flags for flushing output after each format
nounitbuf	O	Reset **unitbuf**

Thus, the **Money()** manipulator shown earlier could have been written like this:

```
// File money.h

#ifndef MONEY_H
#define MONEY_H

#include <iostream>

inline std::ostream &Money(std::ostream &stream)
{
  stream.width(10);
  stream << std::right << std::fixed << std::showpoint;
  stream.precision(2);
  return stream;
}

#endif
```

SUMMARY The built-in manipulators.

Manipulators Taking One Argument

It is possible to write a manipulator that is callable with one or more arguments. Obviously, this allows you to give the manipulator much greater flexibility. To see how this can be done for a manipulator that takes one argument, let's start with a class template called **OutputManipulator**:

```
// File manipulator.h

#ifndef MANIPULATOR_H
#define MANIPULATOR_H

#include <iostream>

template <typename T>
class OutputManipulator
{
    protected:
  typedef std::ostream &OSR;
  typedef OSR(*PTRF)(OSR, T);
```

```
   friend OSR operator<<(OSR stream,
                           OutputManipulator<T> const &arg)
   {
      return arg.ptrf(stream, arg.data);
   }
      public:
   OutputManipulator(PTRF ptrf, T data)
                           : ptrf(ptrf), data(data) { }
      private:
   PTRF ptrf;
   T data;
};
```

```
#endif
```

Although the **typedef**s are encapsulated, they are declared **protected** so that a derived class can use them. The constructor receives both the address of a manipulator and a const-reference to the one argument that the manipulator uses, and it initializes the corresponding data members of the **OutputManipulator** class instance with these values. The insertion operator executes the manipulator to which the pointer-to-function data member points, and passes the one argument to it.

Now we're ready to derive from this class in order to create a class with the name of our manipulator. The name of the base class, **OutputManipulator**, must be specialized to reflect the type of the one argument that the manipulator uses:

```
// File format.h

#ifndef FORMAT_H
#define FORMAT_H

#include "manipulator.h"

class Format : public OutputManipulator<int>
{
      public:
   explicit Format(int size)
                        : OutputManipulator<int>(def, size) { }
      private:
   inline static OSR def(OSR stream, int size);
};

inline Format::OSR Format::def(OSR stream, int size)
{
   stream.width(size);
   stream.fill('*');
```

```
    return stream;
}

#endif
```

The class contains a static member function named **def** that defines the manipulator itself. This manipulator receives the width size in addition to the stream device. The constructor of class Format takes the size and passes to the base class constructor the address of the manipulator and the size.

Finally, we're ready to run a test:

```
// File main.cpp

#include <iostream>
#include "format.h"

int main()
{
    std::cout << Format(10) << 123 << '\n';
}

/* Output:

******123

*/
```

Notice how a function style cast (class name followed by a list of arguments in parentheses) is used to write the manipulator. This invokes the constructor in the **Format** class so that the output line is effectively equivalent to,

```
std::cout << OutputManipulator<int>(Format::def, 10)
                                     <<123 << '\n';
```

and the displaying of the temporary **OutputManipulator** object causes the manipulator code to execute.

 How to write a manipulator taking one argument.

Built-In Manipulators Taking One Argument

Every C++ compiler also comes with built-in manipulators that take one argument, as shown in Table 16.2. As before, they are assumed to exist in the **std** namespace.

TABLE 16.2

Name	I, O, I/O	Description
setiosflags(long mask)	I/O	Set format flags according to **mask**
resetiosflags(long mask)	I/O	Clear format flags according to **mask**
setbase(int base)	I/O	Set the base for integer notation (8, 10, or 16)
setfill(char ch)	I/O	Set the fill character for padding
setprecision(int prec)	O	Set the precision of floating-point values
setw(int width)	I/O	Set the minimal field width

Note that, in order to use any of these, you must include the header file **iomanip**.

Returning once again to the **Money** manipulator, here is how it can be written using only the built-in manipulators:

```
// File money.h

#ifndef MONEY_H
#define MONEY_H

#include <iostream>
#include <iomanip>

inline std::ostream &Money(std::ostream &stream)
{
   return stream << std::setw(10)
                 << std::right
                 << std::fixed
                 << std::showpoint
                 << std::setprecision(2);
}

#endif
```

 The built-in manipulators taking one argument.

EXERCISE 16.1

Write a manipulator called **EndLines** that will output the number of end-of-lines that the argument specifies. For example,

```
std::cout << EndLines(5);
```

would produce five end-of-lines.

17

File Input/Output

Introduction

File input/output in C++ using **iostream** member functions gives you the ability to read an input file, write an output file, or both read and write the same file. To do this, classes have been derived from **std::istream** and **std::ostream** that accommodate anything that the operating system software considers a legitimate file.

 Classes derived from **std::istream** and **std::ostream** accommodate file input/output.

File Input/Output Classes

The classes that have already been defined for you are:

▲ **std::ofstream** (derived from **std::ostream**). Use this whenever you wish to write a file.

▲ **std::ifstream** (derived from **std::istream**). Use this whenever you wish to read a file.

▲ **std::fstream** (derived from **std::iostream**). Use this whenever you wish to update a file.

To use any of these classes, you must include the header file **fstream**.

SUMMARY ▶ Three classes handle writing, reading, and updating a disk file.

File Open Modes

The modes shown in Table 17.1 are all the modes in which a file can be opened. They are declared by class **std::ios_base** as static constant values of the bitmask type **std::ios_base::openmode**.

If the program does not specify the **binary** mode flag when opening a file, the program will try to open the file using text mode by default. Therefore, the bitmask type **openmode** does not define a "text" mode flag.

More than one mode can be used, provided they are bitwise OR'ed together. The valid mode combinations are shown in Table 17.2.

The **ate** and **binary** modes can be OR'ed with any of these combinations.

SUMMARY ▶ The modes in which a file can be opened.

TABLE 17.1

Mode	Effect
in	Open file for reading
out	Open file for writing. Truncate to zero length if the file exists, or create a new file if nonexistent
ate	Start position is at the end of the file
app	Open file for appending
trunc	Delete file content before writing
binary	Open in binary mode

TABLE 17.2

Mode (in std::ios_base)	Effect
out | trunc	Truncate to zero length if the file exists, or create a new file if nonexistent
out | app	Open or create text file for writing at the end
in | out	Open for update (reading and writing)
in | out | trunc	Truncate to zero length if the file exists, or create a new file for update

File Output

Let's start with file output. There are two ways to open an output file:

▲ The first way is to instantiate the class **std::ofstream** and then call the member function **open()**. The first argument to the **open()** function is a **char const *** that points to a null-terminated string that holds the file's name. This argument is required. The second argument is optional and is a bitmask of type **std::ios_base::openmode** that specifies one of the modes or mode combinations shown in Tables 17.1 and 17.2.

▲ The second way is to combine the instantiation and the call to **open()** into one step by passing the same parameters directly to the constructor.

For example:

```
#include <fstream>
// ...
std::ofstream file;
file.open("fileName");
   // or...
std::ofstream file("fileName");
```

SUMMARY ▶ How to open a disk file for output.

The File Name Argument

In both cases, the formal argument that accepts the file name is declared as a pointer-to-const-char (**char const ***); the file's name *must* be specified using a C style null-terminated byte string (NTBS), such as, a constant-valued string literal such as "myfile.txt" or a **char** array that holds the file name as a null-terminated character string. If the file name is stored in an instance of the **std::string** class (discussed in Chapter 18), the program must convert the **std::string** instance into a temporary, **const**-valued, NTBS by calling the instance's **std::string::c_str()** member function:

```
std::string fileName("mydata.txt");
std::ifstream file;
file.open(fileName); // ERROR - std::string not supported
file.open(fileName.c_str());      // Correct
```

SUMMARY ▶ How to specify the file name argument when opening a disk file.

The File Mode Argument

If the program does not explicitly specify an **openmode** value when opening a file with a **std::ofstream** instance, the value **std::ios_base::out** is specified by default. This corresponds to a text mode output file. (Recall that text mode is used by default if the

std::ios_base::binary mode flag is not specified.) Also, the **std::ios_base::out** mode flag is *always* bitwise OR'd into any **openmode** value that the program specifies when it tries to open a file with an **std::ofstream** instance. You are not required to specify the **std::ios_base::out** flag explicitly when configuring the **openmode** value for an **std::ofstream** instance (although you can do so):

```
using std::ios_base;
std::ofstream file("fileName", ios_base::app);
    // The actual openmode value will be:
    //   ios_base::out | ios_base::app
    // even though ios_base::out was not specified
```

 A **std::ofstream** object always has output mode set by default.

Verify That the File Was Opened

Immediately after the program tries to open the specified output file, it should test the **ofstream** instance's **failbit** state flag to determine whether the open attempt was successful or not. If the instance's **failbit** flag is on, the open attempt failed; otherwise, the open attempt was successful and the program can now use the open file.

 You should always verify that a disk file is opened successfully by looking at its **failbit**.

Closing an Open File

The member function **close()** can be called at any time to close an open file. If you fail to do this, it will be called automatically when the **ofstream** instance goes out of scope.

 The member function **close()** is used to close an open disk file. It is called automatically when the disk file object goes out of scope.

An Example of an Output Disk File

Let's start by creating a file with some nice text:

```
// File main.cpp

#include <iostream>
#include <fstream>
#include <cstddef>
using std::ios_base;
using std::size_t;

int main()
{
  std::ofstream outputFile("fileName.dat");
```

```
      if (outputFile)    // or, if (!outputFile.fail()) ...
      {
        char const *data[] =
        {
          "The time has come",
          "The walrus said",
          "To talk of many things,"
        };
        size_t const size = sizeof(data) / sizeof(*data);
        for(size_t i = 0; i < size; ++i)
          outputFile << data[i] << '\n';
        outputFile.close();
      }
      else
        std::cerr << "Open error\n";
    }
```

You can easily verify that the file **fileName.dat** does indeed exist in the current directory on your hard disk by listing it or examining it with your favorite editor.

Just for fun, let's try opening the file in append mode in order to add some more lines:

```
// File main.cpp

#include <iostream>
#include <fstream>
#include <cstddef>
using std::ios_base;
using std::size_t;

int main()
{
  std::ofstream outputFile("fileName.dat", ios_base::app);
  if (outputFile)
  {
    char const *data[] =
    {
      "Of shoes and ships and sealing wax",
      "And whether pigs have wings."
    };
    size_t const size = sizeof(data) / sizeof(*data);
    for(size_t i = 0; i < size; ++i)
      outputFile << data[i] << '\n';
    outputFile.close();
  }
```

```
    else
       std::cerr << "Open error\n";
}
```

Once again, you can verify that the file has these lines appended to it.

File Input

The class **std::ifstream** is used to read a file. Just like class **std::ofstream**, you can attach the file to the object at instantiation time or during the call to **open()**. The default mode for input is **std::ios_base::in**, that is, a text mode input file. Also, the **std::ios_base::in** mode flag is *always* bitwise OR'd into any **openmode** value that you specify when opening a file with an **ifstream** instance. It's not necessary to specify the **std::ios_base::in** mode flag explicitly when configuring the **openmode** value for an **ifstream** instance. Of course, you must still take care to verify that the file was opened successfully before attempting to read from it, and the usual functions associated with the **std::cin** object can then be used.

Now let's read the file that was just created:

```cpp
// File main.cpp

#include <iostream>
#include <fstream>

int main()
{
   std::ifstream inputFile("fileName.dat");
   if(inputFile)
   {
      int const size = 256;
      char buffer[size];
      do
      {
         inputFile.getline(buffer, size);
         std::cout << buffer << '\n';
      }
      while(!inputFile.eof());
   }
   else
      std::cerr << "Open error\n";
}

/* Output:

The time has come
```

```
The walrus said
To talk of many things,
Of shoes and ships and sealing wax
And whether pigs have wings.


*/
```

    An input disk file is always opened in input mode by default. As before, you should make sure that the file is opened successfully.

File Position Markers

In addition to processing a file sequentially from start to end, you can jump around in it by modifying the *file position markers.* For input operations, the *get marker* determines where the next read will occur. For output operations, the *put marker* determines where the next write will occur. Input-only streams do not use the put marker. Likewise, output-only streams do not use the get marker. Streams that perform both input and output use both markers.

For some **iostream** types, the streams' get and put markers operate independently, that is, the get and put markers might point at different locations within the same data stream. For other **iostream** types, most notably the file streams, the get and put markers are "locked together," that is, moving the get marker also moves the put marker, and vice versa, so that at all times both markers point at the same location within the data stream.

When working with input streams, there are two ways to reposition the stream's get marker:

▲ Call the member function **ifstream::seekg()** with one argument representing the absolute byte position within the file, starting at position 0,
▲ Call the member function **ifstream::seekg()** with two arguments. The first argument represents an offset byte position relative to the second argument, which is either **std::ios_base::beg**, **std::ios_base::cur**, or **std::ios_base::end**, meaning the beginning, the current position, and the end of the file, respectively. For example, **seekg(−3, std::ios_base::end)** would represent 3 bytes before the end of the file.

The member function **ifstream::tellg()** returns the current location of the file position marker as a value of type **std::istream::pos_type**.

For example, the following is a repeat of the previous program with **end** representing the number of bytes in the file. Then one byte at a time is extracted and displayed. Note the use of the **static_cast** because the member function **get()** returns type **std::istream::int_type**, not type **char**:

```cpp
// File main.cpp

#include <iostream>
#include <fstream>
using std::ios_base;

int main()
{
  std::ifstream inputFile("fileName.dat");
  if(inputFile)
  {
    inputFile.seekg(0, ios_base::end);
    std::ifstream::pos_type end = inputFile.tellg();
    inputFile.seekg(0);
    for(long begin = 0L; begin < end; ++begin)
      std::cout << static_cast<char>(inputFile.get());
  }
  else
    std::cerr << "Open error\n";
}

/* Output:

The time has come
The walrus said
To talk of many things,
Of shoes and ships and sealing wax
And whether pigs have wings.

*/
```

 CAUTION The analogous functions **seekp()** and **tellp()** exist for the class **std::ofstream**.

SUMMARY The file position markers can be used to read from and write to any position within a disk file.

File Update

The class **std::fstream** is used to instantiate an **iostream** object that "knows" how to open an existing file for updating—for reading and writing the file's current contents.

The default mode is **std::ios_base::in | std::ios_base::out**, so that it is available for both reading and writing.

If you specify your own **std::ios_base::openmode** value when opening a file stream with a **std::fstream** instance, the **std::fstream** class *does not* implicitly enable the mode flags **std::ios_base::in** and/or **std::ios_base::out**. If you want to specify your own **openmode** value when opening a stream with a **std::fstream** instance, you must explicitly enable **std::ios_base:in** and/or **std::ios_base::out** in your **openmode** value.

In the following program, an existing file is opened for update, its contents are truncated (wiped out), and then new data is written into the file. Afterward, the leading commas are replaced with periods (to keep Mr. Donne pacified). Then all records are displayed:

```cpp
// File main.cpp

#include <iostream>
#include <fstream>
#include <cstddef>
using std::ios_base;
using std::size_t;

int main()
{
  std::fstream updateFile("fileName.dat",
      ios_base::in | ios_base::out | ios_base::trunc);
  if (updateFile)
  {
    char const *data[] =
    {
      ",,,and therefore never send to know for whom the "
      "bell tolls;",
      "it tolls for thee."
    };
    size_t const size = sizeof(data) / sizeof(*data);
    // Write the new data into the file
    for(size_t i = 0; i < size; ++i)
      updateFile << data[i] << '\n';
    // Replace commas with periods
    updateFile.seekp(0);
    for(int i = 0; i < 3; ++i)
      updateFile << '.';
    // Read the file's new contents
    updateFile.seekp(0);
    int const length = 256;
```

```
        char buffer[length];
        while(!updateFile.getline(buffer, length).eof())
          std::cout << buffer << '\n';
    }
    else
      std::cerr << "Open error\n";
}

/* Output:

...and therefore never send to know for whom the bell tolls;
it tolls for thee.

*/
```

When opening a disk file for update, you must explicitly specify the mode; there is no default value.

Binary Mode

When performing file I/O with a C++ program, you must never forget that there is *always* another program between your C++ program and the file itself. That "other program" is the operating system (OS):

```
your program <-> operating system <-> file
```

Each time a C++ program opens a file, it tells the operating system whether it should open the file using text or binary mode. This is *very important,* because an operating system might perform "behind the scenes" translations on data that is written to, or read from, text-mode files. For example, some operating systems translate each newline character **\n** into a newline/carriage-return pair **\n\r** when writing data to a text-mode file; these operating systems perform the opposite translation—**\n\r** becomes **\n**—when reading data from a text-mode file. This type of translation is often done to accommodate line printers and video displays that do not have enough built-in "smarts" to convert a newline character into a newline/carriage-return pair on their own.

The newline character is typically the same thing as a "linefeed" character. Documentation that comes with printers and video display terminals (VDTs) often uses the term "linefeed" instead of newline.

These OS-specific translations are not necessarily a bad thing when working with text files, but they wreak havoc on files that store nontext data, such as graphics images. There needs to be a way to disable the OS's text-mode translations when reading from, or writing to, a file that contains nontext data. This is done by specifying the **std::ios_base::binary** mode flag when opening the file stream.

The following program demonstrates these behaviors. It writes out a record consisting of the string literal "C++" followed by three newline characters using both text mode (the default mode) and binary mode:

```cpp
// File main.cpp

#include <iostream>
#include <fstream>
#include <cstddef>
using std::ios_base;
using std::size_t;

void testSize(ios_base::openmode mode = ios_base::out)
{
  std::ofstream file("fileName.dat", mode);
  if (file)
  {
    char const *data[] =
    {
      "C++\n\n\n"
    };
    size_t const size = sizeof(data) / sizeof(*data);
    for(size_t i = 0; i < size; ++i)
      file << data[i];
    std::cout << file.tellp()<< '\n';
  }
  else
    std::cerr << "Open error\n";
}

int main()
{
  testSize();
  testSize(ios_base::out | ios_base::binary);
}

/* Output:

9
6

*/
```

If you happen to be using an operating system that performs newline translations (i.e., **\n** becomes **\n\r**) during file write operations, then **tellp()** will report that exactly nine characters were written in text mode, whereas repeating the process in binary mode writes exactly six characters.

SUMMARY ▶ Open a disk file in binary mode when working with non-text data.

Unformatted Output

Normally, when you write primitive types such as **double** and **int** to an output stream, the binary representations of these values are automatically converted into a sequence of human-readable characters; then the human-readable characters are written to the output stream. For example, the **int** value of 123 is converted into the character sequence '1', '2', and '3', and then these characters are written to the output stream. On the other hand, if you ever need to write out the binary representation of a primitive type as a sequence of one or more bytes, that is, without any primitive-to-human-readable-text formatting taking place, you use the member function **std::ofstream::write()**. This function takes two arguments: the starting address of an array of bytes, and the number of bytes to be read from the array and written to the output stream:

```
std::ofstream &std::ofstream::write(char const *buf,
        std::streamsize bufsize);
```

The program specifies the **buf** argument by taking the address of a primitive object (e.g., the address of an **int** object) and converting that address into a pointer-to-constant-character via a **reinterpret_cast**. In other words, the program is fooling the **write()** function into thinking there is constant-valued **char** array sitting in storage at the specified address. (Of course, you and I know there is actually a primitive object stored in memory at that address, but we won't tell **write()** that.) The **bufsize** argument—the number of bytes that are to be read from the array and written to the output stream—corresponds to the number of bytes of storage that the primitive type occupies (e.g., the size of an **int** object). This value is easily deduced by applying the **sizeof** operator to the primitive object.

For example, the following program writes an unformatted **double** and an unformatted **int** to a file:

```
// File main.cpp

#include <iostream>
#include <fstream>

int main()
{
    using std::ios_base;
```

```
std::ofstream file("fileName.dat", ios_base::binary);
if (file)
{
  // Write the double
  double const avgLevel = -16.2150;
  file.write(reinterpret_cast<char const *>(&avgLevel),
          sizeof(avgLevel));
  // Write the int
  int ovenTemp = 123;
  file.write(reinterpret_cast<char const *>(&ovenTemp),
          sizeof(ovenTemp));
  file.close();
}
else
  std::cerr << "Open error\n";
}
```

There are a couple of items of interest here. First and foremost, when performing unformatted I/O with the **write()** and/or **read()** member functions (note that **read()** is
write()'s counterpart), the **iostream** instance *must* be opened in binary mode. If the
iostream instance is opened in text mode, the operating system software might perform
text-mode translations on the bytes that are being read from the data source or written
to the data sink, which would apparently foul up the byte representation of the primitive
type value that is being read/written.

CAUTION   When you write data to an output stream, the "thing" that ultimately receives the data
from that output operation is commonly referred to as the *data sink*. For example,
std::cout's data sink is typically some kind of video display device:

   std::cout → operating system → video display

In order to drive this point home, let's assume that a particular compiler product
implements the **int** data type as a 4-byte value, and that a program written with this
compiler product has instantiated an **int** value whose individual byte values are
(in hex):

```
F3 5C 0A 33    // hex representation of some 4-byte int value
```

If these bytes are written to a text-mode file, the operating system might incorrectly in-
terpret the byte **0A** as a newline character **\n** and convert it into a newline/carriage return pair **\n\r** (i.e., **0A 0D**) before writing the value to the file:

```
F3 5C 0A 0D 33 // this is what some OSs write into the file
```

Sometime later, another program (written with the same compiler as the previous program) opens this file in binary mode and tries to read in the 4-byte **int** value. Because the

file has been opened in binary mode this time, the OS *does not* translate the byte sequence **0A 0D** back into a single newline byte **0A**. Consequently, the program reads the wrong **int** value, specifically, **F3 5C 0A 0D**, from the input file. Furthermore, the byte **33** is left sitting in the input stream:

```
33 XX XX XX ...
```

Clearly, the program itself and the input sequence are now corrupted. There is no way to predict how the program will respond to the incorrect **int** value it has just read. Likewise, there is no way to predict how the residual **33** byte will affect any remaining read operations on this particular file stream.

The second item of interest in the earlier code sample is this: The program *always* specifies the name of a variable (e.g., **ovenTemp**) as the **sizeof** operator's operand rather than specifying the variable's type (e.g. **int**), which would also be valid. Here's why this is done. Assume that the program uses **sizeof(int)** instead of **sizeof(ovenTemp)**, and that a year from now you (or someone else) decides to change **ovenTemp**'s type to some other integer type, such as **short int**. This change could easily introduce a bug:

```
short int const ovenTemp = 123;
// ...
file.write(reinterpret_cast<char const *>(&ovenTemp),
    sizeof(int));        // whoops!
```

If you need further convincing, assume that **ovenTemp** is implemented as a global variable instead of as a local variable, and that there are hundreds (or thousands!) of uses of **sizeof(int)** throughout the program that specify the size of the global variable **ovenTemp**. If **ovenTemp**'s type is subsequently changed from **int** to some other data type (e.g., **short int**), then someone—probably *you*—must locate and change every occurrence of **sizeof(int)** that specifies **ovenTemp**'s size. Of course, if you miss any of these changes, then the program is broken. Likewise, if you inadvertently change a **sizeof(int)** that does not pertain to **ovenTemp**'s size, the program is again broken. It doesn't take a rocket scientist to realize this is an error-prone task—particularly in a large, complex program. By specifying the variable name as the **sizeof** operator's operand rather than the variable's data type, we automatically avoid such problems.

CAUTION   Changing **ovenTemp**'s type from **int** to **short int** might introduce other problems as well. Note that the **int** and **short int** data types might require different amounts of storage, such as **sizeof(int)** != **sizeof(short int)**. If the previous version of the program created a data file that contains **ovenTemp** values that occupy **sizeof(int)** bytes, the new-and-improved program might not be able to read the existing data file because it expects **ovenTemp** values to occupy **sizeof(short int)** bytes. Correcting this problem is not trivial and is left as an exercise (in frustration!) for the reader.

   How to perform unformatted output when writing to a disk file.

Unformatted Input

In order to read unformatted data from a file, use the member function **std::ifstream::read()**. Its two arguments are a pointer to a nonconstant **char** array, and the number of bytes that are to be read from the stream and stored in the **char** array:

```
std::ifstream &std::ifstream::read(char *buf, std::streamsize
bufsize);
```

As before, the program specifies the **buf** argument by taking the address of a primitive object and converting that address into a pointer-to-char via a **reinterpret_cast**. Likewise, the sizeof operator is applied to the primitive object itself to obtain the **bufsize** value (i.e., the number of bytes to be read from the stream into **buf**).

The following program reads and displays the data that was created in the **ovenTemp** example:

```cpp
// File main.cpp

#include <iostream>
#include <fstream>

int main()
{
  using std::ios_base;
  std::ifstream file("fileName.dat", ios_base::binary);
  if(file)
  {
    // Read the double
    double avgLevel = 0.0;
    file.read(reinterpret_cast<char*>(&avgLevel),
            sizeof(avgLevel));
    std::cout << avgLevel << '\n';

    // Read the int
    int ovenTemp = 0;
    file.read(reinterpret_cast<char*>(&ovenTemp),
            sizeof(ovenTemp));
    std::cout << ovenTemp << '\n';

    file.close();
  }
  else
    std::cerr << "Open error\n";
}
```

```
/* Output:

-16.215
123


*/
```

 How to perform unformatted input when reading from a disk file.

Redirecting I/O

The C++ I/O model is based on the following hierarchy:

```
    +--------------------------------------------------+
5)  | Your C++ code                                    |
    +-= iostream API ---------------------------------+
4)  | iostream-derived classes                         |
    +-= streambuf API -------------------------------+
3)  | streambuf-derived classes                        |
    +== system API====================================+
2)  | "system software" (e.g., the operating system)  |
    +-= system device drivers -----------------------+
1)  | actual data source / sink                        |
    +--------------------------------------------------+
```

In a typical program, the software at any particular level in the hierarchy interacts with only the software at the next higher or next lower level. For example, the **iostream** classes (level 4) interact with your code (level 5) and with the **streambuf** classes (level 3). The **iostream** classes do not interact with level 2 or level 1 code. Furthermore, each layer defines an application program interface (API)—that is, a public interface—that the layers above it must use when communicating with that layer.

In a nutshell, the **iostream** classes (layer 4) provide a program-friendly API that your code (layer 5) can use to read formatted data from, or write formatted data to, a **streambuf** object (level 3). For example, the **iostream** API provides (among other things) a set of **operator>>**() and **operator<<**() functions that "know" how to extract formatted data values from, or write formatted data values to, any kind of **streambuf** object.

The **streambuf** classes (level 3) provide the following two services: They "know" how to manage a contiguous sequence of raw (unformatted) data, and they "know" how to interact with the underlying system software (level 2) when it's time to (a) obtain more raw data from a system-owned data source during an input operation, or (b) output raw data to a system-owned data sink during an output operation.

To help clarify how this all works, consider the following example:

```
int count;
std::cin >> count;
```

Let's assume that **std::cin** gets its input from the system keyboard, and that prior to the **operator>>**() call **std::cin**'s internal **streambuf** object is empty. When the program (level 5) invokes the **operator>>**() call (level 4) on the **std::cin** instance, the **operator>>**() call in turn invokes the appropriate API (member) functions of the **streambuf** class (level 3) as it attempts to read a sequence of unformatted digit characters from **std::cin**'s internal **streambuf** object. Because the **streambuf** object is currently empty, the **streambuf** object invokes in turn the appropriate API functions at the system software (level 2) to cause the system software to obtain another line of data from the system-owned keyboard device (level 1). Let's assume the user now enters the characters '1', '2', and '3' and presses the keyboard's <**ENTER**> key. When the system software detects that the <**ENTER**> key has been pressed, it knows the user is done entering data at the keyboard. The system software copies the user's input (the characters '1', '2', '3', and '\n') from the system-owned keyboard buffer (level 1) up into the **streambuf** object (level 3). Now that the **streambuf** object has some raw data in it (the characters '1', '2', '3', and '\n'), the **operator>>**() call (level 4) begins extracting the raw keyboard data from the **streambuf** (e.g., the digit characters '1', '2', and '3') and converts this raw data into the formatted data value that the program (level 5) expects (e.g., the **int** value 123); finally it stores the resulting **int** value 123 in the **int** variable named **count**.

An **iostream** class instance is nothing more than a programmer-friendly "front end" for a **streambuf** object, so you can theoretically use *any* **iostream** class object with *any* **streambuf** object. In other words, you can "drop" any **streambuf** object into any existing **iostream** object and then use the **iostream** object's API to read data from, or write data to, that **streambuf** object. This is precisely how I/O redirection is programmatically implemented using the C++ I/O model. You start by creating a new **streambuf** object (or borrowing an existing **streambuf** object) that "knows" how to read data from, or write data to, the system-owned data source/sink you're interested in. You then drop that **streambuf** instance into an **iostream** instance and use the **iostream** API to read data from, or write data to, that **streambuf** object.

The following example shows one way to programmatically direct the output of an **std::ostream** instance to one of two **streambuf** objects:

```cpp
// File main.cpp

#include <iostream>
#include <fstream>

int main()
{
  bool useFile = false;
    // false : output is sent to cout
    // true : output is sent to a file

  std::ofstream *outputFile = 0;
  std::streambuf *sb = 0;
  if(useFile)
```

```
  {
    outputFile = new std::ofstream();
    outputFile->open("fileName.dat");
    // if the file open attempt did not fail ...
    if(!outputFile->fail())
    {
      // ... store the address of outputFile's
      // filebuf object in the streambuf
      // pointer 'sb' (n.b. filebuf is derived
      // from streambuf)
      sb = outputFile->rdbuf();
    }
    else
      std::cerr << "File open failed\n";
  }
  else
  {
    // Store the address of cout's streambuf
    // object in the streambuf pointer 'sb'
    sb = std::cout.rdbuf();
  }

  if(sb)
  {
    // "Drop" the streambuf instance into
    // a std::ostream "front end"
    std::ostream output(sb);
    // Use the ostream instance's API to write data
    // into the underlying streambuf instance
    output << "C++\n";
    // Flush the streambuf's buffer contents to the
    // streambuf's data sink (i.e., the display or file)
    output.flush();
  }

  // Housekeeping
  if(useFile)
  {
    // close the output file if it's currently open
    if(outputFile->is_open())
      outputFile->close();
    // deallocate the ofstream instance
    delete outputFile;
  }
}
```

▶ **SUMMARY** How to redirect I/O.

EXERCISE 17.1

Write a C++ program that (1) writes all 256 characters in the collating sequence to a disk file in character, decimal, hexadecimal, and octal formats, and then (2) reads each of the 256 records back in and displays it. (Caution: You might not be able to write number 26, the end-of-file character.)

18

The **string** class and
the Standard Template Library

Introduction

The **string** class and the Standard Template Library (STL) comprise the bulk of the C++ standard library functions and classes. By taking advantage of these functions and classes, you will saving yourself a great deal of time and effort for the simple reason that you will not have to write, test, and debug these functions and classes again and again for your various projects. All you have to do is know how to use them.

The **string** Class

The C++ library contains a class called **string** that encapsulates the notion of a character sequence. If you're thinking that this class is essentially the same as the **String** class that was first shown in Chapter 7, you're absolutely right. But because we've gone to all the trouble to write our own class, one could say that we've "paid our dues" and are now entitled to use the one from the library. As you might suspect, the **string** class that is provided with the standard C++ library has a wide variety of functions that do just about anything to a **string** object that you could imagine, including input and output with overloaded extraction and insertion operators.

The **string** class is defined in the C++ library header file **string**, which is not to be confused with the C library header file **string.h** that contains functions to support C language null-terminated char strings, such as **strcpy()**, **strlen()**, and so on. (The header file **cstring** is the C++ version of **string.h**.)

CAUTION   As a reminder, the header files that accompany the ISO/ANSI C++ standard library *do not* have the ".h" file extension. Also, C++ defines its own set of header files for use with the standard C library. These C++ header files have essentially the same names as their C library counterparts, except that the C++ names start with "c" and they *do not* have the ".h" file extension; the C++ header file **cstring** corresponds to the header file **string.h** in the standard C library; **cstdio** in the C++ library corresponds to **stdio.h** in the C library; **cmath** corresponds to **math.h,** and so on.

Just about everything in the standard C++ library is defined within the **std** namespace, and the **string** class is no exception. The **string** class's fully qualified name is **std::string**. The **std::string** class is one of two predefined string classes in the standard C++ library. The other string class is called **std::wstring**. The primary difference between these two classes is that **std::string** works with **char** values, and **std::wstring** works with **wchar_t** values. The C++ data type **wchar_t** provides support for so-called wide character sets, those character sets that require more storage per character than the **char** data type can provide. Because these two classes are fundamentally similar, it should come as no surprise that they are actually specializations of a class template named **std::basic_string**:

```
namespace std
{
  // ...
  typedef basic_string<char> string;
  typedef basic_string<wchar_t> wstring;
}
```

When the **string** class's member functions allocate storage for an instance of the **string** class, they often allocate more storage than actually required. At any given time, the total amount of storage that a string instance owns (called its *capacity*) will be greater than or equal to the current length of the string value itself. This makes the expansion of a **string** object much more efficient because it's not always necessary to reallocate dynamic space.

Let's start by looking at some of the functions of the **string** class, as shown in Table 18.1. Note that **string::size_type** is an implementation-defined integral type, and **npos** is defined to be −1:

TABLE 18.1

Constructor	Description
string(char const *lit)	Create an object that points to a copy of **lit**.
string(size_t num, char ch)	Create an object **num** bytes in length, each of which contains **ch**.
string(string const &str, size_type pos = 0, size_type num = npos)	Create an object that is a copy of **str**, starting at position **pos** and going to the end of str or using **num** characters, whichever comes first. If **num** is negative, the end of **str** is assumed.

(continued)

TABLE 18.1 (*continued*)

string()	Create an object of 0 size.
string(char const *lit, size_type num)	Create an object that points to a copy of **lit** and continues for **num** characters, even if **num** exceeds the logical length. Any extra space is uninitialized.

Input (nonmember function)	Description
istream &getline(istream & in, string & str, char delim = '\n')	Reads characters from the input stream **in** and stores them in the string object **str**. **str** is erased first, and it is expanded as needed. Reading stops when either the trailing delimiter character **delim** is extracted from **in** (the delimiter is discarded; it is not stored in **str**), or an input error occurs (e.g., end-of-file).

Assignment	Description
string &operator=(string const &str)	Assign the string object **str** to the current string object.
string &operator=(char const *lit)	Assign the string literal **lit** to the current string object.
string &operator=(char ch)	Assign **ch** to the current string object.

Append	Description
string &operator+=(string const &str)	Append **str** to the current string object and assign.
string &operator+=(char const *lit)	Append **lit** to the current string object and assign.
string &operator+=(char ch)	Append **ch** to the current string object and assign.
string &append(string const &str)	Append **str** to the current string object and assign.
string &append(char const *lit)	Append **lit** to the current string object and assign.
string &append(char ch)	Append **ch** to the current string object and assign.

Insert	Description
string &insert(size_type pos, string const &str)	Insert the string object **str** in front of the character at position **pos**.

Subscript	Description
char &operator[](size_type pos) throw()	Fetch the character at position **pos**.
char const &operator[](size_type pos) const throw()	Fetch the character at position **pos**.
char &at(size_type pos) throw(std::out_of_range)	Fetch the character at position **pos**. Throws an **std::out_of_range** exception if **pos** >= **size()**.
char const &at(size_type pos) const throw(std::out_of_range)	Fetch the character at position **pos**. Throws an **std::out_of_range** exception if **pos** >= **size()**.

(*continued*)

TABLE 18.1   (*continued*)

Substring	Description
string substr(size_type pos = 0, size_type n = npos) const throw(std::out_of_range)	Return the string consisting of **n** characters starting at position **pos**. Throws an **std::out_of_range** exception if **pos>size()**.

Concatenation (nonmember functions)	Description
string operator+(string const &str1, string const &str2)	Concatenate **str1** and **str2**.
string operator+(string const &str, char const *lit)	Concatenate **str** and **lit**.
string operator+(string const &str, char ch)	Concatenate **str** and **ch**.
string operator+(char const *lit, string const &str)	Concatenate **lit** and **str**.
string operator+(char ch, string const &str)	Concatenate **ch** and **str**.

Relational (nonmember functions)	Description
bool operator==(string const str1, string const &str2	true if **srtr1** is equal to **str2**.
bool operator!=(string const str1, string const &str2	true if **srtr1** is not equal to **str2**.
bool operator>(string const str1, string const &str2	true if **srtr1** is greater than **str2**.
bool operator<(string const str1, string const &str2	true if **srtr1** is less than **str2**.
bool operator>=(string const str1, string const &str2	true if **srtr1** is greater than or equal to **str2**.
bool operator<=(string const str1, string const &str2	true if **srtr1** is less than or equal to **str2**.

Query	Description
size_type length() const	The logical length of the string object.
size_type size() const	The logical length of the string object.
size_type capacity() const	The physical size of the string object.
bool empty() const	true if the string object is empty.

(*continued*)

TABLE 18.1 (*continued*)

Comparison	Description
int compare(string const &str) const	Returns a negative number if ***this** is less than **str**, zero if they're equal, and a positive number if greater.
int compare(int pos, int n, string const &str) const	Same as above, but compare ***this** starting at position **pos** comparing **n** characters.

Misc.	Description
void clear()	Clear the contents of the string object. (Invoking this function *does not* necessarily deallocate any storage that the string object currently owns.)
void swap(string &str)	Swap the contents of the string object with the string **str**.

The following program provides a test of many of these functions:

```cpp
#include <iostream>
#include <string>
using std::string;
using std::cout;
using std::cin;

void display(string const &str)
{
    char const quote = '\"';
    cout << quote << str << quote << " Length: "
         << str.length() << ", Capacity: " << str.capacity()
         << '\n';
}

int main()
{
    string str1("Typical string");
    display(str1);
    str1 += "s";
    display(str1);
    string str2(str1, 8);
    display(str2);
    str2.append(" are here");
    display(str2);
    str2.clear();
    cout << (str2.empty() ? "Empty" : "Not empty") << '\n';
    display(str2);
```

```
        str2 = str1 + 's';
        display(str2);
        str2.swap(str1);
        display(str2);
        str2[0] = 't';
        display(str2);
        cout << "Enter a new value: ";
        getline(cin, str2);
        display(str2);
}

/* Output:

"Typical string" Length: 14, Capacity: 14
"Typical strings" Length: 15, Capacity: 28
"strings" Length: 7 Capacity: 7
"strings are here" Length: 16, Capacity: 16
Empty
"" Length: 0, Capacity: 16
"Typical stringss" Length: 16, Capacity: 16
"Typical strings" Length: 15, Capacity: 28
"typical strings" Length: 15, Capacity: 28
Enter a new value: Whatever...
"Whatever..." Length: 11, Capacity: 28

*/
```

The Standard Template Library

The Standard Template Library (STL) is a C++ library that provides a set of generic container classes (class templates) and generic algorithms (function templates). The container classes include vectors, lists, deques, sets, multisets, maps, multimaps, stacks, queues and priority queues, and more. The generic algorithms include a broad range of fundamental algorithms for the most common kinds of data manipulations, such as searching, sorting, merging, copying, and transforming. This chapter will give you a taste of the STL by illustrating a few of the more common classes and algorithms (which, of course, are located in the **std** namespace). If you want more information, you can consult some of the STL books listed in the Bibliography in Appendix A.

std::vector Class

A typical container class in the STL (and probably the most frequently used) is called **std::vector**. This class template encapsulates an array of elements of some generic type.

It is defined in the header file <**vector**>. In effect, it looks like a C language array. By definition of the STL, it is a class template and thus able to contain virtually any type of data. For the sake of efficiency, its physical size can be greater than its logical size so that, whenever a new element needs to be added, it probably will not be necessary to reallocate space on the free store.

Because a **vector** is used so often to hold data, we will focus on its member functions, shown in Table 18.2. (Note that the data type **std::vector::size_type** is an implementation-defined unsigned integer type.)

TABLE 18.2

Member function name	Meaning
vector()	Construct an empty vector.
vector(size_type num, T const &val = T())	Construct a vector with **num** elements, each of which has the value **val**.
vector(T *start, T *end)	Construct a vector with (**end-start**) elements, and initialize the vector with the values ***start**, . . . ,*(**end−1**).
vector(vector<T> const &obj)	Copy a vector.
size_type size() const	Return the number of logical entries.
size_type capacity() const	Return the number of physical entries.
bool empty() const	See if the vector is empty.
void assign(size_type num, T const &val)	Assign to the vector **num** elements of value val.
void push_back(T const &)	Add an element to the end of the vector.
void pop_back()	Remove an element from the end of the vector. If no such element exists, the vector will be left in an unstable state.
T &front()	Return a reference to the first element of the vector.
T const &front() const	Return a reference-to-**const** to the first element of the vector.
T &back()	Return a reference to the last element of the vector.
T const &back() const	Return a reference-to-**const** to the last element of the vector.
T &operator[](int pos)	Return a reference to the element at position **pos**.
T const &operator[](int pos) const	Return a reference-to-**const** to the element at position **pos**.
T &at(int pos) throw(std::out_of_range)	Return a reference to the element at position **pos**. Throws an exception if **pos** >= **size()**.
T const &at(int pos) const throw(std::out_of_range)	Return a reference to the element at position **pos**. Throws an exception if **pos** >= **size()**.

Let's start with a simple program that creates a **Vector** and performs various operations on it:

```cpp
#include <iostream>
#include <vector>
#include <cstddef>
using std::cout;

// A vector type that will hold 'int'
typedef std::vector<int> Vector;

// Global function to display a Vector object
std::ostream &operator<<
                (std::ostream &stream, Vector const &vec)
{
  // See if it's empty
  if(vec.empty())
    stream << "Vector is empty\n";
  else
  {
    // Display its capacity
    stream << "Capacity: " << vec.capacity() << '\n';
    // Display the first element
    stream << "First element = " << vec.front() << '\n';
    // Display the last element
    stream << "Last element = " << vec.back() << '\n';
    // Display all elements
    for(std::size_t i = 0; i < vec.size(); ++i)
      stream << '[' << i << "] = " << vec      [i] << '\n';
  }
  return stream << "--------";
}

int main()
{
  // The data itself
  int const array[] = {1, 2, 3};
  // The number of data elements
  std::size_t const size = sizeof(array) / sizeof(*array);
  // Instantiate the class and fill the vector object
  Vector vec(array, array + size);
  cout << vec << '\n';
  // Add an element to the end
  vec.push_back(4);
```

```
    cout << vec << '\n';
    // Delete the last element
    vec.pop_back();
    cout << vec << '\n';
    // Change the first element
    vec[0] = 9;
    cout << vec << '\n';
    // Empty the vector
    std::size_t const count = vec.size();
    for(std::size_t i = 0; i < count; ++i)
      vec.pop_back();
    cout << vec << '\n';
}


/* Output:

Capacity: 3
First element = 1
Last element = 3
[0] = 1
[1] = 2
[2] = 3
---------
Capacity: 6
First element = 1
Last element = 4
[0] = 1
[1] = 2
[2] = 3
[3] = 4
---------
Capacity: 6
First element = 1
Last element = 3
[0] = 1
[1] = 2
[2] = 3
---------
Capacity: 6
First element = 9
Last element = 3
[0] = 9
[1] = 2
```

```
[2] = 3
--------

Vector is empty
--------


*/
```

Iterators

Because each container class has its own internal structure, iterating (i.e., moving across and examining all elements) through a vector object certainly entails a different algorithm than, for example, iterating through a linked list object, and it is certainly different than iterating through a map object. Nevertheless, wouldn't it be nice if these differences were transparent to the user of a container? In other words, your job would be greatly simplified if you could use the same public interface to iterate over the elements within a container, regardless of the type of container involved. In addition, the type of container being used can be changed to something different, with minimal impact on the user's code. Fortunately, the STL does exactly this with the use of *iterators*. All iterators are defined in the header file **iterator**.

An iterator is just a generalized form of a C language pointer. It also acts as an intermediary between algorithms (such as **std::sort**(), **std::find**(), etc.) and the containers they operate on. Each container type, such as **std::vector**, defines its own set of iterators that the program can use to access the elements within that container type. These container-specific iterators can be selected by qualifying their names with the container's name.

Iterator Categories

Different types of containers implement the following five different kinds of iterators:

▲ **Input**—This iterator can be dereferenced in order to retrieve the value at the current position, but not to set (store into) that value. It can be moved forward by one step by using **operator++**().

▲ **Output**—This iterator is similar to an input iterator except that the dereferenced value of the iterator can only be set (stored into), and not retrieved. Standard examples for input and output iterators are the STL stream and stream buffer iterators.

▲ **Forward**—This iterator is a combination of an input and output iterator insofar as it allows both reading and writing of its dereferenced value. This iterator can only be incremented.

▲ **Bi-directional iterators**—This is like a forward iterator with the added ability to be decremented by one step via **operator−−**().

▲ **Random access iterators**—This is like a bi-directional iterator except it adds the capability to increment and decrement the iterator by an arbitrary number of steps via the member functions **operator+(int)** and **operator–(int)**. In other words, they behave just like C language pointers. The natural example for this type of iterator is the **vector** class.

Supported Operators

The overloaded operators that each category supports are shown in Table 18.3.

Iterator Types

Each container class encapsulates iterators that can move in a forward or reverse direction. If you use a reverse iterator in conjunction with **operator++()**, then, in reality, you're starting at the end of the container and moving toward the beginning. Because constant objects must be supported, this means that there are four iterator classes whose names have been **typedef**'ed, as seen in Table 18.4.

For example, to easily refer to all four iterator classes within the (**typedef**'ed) **Vector** class designed to hold elements of type **double**, you could write something like this:

```
typedef vector<double> Vector;
typedef Vector::iterator Iterator;
typedef Vector::const_iterator ConstIterator;
typedef Vector::reverse_iterator ReverseIterator;
typedef Vector::const_reverse_iterator ConstReverseIterator;
```

TABLE 18.3

Iterator	Operators Supported
Input	*, –>, =, ++, ==, !=
Output	*, =, ++
Forward	*, –>, =, ++, ==, !=
Bi-directional	*, –>, =, ++, —, ==, !=
Random Access	*, –>, =, ++, —, ==, !=, +, -, [], <, >, <=, >=, –=, +=

TABLE 18.4

Typedef'ed name	Meaning
iterator	Iterate forward through a writeable collection.
const_iterator	Iterate forward through a read-only (**const**) collection.
reverse_iterator	Iterate backwards through a writeable collection.
const_reverse_iterator	Iterate backwards through a read-only (**const**) collection.

TABLE 18.5

Member function name	Meaning
iterator begin()	Return an iterator positioned at the first item.
const_iterator begin() const	Return a const iterator positioned at the first item.
iterator end()	Return an iterator positioned immediately after the last item.
const_iterator end() const	Return a const iterator positioned immediately after the last item.
reverse_iterator rbegin()	Return a reverse iterator positioned at the last item.
const_reverse_iterator rbegin() const	Return a const reverse iterator positioned at the last item.
reverse_iterator rend()	Return an iterator positioned immediately before the first item.
const_reverse_iterator rend() const	Return a const reverse iterator positioned immediately before the first item.

Iterator Member Functions

In order to obtain an iterator for the container with which it associates, you can invoke any of the member functions shown in Table 18.5.

When an iterator "points" to a valid position inside its container, it can safely be dereferenced (via **operator*()**) to fetch the value stored. However, whereas **begin()** returns an iterator referring to the first element of its container, **end()** returns an iterator referring to the hypothetical element that is *one past* the end of the container. This is perfectly valid, but any attempt to dereference the **end()** iterator can cause a run-time error. Also, because **operator>()** and **operator<()** are not valid for all iterators types, but **operator!=()** (and others) is, the correct way to see if you have reached the end of a container is to compare the incremental iterator against the iterator produced by **end()** for equality.

For example, the following program creates a vector and then iterates across it in both directions:

```
#include <iostream>
#include <vector>
#include <iterator>

// A vector type that will hold type 'int'
typedef std::vector<int> Vector;
```

```
// An iterator type for the container
typedef Vector::iterator Iterator;
// A reverse iterator type for the container
typedef Vector::reverse_iterator ReverseIterator;

int main()
{
  // The data itself
  int const data[] = {1, 2, 3};
  // Compute the number of elements
  std::size_t const size = sizeof(data) / sizeof(*data);
  // Create the vector
  Vector v(data, data + size);
  // Loop forward and display each element
  for(Iterator i = v.begin(); i != v.end(); ++i)
    std::cout << *i << '\n';
  std::cout << "---\n";
  // Loop backward and display the same data
  for(ReverseIterator i = v.rbegin(); i != v.rend(); ++i)
    std::cout << *i << '\n';
}


/* Output:

1
2
3
---
3
2
1

*/
```

Of course, the real power of the **std::vector** class comes through when you have to insert and delete elements; all of this messiness is taken care of for you by the member functions seen in Table 18.6, which all use iterators.

The following program uses these functions:

```
#include <iostream>
#include <vector>
#include <iterator>
#include <cstddef>
```

TABLE 18.6

Member function name	Meaning
template <class Iter> vector(Iter start, Iter end)	Construct a vector containing the elements in the iterator range **start** to **end**.
void erase(iterator pos)	Delete the element at position **pos**.
void erase(iterator first, iterator last)	Delete the elements from **first** to the one prior to **last**.
iterator insert(iterator pos, T const &value)	Insert value after **pos** and return an iterator representing where **value** now resides.
template <class Iter> void assign(Iter start, Iter end)	Assign to *__this__ vector the sequence defined by **start** and **end**.
void clear()	Remove all elements from the vector.

```cpp
using std::cout;

// A new vector type that will hold type 'int'
typedef std::vector<int> Vector;
// An iterator type for the container
typedef Vector::const_iterator ConstIterator;

// A global function to display a Vector object
std::ostream & operator<<
                (std::ostream &stream, Vector const &vec)
{
  ConstIterator begin(vec.begin());
  ConstIterator end(vec.end());
  if(begin == end)
    stream << "Empty vector\n";
  else
    for(ConstIterator i(begin); i != end; ++i)
      stream << *i << '\n';
  return stream << "-----\n";
}

int main()
{
  // Create an empty vector
  Vector vec;
  // The data itself
  int const data[] = {1, 2, 3};
```

```
    // Computer the number of elements
    std::size_t const size = sizeof(data) / sizeof(*data);
    // Fill the vector
    for(std::size_t i = 0; i < size; ++i)
      vec.insert(vec.end(), data[i]);
    cout << vec;
    // Delete all elements
    vec.erase(vec.begin(), vec.end());
    cout << vec;
    // Fill the vector
    vec.assign(size, 4);
    cout << vec;
    // Delete the first element
    vec.erase(vec.begin());
    cout << vec;
    // Delete all elements
      vec.clear();
    cout << vec;
}

/* Output:

1
2
3
-----
Empty vector
-----
4
4
4
-----
4
4
-----
Empty vector
-----

*/
```

Input and Output Iterators

Two kinds of iterators can be attached to input and output streams: **std::istream_iterator** and **std::ostream_iterator**, respectively. The specialization of each iterator indicates the type of data that is to be input or output. For example, **std::istream_iterator<int>** would be used to input successive objects of type **int** from the associated input stream. (If the objects are not valid **int** types, they are simply bypassed.)

The **std::istream_iterator** (an input iterator) reads items from a standard input stream. The constructor takes a reference to the input stream object to which the iterator is attached. Note, however, that the default constructor creates a pseudo end-of-stream marker to detect end-of-file.

TABLE 18.7

Member function name	Meaning
istream_iterator()	Construct an object to serve as end-of-stream marker (i.e., when compared to another input iterator, the result will be true if the stream is at end-of-file).
istream_iterator(istream &)	Construct an object to be associated with the input stream, and cache the first element of that stream.
T const &operator*() const	Return a reference to the currently cached item.
istream_iterator<T> &operator++()	Read and cache the next type **T** item.
istream_iterator<T> const operator++(int)	Postfix ++.

The output iterator **ostream_iterator** is a class that outputs items of generic type to an output stream (such as **cout**). The constructor expecting two arguments outputs the second argument after each insertion.

TABLE 18.8

Member function name	Meaning
ostream_iterator(ostream &stream)	Construct an object to be associated with the output stream.
ostream_iterator(ostream &stream, char const *delim)	Same as above, but also append the null-terminated char string specified by **delim** to every output line.
T const &operator*() const	Send the item referred to by the iterator to the stream device.
ostream_iterator<T>&operator++()	Move the iterator to the next type **T** item.
ostream_iterator<T> const operator++(int)	Postfix ++.

For example, the following program creates a disk file and uses an input iterator to display its content on the output screen. For this example, we'll use the standard library's **std::string** class (which is defined in the header file **string**):

```cpp
#include <iostream>
#include <fstream>
#include <iterator>
#include <string>
#include <cstddef>
using std::string;

int main()
{
  std::fstream diskFile("test.data");
  string const data[] =
  {
    "Two roads diverged in a wood, and I-",
    "I took the one less traveled by,",
    "And that has made all the difference."
  };
  std::size_t const size = sizeof(data) / sizeof(*data);
  for(std::size_t i = 0; i < size; ++i)
    diskFile << data[i] << '\n';
  diskFile.seekg(0);
  typedef std::istream_iterator<string> Input;
  typedef std::ostream_iterator<string> Output;
  Input input(diskFile), eof;
  Output output(std::cout, "\n");
  while(input != eof)
    *output++ = *input++;
}


/* Output:

Two
roads
diverged
in
a
wood,
and
I-
I
took
```

```
the
one
less
traveled
by,
And
that
has
made
all
the
difference.

*/
```

EXERCISE 18.1

Write a program that copies a disk file.

String-Based I/O

In the standard C library, functions such as **sprintf()** and **sscanf()** allow you write formatted data to, or read formatted data from, a **char** array in memory. Unfortunately, using these functions reliably can be tricky. For example, the **sprintf()** function can easily overrun the end of the **char** array that it is writing the formatted output into (e.g., we pass into **sprintf()** a 10-element char array, but **sprintf()** outputs a 20-character string).

Fortunately, C++ provides a better alternative: **std::string** I/O streams. These I/O streams use **std::string** objects as their underlying data buffer. Therefore, they enjoy all the benefits of having an easily manipulated **std::string**–based data buffer at their disposal. For example, if the program is using an output string stream, and an output operation happens to fill the underlying **std::string** object to its current capacity, this is not a problem. The output stream simply resizes the **std::string** object (increase its capacity) and then resumes writing data into it.

The header file **sstream** defines three **string**-based **iostream** classes: an output string stream **ostringstream** (writes data into a string), an input string stream **istringstream** (reads data from a string), and an I/O string stream **stringstream** (read from, or write to, a string). These string streams can be used just like the other **iostream**-derived classes we've seen so far. For example, you can use **operator>>()** calls to extract data from an input string stream, and **operator<<()** calls to write data to an output string stream.

The following program demonstrates one common use for output string streams— generating **std::string** objects that contain detailed error messages:

```
// File main.cpp

#include <iostream>
```

```cpp
#include <sstream>
using std::cout;
using std::cerr;

namespace my
{
  struct error
  {
    error(std::string const &msg) : what(msg) { }
    std::string const what;
  };
}


void hal9000_response()
{
  cout << "HAL 9000: I'm sorry, Dave, "
          "I'm afraid I can't do that.\n";
}


void system_ok(bool ok, int value)
{
  if(!ok)
  {
    // Use an ostringstream object to create a
    // detailed error message in a std::string
    std::ostringstream errmsg;
    errmsg.setf(std::ios_base::boolalpha);
    errmsg << "WHERE: system_ok() [line "
              << __LINE__ << "]\n"
              << "WHAT: Logic error\n"
              << "-- VALUES --\n"
              << "ok   : " << ok << '\n'
              << "value : " << value << '\n' ;
    throw my::error(errmsg.str());
  }
}


int main()
{
  try
  {
    system_ok(true,123);
    cout << "Dave: Open the pod bay "
```

```
                        "doors please, HAL...\n";
          hal9000_response();
          system_ok(false,555);
      }
      catch(my::error const &err)
      {
         cerr << "\n:: ERROR ::\n" << err.what << '\n';
      }
      catch(...)
      {
         cerr << "\n:: ERROR :: Unknown error\n\n";
      }
}


/* Output:

Dave: Open the pod bay doors please, HAL...
HAL 9000: I'm sorry, Dave, I'm afraid I can't do that.

:: ERROR ::
WHERE: system_ok() [line 27]
WHAT: Logic error
-- VALUES --
ok    : false
value : 555


*/
```

One of the many nice features about string streams is that they are completely reusable. To reuse a string stream, place the stream in its "good" error state by calling the stream's **clear**() member function with no arguments, and then load the desired initial value into the string stream. For output string streams, the initial value is usually the empty string "". For input string streams, the initial value is typically the data (in string format) that the program wishes to read from the input string stream. For example:

```
// File main.cpp


#include <iostream>
#include <sstream>
using std::cout;


void f1()
```

```
{
  int ovenTemp = 333;
  std::ostringstream message;
  message << "ovenTemp : " << ovenTemp ;
  cout << message.str() << '\n';
  // Reuse 'message'
  message.clear();    // clear all error flags first!
  message.str("");    // load the initial value
  double pressure = 1.53;
  message << "pressure : " << pressure ;
  cout << message.str() << '\n';
}


void f2()
{
  std::string data = "271";
  int coreTemp = -1;
  std::istringstream in(data);
  in >> coreTemp;
  cout << "coreTemp : " << coreTemp << '\n';
  // Reuse 'in'
  data = "3.52";
  in.clear();                   // clear all error flags first!
  in.str(data);                 // load the initial value
  double ovenHumidity = -1.0;
  in >> ovenHumidity ;
  cout << "ovenHumidity : " << ovenHumidity << '\n';
}


int main()
{
  f1();
  f2();
}

/* Oputput

ovenTemp : 333
pressure : 1.53
coreTemp : 271
ovenHumidity : 3.52

*/
```

Algorithms in the Standard Template Library (STL)

std::min() and std::max()

The STL also contains a generic set of algorithms that can operate on a wide variety of containers. These algorithms are defined in the file **<algorithm>**. Perhaps two of the simplest are **std::min**() and **std::max**(). For example:

```
#include <iostream>
#include <algorithm>
#include "flush.h"
using std::cout;
using std::cin;
using std::cerr;

int main()
{
  do
  {
    cin >> Flush;
    cout << "Enter 2 ints: ";
    int a, b;
    if(cin >> a >> b)
    {
      cout << "\tLesser of " << a << " and " << b
              << " is " << std::min(a, b) << '\n';
      cout << "\tGreater of " << a << " and " << b
              << " is " << std::max(a, b) << '\n';
    }
    else if(!cin.eof())
      cerr << "\tBad input\n";
  }
  while(!cin.eof() && !cin.bad());
}


/* Output:

Enter 2 ints: 5 7
      Lesser of 5 and 7 is 5
      Greater of 5 and 7 is 7
Enter 2 ints: -4 8
      Lesser of -4 and 8 is -4
      Greater of -4 and 8 is 8
```

```
Enter 2 ints: junk
        Bad input
Enter 2 ints: ^Z


*/
```

std::find()

The **std::find()** function searches any kind of container for a specified value. Two iterators represent the starting and (one past) the ending range to be searched. If the value is found, an iterator is returned representing the found position; otherwise, the iterator that is returned will be one past the last one examined. **std::find()** itself is written as:

```
template <class Iter, class T>
Iter find(Iter first, Iter last, T const &value)
{
  while(first != last && *first != value)
    ++first;
  return first;
}
```

The following is an example of **std::find()** that locates an item in a sequence; it shows the power of the STL. Note how the algorithm works equally well on either a **std::vector**, **std::list** or a **std::deque** container object. To switch from one to the other, just *one* line of code needs to be changed:

```
#include <iostream>
#include <vector>
#include <list>
#include <algorithm>
#include <deque>
#include <iterator>
#include <typeinfo>
#include <cstddef>
#include "flush.h"
using std::cout;
using std::cin;
using std::cerr;

typedef int T;
// ** Uncomment the type of container you want **
// typedef std::vector<T> STLType;
// typedef std::list<T> STLType;
// typedef std::deque<T> STLType;
typedef STLType::iterator Iterator;
```

```
int main()
{
  // The data itself
  T const data[] = {1, 2, 3};
  // The number of data elements
  std::size_t const size = sizeof(data) / sizeof(*data);
  // Instantiate the STL type
  STLType v(data, data + size);
  // Create the starting and ending iterators
  Iterator begin = v.begin();
  Iterator end = v.end();
  // See if an element is present
  do
  {
    cin >> Flush;
    cout << "Enter type " << typeid(T).name() << ": ";
    T value;
    if(cin >> value)
    {
      Iterator answer(std::find(begin, end, value));
      cout << value
              << (answer != end
                    ? " was found\n" : " was NOT found\n");
    }
    else if(!cin.eof())
      cerr << "Input error\n";
  }
  while(!cin.eof() && !cin.bad());
  if(cin.bad())
    cerr << "Unrecoverable error\n";
  else if(cin.eof())
    cout << "\nEnd-of-file detected\n";
}

/* Sample output:

Enter type int: 1
1 was found

Enter type int: 2
2 was found

Enter type int: 3
3 was found
```

```
Enter type int: 4
4 was NOT found

Enter type int: ^Z

End-of-file detected

*/
```

EXERCISE 18.2

Modify the previous code example so that type **T** is a user-defined type.

std::count()

The **std::count()** algorithm counts the number of occurrences of a value within a container. The actual count (**answer**) is specified as an input argument. The algorithm itself is defined as the following:

```
template <class Iter, class T, class U>
void count(Iter first, Iter last, T const &value, U &answer)
{
  while(first != last)
    if(*first++ == value)
      ++answer;
}
```

The following example counts the number of 2's in an array and in a **Vector**:

```
#include <iostream>
#include <vector>
#include <algorithm>
#include <cstddef>
using std::cout;

int main()
{
  // The data itself
  int const data[] = {2, 1, 2, 3, 2};
  // The number of data elements
  std::size_t const size = sizeof(data) / sizeof(*data);
  // See how many 2's there are in the array of ints
  int answer = std::count(data, data + size, 2);
  cout << answer << '\n';
  // Do it again for a vector
  typedef std::vector<int> Vector;
```

```
        Vector v(data, data + size);
        answer = std::count(v.begin(), v.end(), 2);
        cout << answer << '\n';
}


/* Output:


3
3


*/
```

std::copy()

The **std::copy()** algorithm copies a sequence beginning at **start** and ending at **end**, and it puts the result into the sequence starting at **out** (which must be large enough). This algorithm is declared as:

```
template <class InIter, class OutIter>
OutIter copy(InIter start, InIter end, OutIter out);
```

The following example creates a **std::vector** of **std::string** objects, then copies the contents to a second **std::vector**:

```
#include <iostream>
#include <vector>
#include <string>
#include <algorithm>
#include <cstddef>
using std::cout;
using std::string;

int main()
{
    typedef std::vector<string> Vector;
    string const data[] = {"One", "Two", "Three"};
    std::size_t const size = sizeof(data) / sizeof(*data);
    Vector input(data, data + size), output(size);
    std::copy(input.begin(), input.end(), output.begin());
    for(std::size_t i = 0; i < output.size(); ++i)
        cout << output[i] << '\n';
}

/* Output:

One
```

```
Two
Three


*/
```

std::sort()

The **std::sort()** algorithm takes as its inputs two random access iterators and sorts the container into ascending sequence. In the following example, an input disk file is created and copied into a vector, after which the vector is sorted and then displayed:

```cpp
#include <iostream>
#include <fstream>
#include <vector>
#include <iterator>
#include <algorithm>
#include <string>
#include <cstddef>
using std::string;

int main()
{
  // Open the input file
  std::fstream diskFile("test.dat");
  // The data itself
  string const data[] =
  {
    "One", "Two", "Three", "Four", "Five"
  };
  std::size_t const size = sizeof(data) / sizeof(*data);
  // Create a disk file
  for(std::size_t i = 0; i < size; ++i)
    diskFile << data[i] << '\n';
  // Create a vector of type string
  std::vector<string> vec;
  // Read lines of text from the input file and put this
  // text into the vector
  diskFile.seekg(0);
  std::string str;
  while(getline(diskFile, str))
    vec.push_back(str);
  // Sort the vector into ascending sequence
  std::sort(vec.begin(), vec.end());
  // Create an output iterator
  std::ostream_iterator<string> iter(std::cout, "\n");
```

```
    // Display the records in the vector
    copy(vec.begin(), vec.end(), iter);
    diskFile.close();
}

/* Output:

Five
Four
One
Three
Two

*/
```

std::swap()

The **std::swap()** algorithm is defined and works just as you would expect:

```
template <class T>
inline void swap(T &a, T &b)
{
    T hold(a);
    a = b;
    b = hold;
}
```

This simple program swaps the content of two **std::string** objects:

```
#include <iostream>
#include <algorithm>
#include <string>

int main()
{
    std::string one("one"), two("two");
    std::swap(one, two);
    std::cout << "one contains " << one << '\n';
    std::cout << "two contains " << two << '\n';
}

/* Output:

one contains two
two contains one

*/
```

Major Containers for the Standard Template Library

The STL supports the following containers. The type of iterator that each one uses is in parentheses.

Sequence containers are objects that store collections of other objects in a strictly linear arrangement.

- ▲ **std::deque**—provides random access to a sequence of varying length, with constant time insertions and deletions at both ends (random)
- ▲ **std::list**—provides linear time access to a sequence of varying length, with constant time insertions and deletions anywhere (bi-directional)
- ▲ **std::vector**—provides array-like random access to a sequence of varying length, with constant time insertions and deletions at the end (random)

Adaptive sequence containers are collections that are built from an existing container type. For example, you could build a **stack** that uses a **vector** as the underlying container type.

- ▲ **std::stack<Container>**—implements a stack (none)
- ▲ **std::queue<Container>**—implements a queue (none)
- ▲ **std::priority_queue<Container>**—implements a priority queue (none)

Associative containers provide for fast retrieval of objects from a collection based on keys. The size of the collection can vary at runtime. The collection is maintained in order, based on a comparitor function object of type **Compare**.

- ▲ **std::map<KeyT, ValueT, Compare>**—manages a set of ordered key/value pairs. The pairs are ordered by key, based on a user-supplied comparitor function (bi-directional)
- ▲ **std::multimap<KeyT, ValueT, Compare>**—supports duplicate keys (possibly contains multiple elements with the same key value) and provides for fast retrieval of values of the user-specified type **ValueT** based on the keys (bi-directional)
- ▲ **std::set<KeyT, Compare>**—supports unique keys (contains at most one of each key value) and provides for fast retrieval of the keys themselves (bi-directional)
- ▲ **std::multiset<KeyT, Compare>**—supports duplicate keys (possibly contains multiple copies with the same key value) and provides for fast retrieval of the keys themselves (bi-directional)
- ▲ **std::bitset<std::size_t N>**—manages fixed-size sequences of bits. The number of bits in a given sequence is specified by the template argument **N** (none)

Comparitor Objects

A *comparitor* object in the STL is an instance of a class in which **operator()()** is defined as a member function. Such an object is sometimes called a *function object,* or *functor.*

Recall from Chapter 10 that **operator()()** is unique in the sense that it can be defined to take any number of arguments, including default function arguments.

When a comparitor object is followed by a set of parentheses, its **operator()()** is invoked. For example, the following comparitor classes each define an **operator()()** that returns **true** if the input argument is less than zero or greater than zero, respectively:

```cpp
template <typename T>
struct LessThanZero
{
  bool operator()(T const &arg) const
  {
    return arg < 0;
  }
};

template <typename T>
struct GreaterThanZero
{
  bool operator()(T const &arg) const
  {
    return arg > 0;
  }
};
```

The following is an example of a **std::map** object (supporting bi-directional iterators) that associates a **std::string** value with a **long** value. The **std::string** objects are kept in sequence according to the particular comparitor type you choose—**less** for ascending sequence, and **greater** for descending sequence. Usage of the subscript operator on the key value yields a reference to its corresponding value. The names **first** and **second** in the **std::map** class hold the key and its value, respectively:

```cpp
#include <iostream>
#include <iterator>
#include <string>
#include <map>
using std::string;
using std::cout;
using std::cin;
using std::cerr;

// ** Uncomment the comparitor type you want **
// typedef std::less<string> Compare;
// typedef std::greater<string> Compare;

// The map will hold a pair of values consisting of a string and
// a long, and will be kept in sequence by the string value
typedef std::map<string, long, Compare> Map;
```

```
typedef Map::iterator Iterator;

int main()
{
  // Create the map object
  Map map;
  // Add 3 elements
  map["Tom"] = 356980578L;
  map["Dick"] = 560945738L;
  map["Harry"] = 468840981L;
  // The starting and ending iterators
  Iterator begin(map.begin());
  Iterator end(map.end());
  // Display all pairs
  for(Iterator i = begin; i != end; ++i)
    cout << "Name: " << i->first
         << " Number: " << i->second << '\n';
  // See if a name is present
  cout << "\nEnter a name: ";
  string name;
  while(getline(cin,name))
  {
    if(map.find(name) != map.end())
      cout << "Number: " << map[name] << '\n';
    else
      cerr << "Error: '" << name << "' was not found\n";
    cout << "Next name: ";
  }
}

/* Output:

Name: Tom Number: 356980578
Name: Harry Number: 468840981
Name: Dick Number: 560945738

Enter a name: Harry
Number: 468840981
Next name: Dick
Number: 560945738
Next name: Eric
Error: 'Eric' was not found
Next name:^Z

*/
```

EXERCISE 18.3

Create a library that contains both books and patrons and that has the ability to check out and return books to and from the library. A book has the following abstraction:

```
// File book.h

#ifndef BOOK_H
#define BOOK_H

#include <iosfwd>
#include <string>

class Patron;
class Book
{
  friend std::ostream &operator<<
               (std::ostream &, Book const &);
        public:
  Book(std::string const &);
  std::string const &getTitle () const;
  Patron *getPatron () const;
  void checkOutBook(Patron *p);
  void returnBook();
        private:
  std::string title;
  Patron *patron;      // Zero if book is available
};

#endif
```

A patron has the following abstraction:

```
// File patron.h

#ifndef PATRON_H
#define PATRON_H

#include <vector>
#include <iosfwd>
#include <string>

class Book;
class Patron
{
  typedef std::vector<Book*> Vector;
```

```
typedef Vector::iterator Iterator;
friend std::ostream &operator<<
        (std::ostream &, Patron const &);
        public:
Patron(std::string const &);
std::string const &getName() const;
void checkOutBook(Book &book);
void returnBook(Book &book);
        private:
std::string name;
Vector books;
};
```

```
#endif
```

A library has the following abstraction:

```
// File library.h

#ifndef LIBRARY_H
#define LIBRARY_H

#include <iosfwd>
#include <vector>

class Patron;
class Book;
class Library
{
  friend std::ostream &operator<<
                        (std::ostream &, Library const &);
  std::vector<Book*> books;
  std::vector<Patron*> patrons;
        public:
  void addPatron(Patron &);
  void addBook(Book &);
  void checkOutBook(Patron &, Book &);
  void returnBook(Patron &, Book &);
};
```

```
#endif
```

Use the following test program:

```
// File main.cpp

#include <iostream>
```

```cpp
#include "library.h"
#include "patron.h"
#include "book.h"

int main()
{
  // Instantiate the library
  Library MLK;

  // Add some patrons
  Patron John("John");
  MLK.addPatron(John);
  Patron Marsha("Marsha");
  MLK.addPatron(Marsha);
  Patron Peter("Peter");
  MLK.addPatron(Peter);

  // Add some books
  Book WarAndPeace("War and Peace");
  MLK.addBook(WarAndPeace);
  Book Exodus("Exodus");
  MLK.addBook(Exodus);
  Book LearningCPlusPlus("LearningCPlusPlus");
  MLK.addBook(LearningCPlusPlus);

  // Display the library
  std::cout << MLK << std::endl;

  // Check out some books
  MLK.checkOutBook(John, WarAndPeace);
  MLK.checkOutBook(Marsha, WarAndPeace);
  MLK.checkOutBook(Peter, LearningCPlusPlus);

  // Display the library
  std::cout << MLK << std::endl;

  // Return some books
  MLK.returnBook(John, WarAndPeace);
  MLK.returnBook(John, LearningCPlusPlus);

  // Display the library
  std::cout << MLK << std::endl;
}
```

```
/* Sample output:

———————— The Library ————————
                        ALL BOOKS:
"War and Peace" is not checked out
"Exodus" is not checked out
"LearningCPlusPlus" is not checked out
                        ALL PATRONS:
John has these books: NO BOOKS CHECKED OUT
Marsha has these books: NO BOOKS CHECKED OUT
Peter has these books: NO BOOKS CHECKED OUT
———————— End —————————

Marsha is attempting to check out "War and Peace"
                        but it is already checked out!
———————— The Library —————————
                        ALL BOOKS:
"War and Peace" belongs to John
"Exodus" is not checked out
"LearningCPlusPlus" belongs to Peter
                        ALL PATRONS:
John has these books: "War and Peace"
Marsha has these books: NO BOOKS CHECKED OUT
Peter has these books: "LearningCPlusPlus"
———————— End —————————

John is attempting to return "LearningCPlusPlus"
                        but doesn't have it
———————— The Library —————————
                        ALL BOOKS:
"War and Peace" is not checked out
"Exodus" is not checked out
"LearningCPlusPlus" belongs to Peter
                        ALL PATRONS:
John has these books: NO BOOKS CHECKED OUT
Marsha has these books: NO BOOKS CHECKED OUT
Peter has these books: "LearningCPlusPlus"
———————— End —————————

*/
```

Appendix A: Bibliography

Anderson, Paul, & Anderson, Gail. **Navigating C++ and Object-Oriented Design**. Upper Saddle River, NJ: Prentice Hall, 1998.

Coplien, James O. **Advanced C++**. Reading MA: Addison Wesley Publishing Company, 1992.

Deitel, H.M., & Deitel, P.J. **C++ How to Program (3rd ed)**. Upper Saddle River, NJ: Prentice Hall, 2001.

Eckel, Bruce. **Thinking in C++ (2nd ed)**. Upper Saddle River, NJ: Prentice Hall, 2000.

Kalev, Danny. **The ANSI/ISO C++ Professional Programmer's Handbook**. Indianapolis, IN: Que, 1999.

Koenig, Andrew, and Moo, Barbara. **Accelerated C++**. Reading, MA: Addison Wesley, 2000.

Langer, Angelika, & Kreft, Klaus. **Standard C++ IOStreams and Locales**. Reading, MA: Addison Wesley, 2000.

Lippman, Stanley. **Essential C++**. Reading, MA: Addison Wesley, 2000.

Lippman, Stanley, & Lajoie, Josee. **C++ Primer (3rd ed)**. Reading, MA: Addison Wesley, 1998.

McGregor, Rog. **Practical C++**. Indianapolis, IN: Que, 1999.

Meyers, Scott. **Effective C++**. Reading, MA: Addison Wesley, 1992.

————. **More Effective C++**. Reading, MA: Addison Wesley, 1996.

Nagler, Eric, **Learning C++ (2nd ed): A Hands-On Approach**. Minneapolis, MN: West Publishing, 1996.

Nelson, Mark. **C++ Programmer's Guide to the Standard Template Library**. Indianapolis, IN: IDG Books, 1995.

Prata, Stephen. **C++ Primer Plus (4th ed)**. Indianapolis, IN: Sams, 2002.

Schildt, Herb. **STL Programming from the Ground Up**. Berkeley, CA: Osborne/ McGraw-Hill, 1999.

Stroustrup, Bjarne. **The Design and Evolution of C++**. Reading, MA: Addison Wesley, 1994.

———. **The C++ Programming Language (3rd ed)**. Reading, MA: Addison Wesley, 1997.

Sutter, Herb. **Exceptional C++**. Reading, MA: Addison Wesley, 2000.

———. **More Exceptional C++**. Reading, MA: Addison Wesley, 2002.

B

Appendix B: C++ Guidelines

Try to follow these guidelines when coding your C++ programs to make sure they are as clean and efficient as possible.

General

1. Prefer Initialization To Assignment (the PITA rule), especially in a constructor definition.
2. Support Constant (and temporary) Objects (the SCO rule).
3. Do not place variables into the global space.

Header files

1. Use the ISO/ANSI C++ header files (e.g., **iostream** instead of **iostream.h**, **cstdlib** instead of **stdlib.h**).
2. Never define variables or noninline functions in a header file.
3. Noninline member functions must never be defined in header files.
4. An inline function *must* be defined in every translation unit that uses that inline function. This applies to both member and nonmember inline functions. Always define an inline function in a header file, and then **#include** that header file into each translation unit that uses the inline function.
5. Put all variable and noninline function definitions, including static data member definitions, into a definition (**.cpp**) file.
6. Do not use **stdio** functions.

Class design

1. Keep class definitions small.
2. Never make a data member public.
3. Prefer objects instead of pointers as data members inside classes.
4. Keep member functions of a class as small and as specific as possible.
5. Initialize nonstatic data members in declaration order, and invoke the base class constructor first in a derived class constructor.
6. Do not expose the private parts of a class by returning a pointer or reference to them. Instead, use message passing and a public interface to provide controlled access to any nonpublic members.
7. Avoid granting friendship to another class unless there is a logical coupling between the two classes.
8. Modularize each class into header and definition files. (If the class has only a few member functions, and these member functions are inlined, then a definition file is not necessary.)
9. Put the **main**() function into its own definition file, not into a class's definition file.

Style

1. When you want a character, write a character, not the ASCII-decimal representation (write "A", not 65, and not 0x41).
2. In a function, defer the declaration of data members until you're ready to use them (think PITA).
3. Use **const** instead of **#define** where applicable.
4. Use **const** whenever possible (the SCO rule), but not at the top level in function parameter types nor at the top level in return types for functions returning nonclass types.
5. When returning a **bool** type, don't write **? true : false** after the test. For example: **return (x > y);**, not **return (x > y) ? true : false;**.

Free store management

1. Use **new** and **delete**, never **malloc**() and **free**().
2. Balance every **new** with a call to **delete**.
3. Write **delete ptr** for single objects, **delete [] ptr** for an array of objects.

Functions

1. Almost never pass a user-defined object into a function by value.
2. Never return a local object (an object with automatic storage duration) from a function by pointer or reference. Instead, you must return it by value.

3. When overloading an operator, make it a member function unless (a) you need to perform implicit type conversion on the left-hand argument, or (b) you are overloading the insertion or extraction operator, in which case it should be a nonmember function.

4. If the function creates some result that must be returned, do not create this result on the heap and then return the dereferenced pointer to it by reference (in an attempt to avoid the copy constructor).

5. Default function arguments must be listed in the function's declaration, not definition, and can not be listed in both.

6. Do not hide data members at class scope with members having the same name at member function scope.

7. Whenever possible, use prefix instead of postfix increment and decrement.

Index